*Iranian and Diasporic
Literature in the
21st Century*

ALSO BY DANIEL GRASSIAN

*Hybrid Fictions: American Literature and Generation X* (McFarland, 2003)

# Iranian and Diasporic Literature in the 21st Century

## A CRITICAL STUDY

### Daniel Grassian

McFarland & Company, Inc., Publishers

*Jefferson, North Carolina, and London*

LIBRARY OF CONGRESS CATALOGUING-IN-PUBLICATION DATA

Grassian, Daniel, 1974–
    Iranian and diasporic literature in the 21st century :
a critical study / Daniel Grassian.
        p.        cm.
    Includes bibliographical references and index.

    ISBN 978-0-7864-7272-7
    softcover : acid free paper ∞

    1. American literature — Iranian American authors —
History and criticism.    2. Persian literature — 21st century —
History and criticism.    3. East and West in literature.
4. Exiles' writings, Iranian — History and criticism.    5. Iran —
Foreign public opinion, American.    6. United States —
Foreign public opinion, Iranian.    7. Blogs — Political
aspects — Iran.    8. Iranian diaspora.    I. Title.
PS153.173G73  2013
810.9'8915 — dc23                                        2012045587

BRITISH LIBRARY CATALOGUING DATA ARE AVAILABLE

Front cover image © 2013 Shutterstock

Manufactured in the United States of America

*McFarland & Company, Inc., Publishers*
    *Box 611, Jefferson, North Carolina 28640*
        *www.mcfarlandpub.com*

# Table of Contents

# Introduction

"States like these [Iran, North Korea, Iraq], and their terrorist allies, constitute an axis of evil, arming to threaten the peace of the world." — United States president George W. Bush, January 29, 2002 (Bush, par. 26)

"Freedoms in Iran are genuine, true freedoms. Iranian people are free. Women in Iran enjoy the highest levels of freedom." — Iranian president Mahmoud Ahmadinejad (Ahmadinejad, par. 157)

When U.S. president George W. Bush declared Iran part of the so-called Axis of Evil in 2002, he met with little to no resistance from the general American public, who, on the heels of the attacks of September 11, tended to lump the Islamic world into one generalized mass of totalitarian despotism. This generalization occurred even though the Islamic Regime tends to allow Iranians more freedoms than their neighbors in countries like Saudi Arabia, with which the United States has a solid economic and political partnership.

Problematic as American misconceptions might be, the rhetoric from the Iranian administration was no better, resting as it did upon dubious statements like the one above from President Mahmoud Ahmadinejad, which disregards the many prohibitions placed upon the Iranian populace, from drinking alcohol to publishing supposedly blasphemous or politically and religiously critical or challenging literature. The most populated Islamic country in the Middle East,[1] Iran is a country rife with contradictions, in many ways caught between the rhetoric and policies of the Western (in some eyes, imperialist or colonizing) world and the ideology and policies of fundamentalist Islam as practiced by Iran's supreme leader, his clergy, and Ahmadinejad's administration.

In recent years, most clearly signified by the riots and demonstrations following the 2009 presidential election, Iran has also revealed itself as a largely divided and contradictory country. While Iran describes itself as a republic and Ahmadinejad is the president of Iran, religious clerics wield most of the power,[2] while a sizeable portion of the Iranian public longs for political, cultural, and economic change. As Reza Aslan explains, despite the fact that Iran describes itself as an Islamic republic, it "is neither Islamic nor a republic" ("From Here" 29). Rather, he describes Iran as "a mullahcracy," which he defines as a "bizarre hybrid of religious and third world fascism that, like fascisms of the past century, has turned into an embarrassing example of populism gone awry" (29). However, as Aslan suggests, and as we will see in the literature of Iranians and diasporic Iranians, most Iranians are generally secular, and certainly less religious than the majority of Muslims in neighboring or adjacent Middle Eastern countries (29).[3] Whereas the Western media tends to categorize Iran as an ethnically, culturally, and politically homogeneous country, and Iranians as blind or oppressed followers of a totalitarian dictatorship, as Lila Zanganeh argues, "In truth, Iranians themselves live in a far more complex and schizophrenic reality, at a surreal crossroads between political Islam and satellite television, massive national oil revenues and searing social inequalities" (xiv). Contemporary Iranian and Iranian diasporic writers capture the tension and danger as well as the transformative possibilities of being caught between these conflicting cultures and realities.

Exploring Iran and its diasporic community is especially important since the Western public generally misperceives Iran and Iranian demographics. Despite being predominantly Persian and Caucasian, Iran is often thought of as being an Arabic nation.[4] Indeed, Iranians and diasporic Iranians often bristle at how Westerners tend to group them with their Arabic neighbors, in part because there still exist vestiges of a centuries-old conflict between Arabs and Persians, the former of whom conquered the latter nearly a thousand years ago and "imposed Islam on a people who followed a number of ancient faiths, including Zoroastrianism" (Ghahramani 21). This previous religion, Zoroastrianism, was "a monotheistic religion that has left indelible traces on Iran, at times causing other Muslims to wonder if Iran ever fully accepted Islam" (Baer 234–5). Herein is another essential contradiction of Iran: it is an Islamic Republic that still has strong cultural and literary connections to a religion other than Islam.

As Robert Baer suggests, Americans (if not most Westerners) tend to think of Iranians as strongly, if not virulently, anti–American, when in actuality, instead of despising American culture or the American people, most Iranians (and many from other predominantly Muslim Middle Eastern countries) tend to despise American foreign policy or "what they consider our occupation of large swaths of the Middle East" (11). In addition to Iraq, this perceived "occupation" would include American military bases in allied countries such as Saudi Arabia and Kuwait, as well as the strong U.S. alliance with and presence in Israel. With a large diasporic population in the United States, England, France, and other Western countries, Iran, whether or not its current administration approves, certainly has strong ties to the West; and the West, in turn, has a history of participating in Iranian political events and has even helped shaped the course of Iranian history.

Westerners also generally lack knowledge and appreciation of Iran's rich cultural and literary Persian heritage. As Nasrin Alavi explains, "Iranians are proud of a literary heritage that has produced names such as Omar Khayyam, Hafez, Saadi, and Rumi (who is currently one of the best-selling poets in the United States)" (93). While poetry, above other forms, has been revered in Persia and in contemporary Iran,[5] this does not mean that most of the following book will focus upon contemporary Iranian and Iranian diasporic poetry. In fact, we will see that, in particular, a significant amount of Iranian diasporic literature and Iranian literature translated into English tends to be in the form of fiction and memoirs. Their dominance may be in part due to how the West, especially in recent years, has come to champion these forms over poetry (a preference possibly related to the fact that poetry tends to be less commercially successful).

Contrary to conventional Western stereotypes, Iran is not a hotbed of Islamic terrorism, nor is it a totalitarian country that strips its citizens of basic rights. While women may not possess as many rights as men in Iran, this should not invite characterizations of Iranian men or the Islamic Regime as backwards, primitive sexists. While Western coverage of Iran frequently focuses on the country's supposed pursuit of nuclear weapons, almost never is it argued that Iran's pursuit of nuclear weapons can be seen as a reasonable (although certainly not, by western standards, desirable) attempt to wield more political power in the region and world. Along similar lines, despite the Western vilification of Ahmadinejad, as we will see later in this study, he has made some progressive advances for Iran and for Iranians. Like the United States, Iran is a complex nation whose culture, people, and political structure largely defy simple classifications and analysis; however, simplified classifications and analysis have effectively worsened Western-Iranian relations and largely demonized a country and a people.

That being the case, the question remains: What is the best manner in which to combat the demonization of Iranians by the West and the demonization of the West by Iran? This book proposes that one of the best ways to combat counterproductive political and cultural dichotomies is through the study of literature. Literature has always served an important moral, ethical, and cultural purpose through its sociological and psychological insight into cultures and human life. As contemporary novelist and journalist William T. Vollmann has argued, literature allows readers to "leap the wall of self," and thereby better understand and appreciate different perspectives and cultures (qtd. in Weissman, par. 38). Given how Iran and the West have been subject to so many false stereotypes, Iranian and Iranian diasporic literature can serve a key function in deconstructing Western caricatures of Iran and Iranian caricatures of the West. However, and unfortunately, U.S. colleges and universities have generally marginalized if not excluded Iranian and Iranian diasporic literature and culture courses.[6] Often not considered Asian enough for Asian or Asian-American studies and not appropriately placed in Arabic or Arabic-American Studies, Iranian or Iranian diasporic literature and culture have seldom been included in Western academic studies or courses.

While technically part of the Middle East, Iran is more accurately described as a peripheral Middle Eastern country or a border country, albeit a border county which may prove to be in one of the most important geographical and political positions in the twenty-first century. It is hardly bold to state that Iran may well be the linchpin holding a post–September 11, post–"reconstructed" Iraq, post–Arab Spring Middle East together. On the other hand, Iran could also, especially if it is successful in producing nuclear weapons, upset the balance of power and the presence of the West in the Middle East.

Much has been written about the Arab Spring and the supposed beginning of a larger democratic transformation of the Middle East. Some writers suggest that the Arab Spring could provide a golden opportunity for Iran to assert itself in the region, while others suggest that, after its quashing of the Green Movement, Iran no longer holds any sway whatsoever for pro-democratic Middle Eastern youth (Kaye and Wehrey 183).[7] However, as the hopes of the Arab Spring have begun to sputter with civil wars, political instability, and ongoing economic problems, it is becoming clear how complex, messy, and time consuming it can be to establish an effective government (let alone a democracy). I submit that Iran, more than most countries in the Islamic Middle East, has a significant potential to transform into a more progressive, Western-style democracy (and, in fact, has already made strides in this direction), despite the West's image of Iran as a totalitarian and oppressive country.[8] With these various factors in mind, the time is ripe for Iranian and diasporic Iranian studies to be welcomed into Western academia.

This is not to suggest that there has been a systematic repression or complete exclusion of these subjects (although I do suggest there has been a marginalization). Diasporic Iranians are an emerging group with the majority having emigrated to the West (especially the United States) rather recently, after the 1979 Iranian Revolution. One can certainly understand why the topsy-turvy, uncertain, and violent post–Revolutionary political climate in Iran may have produced a large number of exiles, a virtual brain drain with as many as "four to five million Iranians" leaving Iran during the 1980s and 1990s (Ebadi *Iran Awakening* 78). Many of these emigrating Iranians ended up settling in the United States "because of its long withstanding ties with Iran and the significant number of U.S.–educated Iranians who have resided historically in North America" (Karim and Rahimieh 7). In the new, significantly more open atmosphere of the West or the United States, some Iranian exiles, many of whom were extremely well-educated, took to writing. After all, many had a considerable amount to say about their native country and their new country, and only now were they free to do so without the fear of censorship or imprisonment. The result was a new Iranian diasporic literature centered mainly in the United States.

Not until the later part of the twentieth century (specifically, 1978) did the first Iranian-American, Nahid Rachlin, publish a novel in English.[9] Iranian and diasporic Iranian writers like Rachlin and Gina Nahai subsequently found a larger audience after the Iranian Revolution in the 1980s and 1990s. As Persis Karim and Nasrin Rahimieh illustrate, "For the generation of Iranian-Americans coming of age in the post-exile, post-revolution period, literature become a vehicle by which to wrestle with their origins and the landscape of their American identity" (11). As one can imagine, the atmosphere for Iranians in the West during the 1980s wasn't entirely welcoming, making it difficult for diasporic Iranians to wrestle with their origins as well as with their new country and its culture. Ardavan Davaran suggests that Iranian diasporic literature can be categorized by "a sense of alienation, together with a nostalgic longing for the lost life of the homeland" (12). Indeed, alienation is a common theme in the various works explored in this book. However, many diasporic Iranian writers and diasporic Iranian characters, both first and second generation Westerners, strive to be and sometimes succeed in becoming something more than alienated exiles. They might not always be able to "assert the dignity of their existence," and formulate "a new consciousness," but, through their depictions, we can see the beginnings of an amalgamation of Western and Iranian worlds (Davaran 12).

Still, being an Iranian expatriate, and more specifically an Iranian-American, comes with its set of challenges. Some of those challenges are common to a new emigrating ethnic group, while others are more specific to the Iranian diasporic community. Ever since the Iranian Revolution of 1979, as Persis Karim and Mohammad Khorrami explain, "Many Iranian-Americans have often felt concerned, ambivalent, and at times even ashamed about revealing their heritage in an atmosphere steeped with media images portraying Iranians as hostile, as fanatical, and above all as terrorists" (21–22). Iranians tended to not be especially race conscious while in Iran (as most considered themselves to be white or Caucasian[10]), but after settling in the West, diasporic Iranians began to become more racially conscious as an increasing number of Westerners questioned and interrogated their ethnic identity. As Iranian-American writer Gelareh Asayesh explains, "I grew up thinking I was white. When I moved from Iran to America, I discovered otherwise" (12). Iranian-Americans are in a particularly challenging position as an ethnic group because they are not easily categorized. They are often misidentified, due to their appearance and their surname, as Latino or Arabic.

Still, in a larger sense, critics like Jasmin Darznik have argued that Iranian-American or diasporic literature, as a new genre or sub-genre, suffers from a "present crisis," generally specific to a new form of ethnic literature (55). Specifically, she suggests that the "crisis" mirrors debates "about authenticity and authority in other US ethnic literatures, for example the debates that arose in the late 1970s and 1980s, following the publication of *Aiieeee!* (1974), the first anthology of Asian-American literature" (55). Further, Darznik suggests that Iranian-American writers have not fully assimilated as other ethnic American writers have.[11] One reason why Iranian-Americans may have more difficultly assimilating to the general mainstream and to the literary mainstream is that they comprise a relatively small literary and ethnic group. Whereas Asian-American literature, from its emergence to the present day, encompasses literally millions of people (and indirectly, billions of people) as well as many distinct nations and cultures, Iranian-American literature is considerably smaller, referring as it does to only one country and to a much smaller ethnic group. Complicating matters is the fact that, along with much of Middle Eastern American literature, Iranian-American literature is often marginalized or excluded because it does not quite fit neatly into a category such as Asian-American literature or postcolonial literature.

Another factor affecting Iranian-American literature, and more specifically, Iranian diasporic literature is the aftermath of the September 11, 2001, attacks, which, Darznik further argues, contributed to how many Iranian diasporic writers resist assimilation or have difficulty assimilating in the West (especially in the United States).[12] Certainly, after September 11 there has been a backlash against Americans who are or who appear to be Muslim or of Middle Eastern descent as well as an increasing amount of prejudice and stereotypes of Muslims as violent, rabid, and intellectually stunted.[13] However, the events of September 11 cut both ways, not only creating divisions between communities and people, but also helping set the stage for a better understanding of, in particular, predominantly Muslim Middle Eastern countries and people. Indeed, after September 11, many Americans who previously had little to no knowledge of Islam or Middle Eastern cultures and nations became interested in learning about the region, its people, and its cultures. This emerging interest can be seen in the increased numbers of memoirs and other nonfiction books published about various countries in the region and in the increased attention for, as well as the critical and commercial success of, contemporary Middle Eastern, Central Asian, and Iranian diasporic literature.[14] For example, after September 11, Azar Nafisi's *Reading Lolita in Tehran* (2003)[15] and Khalid Hosseini's *The Kite Runner* (2004), among other literary and nonfictional works, became bestsellers. Along similar lines, it may be no accident that Shirin Ebadi, an Iranian judge, won the Nobel Peace Prize in 2003, not long after the events of September 11, for her work towards political and personal equity as well as human and civil rights in Iran.[16]

Still, to a large extent, Iran has not benefited from any Western, post–9/11 increased understanding or sympathy for predominantly Muslim Middle Eastern or Central Asian countries. Conventional Western or American views of Iran tend to be less than idyllic and are often the result of generalizations and stereotypes. Indeed, animosity towards Iran was made particularly palpable during the 2008 U.S. presidential campaign when Republican candidate John McCain answered a question regarding what to do about Iran with a modification of the Beach Boys' song "Barbara Ann" to "Bomb Iran" (McCain's chorus being "Bomb-Bomb-Bomb, Bomb-Bomb Iran"). While McCain later claimed that his rendition was just meant to be a "joke" to "amuse old veteran friends," the laughter of those "veteran friends," indicates that, on some level, they agreed with the attitude conveyed by the lyrics (Edwards and Brynaert, par. 14; Gonyea, par. 5). This is only one example of the many ways Iran has been maligned or misunderstood by the Western media and general Western (and American) public. Author, critic, and professor Hamid Dabashi argues that Iran has been homogenized by Western countries like the United States despite being "multicultural, multiethnic, multifaceted, syncretic, and hybrid" (*Iran* 20–21). Dabashi also argues that even Iranian studies itself "is a direct descendent of old-fashioned Orientalism" (21).

Indeed, Edward Said's theories of Orientalism prove helpful when studying Iranian and diasporic Iranian literature. The Western media has helped contribute to caricatures of Iranians and other Middle Eastern Muslims as violent, primitive or backwards (or exoticized as Dabashi suggests) while depicting Iran (and other predominantly Muslim Middle Eastern countries) as aggressive and gendered not as feminine but as hyper-masculine. Still, one cannot completely condemn the Western world and the United States for their stereotypical conceptions of Iranians. As Robert Baer argues, Iran is a very complex country whose governing bodies could be described as "deeply xenophobic and paranoid," in which "all foreign visitors are seen as potential spies," and where "there's no such thing as investigative journalism" (16–17). Indeed, in later chapters, we shall see evidence of a rampant paranoia in the Islamic Republic, which, in itself, can be largely attributed to unwanted Western interference in the political and social structure in Iran. While the West may not be able to proclaim many (or practically any) indisputable truths about Iran, at the very least, the literature of Iranians and diasporic Iranians reveals more holistic, realistic, complex, and disparate perspectives about Iran. In particular, this realism is apparent in the writings by younger Iranians or diasporic Iranians who were born right before or after the Islamic Revolution, as they can speak directly about life in post-revolutionary Iran and in the West, and they also have the most invested in the future of both Iran and the West.

Towards that end, this study focuses on the younger generation of Iranians and diasporic Iranians who were generally born from the early 1960s through the early 1980s.[17] In the United States and other Western countries, this group is generally known as Generation X. In Iran, they are often called the Burnt Generation, a term signifying the amount of strife they grew up with in Iran,[18] from the steep causalities of the Iran-Iraq war, which lasted from 1980 to 1988, to the more recent defeat of the sizeable student-led protests of the late 1990s in Iran,[19] to the thwarted 2009 demonstrations. For most of their lives, those of the Burnt Generation have lived in an environment dominated by war, Western paranoia, and religious dogmaticism. This generation also grew up and continues to live in a bleak economic climate in which "according to the regime's own figures, 15 percent of the population lies below the poverty line and the unemployment rate among young people under 30 is about 28.4 per cent" (Alavi 147).[20] Other accounts of Iran suggest that, along with poverty, there has been an increase in hard drug use and general despondency among Iranian youth.[21] This stark economic reality is worsened by a general, and, as it turns out, a rather accurate sense that the gulf has widened between the rich and the poor[22] in Iran, with many of the newly wealthy being powerful clerics who have become overly materialistic (Afshan, par. 15).

While these formidable challenges might understandably lead to more of a defeated or frustrated generation (and to be sure, some of this exists) in contemporary Iran, the Burnt Generation has proven itself (especially through the 1999 student demonstrations and the 2009 Green movement) to be extremely politically active and motivated. In addition, even though both demonstrations ultimately failed to produce regime change or political upheaval in Iran, they have produced significant results. For instance, a by-product of the 1999 student demonstrations was a more transparent and culpable Iranian government, which "admitted partial complicity in the premeditated spate of killings ... of dozens of intellectuals" during the demonstrations themselves (Ebadi *Iran Awakening* xii). This was "the first time in the history of the Islamic Republic that the state had acknowledged that it had murdered its critics, and the first time a trial would be convened to hold the perpetrators accountable" (Ebadi *Iran Awakening* xiv). In addition, I would argue that the Burnt Generation helped lay the groundwork for the subsequent Arab Spring of 2011.[23] Indeed, the 2009 demonstrations in Iran can be seen as a precursor (if not a catalyst) of the events in Tunisia, Egypt, and other Middle Eastern countries during the spring of 2011. What all of these movements have in common is that they were youth-driven and fueled by new technological platforms like Twitter, Facebook, and blogs. In a later chapter, I will explore the role these new technologies have played (and continue to play) in contemporary Iran.

Perhaps feeling they have little to lose,[24] the Burnt Generation may prove to be instrumental in transforming the Islamic Regime as well as in transforming Western attitudes towards Iran and other predominantly Muslim countries in the Middle East.[25] First, the Burnt Generation has sizeable numbers as over 70 percent of Iran's population was born after the mid 1970s. This means that, as of 2011, the vast majority of the country is under thirty-five years of age (Fang and Whitlaw 21). In addition, members of the Burnt Generation, despite Iran's filtering of the Internet, are much more technologically savvy than previous generations, leading to their use of blogs, Twitter, and other platforms to express their views and bypass the restrictions of the Islamic Regime. Also, with access (albeit limited at times) to global media and (access permitting) the Internet, they have become more cognizant of other cultures and nations,[26] and many have, as Fang and Whitlaw argue, grown "tired of living under repressive rule" (21).[27]

Possibly influenced by the worldwide spread of Western and American popular culture, presumably made all the more appealing by its frequent censorship, banning, and demonization by the Islamic Republic,[28] members of the Burnt Generation also appear more willing to embrace the West. This is noted not only by Iranians themselves, but also in the accounts of Westerners traveling and living in Iran. For instance, in his book *Children of Jihad* (2007), Jared Cohen, a former Rhodes Scholar at Oxford, describes his travels to the Middle East while in his twenties. When he travels to Iran, Cohen notes a desire on the part of youth to rebel against their government and to embrace American popular culture, if not ideology. Cohen writes:

> The vast majority of the Iranian population is under the age of thirty and these young people proved not only eager to talk to me, but also to be forth-

right in their displeasure for the Iranian regime. To this day, the Iranian people are some of the most pro–American people I have met in the entire world. The vast majority of Iranians — especially the youth — have a strong affinity for American culture, products, and entertainment and a substantial portion has at least an element of appreciation for the American government's unwillingness to pander to the Iranian regime [28–9].

Similarly, other critics have identified how members of the Burnt Generation tend to use democratic and Western rhetoric, such as, "We, too, want and deserve the freedom to dress. The freedom to speak. The freedom to assemble. The freedom to love and the freedom to dream" (Afshar, par. 19). Lila Zaganeh also describes young Iranians as "ravenously eager to embrace modernity along with a certain avatar of the American dream" (xiv). This is not to suggest that nearly all members of the Burnt Generation support the West or Western culture, for as Zaganeh argues, there still exists a wide diversity of opinions among younger Iranians with some being "genuinely religious," and believing "in a modern, progressive, and tolerant Islam," while "many — while mesmerized by satellite TVs and American sitcoms — remain skeptical about American values" (xiv). However, the evidence suggests that a sizeable portion of the Burnt Generation (more sizeable than their parents' generation) have, if not embraced the West, then at least resisted its demonization by the Islamic Republic. Ironically, the reverse cannot be asserted about American youth, who are much less informed or interested in Iran and Iranians than Iranians tend to be about the United States and Americans.

Younger diasporic Iranians face a set of problems in some way similar but also distinct from the Burnt Generation. Many in this group were actually born in Iran during the 1960s and 1970s and subsequently moved to the United States (or, in Marjane Satrapi's case, France) when children or teenagers. Others are second-generation Westerners or Americans. In the case of Iranian-Americans, as Persis Karim and Mohammad Khorrami explain, "These children [now adults] have lived not only with the displacing effects of that revolution and their immigration, but also with the fallout from the tense political relations between Iran and the United States" (255). This would include the hostage situation in the immediate aftermath of the Iranian Revolution (post–1979), the aftermath of the Iran-Contra scandal, the current political confrontation with Iran concerning their possible development of nuclear weapons, Iran's general support of Palestinians as well as radical Palestinian groups like Hamas, and Iran's various human rights violations. While Iranian Generation Xers came of age during what Karim and Khorrami suggest are the "multicultural identity politics of the 1980s and 1990s in the United States" (255), they have been largely left out of that conversation. One reason for their exclusion may be that Iranian-Americans have tended to settle in specific parts of the United States, most notably Los Angeles (or Tehrangeles as some call it). Since Iranian-Americans have not, by and large, dispersed around the country as much as other ethnic groups, most Americans have had no direct, first-hand contact or experience of interacting with, let alone knowing, any Iranian-Americans. In fact, as Iranian-Americans are probably not recognizable to most Americans either visually or by name, they have further become an ethnically invisible or marginalized group.

While this book is not a study in Iranian history, it is important, when exploring contemporary Iran as well as its relationship to the West, to consider key events in recent Iranian political and cultural history. In some ways, Iran can be considered a postcolonial country, having gained its independence (debatably) during the 1979 Iranian Revolution from the Western backed monarchy led by the Shah, who, it has been suggested, was put in place by the United States in 1953 in an effort to unseat the steadily more powerful Prime Minister Mohammad Mossadegh, who was believed to be sympathetic to Communism.[29] As Ebadi explains, the unseating of Mossadegh and the subsequent rise to power of the Shah was "a profoundly humiliating moment for Iranians, who watched the United States intervene in their politics as if their country were some annexed backwater, its leader to be installed or deposed at the whim of an American president and his CIA advisors" (*Iran Awakening* 5). Indeed, we will see that the Iranian government is still extremely wary of the West (especially the United States), believing there is a Western or American push for a Velvet Revolution in Iran, for the purpose of installing a Western backed or friendly government.

While Westerners tend to regard the current Islamic Republic under Ahmadenijad as generally totalitarian, repressive, and unmindful of basic human rights, the Western-backed Shah's administration employed many of the same tactics, best illustrated through the Shah's secret police, the SAVAK,[30] which "hounded writers, intellectuals, and political activists and tortured them in prisons" (Hakakian 6). The corruption of the Shah's regime, apparent through the millions of dollars it squandered on celebration of events and monuments commemorating ancient Persia, helped fuel growing resentment as well as the 1979 Iranian Revolution itself.[31] Still, many of these same intellectuals and political dissidents (including Communists and Marxists)[32] that supported and fought for the Revolution found themselves increasingly isolated, discriminated against, and eventually jailed, tortured or executed as Iran became more of a fundamentalist religious state in the early 1980s.[33] At this time, not only did Iranians have to face the devastation caused by the war against Iraq,[34] they grew increasingly anti–Western and anti–American, since the United States and other Western powers were supporting Saddam

Hussein and Iraq and since the United States helped put the Shah in place.[35] After the Iran-Iraq war and the death of the Ayatollah in the late 1980s, the more economically pragmatic Akbar Hashami Rafsanjani served as the president of Iran from 1989 to 1997. While, as we will see with a study of Azar Nafisi's *Reading Lolita in Tehran*, Iran was hardly much more progressive at this time, towards the end of Rafsanjani's term, Iran began a period of gradual political and social awakening and change, culminating in the early 2000s.[36]

This period of political change was heralded by Mohammed Khatami, who served as president of Iran from 1997 to 2005. A well-educated, contemporary Renaissance Man, Khatami "spoke three languages, studied Western philosophy, stood up straight, and spoke eloquently about rights and individual dignity" (Ebadi *Iran Awakening* 147). Azadeh Moaveni, whose memoirs will be explored in a later chapter, describes the Khatami administration as "a speck of light in over two decades of revolutionary darkness," even though, as Ebadi suggests, he was only able to achieve a limited amount of political and social progress due to growing resistance by Iranian clerics (Moaveni *Lipstick Jihad* 131; Ebadi *Iran Awakening* 147–8). Indeed, the Khatami administration marks the beginning of a growing gulf between the Iranian clerics and the general Iranian public. While, at this time, the Iranian administration (headed by Khatami) was more in line with the general Iranian public (as opposed to the clerics), this would change dramatically with the election of Ahmadinejad and his subsequent administration.

Indeed, to a large degree, one of the main reasons the West currently tends to vilify Iran is Ahmadinejad's perceived behavior and actions, exemplified by the supposed increases in human rights violations under his administration, including, but not limited to, how Iran has arrested, incarcerated, and even executed prisoners without due process (or with dubious due process) for "crimes" such as immorality, blasphemy, and demonstrating against the government or administration. As much as the West (and the global community) should justifiably be outraged by these crimes, it is important to recognize that the SAVAK engaged in the same human rights violations during the reign of the Shah,[37] and the West neither made it an issue nor intervened on the behalf of those affected. Also, while other nearby Middle Eastern countries like Saudi Arabia arguably have even longer lists of human rights violations than Iran, they are typically implicated by the West because of their status as an ally or contributor to the West (e.g., Saudi Arabia) or because they are not often perceived as a direct threat to the West (e.g., Yemen).

As we will also see in subsequent chapters, Iran is a country extremely aware of its image as projected by its own media as well as by global or Western media. As Ebadi suggests, enough attention placed upon Iran's human rights violations may indeed help spark political (if not regime) change.[38] At the same time, Iran has demonstrated skill and versatility in using the media to demonize the West, in particular the Untied States, and to combat their own negative portrayal by Western media. As Zanganeh argues, being called "Western" is one of the worst insults in Iran[39] and the Iranian government as well as high ranking clerics often set up ideological oppositions between the West and Iran (xii). Not only can this be seen through Iranian news and television, it can also be seen in how the Islamic Regime prevents certain information or art, often Western or American in origin, from being released to the general population. They do this through the censorship of books, film, and music, as well as through their use of Internet firewalls, and by banning certain television shows and channels (Ebadi *Iran Awakening* 211; Nafisi "The Stuff" 6). However, in subsequent chapters, we will see that these forms of censorship have often failed or backfired, as illustrated by the large number of Iranian blogs (often critical of the Islamic Regime) that exist and flourish, in addition to the number of Iranians who have been surreptitiously able to gain access to all forms of satellite television. At the same time, those who have protested censorship in Iran or who have directly challenged the government have frequently been subject to discrimination, arrest, torture, and even death.

While the United States (as well as the West) does not generally censor art and does not generally limit information access to adults, it too engages in a campaign to indoctrinate its citizens into a totalizing view of Iran as a backward, violent dictatorship. For example, even when Rhodes Scholar Jared Cohen travels to Iran for the first time in 2004 from Oxford, he is "prepared for the worst," presumably due to the depiction of Iran in the Western media. Indeed, when Cohen sees billboards that read "Down with the USA," to a large extent, his initial impressions of Iran are confirmed. Still, as he spends more time getting to know the real Iran and the real Iranian people, Cohen notices a seemingly contradictory, simultaneous embrace and rejection of the West (and the United States) in Iran. In fact, he concludes, "It is more common to see advertisements and products of Western culture than it is messages denouncing America and Israel" (44). Along these lines, in *Journey from the Land of No*, Roya Hakanian argues that Americans thinking of Iran tend to fall into two primary groups:

> The misinformed, who think of Iran as a backward nation of Arabs, veiled and turbaned, living on the periphery of oases and fairly represented by a government of mullahs; and the misguided, who believed the shah's regime was a puppet government run by the CIA, and who think that Ayatollah Khomeini and his clerical cabal are an authentic, homegrown answer to unwarranted U.S. meddling [10–11].

At the same, in recent years, Iranian art and literature have become more popular than ever in the West and in the United States. As mentioned earlier, part of this popularity can be traced to the general public's desire to know more about Iran (and the Middle East) after the events of September 11, but it can also be attributed to Iran's growing political notoriety as notoriety can and often does breed interest. In this case, if notoriety is the main cause, it has had beneficial results in bringing global attention to a number of important Iranian and diasporic Iranian political activists, writers, and artists such as Nobel Prize–winning Shirin Ebadi, Azar Nafisi, Shohreh Aghdashloo (the first Iranian-American actress nominated for an Academy Award),[40] and Iranian filmmakers like Abbas Kiarostami[41] who have become critically acclaimed in the West.

With the exception of Abbas Kiarostami, the activists, artists and writers just listed are female. Given that Iran (like other Islamic Middle Eastern countries) tends to have the reputation of being patriarchal and sexist, readers may find it surprising that the vast majority of contemporary Iranian and diasporic Iranian writers (and artists) are women. While this disparity could, in part, be due to how Iran (and other Middle Eastern countries) may tend to feminize the arts (as opposed to the more supposedly masculine pursuits of medicine and engineering), the role of women in artistic fields is more complicated than such a generalization could explain.

It is hard to deny that Iranian women are, to some degree, oppressed by the Islamic Regime, if not by traditional Iranian or Persian culture. Indeed, Ebadi argues, "In most Iranian households, male children enjoyed an exalted status, spoiled and cosseted by a coterie of aunts and female relatives. They often felt themselves the center of the family's orbit" (*Iran Awakening* 11).[42] Still, the Islamic Regime (and its administration) disputes these depictions of its country and culture as sexist and patriarchal. For instance, in his speech at Columbia University in 2007, Ahmadenijad not only claimed that "in every Iranian family who has a girl, they are 10 times happier than having a son," but also that, "women are respected more than men are" (par. 176). Further, he suggested, "Many of the legal responsibilities rest on the shoulders of men in our society because of the respect, culturally given, to women, to the future mothers" (par. 177). However, contrary to these claims, as demonstrated in subsequent chapters, Iranian women are largely denied the same legal rights as men[43] (when it comes to marriage, divorce, and custody of their children), and they are subject to dress code regulations (e.g., the veil).[44]

Still, this does not mean that the Islamic Regime treats women in a completely sexist manner. First, one could point to how, unlike most predominantly Islamic countries, "more than half of those graduating from university in Iran today are women" (Alavi 10).[45] In addition, there has been some social and cultural progress for women in post–Revolutionary Iran.[46] As Robert Baer explains, "The average age of marriage for an Iranian woman today is twenty-five; during the Shah's last year in power, it was thirteen" (9). Also, Iran is, in some ways, more progressive than neighboring Middle Eastern countries when it comes to sexuality and gender, as evident by how "doctors reportedly perform more sex-change operations in Iran than in any other country except Thailand, with the Iranian government even paying up to half the cost for some transsexuals" (Baer 9). While it may be argued that, especially through its strict dress code and laws against public affection, Iran does not allow its citizens (especially women) free personal and sexual expression, it has been argued that the West's championing of supposedly free sexual expression (especially for women) is more a form of oppression than liberation.[47] During the Khatami administration, women also gained some political power; in the 2003 elections, more women entered the legislature than ever before. As Ebadi explains, "It was the first time since the revolution that the ratio of women to men in the Iranian parliament was similar to that in European countries" (*Iran Awakening* 185).

This is not to suggest that the Islamic Republic is a strong proponent of women's liberation or that there is anything approaching gender equality in the country. For many Westerners, the regulation to use the veil is emblematic of the oppression of Iranian and Islamic women. This view is perhaps best exemplified by Nafisi, who argues, "The mandatory veil was an attempt to force social uniformity through an assault on individual and religious freedoms, not an act of respect for traditions and culture" ("The Stuff" 5). In fact, as discussed in forthcoming chapters, Western publishers use the veil itself to market Iranian and Iranian diasporic literature, with covers sometimes depicting veiled Iranian women, as if to invite Western readers to view Iran as an oppressive, patriarchal, sexist regime, and, as Persis Karim suggests, to further fixate "on the veil as an icon of the essential identity of Iranian women" (xix). Indeed, as Karim argues, this can be seen as a kind of "silencing" (xix).

Still, the question remains: if Iranian women are being silenced, who is silencing them — the West or the Islamic Regime? I would argue that the answer to this question is both. In the case of the Islamic Regime, some of the recent supposed progress for women is more superficial than substantial. Despite the fact that the majority of university students in Iran are women, the Islamic Regime largely denies them the same career opportunities as Iranian men (Ebadi *Iran Awakening* 107–8). Towards that end, while in Iran, American-born Azadeh Moaveni, whose journalistic memoirs I will explore in a subsequent chapter, finds that contemporary Iranian women lack a clear identity or satisfying life goals.[48] Also, Iran sets up nearly contradictory and paradoxical standards for women that only serve to obfuscate matters, exemplified by how, in Moaveni's words, the Islamic Regime suggests "women were liberated but legally inferior; women should be educated but subservient; women should have careers but stick to traditional gender roles; women should play sports but ignore their dirty physical needs" (*Lipstick Jihad* 179).

Still, it can hardly be denied that one of the most notable aspects of contemporary Iranian and diasporic Iranian literature is that women have come to dominate the field, from Marjane Satrapi's graphic novels to the novels of Dalia Sofer and Porochista Khakpour to the works of literary critics and memoir writers like Nafisi and Moaveni. This is even more the case in contemporary Iran itself. As Persis Karim explains, "Even while they have had to endure harsh government censorship, Iranian women have, since the 1980s, written and published in unprecedented numbers. Over the past decade, Iran's best-selling fiction lists have been dominated by women" (xx). As mentioned earlier, one reason for this may be that Iranian men tend to be pushed into "practical" careers (writing not being considered a practical career by many Iranians). Alternatively, after being silenced for so many generations and decades, Iranian and diasporic Iranian women may simply have much more to say than their male counterparts.[49] It is also reasonable to conclude that more diasporic Iranian women may be writing and being published because they feel liberated by the West. Market forces probably also play a part. Western publishers may have discovered that female authors writing about oppression, identity, and ethnicity are more widely received than male writers either because they may be presumed to be less threatening or they may encourage the Western reader to position him- or herself in the role of a savior.

One thing that has certainly had an impact on contemporary Iran, and will no doubt continue to influence the direction in which Iran heads in the future, is globalization. In this case, globalization can be seen as the almost hegemonic advances of American popular culture, not just in Iran but throughout the Islamic Middle East. As Martin Gannon explains:

> Several years ago *Fortune* magazine analyzed the bedrooms of various male teenagers in widely different nations and found the similarities to be much greater than the differences. These similarities included posters of Michael Jordan, basketballs and running shoes, and CDs of the latest popular songs. MTV is a similar example; it has spread quickly throughout the world [37].

Especially since the 2009 Iranian demonstrations and the Arab Spring, many Americans and other Westerners have held high hopes that Iranian youth will want to embrace democracy, in some cases to the point of revolution, and that the Burnt Generation (and subsequent Iranian generations) will make substantial connections with their Western counterparts. To be certain, media and technology, most notably satellite television and the Internet, have helped produce global connections and an increasing interest in Western culture (even though the Islamic Republic has done its best to block certain websites and programming deemed blasphemous or pro–Western).[50] Indeed, Alavi describes contemporary Iranians as being "caught in the conflict between globalization and tradition" with globalization being represented by "satellite television" and the Internet and tradition referring to "Islamic revolutionary values" (18).

Of the two forms, while satellite television has come to play an important role in contemporary Iran, the Internet dwarfs satellite television in terms of its importance. While Iran may not have as many computers per resident as the United States, and "owning a computer remains the luxury of the upper classes," as Jared Cohen explains, "the growing number of Internet cafes has made the Internet widely accessible to a broad swath of Iranians" (56). In fact it has been estimated that by 2003, Iran ranked third in the world in terms of the number of weblogs produced by a single country (Moaveni, *Lipstick Jihad* 128).[51] More recently, it was estimated that "there are more Iranian blogs than there are Spanish, German, Italian, Chinese or Russian" (Alavi 1).[52] As we will see in a subsequent chapter, one of the reasons for the almost exponential rise in the use of the Internet and blogs in Iran is how much Iran has clamped down on free expression. In recent years "as many as 100 print publications, including 41 daily newspapers, have been closed by Iran's hardline judiciary" (Alavi 2). Without the print or tele-visual media functioning in a free, unbiased manner, young Iranians have few to no options other than the Internet to express their views freely and to try to obtain relatively unbiased information.

To be sure, though, the increase in the use of the Internet, blogs, Twitter, and other technological platforms should not mitigate the importance of printed literature. While blogs and other postings may have the potential for more immediate effects, literature provides more potential for lasting change in an audience. Such influence is evident in how works like Azar Nafisi's *Reading Lolita in Tehran* have helped shaped impressions of Iran and Iranians in the minds of a huge number of readers (in some illuminating and restrictive ways). In addition, the same can be asserted of the popular (both in the United States and Iran) memoir *Funny in Farsi* and the graphic novel *Persepolis*. While critics and countries may dispute how best to analyze Iran as a country, most would agree that Iran holds great importance to the larger region (the Middle East), to the West (especially the United States), and to the larger world. With so little known about Iran and so much presumed about it in the Western world, Iranian and Iranian diasporic literature serve a crucial role of educating the Western public about Iran as a country, and, if the texts find their way (legally or illegally) through or by Iranian censorship, providing insight into the West for those living in Iran. Finally, as someone who has regularly taught courses in contemporary Iranian and diasporic Iranian literature and culture, I can attest to the importance of literature (over historical, political, and cultural texts) in helping to shape and transform student attitudes towards Iran and even towards the West.

If it is true that literature can breed understanding and connections among people of disparate backgrounds, as I believe, then the work of Iranian and Iranian diasporic writers can truly be the ultimate diplomatic tool to help erode and deconstruct the damaging and counterproductive stereotypes and generalizations of both Iran and the West as "good" or "evil," "sexist" or "egalitarian," "oppressed," or "free," and "totalitarian" or "democratic." My hope is that this study brings attention to the many Iranian and Iranian diasporic writers who portray Iran and Iranians for what they truly are: a complex country and people who can claim rich cultural and social traditions, but who are also politically torn and in some ways are casualties of the policies of the West. To call Iran part of something "evil"—a label perpetuated by the Bush administration and subsequent political figures as well as various media outlets—is dismissive, counterproductive, inflammatory, and ultimately false. Through literature, we can deconstruct these false dichotomies and uncover the nuanced complexities of contemporary Iran and the Iranian diaspora.

# 1

# The Personal and the Political

*Marjane Satrapi's* Persepolis *and* Persepolis 2

A literary comic book — a graphic novel — about growing up in Iran? On the surface, it sounds almost farcical and counterproductive. Such a style and format could lead to an increasing amount of generalizations and stereotypes about Iran and Iranians. In addition, it could also trivialize crucial and tragic accounts of life in Iran as well as obfuscate any real insights we might glean into the political, cultural, and social structures in contemporary Iran. Who would read such a work? One might imagine that it would not appeal to the stereotypical comic book audience of young, asocial adolescent boys or the more literate, erudite audience of readers who typically shun comics or graphic novels. Yet, Marjane Satrapi's *Persepolis* and *Persepolis 2* (originally published in French in 2000 and 2001 respectively, and published in English in 2003 and 2004, respectively) have been not only critically but also commercially successful.[1] In a way, these works were published at just the right time. Not only has there been an almost exponential increase in comic and graphic novel sales since 2001,[2] there has also been, after the attacks of September 11, a growing desire on the part of the Western reading public to know more about various Middle Eastern countries and cultures.[3] Instead of contributing to the generalizations and stereotypes about Iran and Iranians or trivializing the country and its people, *Persepolis* and *Persepolis 2* do the opposite. They humanize a country and a people, while providing a more holistic account of Iranian culture. In large part, Satrapi does this by writing candidly and thoughtfully about her own life, while depicting concurrent events in Iran, leading the reader to empathy and understanding.

In contemporary Western media and print cultures, dominated by reality television and the search for the "real" and the "true," autobiographies and memoirs from Dave Eggers's *A Heartbreaking Work of Staggering Genius* (2000) to President Barack Obama's *Dreams of My Father* (1995; re-released in 2004) have become increasingly popular. No doubt, one of the appeals of Satrapi's works is its autobiographical nature. In fact, there is an autobiographical element to all of Satrapi's works, which include graphic works such as *Embroideries* (2005) and *Chicken with Plums* (2006), both of which mainly focus upon other members of Satrapi's family. However, I have chosen to focus on *Persepolis* and *Persepolis 2* as they best encapsulate Satrapi's themes and styles, while being the most politically and socially invested of her works. They have also dwarfed her other works in terms of critical acclaim and commercial success.

Born in 1969 in Iran, Satrapi used much of her early life (from the late 1970s to the early 1990s) as the basis for both *Persepolis* and *Persepolis 2*, and their autobiographical nature lends both a sense of authenticity in the sense that it is difficult, if not impossible, for critics to deny some of the power of Satrapi's accounts since they are not fictional. Towards this end, it has been suggested that "autobiography has been accorded a privileged status in postcolonial and diasporic contexts" (Naghibi and O'Malley 223). While it may be a matter of some debate as to whether Iran is or is not a postcolonial nation, I would argue that it is, given the United States' role in the coup of Prime Minister Mohammad Mosaddegh in 1953 and the subsequent reign of the U.S.–influenced Shah. Postcolonial autobiographies can reflect an individual's or a country's desire to assert independence after being dependent upon the colonizer. In addition, *Persepolis* and *Persepolis 2* are diasporic autobiographies, and as such, they can assert or at least help establish one's identity, which can become fragmented or severely altered when one settles in a country with different cultural norms or a country that marginalizes newcomers. The struggle to establish an identity as an exile, according to Satrapi, is only a struggle if one wants to maintain one's cultural heritage. In her own words, "To become integrated, one must forget entirely where one comes from" (qtd. in Kutschera 50).

For Satrapi then, there results an oppositional dichotomy, whereby being an exile offers two main choices: either submitting (assimilating) to the new, dominant culture or always remaining separate from it (at least to some extent). In both *Persepolis* and *Persepolis 2*, Satrapi gravitates back and forth between these polar opposites. For instance, in *Persepolis 2*, Satrapi describes how, when living in Austria, after seeing and hearing rampant negative stereotypes about Iranians by Westerners, she feels alienated. Subsequently, she tries to integrate fully by "denying my nationality" (qtd. in Kutschera 50). However, this does not work, as Satrapi's "friends" who know of her Iranian heritage do not allow her to be anything other than Iranian (which ostracizes her) and they strongly rebuke her for trying to assimilate. They also choose to believe that Satrapi is an opportunistic liar rather than an ostracized victim whose attempt to assimilate is a failure due not to Satrapi herself due to the non–racially egalitarian country (Austria) in which she now lives.

We can view *Persepolis* and *Persepolis 2* from both postcolonial and diasporic contexts since, at heart, both are about identity and independence, not just of the author-protagonist, but also of Iran itself. After all, the 1979 Islamic Revolution purportedly gave Iran its independence after a centuries-long monarchical rule. Even though *Persepolis* and *Persepolis 2* are mainly autobiographies, Satrapi's decision to use the name *Persepolis*, as it alludes to the celebrated city of Ancient Persia, can be seen as reflecting her desire to recapture Iranian history as well as her desire for readers to appreciate the history of Iran and Persia, especially the celebrated time of the city of Persepolis and the rule of Darius and Xerxes the Great, approximately 2500 years ago. Indeed, Satrapi believes, with good reason, that many Westerners have no real knowledge of Iranian or Persian history and culture, focusing instead on the supposed twin demons of terrorism and rampant sexism exemplified by the mandatory use of the veil for women. In her own words, Satrapi emphasizes, "Iran has extremists, for sure. Iran has Scheherazade as well. But first and foremost, Iran has an actual identity, an actual history — and above all, actual people, like me" ("How Can One Be Persian," 23). Indeed, in Satrapi's account, Iran's history after Darius and Xerxes is not always glorious; rather, it reflects, in the words of her father, "2500 Years of Tyranny and Submission" from Arabic and Mongolian invaders to "modern imperialism" (*Persepolis* 11).

While Satrapi devotes little space in *Persepolis* to recounting Iranian history, she does bring it in at important points in the narrative when intertwining the personal with the political. For instance, when describing the reign of the Shah and his father, Reza Shah, instead of merely describing the general suffering the Iranian people endured, Satrapi has her grandmother (who has already emerged as a significant and sympathetic character) tell the story of what life was like then. Satrapi's grandmother recounts how many of Satrapi's family members were put in prison, how "the Shah's father took everything we owned," how her family went hungry, and how the Shah did not keep his promises to the Iranian people (*Persepolis* 26–27). Rather, according to her grandmother, "All the country's money went into ridiculous celebrations of the 2500 years of dynasty and other frivolities" (28).[4] According to Satrapi's grandmother, the celebrations did not bring cultural pride to Iranians. Instead, "the population couldn't have cared less" (28), presumably because many were economically disadvantaged or lived in fear of the SAVAK, the Shah's often-brutal and murderous police force. Satrapi realizes that in order to get her readers to care and to change their established stereotypes and conceptions of Iran, she cannot merely provide dry historical accounts, but rather, she needs to connect the history to the characters in order to help the reader become emotionally invested in Iran. Indeed, as with the recent case of the death of seemingly martyred Neda during the 2009 Iranian demonstrations, personalizing a case, especially in the age of easily dispersed global media, can help galvanize a response, if not a sea-change in attitudes or perspectives.

Related to the idea that personalized images can help galvanize a response, one of the largest selling points of both works is the graphic format, which (like the news media) blends image and text. Satrapi's works all fall into the somewhat nebulous new genre called "graphic novels." As Eddie Campbell points out, the term can be "used simply as a synonym for comic books" (13). Prior to the 1960s, if not through the 1990s, virtually all texts that consistently combined images with words (on every page) were considered to be comics or comic books. As Campbell also explains, "graphic novel" can also refer to a comic book that is bound "either in soft- or hardcover — in contrast to the old-fashioned stapled comic magazine" (13). It can also signify a work "that is equivalent in form and dimensions to the prose that is more than comic book in the scope of its ambition" (13). I would define a graphic novel more as a combination of the last two designations. Typically, comics that are bound tend to be (or at least be perceived as) more substantive in terms of their content, and I would agree with Campbell that the term "graphic novel" has helped give some academic legitimacy to this form, even if it is entirely or almost entirely a semantic difference. Technically, *Persepolis* and *Persepolis 2* would be more aptly described as graphic nonfiction or graphic autobiography; however, this is a term that does not seem to have been widely adopted yet.

In addition, the graphic format of *Persepolis* and *Persepolis 2* can capture the attention of readers who normally do not read much traditional fiction or who gravitate more towards shorter works or even comic books. While graphic works may lack the critical prestige of more traditional narratives, to some extent attitudes towards graphic works have changed in recent years. Some critics point to graphic works like Art Spiegelman's *Maus* (1973) as helping garner critical attention for works previously deemed low art (Notkin 8). Like *Maus*, in Satrapi's work,[5] it is precisely the coupling of images and text that gives her work emotional and intellectual power and substance. Satrapi explains what drew her to the graphic format:

> Image is an international language. The first writing of the human being was drawing, not writing. That appeared much before the alphabet. And when you draw a situation — someone is scared or angry or happy — it means the same thing in all cultures. You cannot draw someone crying, and in one culture they think that he is happy. He would have the same expression. There's something direct about the image [qtd. in Weich, par. 7].

Along these lines, for Western or American readers who may not be interested in learning of or reading about the complicated and often tragic account of contemporary Iran, the graphic novel provides a direct, non-overwhelming entry point, since most Westerners or Americans associate graphic novels with something lighthearted. While *Persepolis* and *Persepolis 2* do have lighthearted moments, they are most powerful in providing images that correspond with tragic commentary, such as showing the means through which Iranian prisoners are tortured (with an iron, for instance) or, in a climactic scene, the look of horror on Satrapi's face when she discovers part of her friend Neda's arm in rubble after Neda's family's home was bombed. In this case, the chapter ends with a blackened-out image box accompanying the words: "No scream in the world could have relieved my suffering and my anger" (*Persepolis* 142). It is precisely the accompanying images that allow the reader to fully empathize, if not experience the same emotions as Satrapi.

It has been suggested that graphic works are quintessentially modern and that their increasing popularity represents "an emerging new literature of our times in which word, picture, and typography interact meaningfully and which is in tune with the complexity of modern life with its babble of signs and symbols and stimuli" (Campbell 13). The irony of *Persepolis* and *Persepolis 2* is that they are not really focused on modern life, at least not in a Western sense, but rather upon Iran and the West as seen through the eyes of the narrator, Satrapi. Campbell also suggests that graphic novels are, in some ways, a post-postmodern form or that they can solve a quintessential postmodern dilemma in that they can help decipher or bring clarity and finality to an endless chain of signifiers, through the specific images. However, to a large extent, the accompanying images only add an additional dimension to this chain.

To further clarify, it is useful to consider graphic works in terms of post-structuralist theory.[6] It would seem that graphic works with pictures (signified) and words (signifier) would help efface the distinction between both as Campbell suggests. In a sense, this is accurate, for graphic works do provide singular images that stand as the signified; however, it is the author (in this case, Satrapi) who chooses what the signified will look like. By choosing which images to use and by choosing the manner in which she presents the images, Satrapi can help determine the audience's reaction. In this manner, graphic works can be somewhat totalitarian in their scope, leading readers towards more definitive conclusions than text-only narratives. In the case of an author who wants to shape or counteract ingrained notions of people, ideas, or concept, the graphic format is ideal as it can help counteract a certain association between a signifier (e.g., Iran) and a signified (e.g., repressive regime, Axis of Evil, etc.).

It has been suggested that graphic works, like comic books (if one accepts that there is a difference between the two), are the domain of the young.[7] If indeed graphic works "induce an enveloping kind of emotional identification that makes them only too congenial to adolescent narcissism" (Schjeldahl 165), the effect may be doubly, if not triply apparent with autobiographical graphic works like those of Satrapi which focus upon her childhood and adolescence, for these years or phases tend to be much more universal than adulthood. That is, to a large extent, regardless of where one grows up, the experience of childhood and adolescence tends to be much more uniform than adulthood. Along these lines, many readers and critics have praised *Persepolis* and *Persepolis 2* for its supposed universality in depicting that the Iranian-born author is indeed like most readers (presumably Western) in her emotional and behavioral responses to often challenging and even traumatic experiences.[8] Related to this apparent universality is the fact that *Persepolis* and *Persepolis 2* tend to defy classification, but rather "can be found in most bookstores in most North American cities under any one of the following categories: autobiography; children's or young adult's literature; graphic novel; middle east history; women's studies" (Naghibi and O'Malley 225). This does not mean that *Persepolis* and *Persepolis 2* encourage a kind of narcissism since, as established earlier, Satrapi does not consistently glorify herself and her actions, although she certainly appears heroic when speaking out against perceived hypocrisy and demeaning and racist behaviors of others.

Another way readers become emotionally invested in *Persepolis* and *Persepolis 2* is through Satrapi's depictions of strong, largely independent women. Satrapi does not want her primarily Western audience to merely see Iranian women as oppressed and as part of Gayatri Spivak's model of colonialism in which white men try to save brown women from brown men. Rather, Satrapi attempts to undo the generalizations and stereotypes of Iranian women as being powerless victims or pariahs.[9] In *Persepolis* and *Persepolis 2*, Satrapi also demonstrates how women can stage small rebellions that might go unnoticed by Westerners not aware of or accustomed to the rules and regulations of the Islamic Regime. For instance, one can tell how progressive an Iranian woman is by how much of her body and hair she shows through her choice of clothing and head covering (less head covering and more tightly fitting clothes suggest a more progressive woman) (*Persepolis 2* 140). This may not seem like a significant rebellion, but as women can be imprisoned for this "offense," it is a meaningful act.

At the same time, Satrapi doesn't fully embrace the notion that the limits placed on Iranian women (presumably by men) are definitely and completely oppressive, even though they would probably seem so to a general Western reader. For instance, when Satrapi attends art college in *Persepolis 2*, she is struck by the segregation of the sexes, especially when it comes to the stipulation that men and women use different staircases, which seems nonsensical since they all end up in the same place: a co-ed classroom. However, Satrapi doesn't directly condemn the practice. Rather, when a classmate, Shouka, explains to Satrapi that the gender segregated staircases aim "to keep the boys from watching our butts while we climbed," at the bottom of the picture, Satrapi writes, "I think she was right" (141). At the same time, Satrapi illustrates the hypocrisy of the Islamic Regime, which seeks to render women asexual in public through conservative dress, but which ultimately fails to achieve its goals, and in some ways backfires by further encouraging men to sexualize women. At another point in *Persepolis 2*, one of the Guardians of the Revolution accosts Satrapi as she is running to try to catch a bus. Even though Satrapi wears appropriate clothes, one of the Guardians tells her, "When you run, your behind makes movements that are ... how do you say ... obscene!" (147). Ironically, the full body chador that Satrapi wears actually encourages these Guardians of the Revolution to scrutinize Satrapi's body even more because of what her clothes withhold. In an act of defiance, Satrapi yells out in response: "Well then, don't look at my ass!" (147). Here we can see that the dictates of the Islamic Regime, when it comes to women and clothing, fail to render women asexual, but rather, seem to encourage a kind of hyperawareness of sexuality because of how intently they try to hide it.

Nima Naghibi and Andrew O'Malley suggest that one of the most important aspects of contemporary Iranian and diasporic Iranian literature is how much of it is written by women, who "have recently been using the genre to challenge the stereotype of the self-effacing, modest Iranian woman and to write themselves back into the history of the nation" (224). Along these lines, Satrapi progresses from being more introverted and self-effacing to becoming bold and assertive by *Persepolis 2*, and she has stated in an interview, "The basic problem of a country like mine, apart from the regime, apart from the government, is the patriarchal culture that is leading my country" (qtd. in Tully, par. 11). Counteracting the patriarchical culture of Iran are the strong, independent women like Satrapi herself as well as her mother and grandmother in *Persepolis* and *Persepolis 2*. Specifically, Satrapi's mother and grandmother tend to guide and correct Satrapi when she goes astray, and it is Satrapi's mother, not her father, who, in *Persepolis 2*, goes to Austria to visit and assist Satrapi. Still, male characters like Satrapi's father as well as her uncle Anoosh, who is imprisoned, released, but later executed as an accused Russian spy, play an important but stereotypical feminine role as nurturers for Satrapi. For instance, Anoosh lavishes a young Satrapi with affection while also becoming an inspiration to a young Satrapi in his non-violent, selfless, and idealistic devotion to Marxism. Satrapi breaks down gender stereotypes with these male characters who exhibit great strength with conventionally feminine attributes.

Along these lines, while she may view Iran as a patriarchy, Satrapi is careful to not give the reader a one-dimensional account of Iranian men as oppressors and Iranian women as oppressed victims. Satrapi may depict most Iranians in power as being men, but she portrays women in Iran as equally capable of oppressing one another. For instance, in *Persepolis*, female members of the Guardians of the Revolution accost Satrapi when she wears Western style clothing (a denim jacket and sneakers) as well as symbols of Western culture (a Michael Jackson pin). They call her a "little whore," and interrogate her at committee headquarters (*Persepolis* 133). Only through Satrapi's act of false but believable pathos to the guards is she able to be released. Similarly, when Satrapi returns to Iran in *Persepolis 2*, one of her former female "friends" suggests that she is a "whore" for having premarital sex (116). This occurs at another point when Satrapi is in art college, and her fellow students likewise condemn her for engaging in premarital sex (*Persepolis 2* 149). In Satrapi's words, "That day, half the class turned its back on me" (149). In these instances, we see how Iranian women have internalized the restrictions placed upon them by the patriarchical system, and end up doing the social enforcement for the patriarchy.

Still, Satrapi does not have a wider purpose of rewriting Iranian history beyond that of her family. *Persepolis* and *Persepolis 2* do not include revisionist accounts of Iranian women helping to shape the country or culture, for instance, nor are there any accounts of contemporary politically active women in Iran such as Shirin Ebadi. While Satrapi's works certainly lend themselves to feminist readings, she even lightly mocks feminist theory in *Persepolis 2*. For instance, after she reads works by Simone de Beauvoir, Satrapi focuses upon Beauvoir's seemingly trivial idea presented that "if women peed standing up, their perception of life would change" (21). As Satrapi explains, "So I tried. It ran lightly down my left leg. It was a little disgusting" (21). Western feminist theory, for Satrapi, turns out to not really be empowering as opposed to practical, real, and significant examples of what female members of her family can and have done.

It is important to also consider that *Persepolis* and *Persepolis 2* are coming of age stories, and as such, they detail a protagonist's (in this case, Satrapi's) attempt to establish a stable, fulfilling identity. It is doubtful that *Persepolis* and *Persepolis 2* would have been as significant or meaningful if the protagonist were an adult. Not only does having a child or adolescent protagonist add a kind of universal appeal, it also allows Satrapi to construct her narrative as a bildungsroman, or even a nearly failed kunstlerroman. In fact, Satrapi's artistic leanings are thwarted time and time again while she is in Iran (which was and is still not open to all forms of artistic expression), and it isn't until after she leaves Iran for good (after the end of *Persepolis 2*) that Satrapi is able to fully realize herself as an artist. Also, a narrative in which the protagonist is a child or adolescent is bound to garner more attention and sympathy from the general reading public, especially a narrative in which the protagonist is exposed to traumas like familial separation and death. As the experience of childhood and adolescence is generally more uniform than adulthood, it also encourages the reader to connect with the protagonist.

Another point of appeal and another way Satrapi universalizes the narrative is how Satrapi humanizes herself by expressing her weaknesses. In fact, Satrapi is more of a flawed heroine who can, at times, be self-absorbed and who makes mistakes but ultimately learns from them. We can see this, for instance, in an important scene in *Persepolis 2*. At this point, Satrapi is dating her future husband, Reza. Because Reza has criticized Satrapi for not being "elegant enough" and for not being "made-up enough," she decides to surprise him by putting lipstick and make-up on when she plans to meet him in public. However, when the Guardians of the Revolution happen to pull up nearby for a surprise raid, Satrapi, fearing, for good reason, that she might be imprisoned or worse for her "immodest" appearance, proceeds to act in a rather amoral manner. She pretends to be an insulted woman and blames an innocent man for saying "something indecent" to her (*Persepolis 2* 131). Thereby, she takes the attention off herself and places it on the innocent man. The man is taken away, while Satrapi escapes harmlessly.

In this scene, not only can we see Satrapi's relative immaturity, we can see the damage that the Islamic Regime does to Satrapi and can do to others. Fear and the impulse for self-preservation drive Satrapi to turn on her fellow citizens, just as her former female "friends" will soon turn on Satrapi when they learn she has engaged in premarital sex. Still, Satrapi displays callousness and selfishness, evident by how she and Reza laugh off the incident, unconcerned with what she has done to an innocent man. Indeed, Satrapi hardly seems to devote a passing thought to the innocent man she condemned and what might happen to him because of the false accusation she made. However, when Satrapi relates it to her grandmother (with no remorse), her grandmother is appalled and calls her "a selfish bitch" (*Persepolis 2* 137). Satrapi's grandmother further chastises her with the following: "Have you forgotten who your grandfather was? He spent a third of his life in prison for having defended some innocents! And your Uncle Anoosh? Have you forgotten him too???! He gave his life for his ideas! What have I taught you?" (137). Here, we can once again see Satrapi's recurring theme of the importance of remembering not only familial but also cultural history as opposed to what the Islamic Regime encourages Iranians to do — to live in fear and thereby live in the perpetual present, only concerned with self-preservation. We can also see the importance of Satrapi's family here. While it is initially painful for Satrapi to hear her grandmother's condemnation, her grandmother's words do sink in and Satrapi realizes the error of her ways.

This is not to suggest that *Persepolis* and *Persepolis 2* only revolve around domestic and familial issues. Although the story is occasionally told in a comic manner, Satrapi depicts many acts of physical and verbal violence in *Persepolis* and *Persepolis 2*. Of course, one would expect depictions of violence in any autobiographical account of Iran in the late 1970s and 1980s, but this violence extends beyond the borders of Iran to Satrapi's depiction of Europe, although the violence there is more verbal, implicit, and harder to perceive. At the same time, violence rips Satrapi's family apart, time and time again. Specifically, it is the fear of violence that ultimately convince Satrapi's parents that Satrapi should be sent abroad (to Austria) in order to complete her education. Satrapi's disdain for violence can be seen most clearly in her depiction of the Iran-Iraq war. As she states in *Persepolis*: "When I think we could have avoided it [the Iran-Iraq war] all. It just makes me sick. A million people would still be alive" (116). Not only is the war completely devastating, internally, the Regime clamps down on any opposition, arresting and even executing those they believe would challenge the government (*Persepolis* 117).

Related to this and as alluded to earlier in this chapter, one of the most shocking and devastating portions of *Persepolis* and *Persepolis 2* is when a bomb hits on Satrapi's street and destroys the house of one of their neighbors, the Baba-Levys, killing a young friend of Satrapi. After the traumatic experience of seeing her now deceased friend's dismembered arm in the wreckage of their house, Satrapi says, "No scream in the world could have relieved my suffering and anger" (*Persepolis* 142). Keeping with Satrapi's belief about the supremacy of the family, it is Satrapi's connections with her family that help Satrapi maintain some level of emotionally stability. Still, it is not enough to counteract the cycle of violence that subsequently ensues. As Satrapi explains, "After the death of Neda Baba-Levy, my life took a new turn. In 1984, I was fourteen and a rebel. Nothing scared me anymore" (*Persepolis* 143). With these words, Satrapi demonstrates how witnessing extreme traumas as children or adolescents can drive them to a kind of aggressive, callous nihilism. One can imagine many disaffected youth in such a state, right before they decide to join a radical religious and political group like al-Qaeda or Hamas. Indeed, this aggressive, rather callous nihilism becomes apparent when Satrapi gets into several heated arguments with the principal at her school. At last Satrapi hits the principal and is subsequently expelled (*Persepolis* 143). Satrapi's anger can be seen in how she challenges another teacher in a new school, who falsely claims that "Since the Islamic Republic was founded, we no longer have political prisoners" (*Persepolis* 144). Consequently, understandably fearing for her life, Satrapi's parents send her away to Austria.

It is doubtful that Satrapi's depiction of violence, trauma, and its aftermath helped make *Persepolis* and *Persepolis 2* commercially successful. Rather, their success is more likely due to the post–September 11 climate in which the general public was more interested in learning about the Middle East and Islam, as well as to Satrapi's engaging literary style and her use of graphics.[10] Further, Satrapi clearly describes her goal in *Persepolis* and *Persepolis 2* as counteracting stereotypes of Iran and portraying a more comprehensive, complicated, and realistic portrayal of Iran. To be certain, Satrapi is not apolitical, and *Persepolis* and *Persepolis 2* contain a fair amount of biting criticism of the Islamic Regime. Perhaps because of this, the Islamic Regime seems to view both works as threats. This can be seen in how neither has been translated into Persian and the works have "been dismissed by the Iranian authorities as Islamophobic," a charge that Satrapi vehemently denies (Hattenstone, Malek 376–7). Still, as Amy Malek explains, "While *Persepolis* is not sold in official bookstores, thanks to the extensive black market and networks between Iran and the rest of the world *Persepolis* has gained a readership within Iran, as indicated by its mention on a number of Iranian weblogs" (376–7).

Even though *Persepolis* and *Persepolis 2* may have "gained a readership in Iran," Satrapi's intended audience is clearly Western. In Western discourse, perhaps no feature has been so discussed and vilified as an emblem of supposed traditional Islamic oppression of women as the veil. In Iran, from shortly after the 1979 Revolution to the present, women have been required to wear a veil that covers their hair. Recognizing the symbolic importance of the veil as well as wanting to critique it as oppression against women, Satrapi begins *Persepolis* with a section that she calls "The Veil." This section displays a portion of Satrapi's class photo in 1980 when she is ten years old. Specifically, Satrapi focuses on four other veiled female classmates. While the reader cannot see Satrapi in this class photo, her classmates look completely identical except for their facial expressions. This demonstrates how the veil strips them of their individual identity. Or does it? When looking closer, one can see important distinctions in their facial expressions. While the eyes of one classmate (Golnaz) look away, her mouth is in the shape of a frown, suggesting anger and defiance. Her classmate to the right, Mahshid, also appears to be frowning; however, her eyes are closed, as if she is trying to block out her unhappy feelings or mentally escape. Meanwhile, the eyes of Narine (the third classmate to the right) are downcast, and her mouth seems twisted into a nervous expression as if she is both defeated and fearful. In contrast, the classmate to the far right, Minna, looks straight at the camera, her mouth vaguely positioned into something like a smile, as if she is trying to demonstrate that she is content with the new regulations in order to please her teachers or the authorities. Through her four classmates, Satrapi shows the range of emotion from defeated resignation to active rebellion. This demonstrates how they have developed different responses to the new seemingly more repressive regime. The fact that they all are responding differently demonstrates the lack of solidarity among them and it can be seen as a microcosm of the fragmentation of Iranian society under the Islamic Regime.

However, one thing her classmates seem to all have in common is, according to Satrapi, their collective resistance to the veil, which they view as nonsensical. As Satrapi explains, "We didn't really like to wear the veil, especially since we didn't understand why we had to" (*Persepolis* 3). Instead, Satrapi portrays her classmates as denigrating the veil by using it as rope, a mask, and as a collar. While part of their disdain for the veil could be attributed to how in the previous year, they attended "a French non-religious school," in comparison to the non-secular Islamic school, the picture of the students at the secular school demonstrates that Satrapi does not necessarily extol the secular over the non-secular school (4). While the students in the secular school are more distinguishable because they are not wearing the veil and they all have different hairstyles, their facial expressions do not illustrate that they are any happier than when they attend the Islamic school. For instance, in the class picture from the secular French school, one student's eyes are closed; another two students are frowning, while one or two appear somewhat content (4).[11]

Contrary to the general stereotype of Islamic fundamentalists coming from impoverished environments, Satrapi also portrays the lure of fundamentalism through a depiction of herself as a middle-class child. Despite growing up in a secular home with parents that tend to have Marxist leanings, Satrapi develops strong religious tendencies exemplified by how she "wanted to be a prophet" as a child (*Persepolis* 6), even though Satrapi's parents encourage her to read books with Marxist or Communist leanings.[12] Like most children (and again, giving *Persepolis* and *Persepolis 2* more of a universal appeal), Satrapi portrays herself as easily influenced by others around her. For instance, she says that she loves "the King [The Shah]" because she believes him to be divinely appointed, which is what she learns when reading her schoolbooks (*Persepolis* 19). However, her mind is changed after she learns of the supposed atrocities of the Shah, such as supposedly burning a cinema down and not rescuing those who were in the building.[13]

In portraying her eagerness to join the budding Revolutionary movement, Satrapi illustrates how easily molded children looking for attention or power can get caught up in political events beyond their comprehension. This can be seen, for instance, in how young boys at Satrapi's Islamic school are given keys and are told "that if they went to war [the Iran-Iraq war] and were lucky enough to die, this key would get them into heaven" (*Persepolis* 99).[14] Given that approximately a million people died in the Iran-Iraq war, it can be surmised that this and other techniques were successful. As further evidence, in *Persepolis 2*, when Satrapi returns to Iran in the mid–1980s, she sees a transformed Tehran in which there are "sixty-five-foot-high murals presenting martyrs, adorned with slogans honoring them, such as, 'The martyr is the heart of history,' or 'I hope to be a martyr myself' or 'A martyr lives forever'" (96). Satrapi also discovers how the streets have been re-named for specific martyrs and she describes the experience as feeling "as though I was walking through a cemetery ... surrounded by the victims of a war I had fled" (97). Ultimately, Satrapi concludes that the Islamic Republic has successfully indoctrinated, if not brainwashed, much of its citizenry during the 1980s. On television, she sees "mothers who were claiming to be overjoyed and gratified by the deaths of their children" (99). However, instead of completely condemning their behavior, Satrapi concludes that it could be an act of "faith" as much as "stupidity" (99). Again, Satrapi disallows the reader from simplistically concluding that Iran is a part of an Axis of Evil and that its residents, in turn, are simple-minded followers or even "evil" themselves.

Nevertheless, Satrapi's disdain of the oppressive dictates of the Islamic Regime as well as the ubiquitous violence of the Iran-Iraq war can be seen in how Satrapi depicts its toll on civilians like her Uncle Taher, who has a series of heart attacks and is refused a permit to leave the country to receive life-saving treatments by a vindictive religious administrator, who was actually a former window washer (*Persepolis* 121). However, this is not to suggest that only in Iran is religion (in this case, Islam) used to harm citizens. Ironically, Satrapi experiences another form of debasement through religion (in this case, Christianity) when she moves to the West. In Austria, she attends a boarding school run by nuns. At one point, Satrapi gets into a verbal confrontation with a nun, which leads to her being expelled. This nun criticizes Satrapi for eating pasta in a pot while she watches television with them. Displaying her prejudicial and racist attitude towards Iranians, whom she seems to view as primitive, the nun tells Satrapi, "It's true what they say about Iranians. They have no education" (*Persepolis 2* 23). Not one to keep silent, Satrapi responds, "It's true what they say about you, too. You were all prostitutes before becoming nuns" (23). When brought in by the Mother Superior,

Satrapi is chastised; however, the Mother Superior only finds Satrapi's comment "unacceptable," not the racist comment made by the nun, and Satrapi is expelled. Satrapi concludes, "In every religion, you find the same extremists" (*Persepolis 2* 24). Through this, Satrapi suggests that religious fundamentalism and the prejudice it tends to engender is not specific to only Iran or to Islam, but can be found throughout the world, even in the supposedly liberated West.

Still, this does not lessen Satrapi's attack upon the religious fundamentalists and patriarchal system she perceives to be debasing Iran. When Satrapi is back in Iran, she finds that the mullahs and religious leaders also dominate and debase the educational system. Students are forced to listen to lectures about morality, in which women are implored to "wear less-wide trousers, and longer head-scarves," to fully cover their hair and not wear makeup (*Persepolis 2* 142). Similar to the scene with the nuns in Austria, Satrapi challenges the rationale of the teachers and mullahs. She writes:

> You don't hesitate to comment on us, but our brothers present here have all shapes and sizes of haircuts and clothes. Sometimes, they wear clothes so tight we can see everything. Why is it that I, as a woman, am expected to feel nothing when watching these men with their clothes sculpted on but they, as men, can get excited by two inches less of my head-scarf? [143].

Ironically, Satrapi is not expelled for these comments as she was in Austria. However, that appears to be due to luck since Satrapi speaks with the same mullah who passed her on her ideological test, mainly because he (rightly) perceives Satrapi to be honest (144). That Satrapi actually finds an honest religious figure in Iran[15] (as opposed to in Austria) also illustrates Satrapi's refusal to simplistically categorize either Iran or the West as morally superior. Instead, she acknowledges that both are complex societies that have their respective benefits and drawbacks.

Ultimately, as explained earlier, Satrapi places the greatest emphasis for hope and change in her family and in families in general. For Satrapi, then, not only can the personal trump the political; it should. Indeed, a common theme throughout Iranian and Iranian diasporic literature is how change can only come from individuals and individual desire as opposed to government mandate or forced legislative change. One reason for this is that the Islamic Regime places so much emphasis on the personal and specifically upon appearance as noted by its guidelines for public clothing and behavior. Further, with Iran's economy steadily eroding in recent years, Iranians have found themselves more understandably concerned with basic economic needs rather than broader social change.

Through depictions of Satrapi's family, the reader can look beyond nationality to see that the primary unit in Iran is the family, just as it is in other countries. Further, the reader can see that it is ultimately the family unit that holds the most potential for change. As Manuela Costantino argues, "The readers' inclusion in Marji's private familial circle makes identification with the young heroine easy and opens a space for negotiations between familiar and unfamiliar cultural and historical issues" (447). In other words, Satrapi encourages the reader to feel like she or he is a part of her family. Through Satrapi's sympathetic depiction of her grandmother, who despite her liberal and secular beliefs, also initially supports the Islamic Revolution because of the extravagant and spendthrift ways of the Shah and his administration (*Persepolis* 28), Western readers are encouraged to go beyond demonizing Iranians or believing them to be misguided fundamentalists who uniformly supported the Revolution. The reader also can see diversity among Iranians who supported the Revolution, not all of whom supported it for religious reasons.[16]

Ultimately, it is Satrapi's family who, time and time again, save her from succumbing to the rhetoric and oppressive climate of the Islamic Regime, which helps breed paranoia, selfishness, and vindictiveness. For instance, amidst frenzy after the Iranian Revolution, Satrapi and her friends aim to attack a classmate, Ramin, because they believe that his father "was in the SAVAK" and that he was responsible for killing "a million people" (*Persepolis* 44). Of course, even if this were true, it hardly justifies attacking Ramin, whom Satrapi portrays as a small, scared boy wearing glasses, hiding behind a tree (45). Still, this depiction helps the reader understand where violent behavior towards others by so-called Islamic fundamentalists can originate. Satrapi suggests that the members of the Regime who prey on others are kept in a kind of perpetual childhood in which they are continually manipulated by rhetoric. In this case, it is only through Satrapi's mother that Satrapi is able to realize the error of her ways, as her mother tells her it's not Ramin's fault and that "we have to learn and forgive" (46). It is doubtful that any of Satrapi's peers have a similar parent who tells them this, and thus, Satrapi portrays herself as the lucky beneficiary of thoughtful parents. All the same, what ensues suggests that the cycle of violence is hardly easy to discontinue. When Satrapi confronts Ramin and aims to "learn and forgive" as her mother encourages her to do, Ramin presumably parrots the rhetoric of his parents by telling Satrapi that his father "is not a murderer," because "he killed Communists and Communists are evil" (46).[17] The scene ends with nothing resolved, indicating how difficult it is to break down miscommunication when the rhetoric of parents or substitute parents (the Islamic Regime) is involved.

As a child and like most children, Satrapi is susceptible to believing virtually all that she hears on television. When Iran goes to war against Iraq, the Iranian media portrays Iraq as the aggressor, leading Satrapi to want to "defend my country against those Arabs who kept attacking us" (*Persepolis* 79). Indeed, when Iraq bombs Iran, Satrapi tells her father, "We need to teach those Iraqis a lesson" (81); she also views the Iraqis as part of an Arabic invasion or colonizing force. However, Satrapi's father claims, "The real Islamic invasion has come from our own government" (81). Whereas Satrapi tends to believe whatever the Iranian media reports, her parents are much more skeptical (83). Satrapi illustrates that without the influence of her more secular, educated, and less hawkish parents, she might have become a violent fundamentalist or at least a stronger supporter of the Islamic Republic and its war on Iraq (like many others in Iran).

Complicating matters is that Satrapi's parents aren't immune to rhetoric themselves, and they are also drawn to continue the cycle of violence. This can be seen even before the Iranian Revolution, after two family friends, both Communists, are released from prison. They both visit the Satrapi family and detail the various ways the Regime tortured them: by pulling their nails out, by whipping the soles of their feet with electric cables, and by burning them with an iron (*Persepolis* 51).[18] Learning of the atrocities that the SAVAK committed, including literally cutting prisoners in pieces, encourages the Satrapis to further support the Iranian Revolution, and even encourages Satrapi's mother to say, "All torturers should be massacred" (52). Hearing this from her mother (instead of a message of forgiveness) leads Satrapi (and her peers) to become fascinated with torture, as evident by how they imagine things like filling someone's mouth with garbage. She reports, "Back at home that evening, I had the diabolical feeling of power" (53). At the same time, Satrapi informs the reader that "it didn't last. I was overwhelmed" (53). This doesn't mean that someone in Satrapi's position would suddenly turn sympathetic or become a pacifist, but rather, she might look for the next method through which she could achieve some level of power.

One way this power may be achieved is through association, by having a family member that one can claim as a hero who has been subjected to imprisonment and torture by the SAVAK and has survived both. Satrapi seems to find this in her Uncle Anoosh who, during the Shah's reign, along with his friends, "proclaimed the independence of the Iranian province of Azerbaijan" (*Persepolis* 55), but ended up fleeing to the then Soviet Union, only to be imprisoned for nine years when he tried to return to Iran after the Iranian Revolution. Uncle Anoosh's imprisonment is the impressive part to Marjane, who thinks to herself that this story will trump the other stories of atrocities told by her peers (60). In a way, this experience foreshadows the way that the

Islamic Regime would help fuel the Iran-Iraq war to come: by creating martyrs that the general populace could idolize and emulate.

Part of the problem, Satrapi suggests, is that many secular, well-educated Iranians like her parents and extended family believed that the revolt against the Shah would be "a leftist revolution" instead of a religious one (*Persepolis* 62). Lack of faith in religious leaders leads many to flee Iran for the United States or Europe (63). However, Satrapi's family resists doing so because of a perceived lack of opportunities they believe will await them should they emigrate to a country like the United States. Her father concludes that going to the U.S. would result in his becoming "a taxi driver," and his wife, Marjane's mother, becoming "a cleaning lady" (64). To be sure, both things might happen if they all decide to emigrate to the West. In that sense, Satrapi does not portray the West as a promised land for many Iranians, even those who are generally secular, like Satrapi's parents.

Along these lines, it has been suggested that *Persepolis* and *Persepolis 2* attempt to deconstruct the generalizations associated with the Islamic Middle East and the secular West.[19] While Satrapi's work resists a dichotomy between the liberal and liberating West and the oppressive Islamic Regime, it is clear that Satrapi's sentiments lie more with the West. This is not to suggest that she portrays Western governments and culture as idyllic. In fact, Satrapi has accused "the west of cultural imperialism," pointing specifically towards how "it always reduces Iran to Hizbullah or 1001 Arabian Nights; the flying carpet or the flying rocket" as evidence (qtd. in Hattenstone Par 3). Satrapi also identifies some rather distressing and totalitarian aspects of Western culture that run parallel to that of the Islamic Regime. In her own words, "The crazy people are not based in one country. They're everywhere. George Bush talks about the Axis of Evil. What's the difference between that and the mullahs talking about the Great Satan? They say, 'read the Koran.' The other one says, 'read the Bible.' The mullah says he's the best friend of God, and George Bush does, too" (qtd. in Bearman, par 31). These statements demonstrate that Satrapi is an independent thinker and wants her readers to see not only beyond the Axis of Evil, but also beyond the conception of the West as a free, democratic Promised Land.

Still, Satrapi portrays herself, while an Iranian child and teenager, as having an almost insatiable desire for Western culture (much of which had been banned in 1980s Iran) when she is growing up in Iran. While it is unclear if Satrapi wants us to see her as a representative Iranian child or adolescent, writers like Jared Cohen and Azadeh Moaveni,[20] among others, have established that Western popular culture holds strong cache and heavily influences Middle Eastern youth. Indeed, when Satrapi's parents go on a trip to Turkey,

Satrapi specifically asks for a Western style denim jacket, as well as two posters, one of the heavy metal group Iron Maiden and the other of pop singer Kim Wilde. Satrapi's obliging parents return to Iran after smuggling in Satrapi's requests as well as Nike sneakers and a Michael Jackson pin (*Persepolis* 130–131). This is an act fraught with danger, for as we learn earlier, as the division between church and state erodes in Iran after the Iranian Revolution, animosity towards virtually everything perceived to be Western (including segments of higher education, thought to be little more than Western dogma) increases. This animosity can turn violent, as Satrapi's mother indicates when she tells Satrapi how one of their friends received seventy-five lashes when some Guardians of the Revolution searched their house and found Western "records and videocassettes," among other things. This, according to Satrapi's mother, resulted in the male friend not being able to "walk anymore" (*Persepolis* 105).

However, the severity of the danger her parents put themselves through does not seem to register with Satrapi,[21] who, instead of appearing thankful, asks her mother, "What about my posters?" and seems distraught only when she thinks they will be photos instead of posters. Further, a naïve Satrapi proceeds to put her Nike sneakers on as well as her denim jacket, and goes outside, ignoring or not being cognizant of the serious dangers she faces for her appearance (*Persepolis* 130–131). Perhaps not surprisingly, Satrapi's Western clothing and Michael Jackson pin nearly get her in serious trouble as she is accosted by two female members of the Guardians of the Revolution, who object to her appearance. They take her to the Committee headquarters, where Satrapi manages to be released by lying about having a cruel stepmother who would "burn me with the clothes iron," and who would "make my father put me in the orphanage" if Satrapi receives a reprimand (*Persepolis* 134). However, when Satrapi gets home, she doesn't think too much about how lucky she has been but rather proceeds to dance to the Kim Wilde song "Kids in America" which she had just purchased (134). Here, then, the West represents for Satrapi a kind of blissful alternative to the Islamic Regime, a kind of hedonistic utopia, one whose perceived pleasures, or even just the ability to associate with those perceived pleasures, outweigh virtually everything. It is not hard to see how, in a conservative, religious country, a much more permissive Western country like the United States might be seen as sinful and hence an evil empire.

This is not to suggest that Satrapi's parents install within her fervent anti–Islamic Regime and pro–Western sentiments. Even when Satrapi's parents grow disenchanted with the Iranian Revolution and Satrapi's father compares the subsequent taking of the American hostages to "a James Bond movie" (*Persepolis* 72), he still persists in calling Americans "dummies" (72). In fact, if anything, it seems like Satrapi's father only criticizes the hostage takers as merely following the formulas of trite Western films. Also, in *Persepolis 2*, Satrapi's father claims that the Iran-Iraq war was "just a big setup to destroy both the Iranian and the Iraqi armies. The former was the most powerful in the Middle East in 1980, and the latter represented a real danger to Israel" (99). He further argues, "The West sold weapons to both camps and we, we were stupid enough to enter into this cynical game ... eight years of war for nothing!" (99). For Satrapi's parents, then, both the West and the Islamic Republic have significant problems and they place little hope in either.

In *Persepolis 2*, Satrapi further complicates the dichotomy of the West as liberator and the Islamic Republic as oppressor and demonstrates that "freedom" can come with a rather heavy price. At first, upon her arrival to Austria as an incoming boarding school student, Satrapi stays with her mother's best friend, Zozo, and her daughter, Shirin, fellow Iranian expatriates. However, Satrapi becomes put off by the seemingly superficial behavior of Shirin, who has become Westernized. When Shirin talks to Satrapi about lipstick, scented pens, and other fashionable items, Satrapi thinks to herself: "What a traitor! While people were dying in our country, she was talking to me about trivial things" (2). In a sense, Satrapi's thinking resembles that of the Islamic Regime, which tends to criticize all things Western as decadent, immoral, and superficial. This is not to suggest that Satrapi is defending the Islamic Regime, but rather, she is illustrating the negative aftereffects of Western "liberation." In this case, it seems to breed a certain selfishness. Life in the West is also not any better for Shirin's parents. Whereas Shirin's father, Houshang, was a CEO in Iran and Zozo was his secretary, in Austria, Houshang doesn't have a job and Zozo is a housekeeper. Further, because of their financial problems, Houshang and Zozo's relationship deteriorates. Ironically, Satrapi's parents, despite living in supposedly oppressive Iran, are able to maintain a healthy relationship and Satrapi's father manages to keep his occupation.

In *Persepolis 2*, when Satrapi is enrolled in a private school in Austria, we see how the supposedly liberated West can produce spoiled and selfish adolescents. To be sure, Satrapi is initially enchanted by the availability of goods while in the West as well as by the seemingly free and nonchalant behavior of her new European friends. At first, Satrapi believes the Western or European friends she makes are legitimately rebelling against the wealth and luxury around them. However, as she stays in Austria longer and gets to know her "friends" better, she becomes disenchanted. This first becomes clear when Satrapi's new "friends," who grew up in privileged environments, appear spoiled when they discuss their Winter Break plans and complain about things like being "bored crazy in the Alps" (14). Despite the fact that they seem drawn to Satrapi when she tells them she is from Iran and has seen violence and war,[22] when Satrapi tells them that "in Iran, we don't celebrate Christmas," and that the Iranian "new year is March 21" (14), her "friends" seem uninterested in learning anything substantive about Iranian culture. Rather, they seem drawn to Satrapi as a way to appear more authentically rebellious and because they view her as an exotic curiosity. Satrapi's exoticization continues when she spends Winter Break with her roommate Lucia's Austrian family, who are enchanted with Satrapi because they "had never seen any Iranians" (18). However, Lucia's family do not seem to truly want to get to know Satrapi (although they may be hampered by language issues since they only speak German, a language Satrapi does not speak, and need a translator — usually Lucia — to speak to one another). Instead, it seems they only want to keep Satrapi as an exotic curio and thereby demonstrate their supposed tolerance and worldliness. One member of Lucia's family concludes, "It's wonderful to have international friends" (18). Even though Satrapi's European friends seem erudite, Satrapi also discovers that they are mainly intellectual posers who make references to theorists like Bakunin without really reading, let alone understanding his works. Meanwhile, Satrapi tries to read Bakunin while her "friends" have parties and socialize.

Ironically, while in Austria, Satrapi also learns to appreciate some Iranian customs, most specifically, respecting her elders as well as romantic and sexual conservatism. In that sense, the influence of the West ironically pushes Satrapi closer to the morals and policies of the Islamic Regime. Satrapi, when living with her European friend Julie, sees how Julie treats her mother in ways that she would never have treated her parents. In Satrapi's own words: "In my culture, parents were sacred. We at least owed them an answer" (*Persepolis 2* 26). Despite seeming to be a liberated woman who has already had sex with eighteen men, Julie hardly seems any happier than Satrapi; however, in her desire to integrate, Satrapi decides to adopt the seemingly liberated behavior of her friends. As Satrapi tries to do what others around her are doing (e.g., drinking, trying drugs, and having sex), she hesitates, concluding, "The harder I tried to assimilate, the more I had the feeling that I was distancing myself from my culture, betraying my parents and my origins, that I was playing a game by somebody else's rules" (39). At one point, Satrapi even pretends to not be Iranian since she has come to see her nationality as a burden more than an asset.[23]

However, Satrapi discovers that she can never really assimilate into Western culture due to Western reactions to her as both a foreigner and as an Iranian. At a climactic point in *Persepolis 2*, Satrapi learns what her "friends" truly think of her when she overhears them criticizing her for pretending to be

French, for being a liar, and for being "ugly" (42). Instead of taking the time to understand the pressures that Satrapi feels as foreigner in Europe and appreciating her distinct appearance, they reject her. This leads to Satrapi yelling out: "You are going to shut up or I am going to make you! I am Iranian and proud of it!" (43). Subsequently, Satrapi reports feeling "proud" for "the first time in a year" (43). She concludes: "I finally understood what my grandmother meant. If I wasn't comfortable with myself, I would never be comfortable" (43). It is ironic that it takes moving to the West for Satrapi to appreciate Iran (or at least to appreciate some aspects of Iran), instead of fully embracing her "liberated" existence in the West. However, this shows how, once again, Satrapi refuses to subscribe to the simplistic dichotomy of the "good" West and the "evil" Islamic Middle East, or in this case, Iran.

However, even after this incident, Satrapi cannot really escape the pull and influence of the West. Even though she states that she has started to become more accepting of her Iranian heritage, Satrapi actually tries harder to assimilate, presumably because of how alienated she feels. At this point in the narrative, Satrapi dates Westerners who seem clueless about intellectual and social matters (which can be seen as a commentary on the selfish hedonism of Western youth), like Enrique who invites her to an "anarchist party" (*Persepolis 2* 55). This party turns out to be completely non-political, more of a fraternity and sorority party with "a group of adults chasing one another and shouting" (56). Still, Satrapi doesn't portray herself much or any better than her European friends; she still says that she loves Enrique and seems to be satiated by the food and music at the party (57). Also, continuing to adopt a more self-involved hedonistic Western lifestyle, Satrapi takes an increasing amount of drugs, and eventually sells them for money. As evidence for how submissive and placated Satrapi has become in the West, after becoming involved with a native Austrian, Markus, and being criticized by his mother for her ethnicity, she doesn't even respond back verbally as she had previously to authority figures in Iran and in Austria.

Satrapi also portrays Austria (and with it, the West) as hardly an all-embracing, liberated, and peaceful nation. At the time of her story, Kurt Waldheim, who affiliated with Nazis during World War II, is the president of Austria, where there is a growing skinhead movement (*Persepolis 2* 73–4). Added to this sense of fragmentation is that, after Satrapi discovers that Markus had been cheating on her, she leaves and begins living on the streets, where she grows increasingly sick, and nearly dies from a case of severe, untreated bronchitis. Even though Austrian doctors eventually save her, it appears that Western culture metaphorically almost kills Satrapi. On some level, Satrapi may realize this, or at the very least, that she cannot really integrate or assimilate to Western or Austrian life as she subsequently makes the decision to go back to Iran. It is not so much that Satrapi decides that she prefers life in the Islamic Regime, but rather that she seeks the comfort of her family. Without family, Satrapi comes to realize, "freedom" is really just alienation for her in Austria, and one of the larger themes in both *Persepolis* and *Persepolis 2* is how family trumps nationality.

Further, Satrapi portrays Iranian nationality as increasingly muddled and contradictory. For instance, when she returns to Iran, Satrapi discovers that her former female Iranian friends, who appear heavily made-up in the corresponding pictures, have become an amalgam of Islamic and American values, chaste in behavior but dolled up or Westernized in appearance. In Satrapi's words, "They all looked like the heroines of American TV series, ready to get married at the drop of a hat, if the opportunity presented itself" (*Persepolis 2* 105). Ironically, her old Iranian friends are surprised by the even more traditional looking Satrapi, who is not wearing make-up. One asks her, "Why do you look like a nun? No one would ever guess that you lived in Europe" (105). Displaying their own stereotypes about life in the West, they also ask Satrapi about nightclubs in Austria and seem shocked and dismayed when she tells them that she didn't go to any (105). Satrapi concludes that: "When something is forbidden, it takes on a disproportionate importance. Much later, I learned that making themselves up and wanting to follow Western ways was an act of resistance on their part" (105). However, at the bottom of the picture, Satrapi writes that "Nevertheless, I felt terribly alone," with her friends in background, in silhouette, not talking to her (105). One reason Satrapi may feel so isolated is that she is now really in limbo between Western and Iranian values and culture. Later, Satrapi's old Iranian "friends" criticize her when they find out that she has had sex with more than one man, even though she dresses in a much more demure manner than they do. One even says, "So, what's the difference between you and a whore???" (116). Satrapi concludes that the heavily made-up appearance of her female Iranian friends is just that, an appearance or facade. As she explains: "Underneath their outward appearance of being modern women, my friends were real traditionalists" (115). She also concludes, "To them, I had become a decadent Western woman," even though she did not do some of the things they said they wanted to do and her friends dress in more decadent ways than Satrapi does (116).

Satrapi's readjustment to life in Iran is not a smooth one, and her feeling of being excluded from both the West and the Islamic Regime drives her into a deep depression.[24] She tells a therapist, "When I was in Vienna, my life didn't matter to anyone and that obviously had an effect on my own self-esteem. I was reduced to nothing. I thought that in coming back to Iran, this would change" (*Persepolis 2* 117). However, it doesn't seem to work; nor do the pills prescribed to her by her therapist. She concludes that she is "nothing," and that "I was a Westerner in Iran, and Iranian in the West. I had no identity. I didn't even know anymore why I was living" (118). At this point, Satrapi makes an attempt to take her life, which demonstrates how important establishing a stable identity has become to her, and how both cultures disallow her from establishing one. In a larger sense, Satrapi demonstrates how life in Iran largely prevents Iranians (especially women) from establishing a stable, fulfilling identity, and that being an exile offers no better alternative. The only real solution is finding one's self and one's values through nurturing familial and personal connections, which trump nationality.

The condemnation of the West by the East (and vice versa) backfires for Satrapi and her peers. Consequently, just as Satrapi seemed to gravitate towards Iranian culture and customs while in the West, now, when back in Iran, she gravitates towards Western culture again, after her botched suicide attempt. She does this by trying to put her life in order in a manner influenced by Western culture and guiding principles. For instance, she writes: "Body hair being an obsession of the Oriental woman, I began with hair removal" (*Persepolis 2* 120). It is significant that Satrapi tries to change herself by changing her body, as it is the only thing she feels she can really change, just as people who suffer from eating disorders or body dysmorphia often seek some perceived measure of control over their life. Satrapi also gets "a modern wardrobe," "a fashionable haircut," and begins wearing makeup, with her ultimate aim to become "a sophisticated woman" (120). Also, possibly influenced by American culture, which helped spawn an aerobics movement in the 1980s, Satrapi becomes an aerobics instructor herself, again, in an attempt to exert influence over her body since she is held helpless by the Islamic Regime.

In a way, Satrapi begins to discover a more substantive identity not so much from the classes she attends while in college in Iran nor from living in Iran itself, but in rebelling against the often arbitrary and nonsensical dictates placed upon her as an art student. For instance, in order to gain admittance to the College of Art, Satrapi must submit a drawing. Knowing that the admissions committee would be most impressed by drawings that express religious devotion or devotion to the Islamic Regime, Satrapi submits a drawing in which she reproduces Michelangelo's *Pietà*, "by putting a black chador on Mary's head, an army uniform on Jesus," and then adds "two tulips, symbols of the martyrs, on either side so there would be no confusion" (*Persepolis 2* 127). Satrapi writes at the bottom of the caption that she "was very pleased with my drawing," but she was probably more pleased at being able to successfully hoodwink those judging her for admittance into believing in her false religious devotion (127).

Still, Satrapi can only play this charade for so long, and she only begins to truly discover herself when she begins to speak out in honest terms about the Islamic Regime. Rebelling in this way gives Satrapi an identity and a purpose. Her first act of major defiance occurs when she has to take "an ideological test," in which she is expected to "pray in Arabic," and to know "the names of all of the Imams, their histories, the philosophy of Shiism, etc" (*Persepolis 2* 129). Satrapi begins to study for the test, but gives up and decides to be honest with her interrogator by expressing her resistance to the veil and admitting that she cannot pray in Arabic (130). Unexpectedly, Satrapi is, in a way, rewarded for her rebellious behavior as she is accepted because the interrogator, a mullah, had been impressed by Satrapi's honesty (130). Satrapi also begins to speak out against the manner in which she is taught. Specifically, the absurdity of the dictates of the Islamic Republic become especially apparent in art class when Satrapi and her fellow students are asked to draw a man without looking at him and to draw veiled women (144–5). While it may seem that, at this point, Satrapi is reinforcing overtly negative images of Iranians, it is important to keep in mind that she did not previously present the West as a significantly better alternative to Iran, and the fact that she speaks out against the dictates she disagrees with Iran can also indicate her love for the country.

For Satrapi and others, rebellion circa 1990 in Iran has morphed into mainly surreptitious, private acts. Due to the fear of imprisonment and execution, young, rebellious Iranians like Satrapi move towards small acts of rebellion such as showing their wrists, laughing loudly, and using a Walkman (*Persepolis 2* 148).[25] Gradually, there develops a bifurcation between their public and private lives, with the status of one contributing to the status of the other. The more repressed and fearful they feel in their public lives, the more they feel a need for private releases, mainly by throwing nightly parties. These parties symbolize decadent Western culture and suggest that the more Iranians are restricted and repressed by the Islamic Regime, the more they gravitate towards Western culture. Towards this end, Satrapi and her friends start to hold parties in which they dress provocatively, drink alcohol, and act impulsively. It is not so much that they are able to express their true selves in these parties, but rather, as Satrapi puts it, they are able "to find a semblance of equilibrium" through these wild and impulsive parties that counteract the nearly totalitarian policies enforced by the Islamic Regime (152). Still, the dangers of these parties are palpable. While usually they are able to merely pay off members of the Revolutionary Guard who sometimes interrupt their parties, one night, the Revolutionary Guard arrests several people and one person dies while trying to escape from the Revolutionary Guard by leaping across a building on the roof. Satrapi includes no words, only pictures to emphasize the acts. However, Satrapi and her friends do not stop their parties, because to do so, in their view, would be to capitulate to those in power.

The sense of being helplessly caught between the West and the Islamic Republic continues in Satrapi's account of the early 1990s in Iran. After the Iraqi invasion of Kuwait and the subsequent beginning of the Gulf War, Satrapi and other Iranians feel ambivalent. After suffering years of devastating war with Iraq, they are happy to just not be attacked (*Persepolis 2* 166). Also, in the repressive and dangerous climate of Iran, most Iranians understandably just focus on the personal and the immediate. Satrapi's family questions the intentions of the West (particularly the United States) in the ensuing Gulf War as being economically driven instead of ideologically driven by a desire to protest the rights of the Kuwaitis.[26] Supporting this is how Satrapi does not portray the Kuwaitis in a positive light. Rather, they are portrayed as mainly callous, wealthy, and sexist with one mistaking Satrapi for a soliciting prostitute merely because she is drinking a Coke in public (166). Added to Satrapi and her friends' rather complacent and ambivalent attitude towards the West is the introduction of satellite television. While, at first, Satrapi has high hopes that satellite television will help her and others "finally experience a view different from the one dictated by our government," the end result is not a greater political awareness, but rather a blasé complacency exemplified by how Satrapi watches a huge amount of television in a mindless, passive manner (170).

In keeping with one of Satrapi's overarching themes, namely the importance of the family in providing people with a stable identity and trumping nationality and culture, once again, it is a member of Satrapi's family, in this case her father, who helps wrest Satrapi out of complacency. He does so by making her closely examine her failing marriage. Satrapi had married another art student, Reza, mainly because it is so difficult to be an unmarried couple in Iran. In fact, Satrapi's failed marriage can be seen as a commentary on how Iran's sexual and romantic conservatism ultimately fail in practice as Satrapi's constraining marriage becomes another way that she is thwarted from establishing a stable, fully developed identity.

Ultimately, Satrapi comes to the conclusion that in the Islamic Republic, women are effectively prevented from becoming full human beings as they are doubly oppressed both by the Regime and by their husbands who typically treat them as inferior servants. In this case, they have the law on their side for, as Satrapi explains: "If a guy kills ten women in the presence of fifteen others, no one can condemn him because in a murder case, we women, we can't even testify. He's also the one who has the right to divorce and even if he gives it to you, he nonetheless has custody of the children!" (*Persepolis 2* 183). Realizing this leads Satrapi to conclude, "I can't take it anymore. I want to leave this country" (183). The revelation Satrapi has is that she can never, try as she might, develop a satisfying and stable identity in Iran as either an Iranian or a woman. Therefore, she leaves Iran once more after getting a divorce, this time for France, presumably for good, at the end of *Persepolis 2* with the blessings of her parents.[27] *Persepolis 2* ends by saying "freedom has a price" and for Satrapi, the price is not being able to see her family often; in fact, she is only able to see her grandmother once more before she dies (187).

While Satrapi's decision to seemingly become a permanent exile appears to be a wholesale rejection of Iran and an embrace of the West (especially her use of the word "freedom"), it is not because she views Iran as beyond redemption or the West as a polar opposite that offers her complete liberation as a woman and as a human being. After all, Satrapi has already lived in the West, and she knows (and has portrayed) how the freedoms promised by the West can sometimes be more like chimeras. At the same time, she realizes that there are very few opportunities afforded to her as woman in contemporary Iran, and that the only chance she has to have a fulfilling life and career would be to leave Iran. As it turns out, Satrapi was entirely correct in the sense that were she to have tried to become an artist and writer in Iran, her works would, by and large, have been censored or banned — as indeed they have been. Yet, it is through this same writing that Satrapi helps her mostly Western readers understand and appreciate not only the long and proud history of Persia and Iran, but also the complexities of nations and peoples — not just of Iran, but also of Western countries. Doing so, she believes — and she has every reason to believe it — creates a communicative bridge between Iran and the West, and leads to a better understanding of both cultures and both peoples.

## 2

# Muslims and Jews in
# Contemporary Iran

### *Dalia Sofer's* The Septembers of Shiraz

It is neither groundbreaking nor controversial to suggest that one of the most pressing conflicts in the Middle East is Muslim-Jewish or Arab-Israeli relations. To many predominantly Islamic Middle Eastern countries, Israel is an interloper, an oppressor and butcherer of Palestinians and their ire is doubly reinforced by their common belief that the West (especially the United States) heavily supports Israel over them. On the other hand, Israelis generally feel that they are still, over sixty years after the establishment of Israel, fighting for their sovereignty amidst a sea of neighboring, largely hostile countries whose fringe elements regularly commit terrorist acts against them. Consequently, Israel has taken Iran's purported progress towards developing nuclear weapons as extremely serious to the point of considering military action. Despite the fact that Iran is not an Arabic country, unlike nearby countries like Saudi Arabia, Syria, and Lebanon, for its part, Ahmadinejad has also exacerbated the conflict between Muslims and Jews with his heated rhetoric as exemplified by calls for Israel to be "wiped off the map" and denial of the Holocaust (Peterson 1).[1] Such rhetoric may be intended to ally predominantly Arabic Middle Eastern countries to Iran or it may simply be rhetoric intended to display aggressive defiance of the West.

Given the Western media's focus upon Ahmadinejad's rhetoric about Israel and Jews, it would probably be surprising to most Westerners to know that not only do more Jews live in Iran than in any other predominantly Islamic Middle Eastern country, but Iran has offered Jews a larger amount of social and governmental inclusion than in many neighboring or nearby Arabic or Muslim countries (Hakanian 7; Peterson 1).[2] Indeed, Iran's attitudes towards Jews is conflicted and almost paradoxical, as noted by Ahmadinejad's rhetoric, on one side, and on the other side, how "one of the most popular dramas on Iranian state television is about an Iranian diplomat who saves French Jews

45

from the Nazis during World War II" (Baer 9). Further, in contemporary Iran, Jews are allowed some level of autonomy. According to Michael Theodoulou, Iranian Jews "elect their own deputy to the 270-seat parliament and have certain rights of self-administration" (6). However, Iranian Jews have recently complained about an increasing amount of prejudice and racism directed towards them in contemporary Iran.[3] If it is indeed true that the problems of the Middle East will never really be solved or significantly improved until there is a real amelioration of Muslim-Jewish relations, it is helpful to look at the relations of these two groups in an Islamic country (Iran) that has a history of both including and excluding Jews, as well as both welcoming and demonizing them. Along these lines, Dalia Sofer's *The Septembers of Shiraz* (2007) explores Muslim-Jewish relations both prior to and after the 1979 Iranian Revolution while revealing the many religious and other layers, dimensions, and contradictions involved in these important relationships and communities.

Through her carefully wrought characters both in Iran and in the United States, Sofer refuses to demonize or glorify Iranian Jews or Muslims. At the same time, she reveals that the United States, its overtures to the contrary, is not considerably more welcoming of Jews than Iran. To some extent, *The Septembers of Shiraz* is an almost oppositional text to Satrapi's *Persepolis* and *Persepolis 2*. Aside from the obvious difference in that one is a graphic work and the other is a traditional novel, Sofer's writing is much more serious, less personal, and involves the use of multiple perspectives. However, like *Persepolis*, *The Septembers of Shiraz* has autobiographical elements to it, although not nearly as much as *Persepolis* does.[4] Like the main characters in the novel, Sofer comes from an Iranian-Jewish family, and while she reports that attitudes towards Jews in Iran by Iranian Muslims were and currently are not horrible (although neither are they especially warm), she did grow up in an environment that, at the very least, allowed for anti–Semitism, if it did not encourage it to thrive.[5] At the same time, for the newly powerful in post–Revolutionary Iran, their anti–Semitism becomes intertwined with anti-capitalist and anti-Western rhetoric.

By and large, *The Septembers of Shiraz* was met with critical acclaim when it was published in 2007. Among the most prestigious honors and awards Sofer received include a designation from *The New York Times Book Review* as a Notable Book of the Year as well as the Sami Rohr Prize which "recognizes the unique role of contemporary writers in the transmission and examination of Jewish values, and is intended to encourage and promote outstanding writing of Jewish interest" (Jewish Book Council, par. 2). Indeed, *The Septembers of Shiraz* sheds important light on the Iranian-Jewish community both before and after the 1979 Revolution. In order to comprehend the role that Jews have played in Iran both before and after the Iranian Revolution, it is helpful to consider the history of Jews in Iran. Perhaps few Westerners know that Jews lived in Iran for over a thousand years before Islam was adopted there (Peterson 1). In addition, one of the most celebrated Persian kings, Cyrus the Great, freed Jews from slavery when he conquered the area around Iran, approximately 2500 years ago (Peterson 1). In subsequent years, Jews continued to settle in Iran, and by the nineteenth century, there were vibrant Jewish communities in various areas of the country, with the total Jewish population at this time estimated to be anywhere from 19,000 to 50,000 (Masliyah 391). This is not to suggest that Iranian Muslims fully integrated or fully accepted Iranian Jews since, as non–Muslims in a predominantly Muslim country, Iranian Jews "faced religious pressure and attendant social discrimination," and they were largely separated from the majority Muslim population (Masliyah 391, 393). In particular, some especially religious Shi'ite Muslims viewed Jews (as well as most Muslims) as "unclean," and these individuals tended to prevent "Jews from holding influential posts in the political and socio-economic life of the country" (Masliyah 396). As an example of this anti–Semitism, during this time, in certain areas, Jews were not allowed to leave their house when it would rain "as the water might touch a true believer and defile him after it had touched a Jew" (Masliyah 396).

Ironically, some of these restrictions against Jews and allied anti–Semitism were lifted or lessened with the reign of Reza Shah (1925–1941) and his son, Mohammad Reza Pahlavi, otherwise known as the Shah of Iran (1941–1979).[6] Both Shahs brought a level of Westernization to Iran (although they have subsequently been implicated in corruption and condemned for being, at least partially, Western puppets). With the rise of Ayatollah Khomeini and the subsequent Islamic Revolution of 1979, a fervent anti–Zionist (anti–Israel) sentiment grew amongst Iranian Muslims. However, when Iran was declared an Islamic Republic, this did not result in rampant targeting of Jews as the Ayatollah preached "tolerance" of the Jews "as people of the book" and subsequently "issued a fatwa, or religious decree, that they must be protected" (Theodoulou 6). One reason for the Ayatollah's behavior may be that a good many Jews helped in the more secular Iranian Revolution (alongside Marxists, Communists, and those who despised the perceived corruption of the Shah and his minions), before the movement became overly Islamic and fundamentalist (Peterson 3). While it may be difficult to understand why Jews might support an Islamic Regime, when the Revolution was occurring in 1979, it was not clear that Iran would become a non-secular Islamic country. Rather, many (like Marjane Satrapi's parents) felt that they were fighting for Iran's independence or at least against what they viewed as a corrupt and dangerous regime.

This, however, does not mean that all Jews were, in fact, protected by the Ayatollah's decree. After the Revolution, the Jewish community in Iran gradually began to fall "into disarray" (Hakakian 7). While some Iranian Jews fled to Israel and the United States after the Iranian Revolution took hold, a good many continued to live in Iran. Since there was a rapidly growing anti–Israel (if not anti–Semitic) movement in Iran, Jews who were thought to be assisting Israel (labeled Zionists) were often imprisoned or worse. In fact, this is exactly the situation of the main protagonist of *The Septembers of Shiraz*, Isaac Amin, a wealthy Iranian Jewish gem smith. From the beginning, *The Septembers of Shiraz* reads like a Kafkaesque novel in which an incarcerated protagonist (Amin) suffers in a labyrinth-like, fascist, bureaucratic system, receiving no due process, nor even being provided with the reasons for which he is arrested. The novel takes place during the aftermath of the Iranian Revolution, specifically 1981–2. The time period is important in the sense that the novel details Iran at a transition period between the rule of the Shah and the firm establishment of the increasingly fundamentalist Islamic Regime. At this point, there has not yet been a complete and thorough crackdown on Iranian political dissidents, those who were loyal to or who profited from life under the Shah, and those suspected of assisting Israel or the Zionist movement, although this crackdown has clearly begun. Some Iranians, like the Amins, cling to the hope that the political and religious changes in Iran may be temporary or that their families may be spared. What many don't realize yet is that to the Revolutionary Guard, Isaac and others like him represent all that the previously poor and sometimes previously jailed and tortured Revolutionary Guard (under the Shah) have come to despise about the West: wealth, amorality, atheism, and support for Zionism. To the Guard, the truth or the relative truth of these Western comparisons hardly matters because those that they arrest tend to be wealthy whereas they (the Revolutionary Guard) tended to be poor, vulnerable, and at times, seriously abused or tortured during the Shah's reign. Therefore, in the Guard's eyes, they are guilty.

Along these lines, in many ways, *The Septembers of Shiraz* is a novel about transformation. On the surface, it depicts how Iran transforms from a monarchy to an Islamic Regime. At the same time, the novel depicts the beginning of a social and economic transformation whereby the rich, who benefited under the Shah, gradually lose their power, money, and security. Unlike the relatively quick change of power during the Iranian Revolution of 1979, the hierarchy of Iranian society was slower to transform. Even during the time that Isaac is in prison, his family (his wife, Farnaz, and daughter, Shirin) are able to continue, if not the lavish lifestyle that they experienced during the Shah's reign, then at least a comfortable one. For instance, they are able to retain a domestic servant, Habibeh, and a gardener, Abbas. Also, despite Isaac's incarceration, things proceed in a relatively normal fashion at the Amin household. Farnaz is still able to complete basic household tasks while Shirin is still able to go to school, and, at least at the beginning of the novel, they have maintained most of their money and assets.

Another of the more important aspects of *The Septembers of Shiraz* involves Sofer's portrayal of the gradual erosion of previously demarcated economic classes, as well as the slow rise of lower class and underprivileged Iranians. The vestiges of this class system still appear in that the Amins employ servants; however, even these distinctions are beginning to erode. Sofer makes that point by showing how the Amin's servants and the Amin family no longer sit in demarcated positions (e.g., the furniture for the Amins and the floor for the servants) (89). While Isaac is in prison, Farnaz's relationship with Habibeh illustrates the deterioration of economic classes in Iran as well as the different perspectives of the formerly rich and powerful and the formerly poor and powerless. For her part, Farnaz feels that she and Isaac have treated their help well and included them in their family. However, this seems to be only Farnaz's perspective and not a wholly accurate one at that. For instance, when Farnaz notices some valuable items missing at their home, she immediately suspects Habibeh (as opposed to her own family members), when it is later revealed that it was actually Isaac's brother, Javad, who stole the items. Habibeh also claims that Farnaz belittles her, and, indeed, this can be seen in how Farnaz mocks Habibeh when Habibeh mistakenly believes Yves Saint Laurent to be a real saint (78). Also, Farnaz doesn't consider Habibeh as anything approaching an intellectual equal, but rather as more of a simple minded woman who is in danger of allowing "people" to "put ideas" in her "head" (77). For instance, when Habibeh legitimately states that "there is a lot of injustice that needs to be set right," namely the capitalists who profited under the Shah at the expense of less fortunate others, Farnaz responds by calling it "Marxist gibberish" (78).

The erosion of class distinctions also appears to bring out the worst in Farnaz, who reacts with anger and displays a propensity for violence. For instance, when Habibeh's son, Morteza, whom Isaac employed as more or less another servant, also begins acting in a rather insubordinate manner to Farnaz, Farnaz's response is to call her brother Keyvan. Sofer which illustrates the extent to which the Amins may have been complicit with the Shah or SAVAK: "In the old days Keyvan, with one phone call to his father, could have had someone like Morteza imprisoned for life" (159). For her part, Farnaz fails to see the irony in that what Keyvan used to do is identical to what others have just done to her husband — Isaac. She fails to see the human consequences of actions unless they directly pertain to her family. From Farnaz's rather capitalistic and demeaning perspective, Isaac's workers, including Morteza, "were all unemployed gypsies when Isaac hired them. He took them in, paid for their education, gave them salaries they probably didn't deserve" (162). While the former of her claims may be somewhat truthful, the latter of her comments represent Farnaz's continued feelings of superiority towards her subordinates. Despite Farnaz's belief that she and her family have privileged their servants, Morteza believes that they have been exploited. While the Amins may have exploited their servants in the sense that Isaac has profited from their labor, and he may not have generously compensated them in turn, one could also argue (as Farnaz does) that Isaac provided a better life for them than they had before they began working for him.

In essence, the relationship between Isaac and Farnaz with Habibeh and Morteza is more like one between parents and children. Indeed, Isaac claims to have treated Morteza as his son, and while there may be some truth to that in the sense that Isaac has not only employed Morteza, but allowed him to use their car, it is also not accurate in the sense that Isaac never exhibits love and affection towards Morteza as he does to his daughter, Shirin, or to his other family members. Those like Morteza, perhaps understandably, want the tables to be turned, and they want retribution for what they have come to see as "the sins of a whole collection of men" (186). However, ardent capitalists that they are, or at least are up until Isaac is incarcerated, neither Isaac nor Farnaz can see the consequences of their actions in pursuit of money. Ironically, the religious Morteza clings to a Marxist analysis (as Islamic officials were beginning to condemn Marxism and Communism at this time), viewing Isaac as a "corrupt" part of the bourgeoisie, who pursued wealth while ignoring the plights of less fortunate or even abused others (163). In truth, Morteza's motivation appears to be at least partially personal and he may use the guise of being religious for personal self-aggrandizement. Further, appearing religious now brings Iranians a greater amount of respect and power, as demonstrated by how Leila's father, who had previously been a humble but devout mortuary worker before the Revolution, is now a highly respected member of the Revolutionary Guard. In this new religious atmosphere, many people like Morteza became religious (in some cases, superficially so) in order to capitalize on the hierarchy of the new Iranian order.[7]

Still, there are signs that the privileged life that the Amins have grown accustomed to in Iran is gradually disappearing. Not only have "the most mundane items — eggs, cheese, soap," become "worthy of celebration," Farnaz recounts how violent her community has become, as evident by the sight of "the charred body of a prostitute ... paraded down the street" by a "euphoric" mob (69). We can also see a transformation in Iran when it comes to class, power, and religion. For instance, when Farnaz first goes to Evin Prison to try to locate Isaac, a young soldier rebuffs her and shows her no remorse or compassion, presumably because Farnaz does not dress in a sufficiently conservative manner or she appears wealthier than he. This becomes especially apparent when Farnaz goes back to the prison again, but this time with her domestic servant, Habibeh. Presumably because the more demure and lower class Habibeh is there, another guard is more responsive to Farnaz's requests.

However, the largest transformation in the novel is more of a personal one, and it occurs in Isaac while he is in prison. When Isaac enters Evin, he is far from a completely sympathetic character. Rather, he appears quite materialistic to the point that he seems to value his money and assets nearly as much as, if not more than, his well-being or the well-being of his family. Possibly because of this, Isaac's family life also seems to be suffering. Right before he is imprisoned, Isaac describes his relationship with his wife, Farnaz, as rather strained; on most nights, "they would say little to each other, a few words about the day or Shirin or some explosion somewhere" (5). Despite the deterioration of Iran after the Iranian Revolution and the stories Isaac hears about his peers (not all Jews) being imprisoned or killed, he does not leave Iran, mainly due to pride in his accomplishments as well as "his belief— very naive he realizes now — that things gone wrong are eventually set right" (10). Similarly, Isaac's brother-in-law, Keyvan, and Isaac's sister, Shahla (also both Jews), do not want to leave Iran because of materialistic reasons, even though they are both in danger due to Keyvan's "connections to the shah" (53).

While a critic might suggest that Sofer's portrayal of the materialistic Amins contributes to stereotypes of Jews as overly greedy and money-obsessed, materialism is not the only motivating factor for the Amins and their extended family. The fact that the Amins appear to fit so neatly into this Jewish stereotype makes them especially vulnerable to the generally anti–Semitic Revolutionary Guard as well as to the guards and interrogators in Evin Prison. Still, despite being Jewish in a country that does not always respond favorably to Jews, they feel that Iran is their home, and they feel culturally tied to it. For instance, Shahla explains that she does not want to leave Iran because of things like her emotional and cultural connection to a painting made by her great-grandfather, which she would have to leave behind were they to flee Iran. While this might seem to be a trivial reason, the painting represents "family history" to Shahla (55).

Still, Sofer does not want the reader to view the Amins one-dimensionally as victims or oppressors, for in a way, they can be seen as both, just as Sofer will later illustrate how the more fundamentalist Revolutionary Guards and actual guards at Evin Prison can also been seen as both oppressors and a formerly oppressed people. Towards the beginning of the novel, the members of the Amin family seem to look back upon the Shah's reign with some measure of nostalgia, for, after all, they lived well during this time. They do not think about those who were less fortunate, those who were tortured or whose lives were ruined or even ended. For those who suffered under the Shah, such ignorance is inexcusable, and they make no distinction between those who committed the crimes and those who ignored the crimes while they occurred or did nothing to stop them. As Mohsen, Isaac's interrogator, points out, "To live well under the shah means you had to shut your eyes and ears. You had to pretend the secret police did not exist" (124). It is very likely that the Amins did exactly this.

Indeed, a good deal of the conflict among characters in *The Septembers of Shiraz* revolves around how they lived and what they did during the Shah's reign. While Isaac acknowledges that the Shah tortured Iranian citizens, he believes rather naively that they did so "to get information and discourage future subversives" (124).[8] The irony of this rationalization, which Isaac does not seem to realize, is that this is the same reason the Revolutionary Guard now uses to justify torturing Isaac himself. Therefore, in essence, Isaac has switched roles with those who now incarcerate him. Isaac may believe that the new Islamic Regime "simply wants to destroy human beings" (124); however, he fails to appreciate that the end result is the same for the Shah's regime, SAVAK, and the new Iranian Revolution: maiming and the deaths of innocent people.

Evin Prison, where Isaac is sent, is generally considered to be Iran's most vicious prison — comparable to or worse than Abu Ghraib or Guantánamo Bay — where prisoners can be and often are denied due process.[9] It is also a prison where inmates can be left to the mercy (or lack thereof) of their guards and interrogators, who sometimes torture or even execute their prisoners for innumerable reasons. As one might imagine, living in such an environment can be devastating and life-shattering, and a good deal of the emotional weight of *The Septembers of Shiraz* rests in the depiction of the prison, which includes political prisoners like Mehdi. Even underage political prisoners, like sixteen-year-old Ramin, are common. Both Mehdi and Ramin were imprisoned largely due to their Marxist or Communistic leanings. The imprisonment of inmates such as Mehdi is ironic in that he, and others like him, fought side by side with his current captors (or the like) to depose the Shah. After the Iranian Revolution succeeds, though, religious groups take control of Iran and they condemn the Communists and Marxists for their perceived atheism and amorality, even those these same individuals had just fought with them. This hardly seems to matter to the more religious captors who now hold the most power and who incarcerate and torture Mehdi and others in Evin.

As horrific as the conditions may be for Isaac and other prisoners at Evin Prison, it is not Sofer's intention to demonize the guards and interrogators there, who terrorize and torture the inmates. While Sofer includes graphic depictions of torture upon inmates like Isaac who are burned with cigarettes, severely beaten on their feet, and subject to mock executions (among other things), she also depicts some of the interrogators and guards in the prison as being, if not somewhat good-hearted, then at least partially victimized by their own experiences under the Shah's reign. For instance, one of Isaac's guards, Hossein, who was possibly imprisoned himself during the Shah's reign, agrees to try to help Mehdi with his gangrenous foot and offers advice to Isaac and others such as how best to navigate their way through the Kafkaesque prison and how to avoid torture or death.

While Sofer humanizes the guards, she does not ultimately portray them as being as sympathetic as the prisoners themselves. Even the seemingly kindly Hossein employs a kind of cold calculus in his analysis of the prison. When Isaac points out to him that some innocent people are put to death in the prison, Hossein responds, "Some innocents die, that's true. And some guilty ones get away. In the end, it balances itself out" (195). For Hossein, the ends justify the means, and it is quite probable that he and other guards and interrogators have grown this callous from the years spent under the Shah or at Evin Prison themselves. Hossein and other guards or interrogators feel that in their own way, they are helping to build a more perfect union in Iran by taking "the weeds out of the soil" (196). Ultimately Sofer does not completely condemn their logic as much as the means to their ends, which involve torture and even unwarranted executions. While it might be relatively easy to understand and appreciate Hossein's logic and position, Isaac's main interrogator and torturer, Mohsen, lacks Hossein's idealism and is motivated more by a personal vendetta against those who supported the Shah, whom he views as accomplices in the torture that Mohsen himself experienced himself when in prison under the Shah's reign. Still, despite the fact that he is the one that orders the torture that Isaac and the others endure, Sofer does not want the reader to demonize Mohsen. Not only was Mohsen tortured by the SAVAK, Sofer depicts him as a doting father (210). While this, of course, does not justify Mohsen's behavior in the least, we are able to see the aftermath of the vicious cycle of violence, which the American-backed Shah's regime helped engender.

As with the Iranian Revolution, the struggle between Mohsen and Isaac is ideologically and religiously based. While their struggle can be seen as a microcosm of the struggle between more secular and non-secular Iranians right after the Iranian Revolution, to Mohsen and others, the real struggle is between what they perceive to be the Zionist influenced, amoral, decadent West and the religious, moral, and conservative atmosphere they seek to establish and then secure in their newly established Islamic Regime. Although Iran may have maintained a relatively sizable minority population of Jews, Iranian administrators do distinguish between "good" and "bad" Jews (bad being those perceived to be "Zionists" and "good" being those perceived to be deferential and apolitical).[10] Mohsen, though, appears to view Jews and Zionists as virtually one and the same, or, at the very least, Jews like Isaac are presumed to be antagonistic Zionists unless proven otherwise. Indeed, from the very beginning of his interrogations, Mohsen suggests that Isaac has assisted Israel, and hence is a Zionist. He points out certain facts that Isaac cannot deny, for instance, that Isaac has relatives in the Israeli Army[11] and a brother, Javad, who has engaged in illicit smuggling activities. As both of these statements are accurate, to some extent one can understand why Mohsen may be suspicious of Isaac. Further, Mohsen views Isaac and his family as virtual lackeys of the Shah and the West, claims that are not entirely without reason. Mohsen also takes issue with the fact that Isaac's wife, Farnaz, has written articles about Western-type activities like ice skating and skating rinks which Mohsen views as "a haven for sin" and evidence of the Amins being pro–Western (15). Again, while there is some logic to Mohsen's claims, such claims also illustrate how, in the climate of the new Islamic Regime, one can and often is found to be guilty of being Western merely by association.

While Mohsen and Hossein may be guilty of rationalizing when it comes to their treatment of prisoners at Evin, Isaac too can be seen as rationalizing, if not acting in a rather non-compliant way in his interactions with his guards and interrogators. To some extent, this is, of course, understandable, as Isaac may not want to accept responsibility for anything, for doing so may put him in greater peril than he already is at this point. However, Isaac believes that he is innocent of any wrongdoing whatsoever, and at the beginning of his incarceration, Isaac fails to realize how his wealth leads to immediate negative regard in the eyes of Mohsen and others like him, who grew up in relative poverty and suffered during the Shah's reign. Isaac tells Mohsen that he is a "simple man," which Mohsen rejects for some compelling reasons, since Isaac was both wealthy and successful under the Shah (60). It is indeed hard to dispute Mohsen's conclusions and to some extent, one can understand his suspicion of Isaac. Also, Isaac does have dubious connections with his brother,

Javad, an illegal smuggler, and his brother-in-law, Keyvan, both of whom supported the Shah.

The conflict between Isaac and Mohsen, which forms the heart of the novel, is not only a conflict between Muslims and Jews, between the Iranian monarchy and the Islamic Republic, but between civilizations and cultures (with Isaac representing the West and capitalism, and Mohsen representing fundamentalist religion). Their conflict is also a struggle for power as well as a way for the guards to condemn capitalism. Mohsen, who himself came from humble upbringings and was previously imprisoned under the Shah, wants Isaac to experience what he did, not only through torture but also through personal debasement. Towards that end, Mohsen insists that Isaac is "nothing" and that "resistance is pointless" (62–3). Similarly, when Farnaz goes to the prison for a second time, she too challenges the guards who condemn Isaac for his financial aggrandizement. Her response reveals her essential belief in capitalism: "Brother, the money did not fall out of the sky. He earned it!" (75). However, her reasoning meets deaf ears as the guard explains: "It's time you understood, Sister Amin, that the days when people like you could demand things from us are over. Now it's our turn" (76).

It is telling, though, that between Mohsen and Isaac, only Isaac is the dynamic character, capable of changing and of learning to empathize with the less privileged. This, perhaps more than anything else, illustrates that Sofer views Isaac as being a worthier character and human being than Mohsen (or others like Mohsen). While it is difficult to determine the extent to which he is telling the truth, Isaac eventually breaks down to Mohsen and accepts that he "looked the other way" and was a kind of "an accomplice" to those who harmed Mohsen and others during the Shah's reign (249). Still, Sofer is not completely criticizing capitalism, for in this case, Isaac's capitalistic tendencies literally save his life (and possibly the lives of his family as well). Ironically, the money that condemns Isaac, according to Mohsen, ends up saving Isaac's life, illustrating that despite their overtures to the contrary, his captors are at least partially capitalists themselves. Specifically, Isaac's offer to donate his entire savings to "the cause of the revolution" (250) turns out to be enough to set him free. It is doubtful that the money will all be used towards the Revolution, as evidenced in the actions of the self-aggrandizing Revolutionary Guard when they ransack the Amins' house and take expensive items like Isaac's cufflinks, presumably for themselves and not for the Regime. Also, when Isaac is brought back to his home to retrieve the materials necessary to withdraw his life savings from his bank, another Revolutionary Guard takes an expensive antique sword, again presumably for himself and not for the Regime.

In this new Iranian order, to be sure, all religions are not treated or respected similarly. The Amins are easier targets because they are Jews and their pursuit of money fits the Jewish stereotype and in turn helps contribute to growing anti–Semitic rhetoric in post–Revolutionary Iran. This can be seen, for instance, in how, after a heated confrontation with Farnaz, Morteza calls Farnaz a "dirty Jew" when he has no real response to her condemnation of him (163). Also, when one of the Revolutionary Guards uncovers a silver teapot that Farnaz had thought missing, "she thanks them for finding it" (137). The guard responds: "Look how happy a piece of silver makes you.... There is no cure for your kind" (137). It is easy to see vestiges of early Nazi Germany in this sort of anti–Semitic rhetoric and behavior. Still, the Amins are caught in a contradictory bind: the Revolutionary Guard or Islamic Regime will presumably condemn them for being Jews but they will also presumably condemn the Amins if they attempt to be secular.[12] Even one of the prisoners berates Isaac for being a materialistic, secular Jew: "As long as you can buy your Italian shoes and your fancy watches and your villas by the sea, you're happy" (100). It is true that when he is first incarcerated, Isaac acknowledges that "he does not have beliefs" (100). In that sense, he represents more of a calculating (and possibly amoral) Western capitalism than Zionism. At the same time, being in prison does seem to make Isaac if not more religious, then at least more appreciative of religion. In this unjust atmosphere in which death may occur at virtually any moment, Isaac concludes that "in order to hold on to hope, he feels he must believe in something" (128). Towards that end, while in prison, Isaac does begin to pray, but, at least at first, he does so mainly to ingratiate himself to his captors.

Isaac's time in prison does not necessarily lead him to become more religious,[13] and it is not Sofer's intention to simplistically demonstrate how Isaac and the Amins rediscover their Jewish roots, are healed by their newfound religious beliefs, and subsequently seek shelter in a Jewish community elsewhere. While Isaac does discover that Iran has become a more hostile environment for Jews after the Iranian Revolution, the attendant solution is not, according to Sofer, to embrace Judaism in response. At the same time, Sofer demonstrates that Isaac's incarceration helps distance him even more from his religious and cultural heritage as a Jew. In fact, he implicates Judaism to some degree for being responsible for his incarceration. To Isaac, Judaism appears have "become more of a liability to him than a salvation" (211). He wonders "why must he bear the burdens of this religion," when he has "led a secular life" (211). Even after he is incarcerated, Isaac regards religion in a pragmatic and utilitarian manner. Isaac, in fact, decides to start reading the Koran in order to gain some leverage with his captors. This, in fact, seems to work as, after Isaac quotes from the Koran, Mohsen seems to be more respectful towards him.

Still, it is not Sofer's intention merely to explore the role that Islam or fundamentalist Islam has upon Iranians and the place, or lack thereof, that Iranian Jews have in post–Revolutionary Iran. She also explores Judaism in general as well as orthodox Judaism in the United States. Towards that end, *The Septembers of Shiraz* also follows Isaac's son, Parviz, who now lives in New York City and is, like his father, a secular Jew. Through Parviz, Sofer details the difficulties facing new Iranian-American immigrants. In that sense, like Satrapi, Sofer does not portray the West (in this case, the United States) as a democratic Promised Land. It certainly does not seem as such to Parviz, who, at least initially, views America and Americans as uncomplicated, privileged, and spoiled (37). Like Isaac, Parviz seems to not realize his own arrogance and that he is also the product of a rather privileged upbringing. While Parviz is not imprisoned like his father, when he first settles in New York City, Parviz too is stripped of his material possessions. Consequently, for Parviz, New York City appears like a prison and he starts feeling almost like a prisoner condemned to solitary confinement. As Sofer explains: "Friendship had once come naturally to him. Now he cannot recall how he managed it so effortlessly. His mutation has been insidious, creeping up on him like a disfiguring disease" (37).

Still, in a way similar to Isaac, Parviz experiences a kind of transformation while in New York City, and this is largely due to interactions with his Jewish landlord, Zalman Mendelson, and Mendelson's family. Ironically, it takes an exile in a secular country, the United States, for Parviz to begin to appreciate and connect with his religious and ethnic roots, just as it takes incarceration in a brutal, dehumanizing prison to humanize Isaac. Still, when Sofer first introduces Parviz to the reader, he is similar to Isaac, who appears somewhat dismissive or resentful of his Jewish heritage. Specifically, Parviz appears to harbor some prejudices, if not animosity towards certain Jews, most notably Hasidic Jews. Parviz calls them "those beardies from Poland," and describes them in a rather anti–Semitic manner as having a "moldiness about them, a certain mustiness in their black suits and stockings and wigs" (41). Parviz encounters Hasidic Jews on a more personal level when he rents a downstairs apartment from the Hasidic Mendelson family. Parviz's rather judgmental and arrogant attitude towards the Mendelsons can be seen in how he attempts to distance himself from them. For instance, he concludes that "to enter their apartment would be like relegating himself to a ghetto, where the memories of all the wrongs committed against Jews simmer year after year in bulky, indigestable stews" (41–2). Instead of appreciating that there have been

"wrongs" committed against the Jews, Parviz wants merely to forget and assimilate. However, he soon discovers that doing so is not nearly as easy as he
imagined it to be.

Sofer allows us to see that it is not just Parviz who harbors anti–Hasidic
sentiments in the supposedly welcoming melting pot of New York City, nor
is it only Parviz who has difficulty adjusting to life in the West as an Iranian
immigrant. For instance, Parviz meets another Iranian Jewish exile, Mr.
Broukhim, who was formerly a respected cardiologist in Iran. However,
because his medical license is not honored in the United States, Mr. Broukhim
becomes a rather impoverished flower seller (227). An embittered Mr. Broukhim tells Parviz, "In this country, I feel like a ghost" (227). Similar to Parviz,
Mr. Broukhim also harbors some resentment towards the Hasids (which may
be projected resentment from his loss of wealth, respect, and position as an
Iranian exile). He tells Parviz, "I don't like these religious beardies. I can't
wait to save enough money so I can get out of this neighborhood" (144). At
the same time, Mr. Broukhim acknowledges that the Hasids "helped" him
out, just as Parviz will benefit from the generosity of the community of Hasidic
Jews in New York City (144).

While Sofer does not directly promote orthodox Judaism in *The Septembers of Shiraz*, she does portray the lives of the Hasids as being much more
stable and satisfying than the lives of secular Jews like Parviz. While Parviz
appears quite unhappy in his secularism and somewhat self-destructive in his
predilection for alcohol, Sofer portrays Zalman Mendelson as generally content
and secure. Sofer also displays the genuine concern and compassion other
Hasids show Parviz because he is a fellow Jew. Despite the fact that they know
Parviz is a secular Jew, Zalman and other religious Jews take pity on him and
allow him to use credit when he runs out of money. Zalman, in fact, gives
him a job in his hat shop. Still, Parviz, who grew up rather privileged and
seemingly arrogant as a result of his upbringing, at first feels that he debases
himself by working and associating with Zalman, which "fills him with sadness," and "is proof of his fall from son of a wealthy man to starving shop
boy" (88). However, just as his father, Isaac, broadens his imagination and
transforms while in prison, so must Parviz in New York City.

In a way, Sofer's depiction of a more welcoming (though not without
faults) orthodox Judaism as represented by Zalman forms a counterpoint to
her depiction of a less welcoming fundamentalist Islam in Iran as well as to
Isaac. In fact, the lesson that Isaac starts to learn while in prison is one that
Zalman has already take to be a basic truth: that the majority of the world is
hostile towards Jews. Indeed, we can see a similar historical cycle in that just
as Parviz's father, Isaac, is incarcerated, Zalman's own father was incarcerated

in Russia due to anti–Semitism there. Still, despite the generosity of Zalman and other Jews towards Parviz, it is not Sofer's intention to oversimplify religious matters, nor is it her intention to idealize orthodox Judaism. In fact, orthodox religion can and does get in the way of personal relationships and love. This becomes apparent in how Parviz finds out that Zalman once loved and was going to marry a Muslim girl, but Zalman decided to break off their engagement due to their religious differences (274).

Sofer also does not portray orthodox Judaism as especially empowering for women. Certainly she depicts it as no more empowering that orthodox Islam.[14] Not only does Zalman's wife, Rivka, not seem to be allowed to work, their teenage daughter, Rachel, is barely allowed to speak to any unmarried men, let alone touch them (including a simple handshake). Indeed, this dictate runs parallel to the current rules in Iran that unmarried men and women should not hold hands or display affection to one another in public. In this parallel, Sofer illustrates how orthodox followers of any religion can have similarly oppressive dictates and expectations. However, it is Rachel to whom Parviz is eventually drawn, but his attention can be attributed mainly to his desire to experience the kind of peace that he believes Zalman has found, since Zalman has surrendered himself to what he considers to be "God's will," and believes "things happen for a reason" (142). As Sofer explains, "Her [Rachel's] religiosity, which not long ago would have repelled him [Parviz], now offers him something no one else has since his arrival: quietude" (170). When Zalman eventually learns of Parviz's interest in his daughter, he tries to put a stop to it because Parviz is not religious. For Zalman, religion trumps everything. Not dissimilar to Mohsen, Zalman looks at himself "as an individual, but as piece of a whole, as a brick in the house. A few broken bricks and the whole house falls down" (313). Whereas Zalman does not torture people like Mohsen, and in that sense can certainly be seen as morally superior to Mohsen, Zalman has also not been directly tortured himself as Mohsen has. Both Zalman and Mohsen stubbornly insist that their religion is the right one, creating divisions between people and self-segregated communities. Indeed, in language ironically and disturbingly similar to that of the Nazis, Zalman believes that if Parviz marries Rachel the couple would "dilute the religion," since she would most likely not carry on the traditions (313).

Sofer does not ultimately portray religion or anything specific as the answer or answers to the dilemmas facing the various characters in *The Septembers of Shiraz*. In a larger sense, she does illustrate how identity can be transitory and in flux, or an "illusion" as Farnaz concludes (207). Sofer also suggests that the atmosphere in Iran will only get worse, as indeed it literally does with the subsequent Iran-Iraq war. On a personal level, this can be seen in how Isaac's sister, Shahla, is attacked for having a loose headscarf, with one attacker throwing acid on her and subsequently disfiguring her (230). Still, out of this same violent and instable environment come opportunities for individual and personal transformation. Ironically, the horrific dehumanization Isaac and others experience while in prison ends up producing the exact opposite in prisoners like Isaac: greater humanization and a greater community among the prisoners. For Isaac, this transformation begins almost from the moment he is incarcerated. Whereas, before his incarceration, Isaac seemed more materialistically concerned with his belongings and his family's well-being, now, with no more material objects or even a worthwhile and stable identity, he and other prisoners begin to bond. As Sofer explains, while in prison "stripped of their ornaments and belongings, they are nothing more than bodies, each as likely as the next to face a firing squad or to go home, unscathed, with a gripping tale to tell friends and family" (8).

While Evin Prison might seem to be a wholly dehumanizing atmosphere in which nothing good could arise, the opposite actually turns out to be true. Rather, it is in Evin that former foes, such as Mehdi, a former professor who opposed the Shah, and Isaac, who supported the Shah, find common ground. Isaac's concern for Mehdi can be seen in how he tries to get Mehdi help for his gangrenous foot (caused by severe lashings). It can also be seen in how Isaac comforts and nurtures his sixteen-year-old cellmate, Ramin, who is devastated after learning that his mother has been executed. As Sofer describes, "It occurs to him [Isaac] that he hasn't held his own children like this in years" (175). It is not only Isaac who appears to be changed by his time spent in prison. At one point, Mehdi tells Isaac that he would have hated Isaac before the Revolution, but "now I don't know. We have more in common than I would care to admit" (124). Isaac's time in prison also helps him re-prioritize his life and reconsider his own identity, which, he comes to realize, was largely determined by material objects. Indeed, when Isaac sees his prison interrogator, Mohsen, for the last time after being tortured on several occasions, Isaac tells him that he "followed the wrong path in life. I pursued material wealth, which in the end brought me nothing" (248). There is no reason to believe Isaac is merely stating this for effect.

Isaac's transformation also is apparent when he is released from prison after donating a significant portion of his life savings to the Islamic Regime.[15] Whereas previously Isaac might not have been concerned for others beyond his immediate family and merely given the money to protect them without any further thought, he does now have more of a conscience. This can be seen in the questions he asks himself after donating money to the Regime: "How will my money be used? To build more prisons, to buy more bullets?

In buying back my own life, will I facilitate the deaths of others?" (252). However, Isaac concludes that "a man has a right to want to live" (252).

When Isaac finally gets back home after being released, he "wonders if something of him remains in those rooms, if a curtain pulled open so many years ago to reveal a sunny provincial day still holds his fingerprints in its folds, as if to say, Isaac Amin was here" (247). On the one hand, Isaac describes himself "like a dead man resurrected," but he also insists that "I am the same man" (287). As time progresses, though, it becomes clear that Isaac had understandably been shaken and shattered by his time spent in prison as evidenced by how, after his release, when he takes his family on a spring vacation to an area near the Caspian Sea and finds that a house they own there has been confiscated by the Revolutionary Guards, Isaac accepts this turn of events without any real protest and rents another house instead. There are other indications that Isaac has become less materialistic after his incarceration. While on their way out of Iran, Isaac's family receives special treatment because of the amount he pays them, but this time he feels some culpability, prompting a series of introspective questions:

> Why is it, he wonders, that wealth must always be accompanied by guilt, if not shame? Had he not worked hard for it, and had it not, in the end, saved his life? Had it not ensured his family's comfort, as it does not — his wife and daughter the only ones of the group seated safely inside the truck? Why the constant indignation at a man who dares to live well? Does living well imply selfishness? Was he — Isaac Amin — a selfish man? [332].

As evidence of Isaac's increasing empathy, he tries to comfort and financially assist a pregnant woman who is also trying to leave Iran along with them, even to the point of endangering himself. In that sense, we can see how Isaac has transcended the violent and vindictive environment of post–Revolutionary Iran.

Ultimately, Sofer illustrates how Iran suffers from and is caught in a vicious circle of violence, which could easily be traced back to the SAVAK (if not earlier), whereby the tortured and oppressed groups of each new regime aim to do the same thing to the group they feel oppressed and tortured them when in power. Sofer also suggests that the only way to break the cycle is for a person to forgive the aggrieving party and resign himself to an uncertain future, or to leave Iran for good. The first option is not easy, even for someone like Isaac, who seems to achieve a kind of dispassionate state whereby any real desire for revenge against those who tortured him has largely dissipated. For indeed, Isaac still has to try to establish a safe and satisfying life for his family.

To a large extent, Sofer suggests that the most appealing solution for the

Amins or any Iranian family (especially Jewish families) who lived well under the Shah is to leave Iran. As Farnaz concludes: "This has become a country of informers.... To survive, one must either become one — or disappear" (167). Especially since in the rather anti–Semitic climate of post–Revolutionary Iran, the Revolutionary Guard and the Islamic Republic itself would never trust the Amins completely, they feel they do not have any real option except to leave. After an arduous journey that takes them through the remote mountains of Iran into Turkey, the Amins do exactly that. Towards the end of the novel, Isaac concludes that he and Farnaz have "shared an education in grief" (338). The fact that Farnaz uses the word "education" is telling. Despite the loss of virtually everything they held dear, the Amins have never been as close as they become during and after their ultimately successful escape from Iran. Still, the Iran that they leave, Sofer illustrates, is not an evil country full of villainous, atavistic, and violent people, but a deeply traumatized country in the throes of an attempted, ultimately violent reconstruction. In Sofer's account, post–Revolutionary Iranians of the early 1980s may feel that they are building a more perfect union, but so many of them have become so blinded by their own internal turmoil and trauma that they do not have the ability or the security to imagine anything like an inclusive, democratic country. Having witnessed violence, corruption, and colonialism for much of their lives, they cannot see much beyond these things even when they are trying to counteract them. Therefore, the oppressed becomes the oppressor; the victims become the aggressors, and the tortured become the torturers.

# 3

# The Iranian-American Exile and the Exiled Iranian

*Porochista Khakpour's* Sons and Other Flammable Objects

Generally, most Westerners have little to no first hand interactions with diasporic Iranians, nor the ability to distinguish diasporic Iranians based on name or appearance. For many Westerners, seeing a name like Farnaz might indicate someone of Middle Eastern and Arabic descent, when in fact, Farnaz would more likely suggest Iranian of Persian descent. Along similar lines, most Westerners, after seeing the name Roya Hakanian (author of the Iranian memoir *Journey to the Land of No*), would probably presume that she is Armenian rather than Iranian (she is Iranian). Possibly because of the difficulty of categorizing diasporic Iranians by name and by sight as well as the more heterogeneous nature of Iran itself, it is relatively easy (at least compared to other major ethnic groups) to be presumed Iranian if one studies and presents in the subject matter and has a vaguely Middle Eastern sounding first or last name. Indeed, this happened to me on multiple occasions while presenting my research on Iranian and Iranian diasporic literature and culture at various academic conferences. Specifically, panelists and audience members have asked me how my family was coping with the recent turmoil in Iran, assuming that due to my presentation, my last name, and possibly my appearance that I am Iranian when I am actually of Sephardic and Ashkenazi Jewish descent.[1]

This example demonstrates the great amount of confusion and the lack of knowledge most Westerners have about diasporic Iranians. Names alone are insufficient to demarcate who is or who is not Iranian, which contributes to how diasporic Iranians have become an even further marginalized or invisible minority. Because most Americans and Westerners have little to no knowledge of the origins, meaning, and important of Iranian culture and history, writers like Marjane Satrapi and Porochista Khakpour place a high premium on names and upon recovering Persian history. In the case of the former, the titles of her two graphic novels, *Persepolis* and *Persepolis 2*, allude to Iran's (Persia's) ancient, glorious empire, now largely forgotten or marginalized by the West. Indeed, while a sizeable number of Westerners probably know about the empires and achievements of the Ancient Greeks and Romans, fewer know of the empires and achievements of the Ancient Persians. Along similar lines, Khakpour names her two main characters in her debut novel, *Sons and Other Flammable Objects* (2007), Darius and Xerxes Adam. These names allude to the two most celebrated emperors of Ancient Persia. Still, it is not Khakpour's intention (nor was it Satrapi's intention) to merely provide the reader with a history lesson about Ancient Persia. Rather, Khakpour illustrates the contemporary status of diasporic Iranians (in this case Iranian-Americans) both pre– and post–September 11, 2001, as being akin to an uncomfortable limbo in which they are caught between nations, stereotypes, ethnicities, and cultures.

*Sons and Other Flammable Objects* can be considered part of a new Iranian diasporic literature mainly centered in the United States. While Khakpour is certainly not the first celebrated Iranian-American novelist as there have been others before her like Gina Nahai,[2] Khakpour represents a new, younger group of Iranian-American authors[3] who write a more complex and contradictory diasporic literature that invokes globalization, fragmentation, the constraining and liberating power of popular culture, as well as the seemingly contradictory hegemony and liberation of American feminism and multiculturalism, while detailing the turn in the United States, especially for Middle Eastern Americans, post–September 11.

Whereas critics have suggested that one hallmark of diasporic literature is "alienation" and a "nostalgic longing for the lost life of the homeland," *Sons and Other Flammable Objects* exposes much more than simple, generic alienation in the lives of the Adam family (Davaran 12). Rather, Khakpour illustrates the ways the Adam family is caught between two cultures (American and Iranian), unable to embrace nor relinquish either one. Further, their perceptions of each culture are unreliable, tainted by media stereotypes and presuppositions. To various members of the Adam family there is both an idealized and reviled United States and Iran. Largely unable to reconcile their conceptions of both countries and cultures with their respective realities, the Adam family turns upon one another and their family subsequently fragments. At the same time, the members of the Adam family, both first- and second-generation Americans, try to become something more than an alienated exile. They might not always be able to "assert the dignity of their existence," and formulate "a new consciousness" as is thought to be typical of diasporic literature, but, through their depictions, we can see the beginnings of an amalgamation of Western and Iranian worlds (Davaran 12). *Sons and Other*

*Flammable Objects* also touches upon many common themes in contemporary Iranian and diasporic Iranian literature: the tension between assimilation and isolation; the rift between first and second generation diasporic Iranians; Western perceptions of Iran; the effects of September 11, 2001; and gender and class struggles, to name just a few.

Most recently (2012) a core faculty member in the M.F.A. program at the University of Tampa, Khakpour, though only in her early thirties, has already received numerous awards and accolades, including writing fellowships from Johns Hopkins University and Northwestern University.[4] Khakpour was born in Tehran in 1978, but as she only briefly lived there, she would more aptly be described as Iranian-American. More significantly, Khakpour grew up in a less diverse area of Southern California: Pasadena (Khakpour "What I Saw" par. 19). Unlike certain sections of Westwood, Bel Air, and Brentwood, Pasadena does not have large enclaves of Iranian-Americans, and this may have led to an easier (and at the same time more difficult) assimilation period for Khakpour. On the one hand, Khakpour did not grow up within an Iranian-American community, which may have pushed her to assimilate more quickly.[5] Due largely to not having a nearby ethnic community of Iranian-Americans, Khakpour describes how she developed a DuBoisian double consciousness as well as a strong desire to assimilate. In her own words:

> For the first two and a half decades of my life, my inner life was devoted to rehearsing for American Girl roles — working the mercilessly flat-ironed hair, generic pale-olive skin and "brown-eyed girl" for "passing" glory — while an impossible *Po-ro-chis-ta* cultivated credible Valley Girlese that would eventually put even Moon-Unit to shame. Like many immigrants, I focused adamantly on looking forward and never back; like many "hyphenates," I felt the existential confusion of a two-pronged identity [Khakpour "What I Saw" par. 2].

It is this double consciousness or two-pronged identity which characterizes all members of the Adam family. In a larger sense, Khakpour suggests that Iranian-Americans cannot find a stable and fulfilling identity for themselves until they are able to synthesize their two identities as Iranian and American. That, Khakpour suggests, is only possible when Iranian-Americans transcend idealizing or demonizing either their Iranian or Persian identity or their American nationality, a process made especially difficult by the way each country tends to demonize the other. Ignoring or repressing one's Iranian culture, Khakpour suggests, only leads to further disappointment, rage, or misdirected anger.

These emotions are something not easily addressed by the male figures in *Sons and Other Flammable Objects*, and hence, the title of the book alludes to the relationship, both fragile and dangerous, between fathers and sons or, in this case, Iranian and Iranian-American fathers and sons. Western countries often describe or depict Iran and many Middle Eastern countries as being both patriarchal and sexist.[6] Indeed, it will be demonstrated in a subsequent chapter how Azar Nafisi's *Reading Lolita in Tehran* has engendered a debate as to whether Iran and other predominantly Islamic Middle Eastern countries are indeed patriarchal and sexist or whether, as others argue, categorizing Middle Eastern countries as such is a Western presumption and distortion of life in these cultures. *Sons and Other Flammable Objects* can certainly be read as support for the argument that Iran is more patriarchal and sexist; however, the "liberation" that the major female character (Lala Adam) in *Sons and Other Flammable Objects* experiences in the West seems illusory and transient. While there may be an equal amount or even more occupational stratification in Iran than in the United States, with more Iranian men than women working in science, engineering, and medicine,[7] in *Sons and Other Flammable Objects*, Khakpour illustrates more of a non-ethnically specific conflict and rivalry between men and their sons. After all, she did not mention Iran, let alone the Middle East, in the title. At the same time, in *Sons and Other Flammable Objects* the inability for both father (Darius) and son (Xerxes) to synthesize their Iranian heritage with their American nationality further aggravates their relationship to the point of implosion. This, we will see, is caused by both internal and external factors. In essence, Khakpour illustrates that the environment in the United States is as much to blame as anything else (including Iran) for the damaged and fragmented Adam family.

To be sure, many works of American literature, ethnically or non-ethnically specific, concern the relationship or lack thereof between fathers and sons. As American ideology tends to champion the self-made man, it makes sense that many works of American literature focus upon a male protagonist who either rejects or rebels against a father or father figure (e.g., authority or society).[8] As critic Josep Armengol-Carrera suggests, "Fatherhood in American literature, when/if present at all, has traditionally been represented as distant and authoritarian" (222). While Khakpour portrays Darius (the father) as being rather domineering, if not totalitarian, this may not have anything do with his ethnicity as Iranian-American or with a supposedly patriarchal Iranian culture, but rather with his non–ethnically specific identity as a man and as a father. At the same time, Khakpour's emphasis upon father-son relationships may hold significance in relation to Middle Eastern culture. For instance, Syrine Hout, in an article outlining contemporary diasporic Lebanese literature, argues that a primary focus in such works "is the father-son relationship" (286).[9]

In the case of *Sons and Other Flammable Objects*, what we see is Xerxes's attempt to become a self-made man in that particular American idiom, but his ethnicity as an Iranian-American holds him back as well as his father, who fears that his son may displace him as the patriarch. To some extent, the father-son relationship in the novel goes beyond issues specific to Iranians (or Muslims) and represents general differences between first and second generation Americans. Darius, who was born and raised in Iran, finds it difficult to adjust to life in the United States, unwilling (and to some extent possibly unable) as he is to embrace American culture or to live nostalgically in the past (Iran). In the United States, Darius, the patriarch of the Adam family, palpably feels this loss of power in American culture. The only place he can safely assert his dominance is through his position as head of household. However, to his son, Xerxes, who aims to dissolve his Iranian identity completely, Darius is that which he (Xerxes) rejects. Throughout the majority of the novel, the two remain at loggerheads.

The title of the novel, *Sons and Other Flammable Objects*, indicates the extent to which Darius objectifies Xerxes, as well as the fragility of their relationship (and specifically of Xerxes himself). For Darius, completely accepting Xerxes would mean acknowledging that in the United States, the younger and more assimilated Xerxes has become more powerful than Darius. The "flammable objects" in the title also refer to an act in Darius's youth in which he and some friends, in an attempt to show their supposed power and masculinity, set fire to doves. From Xerxes's perspective, throughout much of the novel, Darius's acts towards him are akin to this violent act: intended to establish Darius's masculinity and authority at Xerxes's cost. Through this and many more examples, Khakpour displays how intra-ethnic fighting (and later inter-ethnic fighting) threatens the marginalized Iranian-American community.

By and large, the conflicts that shape the book between Darius and Xerxes Adam are manifest in the historical implications of their names, which can also be seen as expressing some generalizable differences between, or even stereotypes of, Iranian and American cultures. While historical accounts of Darius and Xerxes may differ, it is generally accepted that Darius was more of a successful ruler than Xerxes, under whose reign the Persian Empire arguably began to disintegrate. According to Khakpour, "Darius was a solid guy," and "Xerxes, while interesting, ruined just about everything" (64). Given this, it would seem that Darius, who named or at least played a role in naming Xerxes[10] helped sow the seeds of his own disintegration, or that he would do so in order to put himself in a more powerful patriarchal position. Yet, at the same time, Darius's naming of Xerxes may also indicate Darius's desire to maintain his superiority over his son, who indeed, comes to blame Darius for many of his personal problems. At the same time, Xerxes can be seen as analogous to how many in the Muslim world view the West or the United States in that Khakpour portrays the historical, and to some extent, the contemporary Xerxes as both "spoiled and rottened" (64).

Along parallel lines, just as Darius and to some extent, Xerxes, can be seen as patriarchs of the Persian empire, so can the biblical Adam be seen as the ultimate Western patriarch. With the names Darius and Xerxes Adam, we see an attempted merging between a Persian East (Darius and Xerxes) and the Judeo-Christian West (Adam). While the Adams are not Christians or Jews, they adopt this surname, Adam, upon immigrating to the United States. Like other American immigrants, Darius himself chooses to Westernize his last and first names when he and his family arrive so that they might assimilate more smoothly. Originally named Darreyoosh, he shortens his name to Darius. More significantly, he also decides to change their last name, pronounced Odd-damn, to Adam. According to Darius, choosing Adam as a surname makes sense because both Adam and Odd-damn mean or suggest "man" or "human" (41). However, his primary motivation for taking the Westernized name Adam can be attributed to Darius's rather misguided arrogance, whereby he feels that he can resuscitate the original secular nature of the name from its Judeo-Christian Western allusions and implications (41).

In a way, Darius's naïveté can be seen as a manifestation of the American ideal of the cultural and ethnic melting pot, which suggests that the merging of cultures is a simple and smooth process. However, Darius's attempts to forge a secular and assimilated American identity through his surname ends up backfiring. After feeling defeated by mispronunciation after mispronunciation, Darius eventually gives in and accepts the more American pronunciation of "Adam" and the allied Christian implications of the name. This leaves the Adams with two names that are not integrated, a Persian/Eastern name and a Christian/Western name. These two names, like their two identities as Iranian and American, also conflict and clash with one another. The name "Adam" suggests they are Christian, which they are not, and the names Darius and Xerxes make a historical allusion that few Americans would recognize. Even if the historical allusions of their names were realized, these two names hardly represent the contemporary state of affairs in Iran. Despite this, Darius tries to provide Xerxes with cultural understanding of their last name: "It is not an American name. You must remember that. You are Persian. If not Persian, then Iranian. Two choices" (40). Thus, Darius tries to instill in his son, from an early age, a resistance to assimilate to American life and culture. However, his intentions are questionable. Darius has come to believe that he cannot really assimilate in the United States and may not want Xerxes to do so because this might help Xerxes to unseat him as the patriarch of the family.

As mentioned earlier, Darius's attempt to engender in a young Xerxes a resistance to Western assimilation ends up backfiring, and others perceive his seemingly aloof demeanor as a manifestation of arrogance. Khakpour suggests that taking pride in one's ethnic heritage, a common attribute of contemporary multiculturalism, can have some unfortunate consequences, especially for children and teenagers. For instance, when he is young, Xerxes befriends a white child whose first name is the same as Xerxes's last name — Adam. However, as instructed by his father, Xerxes pronounces his last name as Odd-damn. Xerxes's friend, Adam, interprets Xerxes's pronunciation of his last name as an arrogant act. According to Khakpour, Adam's interpretation is not far off the mark because at that point, Xerxes truly believed that "he *was* special" (69). In addition, Xerxes believed that "he was *quite* different and he had the suspicion that it was the better part of different" (69). It is reasonable to assume that Xerxes's feeling of superiority is one that is shared by Darius, who helped instill this in his son.

While Khakpour does not devote much time to it in the novel, one of the most significant events in *Sons and Other Flammable Objects* is an act of racism directed towards Xerxes when he is a child. Here we can see the often hidden costs of asserting one's ethnic pride as that seems to be the motivating factor in Adam's decision to send Xerxes a racially demeaning Christmas card in which Adam draws a camel. The camel has a history as a racial epithet in American culture, used against Arab-Americans or someone perceived as being of Arabic descent as Adam presumably believes Xerxes to be. One American stereotype of Arabs and Arabic Americans derives from the belief that certain nomadic male Arabs are sexually attracted to or even intimate with camels (as suggested by the racial epithets "camel humper" or "camel jockey"). In addition, some view the camel as the bastard stepchild of the American horse, and in using the racial epithets "camel," Arabs or perceived Arabic Americans are debased as primitive or deficient. In addition, the term "porch camel" has also been used to debase those of Middle Eastern origin much like "porch monkey" was used against African Americans. In all of these cases and through the specific card, the camel represents a dehumanization of Xerxes as both a foreigner and as subhuman.

The effect of a racist act upon children has been well documented in literature, perhaps best exemplified by Countee Cullen's poem "Incident," in which an older narrator recalls how a white child's racial epithet shatters the narrator's carefree happiness and childhood innocence. Along similar lines, despite Xerxes's youth, he immediately appreciates the significance of the card. As Khakpour explains, "How clearly he understood, as just a young kid, what the camel symbolized. It had left him in a daze for the rest of the day. He avoided Adam like the plague, hid in the bathroom for recess, and at 3:15 when the final bell shrieked, he sprinted into his father's car" (70). The extent to which the incident affects Xerxes can be seen in how Xerxes never speaks to Adam again.

The fact that neither Darius nor Xerxes confronts Adam about the card, nor do they notify the school, also illustrates how both feel powerless against the dominant white majority, and how neither wants to do anything to spoil the comforting and idealistic vision of the United States as a welcoming melting pot. While Darius may be correct when he tells Xerxes that "camels have nothing to do with us" (71), neither is able nor wants to accept how this act is a racist representation of their false recognition as Arab-American instead of Persian. Like Xerxes, Darius internalizes the act, never forgetting it and keeping "the card in his files forever" (71). Their anger and frustration have no real outlet other than to be misdirected upon themselves and their family. Initially, this racially motivated act encourages a teenaged Xerxes to assert his ethnic identity, as shown by how, when asked by non–Iranians about the meaning and origin of his first and last names, he provides them with "a lesson in Farsi" (181). However, Xerxes eventually realizes that his efforts to counteract inaccurate stereotypes have no perceptible effect, are not worth the effort, and eventually are "better left unsaid" (181). Ultimately, with no encouragement or desire to embrace his Iranian heritage or Iranian culture, and in the face of potential and actual racism, Xerxes moves towards an outright rejection of both.

It has been suggested that first-generation immigrants like Darius tend to be more ambivalent about their host and native cultures, whereas second-generation immigrants tend to have an easier time acculturating to the United States.[11] However, the conflicts between native and host country can be more severe for those from the Middle East. As Hasan Kaplan argues, recent Middle Eastern immigrants tend to face "two separate identity crises" (3). The first, he suggests, is "the crisis of maintaining already formed and inherited traditional (ethnic and religious) identity experienced and voiced by the parent generation" (3). The second, he suggests, is "the crisis of forming a new identity between two seemingly conflicting (family tradition and Western/American way) cultures, experienced by the second generation" (3). Indeed, the Adam family faces both of these struggles in the novel. With no real connection to anything approaching an Iranian-American community in Pasadena and a shared sense of ambivalence towards both American and Iranian cultures (as well as a growing disdain on Xerxes's part for Iranian culture), each member of the Adam family is caught in an identity limbo in which they are not able to establish a stable sense of self while in the United States.

In the absence of a stable, fulfilling identity, one response is to exaggerate and amplify one's own sense of importance, to assert one's superiority over others, because of isolation, alienation, and misdirected generalized hatred of others. Darius does this when he moves to the United States. Specifically, after viewing the commercialization and the superficial manner through which Americans regard and celebrate religious holidays like Christmas, Darius concludes that the United States is "absolute glorious bullshit" (26). While it is immaterial whether or not Darius's conclusion is justified, he appears motivated by a desire to validate his own sense of superiority, not to champion his Iranian heritage. This can be seen in how Darius, without the assistance of his Iranian heritage, believes that he has the wherewithal to see beyond this "glorious bullshit." Further, Darius does not regard Iranian culture as being any more fulfilling than the superficiality he perceives in American culture. For the most part, Darius does not self-identify as Iranian because he believes he only has individual allegiance to himself, not to any country. In truth, though, like Xerxes, Darius realizes that self-identifying as Iranian or Middle Eastern in the United States puts him in a more vulnerable position. It is telling that Darius acts in a rather hypocritical manner when he sees other generally non-white immigrants. At these times, he appears disdainful towards them if they describe themselves as Americans because he believes they do not have the strength either to maintain their native culture[12] or to rise above nationalism. In this manner, we can see how Darius, as an Iranian-American, is caught between a rock and a hard place, unable but attempting to convince himself that he is unwilling to assimilate to the United States while separating himself from other ethnic minorities whom he often demeans. In essence, Darius has become utterly and completely isolated.

It is often accepted as a given by most Westerners that embracing one's ethnic heritage is unquestionably positive. However, Khakpour illustrates not only the negative aftereffects of doing so, but how within minority groups, there can be inter-ethnic fighting on the basis of the extent to which one supposedly embraces one's heritage. For instance, Darius comes to believe that Xerxes is trying to deny his Iranian heritage (while Darius does not realize he is essentially doing the same thing) as well as his family. Indeed, it is true that Xerxes leaves his parents to attend a liberal arts college in the East, and when Xerxes does this, Darius calls it a "crime" (21). However, the reason that Darius may call it a crime is because he is secretly jealous of Xerxes's attempt or even his seeming ability to shed his ethnic heritage, which is easier and more appealing than maintaining one's ethnic identity as Iranian or Iranian-American. Even after graduation, Xerxes stays away from his family and settles in New York City, where he eventually cut off ties with his parents. Darius derides Xerxes for his supposed decision "to be of no past" (33), yet Darius does not realize that he is attempting to do the same thing as Xerxes by neither asserting nor celebrating his own Iranian heritage. Darius claims that attempting to assimilate completely and rejecting one's ethnic heritage, as he believes Xerxes attempts to do, "doesn't work" (33).

While Darius may be right that it is not possible for him or Xerxes to assimilate completely, he is wrong about the reasons. Rejecting the possibility of effectively assimilating gives Darius an excuse to avoid the attempt to change his identity and his life as Xerxes does. In denying Xerxes's attempt to assimilate but not providing Xerxes with an adequate sense of his Iranian heritage, Darius has essentially put Xerxes in an impossible situation. As Xerxes explains, in an imaginary conversation with Darius in his head: "You didn't want me to belong to this country, but yet you wouldn't let me have the ease and clear conscience to belong to you, and so what happened? I ran away" (211). Neither Xerxes nor Darius considers implicating dominant white American culture for putting them in this seemingly impossible position of not being able to fully embrace, let alone accept, their Iranian heritage without being stigmatized, stereotyped, and possibly discriminated against. They do not realize that they will never really be able to assimilate completely because of their appearances and names, which will continually mark them as the Other in the United States (especially in a post–September 11 United States).

For Darius, who was born in Iran, the dilemma is even more pronounced since he spent his formative childhood, adolescence, and young adulthood in Iran. While Darius berates Xerxes for supposedly forsaking his Iranian heritage, it is important to recognize that Darius, although he does not acknowledge it, does the same thing, in fact even more so given that Darius lived in Iran so much longer than Xerxes. For Darius, his Iranian heritage is just a crutch that he turns to in times of personal turmoil. At the same time, instead of seeking out an Iranian-American community (or other specific Iranian-Americans), Darius drives to Middle Eastern convenience stores where he would "rush for the packets of saffron and sumac and hold them hard in his hand, sniff deeply, and stumble out, like a madman in a nonsensical dream" (125). That Khakpour describes him as a "madman in a nonsensical dream" indicates that when Darius is thinking of Iran, he is not doing so in a rational manner; rather, he immerses himself in presumably hyperbolic memories aimed at making himself feel better. In other words, his ethnicity becomes an escape valve, a way to assert his Iranian identity in the most "abstract" way possible (126). If being Iranian is abstract to Darius, this means that he does not really have a sense of what his ethnic identity should or could mean. To be sure, this is not an issue solely specific to Darius, because not only do most Americans not have a clear sense of Iranian culture or identities, even Iran itself is not that homogenous; rather it is both ethnically heterogeneous and rife with social and political contradictions. Finally, as a largely invisible minority group, Iranians, unless they live in certain heavily populated areas of Los Angeles (such as Westwood), tend to have no distinct community of their own around them.

Whereas Darius tends to be critical of American culture, Xerxes makes more of an effort to embrace his American identity. Still, what separates Xerxes from other second-generation American immigrants is the extent of his animosity towards his native country. To some extent, Xerxes develops a rather simplistic oppositional analogy in which he compares Iran to death and the United States to life. In doing so, he elevates the United States while he debases Iran.[13] For instance, when considering how his grandparents die: *"The Iranians*, Xerxes thought, *were always wishing things dead, imagining death, wondering about the dead, ready to curse everything with dead-stuff. Death was everywhere"* (52). While Khakpour does not directly state the cause of Xerxes's animosity towards Iran, it can be attributed to several factors. First, it may be a manifestation of a general American animosity towards Iran during the 1980s (when Xerxes would have grown up) in the wake of the hostage and Iran-Contra crises. It also might be a response to the acts of racism Xerxes experiences as a child such as the Christmas card. Instead of considering the difficulties his grandparents had to face (and the difficulties his parents faced in Iran), Xerxes generalizes that *"the Iranians ... were made for tragedy, always trapped in some sad dramatic past, generational pain, familial anguish, personal turmoil, a collective tragic disposition, an almost genetic mass pessimism"* (59–60). It is important to recognize that when Xerxes uses the words "The Iranians," he does not include himself in this group. He also does not consider the poverty and atrocities suffered by many Iranians during the Shah's reign. However, it would not be entirely fair to condemn Xerxes for this since Darius is so reticent to speak of his experiences in Iran, let alone their Iranian heritage and culture.

Throughout the novel, Xerxes attempts virtually everything imaginable to shed his Iranian identity and completely blend into the supposed American melting pot. Still, to a large degree, assimilation proves to be next to impossible for Xerxes who finds that he cannot merely become American, nor can he completely shed his Iranian identity. Instead, even as a young teenager, Xerxes compartmentalizes and bifurcates his two identities, concluding that "he lived in two worlds and part of the dual-citizenship agreement was that he could not allow those worlds to mix" (136). One question Khakpour leaves unanswered is why Xerxes has concluded that it is impossible to integrate his Iranian and American identities. It could be that racist incidents have forced a double consciousness upon Xerxes from which he can never truly escape. It may also be that, when he becomes a teenager, Xerxes also experiences another, almost opposite form of stereotypes and prejudice, what Frank Chin and Jeffery Paul Chan might call "racist love"[14] or exoticization. This occurs when Xerxes is a teenager and a white, female, rebellious, punk-rock tomboy, Sam, befriends him. For Sam, Xerxes's appeal is not only his status as an ethnic other, but his status as part of an ethnic group that has been largely vilified. Her association with Xerxes fits with her image of herself as a rebel. At some level, Xerxes knows that Sam is objectifying him, which only serves to enhance his double consciousness. This becomes especially apparent when Sam visits the Adam household, and Xerxes begins to scrutinize and seems embarrassed by the Iranian things they own and display (138).[15]

While there are multiple reasons why Xerxes seems to be unable to truly assimilate to American life (e.g., racism, prejudice, and exoticization), he tends to direct his animosity towards his father, Darius (just as Darius turns his own animosity upon his family). As mentioned earlier, one reason for Darius and Xerxes's misguided animosity is that neither truly feels able to critique the dominant (white) culture, and hence, they misdirect their frustrations upon one another. This, however, is not an irrational response since they have little autonomy nor the ability to defy the dominant culture. Thereby, instead of implicating Adam who sends Xerxes the racist Christmas card or Sam for exoticizing him, Xerxes implicates his father, Darius, who he describes as being "the agent of ghosts," and reeking "*of history*" while wanting to "*suffocate us with the bad parts*" (211). Instead of considering the comparatively difficult time Darius had growing up and becoming an adult in Iran, Xerxes only thinks of castigating his father for the supposed cultural baggage he passes on to Xerxes. Again, we see the forces of exclusion serve to turn members of the Adam family against one another.

It is ironic that Xerxes would implicate Darius for reeking of history when Khakpour presents Darius as seldom discussing his past in Iran and only doing so in a significant manner once.[16] It also demonstrates the lack of communication between the two, which can largely be attributed to the desire of both men to shed their respective Iranian identity. The one story Darius tells Xerxes about his past in Iran concerns an incident when Darius was young, when he and his friends would capture doves. Traditionally, doves serve as symbols of peace, and in that sense, Darius's act can be seen as a bellicose expression to prove his strength and masculinity in a more impoverished community where appearing tough may be respected. It is Darius's retelling of this act to Xerxes while visiting a post-collegiate Xerxes in New York City shortly before the events of September 11 that helps force what seems to be the final wedge between the two.

Ultimately, it is both Xerxes's inability to understand the culture from which his father comes and Darius's inability to explain or transmit native Iranian culture to Xerxes that undermine their relationship. Xerxes can only see Darius's story as part of "his father's cruel and unusual past" (34). Instead of trying to understand how the environment Darius grew up in (an impoverished region of Iran) may have engendered a certain "cruelty" in him, Xerxes implicates Darius in cruelty and considers this story as "another reason, any reason, a final reason, to hate himself and his family" (34). Xerxes's response to Darius also illustrates the underside of second-generation American immigrants, who may reject their parents as excess and weighty baggage that holds them back from fully acculturating. A child of greater privilege, Xerxes cannot understand what might drive his father to commit an act of such seemingly wanton cruelty. For his part, Darius tries to explain to Xerxes how lighting the doves ablaze, calling them "shooting stars," was an attempt, however misguided, to see something like "hope burning bright," and to achieve some level of agency in an environment that offered little promise. This is evident in how Darius tells Xerxes: "For once, it was in our hands" (31–2). In this case, the "it" would be their lives. Growing up in a rather oppressive environment without much promise for the future, burning and killing the doves became for them, as children, an act of perverted hope.

However, Xerxes cannot see it this way, but rather concludes that Darius has merely "unloaded" and "burdened" him with this story, when it was actually Darius's attempt to connect with Xerxes (34). Still, it is not the story so much as both Xerxes's and Darius's inability to integrate their American and Iranian identities that is ultimately responsible for seemingly destroying their relationship. Xerxes concludes that his main problem is that he has "let the worlds mix" (34) — that is, his Iranian heritage, manifested through his father, who visits Xerxes in New York City, and his attempted (white or post ethnic) American identity, divorced of ethnicity. Both Xerxes and Darius take this failed discussion about the dove burning as an opportunity to stop communicating with one another not so much because of the story itself, but because their relationship had reached a breaking point due to years of miscommunication and the inability of both to establish a stable Iranian-American identity from a synthesis of the two cultures. Again, this should not be seen as merely failures on the part of Darius and Xerxes, but rather a by-product of an environment not particularly welcoming to Iranian-Americans as well as of a generally misguided belief in the transformative possibilities of the supposed American melting pot.

To be sure, Khakpour does not demonize the United States, and, as much as Darius critiques American culture and positions himself as superior to it, it is in the United States that Darius moves towards a kind of redemption. Haunted by his vicious childhood act of helping burn doves alive in Iran, Darius tries to counteract this trauma through his attempt to save blue jays in his apartment complex by placing collars with bells on the neighbors' predatory cats. In many ways, though, this act backfires. Not only does no one realize that Darius has grown more compassionate and considerate of less powerful victims, white American cat owners in his apartment complex find out what he has done and one aggressively confronts Darius. In this scene, the white, female American cat owner chastises Darius for putting bells on her cats' collars. Darius, the foreigner, then takes on the role of the hunted vulnerable blue jays while the white woman takes on the role of the aggressive, predatory cat. The white woman condescendingly speaks slowly to Darius and demeans him, but Darius never backs down nor admits guilt.[17] While Khakpour stresses that for Xerxes this was "one of the most moving memories of his youth, one of the only ones that didn't paint his father as a full-on asshole but just a confused, okay-hearted, perhaps bored man," Xerxes is hardly appreciative or admiring of Darius (19). Instead, Xerxes sides more with the white woman, ultimately feeling embarrassed by his family as noted by how he denigrates them for their "social anxiety" when the woman knocks on the door, instead of considering the more understandable reasons for their social anxiety — namely, fear of racism and non-acceptance due to their Iranian ethnicity and status as recent immigrants (10).

Later in the novel, Xerxes identifies with the doves that Darius helped burn alive instead of identifying with the blue jays Darius tried to save, because to do the latter would be to acknowledge that he, along with his father, remains vulnerable and relatively powerless in comparison to dominant whites. One reason this is so is because Xerxes has become rather self-absorbed and cannot see beyond himself. Whereas when Darius was a teenager in Iran, he "became responsible for his sister and brother and even his mother" (53), Xerxes only has to care about himself. Due to his hardscrabble upbringing, Darius has consistently lowered expectations of the world around him. In that sense, Darius's pessimism is almost diametrically opposed to the optimism so prized and much more commonplace in the United States, which Xerxes emulates. To Darius, this makes Xerxes naïve, a representation of a self-deceptive United States. He tells Xerxes: "You're still young apparently. One day you will see the world for what it is: disconnected and chaotic. Not everything is linked" (41). While Darius feels he is right in his perspective, this is not necessarily the case. Rather, by setting up a clear demarcation between himself and the outside world ("they" — possibly Americans), he absolves himself of any need to adjust, let alone assimilate to life in the United States.

As a second-generation American immigrant, Xerxes believes he can only acculturate by rejecting his less acculturated parents. Just as Darius became an alienated isolate by removing himself (or being removed) from both Iranian and American culture, Xerxes too becomes or rather seeks a new, almost post-ethnic space. While Darius rejects Xerxes's post-ethnic goal as idealistic and impossible, it is not necessarily so. If we view ethnicity and post-ethnicity as a range instead of as a mutually exclusive dichotomy, it is possible that Xerxes may move closer to a non–ethnically specific identity and his attempts, there-fore, may not entirely be in vain. Even Xerxes acknowledges that his attempt to achieve a post-ethnic, post-nationalistic, post-familial identity may fail, but what he doesn't realize is that establishing such an identity is not com-pletely feasible.

While such an identity may not be available for the two male members of the Adam family, to some extent there seem to be more opportunities for Darius's wife and Xerxes's mother, Lala. As mentioned previously, Westerners tend to believe that Iran is a patriarchal and sexist country and through this perspective the dominant male father figure, Darius, might be seen as a sexist patriarch who has trouble adjusting to a more egalitarian United States. Indeed, most Western scholars writing about Iran and the Islamic Middle East take it as a virtual given that these countries are patriarchal and sexist. Syrine Hout describes Lebanon as being "patriarchal" (286), while Haideh Moghissi argues that "the modern constitutions of almost all Middle Eastern states contain prohibitions against discrimination on the basis of sex." (542).[18] Another critic suggests that in Islamic Republic era Iran, "women's bodies became a locus of contention and a battleground between advocates of moder-nity and religious fundamentalism" (Talattof 43). Entire books alluding to Iran's supposed oppressive patriarchal system have been published such as Minoo Moallem's *Between Warrior Brother and Veiled Sister: Islamic Funda-mentalism and the Politics of Patriarchy in Iran* (2005). While there may be some truth to these criticisms of contemporary Iran and the Islamic Middle East, one could also argue that Western countries, including the United States, are nearly if not equally patriarchal, albeit in different ways.

While it has been frequently suggested by Western writers and commen-tators that Islamic women in the Middle East are subject to oppression and sexism whereas their female counterparts in the West (in this case, the United States) experience a more egalitarian and liberated life, in *Sons and Other Flammable Objects*, Khakpour complicates this dichotomy. Instead, Khakpour suggests that while Islamic women from the Middle East can experience a greater liberation of sorts while living in the West, this "liberation" can be an additional form of oppression. Along these lines, Khakpour's novel follows Darius's wife and Xerxes's mother, Lala Adam, who experiences, or seems to experience, more transformative possibilities while living in the United States; however, these transformative possibilities tend to be more illusory than real.

As a woman previously delimited by societal expectations based on gender expectations in Iran,[19] Lala seems to have many more opportunities in the United States.[20] Unlike Darius, Lala has not been able to assert her identity while in Iran, so she does not carry as much psychological baggage as Darius. She has also learned to subvert her desires, and it is because of this that she adjusts best to the United States of the three in the Adam family. It is in the United States that Lala appears to learn to express and fulfill her desires. However, doing so is not necessarily liberating in any sense. As Khakpour explains, "She was happy in America, she claimed, America with its Disneyland and Las Vegas — her two favorite destinations — home to ignorance and bliss, a land unloaded, haven without baggage, a fresh starting point for people to lose their minds!" (61). From this, it appears that Lala's greatest desire is to experience a kind of blank hedonism, which is hardly a form of liberation, but rather, a different form of oppression. At the same time, it is in America that Lala is able to reinvent herself as Lala, for her actual Iranian name is Lalah (Darius changed his name as well). This turns out to be Lala's first act of independence. In addition, despite Darius's protestations, Lala begins to work on occasion, but her jobs never seem to last too long, in part because they tend to be menial and unfulfilling, and also because Lala is ambivalent about achieving a significant level of independence. She still feels that her job as a homemaker is "a place where she apparently belonged," but now it is also a place she "was constantly fantasizing about leaving" (78–9).[21]

However, unlike Darius and Xerxes, who remain social isolates throughout most of the novel, Lala does venture outside the Adam family and begins making connections with non–Iranian Americans (but still minorities) — namely, a Hispanic housekeeper named Gigi and Marvin, a homosexual African American. Through this grouping Khakpour seems to suggest that, in the United States, there can be solidarity and mutual support through inter-ethnic minorities groups like the one that these three form. However, the solidarity and support that Gigi and Marvin seem to provide for Lala is not that empowering, if at all. Gigi encourages Lala to be more independent, but it is an independence mainly based on superficial frivolities.[22] Towards that end, Lala describes the time she spends with Gigi as a kind of adolescence or pseudo-feminism which "reminded her of the lifestyle of schoolgirls" (97). Khakpour neither encourages nor condemns Lala's adolescent-like actions, since Lala never really had a first adolescence to begin with when she lived in Iran. In order to achieve anything approaching independence, Lala may need to revert back to a form of adolescence. Still, the fact that Lala never really achieves a fully independent adult stage while in the United States is indicative that the attempt to establish her own identity ultimately failed.

Along these lines, the freedom that Lala experiences with Gigi and Marvin appears illusory, hedonistic, and based largely on consumerism. In that, Khakpour suggests that contemporary American or Western women, often thought of as being fully liberated, are actually subjugated through a Western preeminence placed upon appearances, frivolities, and hedonistic behavior.[23] That Lala's progression towards a kind of adolescence halts after the events of September 11 also indicates the rather illusory or insubstantial nature of her newfound identity. Lala turns inward to her family in times of distress, and Gigi and Marvin's inability to understand this leads them to denigrate Lala, even debasing her and Darius with racial epithets about Arabic terrorists[24] (which they now ascribe to the Adam family despite the fact that the Adams are not Arabic) when Lala no longer wants to spend time with them. It also indicates the weak nature of inter-ethnic communities in the United States.

With all three members of the Adam family essentially failing in their attempts to acculturate, to form stable and fulfilling individual identities, and to find a cohesive community or family, their collective response is to withdraw further from one another and retreat to a private fantasy world.[25] For Darius, this private fantasy world involves his imaginary visions of "a perfect" daughter he names Shireen, who listens to Darius and confirms Darius's already established beliefs about virtually everything (23). Feeling powerless and vulnerable in the United States, Darius seeks the comfort and validation of an unconditional love, which he feels unable to receive from his son or his wife.

Along parallel lines, Xerxes also retreats from his family into another fantasy world — that provided by television. Much has been written about the importance of television as a means of escape and also as a tool of acculturation and identity.[26] This, however, is not just specific to Xerxes and other diasporic Iranians. As David Foster Wallace argues in his essay "E Unibus Pluram: Television and U.S. Fiction," for younger Americans, television serves as a focal point for ideas, topics, and conversation, even if those topics may be somewhat superficial or trivial.[27] Xerxes latches onto American popular culture, specifically television, in a similar way to how Darius latches onto the imaginary Shireen. As Khakpour explains, watching television is "The only time that Xerxes believes he was close to happy" (109). Khakpour also explains that Xerxes learns American English mainly through television; however, this hardly helps him communicate better with others, but rather obfuscates genuine communication (85). For Xerxes, "Television was the icebreaker, the playground unifier — if there was nothing to say there was always TV talk" (88). Thus, while Xerxes learns the cultural currency of his peers, he does not learn how to communicate effectively with others. This, however, is not ethnically specific to Xerxes as an Iranian-American, but more to his generation (Generation X).

As Xerxes ages, television becomes more than just a unifier and an icebreaker; rather, it also helps shape Xerxes's conceptions of his heritage as well as his fantasies. The show that ends up affecting him the most is *I Dream of Jeannie*. Khakpour describes it as "a show that shaped him, his character, his future aesthetic sensibility, his sense of not just the world, but its possibilities, a show that made his everyday hell in this supposed Eden a heaven" (89). There are several significant reasons why Xerxes may gravitate towards this show. First of all, he may be drawn to its vaguely Middle Eastern references. After all, Jeannie is literally a genie, and the show is based upon the story of Aladdin and his lamp. However, the genie in this case is the physical epitome of everything not typically associated with the Middle East or with Muslims. In particular, Aryan or Nordic looking Barbara Eden is the virtual antithesis of the conventionally darker skinned, darker haired stereotypical Middle Easterner. Eden's Jeannie does, however, wear the accoutrements of a stereotypical, midriff-baring Middle Eastern or South Asian belly dancer. As a woman, she is also subservient in a conventional, orthodox manner that might conform with Western conceptions of Islam. In essence, she is a bleached, bronzed, and sexually exoticized version of the generalizations of Iranian or Islamic women. For these reasons, Khakpour points out that Xerxes's love for Jeannie "involved what she was *not*" (94). Instead of what Xerxes no doubt perceives as Western generalizations of Iranians as "dark, doom-loving, heavy with the weight of history," Jeannie becomes for Xerxes "an escape, an impossibility, an out from the realm of heartache and sighs and moans and bawls and screams and breast-beatings and hairtearings" (94).

In a way, Jeannie is what Xerxes wants to become — an Aryan or Nordic, sterilized version of the superficially appealing and sanitized features of Middle Eastern and Islamic culture. At the same time, Jeannie becomes a representation of all Xerxes comes to desire — namely, a subservient white woman who can help dilute or remove the stigma of being Iranian-American. In that sense, Xerxes's Jeannie and Darius's Shireen mirror one another; they are both imaginary, subservient incarnations of the stereotypical, subservient Islamic woman. That Jeannie is Nordic or Aryan looking whereas Shireen appears Iranian also signifies Xerxes's desire to assimilate (despite his protestations otherwise) as well as Darius's resistance towards assimilation. That Khakpour never describes Lala as having anything approaching an imaginary, fantasy man or son could be indicative of Lala's being the most adjusted of the three to life in the United States, or it could also be the after-effect of her upbringing, which presumably stresses repression of her desires.

Still, the effects of popular and general American culture are no match for the events of September 11, 2001, which serve not only as the turning point of the novel, but also as the catalyst for change. To be certain, the events of September 11 had a profound effect upon the United States (particularly for Muslims and Middle Eastern Americans) as well as the entire world order. It is largely accepted as a fact that after the events of September 11, the Muslim American community suffered a backlash of hate crimes and discrimination.[28] Anny Bakalian and Mehdi Bozorgmehr argue that this backlash manifested itself in three primary ways: through "scapegoating," the propagating of "negative stereotypes," and by state sponsored "targeting" of Muslim and Arab Americans (7). While it might be assumed that the effects of the September 11 attacks upon American Muslims were uniformly negative, in reality, the effects were multifaceted and complex, neither fully negative nor fully positive.

While the Adams were not really practicing Muslims before September 11 and do not become so after September 11, in *Sons and Other Flammable Objects*, Khakpour illustrates the complexities of the aftermath of September 11 upon the Adam family. Ultimately, the aftermath sparks a chain of events that threatens to dissolve the Adam family and fray already strained familial relationships, but ultimately provides the impetus to bring them together. Initially, the Adams seem shell-shocked and fearful after the attacks, and for good reason. It should go without saying that September 11 greatly affected Americans and American domestic and international policies, but it affects the Adams even more than most since they are Iranian, and they are understandably fearful that there could be a backlash against them because of their ethnicity or falsely perceived ethnicity as Arabic. As Aisha Pena argues, "Since the events of 9/11, American Muslims have been dealing with issues brought about by rising xenophobia" (202). Indeed, the Council on American-Islamic Relations (CAIR) "[reported] hate crimes against Muslims in the United States increased by more than 50 percent" in the first few years after September 11 (Pena 205).[29]

This has included anything from verbal threats to vandalism and discrimination (Economist 36; Abdelkarim "Arab and Muslim Americans" 55).[30]

At the same time, the events of September 11 helped to both galvanize and bring Muslim Americans closer together. As Fait Muedini argues, "Because of the decreased level of comfort within American society, American Muslims began to turn to one another for support" (45).[31] With the threat of discrimination and possible hate crimes looming over them, the Adams are actually driven closer together by the events and aftermath of September 11. Not only do the Adams begin to appreciate the importance of family and the fragility of life more, they also begin relying on one another more because they are presumably fearful of any racial animosity directed towards them as Iranians.[32] This does not mean that Khakpour views September 11 to be the catalyst for substantive change in the Iranian community. While September 11 motivates Xerxes to call his family after ignoring them for months, this is more like a baby step towards reconciliation, evident by how Xerxes doesn't go home, despite initially thinking "it was time to go home" (120) and by how Xerxes does not reply back to Darius who, for the first time, writes Xerxes a letter shortly after September 11.

The events and aftermath of September 11 do not only spark the beginning of what appears to be a reconciliation between Darius and Xerxes, they also drive Xerxes to come out of his largely self-created isolation and help foster a relationship with a woman — Suzanne. It is not unusual that tragedies bring people together, and here, Khakpour is not suggesting that such behavior is necessarily ethnically driven (Suzanne, as it turns out, is part Iranian, but Xerxes does not initially notice that). That Khakpour stresses September 11 to be the primary catalyst for their relationship is evident in how they first meet on that very day while on the roof of their apartment building, surveying the damage wrought upon New York City. Just as with the Adam family, the events of September 11 drive people together through what Khakpour describes as "the most desperate and vital and delusional emergency "love"" (177). However, if this "love" experienced by Xerxes and Suzanne is indeed "delusional" and motivated by a perceived "emergency," then it follows that this "love" is only temporal, which it may turn out to be.

In the last section of the novel, familial, romantic, and ethnic identifications and relationships are precipitously balanced with one another. For every time that Xerxes and Suzanne seem to get closer, there is another stumbling block. Along similar lines, for every step that Xerxes and Darius get closer, they also suffer a setback. These two relationships (Xerxes and Darius along with Xerxes and Suzanne) run parallel to one another, but they are eventually trumped by ethnic identity and nationalism. Ultimately, one of

the most significant aftereffects of the events of September 11 is that it leads
to a chain of events prompting both Xerxes and Darius to reconsider their
heritage and to consider visiting Iran.[33] In this part of the novel, Khakpour
suggests that both Xerxes and Darius must confront or at least attempt to
confront their conflicted feelings towards Iran as well as towards their heritage
before they can reach any sort of resolution with one another. Prior to September 11, Darius had considered going back to Iran, but he reconsiders doing
so due to ominous Western media representations of Iran. As Khakpour
explains, "his homeland had become a cheap, grim, grainy, black-and-white
horror movie" (270). However, the events of September 11 change this and
Darius concludes that "Iran felt like the precise remedy to fill all the many
holes in his life" (269).

It is important to recognize that Darius wants to utilize Iran for a self-
serving purpose — to heal himself— rather than for any altruistic reasons. In
that, his quest to visit Iran is really a quest for his own identity, which has
been in flux for so many years. At the same time, it can be surmised that one
of the most significant holes in Darius's life is his seemingly failed relationship
with Xerxes. Darius's newfound desire to go to Iran can be seen as a manifestation of his desire to salvage his relationship with Xerxes. While Iran may
be the superficial connection that begins to bond Darius and Xerxes, this connection proves to be much more than superficial in the post–September 11
world. As it turns out, it is Iran that ultimately defines Darius and Xerxes,
while potentially bringing them closer together or tearing them apart. Indeed,
to a large extent, Darius and Xerxes's conflicted and buried feelings about
their homeland and heritage drive a wedge between them. As neither can
communicate in a satisfactory manner with the other, Darius, on some level,
wants Iran to be an intermediary for them, a shared, joyful experience[34]
from which the two can begin to repair their relationship and their own identities.

Not only does Darius use nationality and ethnicity as means to salvage
his relationship with Xerxes, so does Suzanne. As Xerxes and Suzanne's relationship begins to deteriorate as more time elapses after September 11, she too
looks to Iran in not only an overly romantic manner but also as a way to
reconnect with Xerxes. As a surprise present, she purchases them both tickets
to Iran. However, when she gives Xerxes the tickets, it infuriates him to the
point that he slaps Suzanne. From Xerxes's perspective, this gift demonstrates
that Suzanne "had betrayed him by going somewhere that it had always been
clear she was not allowed to go" (293). Throughout Xerxes's entire life he had
tried to separate, compartmentalize, and even reject his Iranian heritage.
Suzanne's gift sparks Xerxes's latent hatred of Iran, a country he blames for

having "ruined his life, both by birth and by escape" (293). Yet, it is not Iran, as much as it is Xerxes's own feelings of difference and alienation as an Iranian-American that spark his desperate and angry feelings. Once again, he does not consider implicating the more prejudicial (white) Americans he has known who may have denigrated or excluded him because of his heritage, nor does he consider that he may be using Iran as a scapegoat for his non–ethnically related personal problems. Later, Xerxes does consider how Suzanne's gift (the trip to Iran) seems to "threaten" (295) him, but he never really is able to see how the threat is grounded in his own fear of acknowledging his Iranian heritage or identity, which marks him as the Other and as more vulnerable.

It is also important to note that Xerxes's violent act towards Suzanne mirrors Darius's violent acts towards both Xerxes and Lala, demonstrating how close father and son are to each other, despite their attempts to assert the contrary. Consequently, after the slapping incident, Xerxes comes to believe that he "had become his father" (291). In many ways, when both men fail to communicate and when they are reminded of painful aspects of their family and heritage, they are drawn to respond with violence, or, as occurs with both men in the novel, they succumb to a deep depression. Indeed, after slapping Suzanne, Xerxes becomes so despondent that he reaches a point at which he wonders, *"What the hell do I have to live for anywhere?"* (304). Instead of completely defeating him, suicidal thoughts like this actually push Xerxes in the opposite direction, and Khakpour describes him as having "suddenly snapped out of it [his depression]" (304). However, she also stresses that "in reality, he was manic at most" (304), no longer caring what happens to him or content to let Iran be his executioner (which is how he views his home country and heritage).

Still, Khakpour demonstrates how both Darius and Xerxes use their ethnicity and nationality as pawns in a kind of calculating and potentially destructive chess game they play with one another. As time progresses, it becomes even more than a cold, calculating chess game; rather, visiting Iran becomes more like a game of chicken in which both Darius and Xerxes challenge one another to do what they dread the most — go to Iran and come to grips with their Iranian identity — because subconsciously they both know they need to do so in order to integrate their conflicting and oppositional identities as both Iranian and American. Also, as neither feels he has the agency to confront the American (white) mainstream, they can only cannibalistically feed on each other. Consequently, when Darius learns that Xerxes plans to go to Iran with Suzanne, Darius, who proposed taking such a trip in a previous letter to Xerxes, takes it as Xerxes's not only striking out on his own without him (Darius), but also usurping the dream that Darius feels he has harbored for much longer. In fact, after learning about the proposed trip, Darius is stunned and thinks, "His son once again managed to kill him without even thinking of him" (317). To counteract what Darius perceives as a hostile act towards him, once Darius learns that Xerxes and Suzanne are going to Iran, he decides that he will go as well, and he manages to align his travel plans with theirs. While Xerxes initially is put off by the idea that Darius may accompany them, he comes to accept it, concluding, in an imaginary conversation with Darius: "In a way, from the beginning, this was how I saw it ending. This is the only way I imagined it. You and I could never understand each other anywhere else" (320). One reason that Xerxes (or Darius) may feel this way is because he is (or they both are) aware that they will not really feel at home or comfortable in Iran, and that there, they may be forced to honestly interact and communicate with one another because they will have no viable options in difficult, challenging, and even hostile surroundings.

To be sure, Khakpour does not allow the novel to be wrapped up in a neat, happy ending whereby Iran serves as deus ex machina, allowing all three to reconnect with one another and become a happy, well-adjusted family. Ultimately, it is Xerxes, the second-generation American, who ends up having cold feet, presumably because he has the most to lose and the most to gain by going to Iran and reconciling with his father. Unlike Darius, Xerxes has come to believe that if he cannot have a post-ethnic identity (towards which he previously aspired), then he can at least generally assimilate. Indeed, as a younger, second-generation immigrant, Xerxes does have a greater ability and more opportunities to assimilate than does Darius. Embracing and accepting his father would also mean that all Xerxes has struggled for during his adolescence and early adulthood — namely a separation of his Iranian and American identities — would be for naught. As doing this not only would be tantamount to admitting defeat, but could also shatter his fragile identity, Xerxes understandably has second thoughts. At first, he hides away in a bar the day of his flight, but eventually he takes a later flight to meet both Suzanne and Darius in Frankfurt, Germany.

It is in the Frankfurt Airport, a virtual no man's land between the United States and Iran, a kind of space devoid of nationality, that pivotal events occur, leading the book towards its final conclusion. It seems that only in this environment can a final crisis or culmination occur. One significant thing that occurs is that when Darius meets Suzanne in the Frankfurt Airport (as they wait for Xerxes to arrive), he thinks she looks exactly like his vision of Shireen, and the two of them bond to the extent that when Xerxes finally gets into Frankfurt and calls Suzanne, she calls Darius (while talking to Xerxes) "Dad" (374). To a large degree, this becomes the final straw for Xerxes, whom

Khakpour describes as being "beyond disgusted" (374). Believing Darius to have damaged everything worthwhile in his life, Xerxes cannot take what he sees as a final betrayal not just from Suzanne, who does not partake in Xerxes's animosity towards his father, but also from Darius, who seems to be usurping Suzanne's affection. Subsequently, Xerxes locks himself in an airport bathroom, and thinks of an example his father once told him about monkeys that sacrificed their children. He comes to believe that Darius will do this to him, just as Darius, for all effects and purposes, believes Xerxes would like to do to him (377).

Feeling excluded from his family, his girlfriend, and his native country as well as his adopted country, Xerxes experiences a kind of existential crisis in which he concludes that he wants to "disintegrate gracefully" (377). Not being able to do so, Xerxes decides that he will go back to the United States, even though he knows it would probably mean the end of his relationship with Suzanne and his father. He even resorts to telling a counter person at the Frankfurt Airport that his father has died, which, at this point, is probably his subconscious wish. It is here that the events of September 11 play a role, helping to shape Xerxes's fate. Acting erratically and increasingly upset at his inability to get a ticket back home, Xerxes is approached by a suited man who asks him where he is from. In the post–September 11 environment, Xerxes's response of "Iran" along with his emotionally distraught behavior is enough to convince this man to call security, who takes Xerxes away for questioning.

Were it not for Xerxes's subsequent detaining, it can be presumed that his relationship with Darius and Suzanne would have ended. This would not be particularly surprising as it would take strength beyond Xerxes's means (or most people's means) to demolish his old identity and create a new one. Rather, it takes a force beyond either Xerxes or Darius to shatter Xerxes into submission. This force, as it turns out, is the United States government, who keeps Xerxes under custody for several days (presumably through new powers allowed by the Patriot Act). As harrowing as this experience turns out to be for Xerxes, it does finally force him come to grips with his Iranian identity. This is not to suggest that Khakpour is encouraging the enhanced interrogation techniques of the post–September 11 Bush administration, especially considering that government officials have no real evidence that Xerxes is anything approaching a terrorist.

At the same time, being identified as the Other, or in this case as Iranian, makes it easier for Xerxes to accept his identity since he does not really have a viable alternative. It is telling that when Xerxes's mother, Lala, first sees Xerxes after he is released, "she found a version of her son she hadn't seen — shaking, exhausted, wasted, *grateful*" (394). That Khakpour italicizes "grateful" indicates that it is this attribute above the others that Lala finds surprising to see in Xerxes. While it is never explained, it could be that Xerxes now sees that whatever damage Darius may or may not have done to him pales in comparison to what the American government (or for that matter any government) might do to him. Also, Xerxes may realize the importance of family in times of crisis, or when he is identified as the potentially dangerous Other. For his part, Darius comes to appreciate Xerxes as he (along with Suzanne) searches frantically for him while they are in Frankfurt. Realizing his and his son's precarious place in the West and the world as post–September 11 diasporic Iranians, Darius desperately fears for the safety of Xerxes, and only wants to ensure his safety. Still, Khakpour does not neatly wrap up *Sons and Other Flammable Objects* into a complete reconciliation of the Adam family, but rather, the end of the novel marks a possible new beginning or re-birth for them. This is evident in how Xerxes purposely chooses to begin his conversation with Darius using "his oldest word, his best one, his first one" (395).

This word, "Dad," is the last word in the novel, and the fact that it was Xerxes's first word indicates that Xerxes appears finally ready to start over and begin his life once more, but this time with his two identities (Iranian and American) more fully integrated. Khakpour leaves it an open question as to how the Adam family will progress, not only in terms of their relationships with one another, but also in terms of their identities, self-images, and relationships with their home and adopted countries. It may indeed prove to be a painful re-birth for both Darius and Xerxes, and their reconciliation may ultimately be doomed to fail. Yet, through this ending, Khakpour suggests that both first- and second-generation Iranian-Americans must accept their Iranian identities, especially in the aftermath of September 11 which largely disallows them, or any other Muslim Americans, from fully assimilating. Still, unlike other critics, Khakpour does not suggest that being prevented from assimilating (or even being profiled or discriminated against) is wholly debilitating or tragic. Rather, it allows for Iranian-American (or Muslim American) families and communities to grow tighter, more centralized, and stronger.

# 4

# Savior or Villain?

## *The Case of Azar Nafisi's*
## Reading Lolita in Tehran

Running parallel to the commercial explosion of reality television, in recent years, the memoir form has become a commercially viable form of literature. It also mirrors the public's desire to witness something authentic or "real." Additionally, this may be the case for the post–Watergate American generation (Generation X and beyond), who may feel perhaps cynically or realistically that so much of what is put in front of them for consumption is staged or manipulative.[1] In many ways, it has never been as lucrative to become a memoir writer as it now is in the early twenty-first century west. For instance, critically acclaimed and commercially successful writers such as Dave Eggers and David Sedaris have essentially built their literary careers upon their memoirs. It has been suggested that memoirs are often published or become successful due to the amount or quality of their "shocking details" (Motlagh 27). In other words, extreme or sensationalized memoirs can sell. In the case of Eggers, his brazen, eye grabbing title, *A Heartbreaking Work of Staggering Genius* (2000), as well as the subject matter (specifically how he coped with the deaths of his parents to cancer in his early twenties while taking charge of his younger brother and trying to establish a career and personal life for himself) helped generate an initial buzz of interest which ultimately led to commercial success.

Iranian and Iranian diasporic memoirs certainly tend to contain shocking or sensationalized material, whether it is the depiction of torture, death, warfare, extremism, or the perceived oppression of women. However, thus far, one Iranian or Iranian diasporic memoir has outstripped the others in terms of commercial success, namely *Reading Lolita in Tehran* (2003), which will be explored at length in this chapter. After the September 11 attacks, due in large part to the increased interest in learning on the part of Westerners (especially Americans) about Islam and the Middle East, many Iranian and Iranian diasporic memoirs (along with other Middle Eastern memoirs) were published. Still, as much as there seems to have developed a generic Western interest in

Iranian and Iranian diasporic memoirs, it is important to put it in context and to consider that they do not, with the exception of *Reading Lolita in Tehran*, compare to the commercial success of the memoirs by Bill Clinton, Barack Obama, and Sarah Palin, amongst others.[2] Iranian and Iranian diasporic memoirs should be considered an important, but not vastly widespread, sub-genre of the memoir form.

While memoirs can serve the important function of informing readers about significant and previously little known or unknown situations, environments, and cultures, they can also encourage or help establish stereotypes of groups, persons, or countries. Contemporary Iranian and Iranian diasporic memoir writers have met both strong praise and criticism for both of these two general reasons. Some critics argue that Iranian memoirs "run the risk of Orientalizing contemporary Iran and offering voyeuristic and exoticizing views of Iranian women" (Karim and Rahimieh 15).[3] Indeed, there is some evidence of Orientalism apparent in some of the memoirs explored in this chapter. Other critics suggest that Iranian and Iranian diasporic memoir writers may prey upon the Western public's fascination with and focus upon the veil both as an object of perceived oppression and as a device to show something "real" by "lifting the veil off Iranian women's lives" (Darznik 57). Indeed, Iranian and Iranian diasporic memoir writers often meet this literal and proverbial goal by tempting the prospective reader with pictures of half-veiled women on the cover of the book as if enticing the reader with an implicit promise that, in the memoir, the author will lift the veil completely, metaphorically and literally.[4] At the same time, these memoirs beg the question: Is there anything intrinsically wrong with the metaphoric attempt to lift the veil off the lives of people in order to expose something more authentic or truthful? This question leads to a complex debate, which revolves around two main viewpoints. On the one hand, Iranian and Iranian diasporic memoirs can been seen as activist texts that authentically give voice to the previously voiceless while exposing and trying to address perceived human rights violations in the Islamic Republic. On the other hand, these memoirs have also been seen as colonialist texts that debase the subjects they supposedly seek to liberate and contribute to further denigrating generalizations and stereotypes about Iranian and diasporic Iranians. Ultimately, both viewpoints are somewhat accurate but extreme and neither is comprehensively accurate.

Since no other Iranian or diasporic Iranian memoir has received as much attention or has been as commercially successful as Azar Nafisi's *Reading Lolita in Tehran* (henceforth abbreviated *RLT*), it would make sense to begin a discussion with this text. A number one bestseller on the *New York Times Book Review*, *RLT* remained towards the top of this list "for a year and a half"

(Donadey and Ahmed-Ghosh 623). Also, by late 2004, only a little over a year after its publication, *RLT* "ranked second on the list of most-read books on college campuses" and "was the fifth-most-borrowed nonfiction book in U.S. libraries" (Donadey and Ahmed-Ghosh 623). Lastly, by this time (late 2004), *RLT* "was in its fifteenth printing and was being translated into ten other languages" (Donadey and Ahmed-Ghosh 623).

Clearly then, *RLT* was a book that garnered almost immediate commercial success. As established earlier, *RLT*'s commercial success can be at least partially attributed to the general public's desire, post–September 11, to know something more about the Middle East and about Islam as well as President Bush's declaration of Iran being a part of the "axis of evil" (along with Iraq and North Korea). In addition, the critical praise lavished upon *RLT* immediately after its publication (in 2003)[5] also helped increase public interest, and with that, sales. The first reviews of *RLT* tended to praise it for several reasons. First, some critics lauded what they saw as the didactic nature of the text in illustrating and arguing for the value of literature, especially to "nourish free thought in climes inhospitable to it" (Hewett 17; "Reading Lolita in Tehran" 289). Along similar lines, other critics suggested that the book promotes "the redemptive power of the human imagination" through its "championing of literature as a transformative agent" (Bordewich 119; Ratliff 98). By connecting the lives of her students to that of literary critics, another critic suggests that *RLT* can be seen as "teaching us how to construe literature in a new, more meaningful way by relating the quandaries of the fictional characters to our own" (Roncevic 100). These are all understandable and justifiable points of praise in the sense that valued literature can promote imagination, empathy, and understanding. Even *RLT*'s most ardent critics tended to recognize that if the book had praiseworthy features, it was through Nafisi's celebration of the power and importance of literature.

However, it is notable that none of the initial reviewers of *RLT* seem to discuss, let alone identify, that Nafisi's book focuses upon Western literature as opposed to Persian or Iranian literature, or more broadly Arabic or Middle Eastern literature. Critics of *RLT* might point to this as further evidence of the Eurocentrism of the reviewers, and, indeed, this is a valid point in the sense that the reviewers, themselves writing for Western journals or newspapers, may have unconsciously or consciously come to equate classic, quality literature with the authors that Nafisi focuses upon: Henry James, F. Scott Fitzgerald, and Vladimir Nabokov. If Nafisi had chosen classic Persian or contemporary Iranian literature, it is safe to presume that most Western readers would not assume that the works were anything approaching the perceived literary masterpieces of James, Fitzgerald, and Nabokov.

Despite the fact that Nafisi does focus upon Western literature, it is important to recognize that, at least according to Nafisi, before she begins assembling the class that formed the basis of *RLT*, for years she participated in "a small class who came together to read and study classic Persian literature" (175). As Nafisi explains, "Even when our personal and political differences alienated us from one another, the magical texts held us together. Like a group of conspirators, we would gather around the dining room table and read poetry and prose from Rumi, Hafez, Sa-adi, Khayyam, Nezami, Ferdowsi, Attar, Beyhaghi" (172). Yet, Nafisi devotes a scant page or two of her three-hundred-page book to these writers. While this could be due to her devaluation of these writers, her commentary suggests otherwise. Rather, she becomes drawn even more to Western literature because she seeks literature as an escape from what she perceived to be an oppressed Iran.

While living in what Nafisi perceives to be an increasingly totalitarian Iran, Nafisi and her students seem more drawn to Western literature especially when the Islamic Regime begins to increasingly clamp down on it through censorship. Though this also does not comprise a large part of *RLT*, Nafisi's class, as described in *RLT*, does begin with "Persian classic literature, such as the tales of our own lady of fiction, Scheherazade, from *A Thousand and One Nights*" (2). Despite that it is again true that Western literature gets center stage in *RLT* and the inclusion of the canonical text, *A Thousand and One Nights*, could be considered both a token and a text that contributes to Orientalism, Nafisi does not only expose her students to Western literature. In addition, there is also a larger defense of Nafisi's choices. In one sense, a person can assign literature from a different culture or perspective in order to help readers better understand other cultures and nations as well as one's own. Also, just as there developed a keen interest in the Middle East and Islam in the United States after the events of September 11, Iranians and other people in predominantly Islamic Middle Eastern countries appear to have developed a keen interest, if not a fervent interest (even if that interest may be a product of disdain) about the West and specifically about the United States.

A significant portion of the critical debate about the value and content of *RLT*, as we will see, hinges upon the extent to which one views *RLT* as a colonizing text and a text that seemingly imposes Western values and preferences over that of the native culture (Persian and Iranian) instead of encouraging readers to question and critique (as opposed to passively accepting and receiving Western "wisdom" and culture as intrinsically superior). In other words, to what extent (if at all) does *RLT* encourage the reader to view the West or the United States as morally, governmentally, and ethically superior to the Islamic Regime? It will be demonstrated in this chapter that Nafisi harbors a good deal of hostility (some of which may be justified) against the Islamic Regime, while she holds a great deal of affection for the United States (some of which may also be justified). *RLT* manifests this through conscious and unconscious valuing of Western literature and culture over that of Iran and the general region. This is, of course, Nafisi's perspective, and it is a perspective shared by other political writers and literary critics as well as by prominent public officials who feel that the United States is in some or all ways governmentally, morally, or ethically superior to a country like Iran. According to Nafisi, another reason for her choice to focus upon Western literature is that her class represented "an active withdrawal from a reality that had turned hostile" (11). She also explains that she "wanted very badly to hold on to my rare mood of jubilance and optimism" (11). Thereby, instead of assigning literature that directly explored Iran, Islam, or the Middle East, Nafisi chose a more escapist route by assigning Western literature. Through *RLT*, it becomes clear that Nafisi associates the United States and its representation through American literature with "jubilance and optimism." It is this "jubilance and optimism" that she wanted to give not only to her class, but also to herself, instead of a more pessimistic realism. It could certainly be argued that leading students towards this optimism through literature could lead them towards change, but at the same time, it could lead to further personal dissatisfaction if one is not able to achieve that level of jubilation and it could also lead towards disdain towards one's native culture. In Nafisi's case, it leads her to a self-chosen exile in the United States.

Reviewers praised *RLT* for Nafisi's depiction of Iran, specifically as social criticism of a perceived totalitarian, "stifling," or fanatical regime that has the power "to ruin the lives of decent people." (Byrd 126). Along similar lines, the preeminent contemporary reviewer of literature for *The New York Times*, Michiko Kakutani, described *RLT* as "an eloquent brief on the transformative powers of fiction — on the refuge from ideology that art can offer to those living under tyranny, and art's affirmation and subversive faith in the voice of the individual" ("Reading Lolita," par. 2). That the Pulitzer Prize–winning Kakutani described people in Iran as "living under tyranny" indicates the extent to which, at least in 2003, Americans tended to think of Iran as a totalitarian, even possibly evil regime (in lines with former president Bush's rhetoric). Additional book reviews echo Kakutani's position by describing the Islamic Republic as "radical, barbaric tyranny," built upon "repression and fear" (Munson 72). For these critics, *RLT* can be seen as a quintessential depiction of "an insatiable desire for intellectual freedom in Iran" (Lyons 05d). In these reviews, there is a clear juxtaposition, which subsequent critics of *RLT* would later attempt to debunk and deconstruct, between the supposedly free and morally upstanding West and the supposedly barbaric and oppressive East and Islamic Republic.

This is not to suggest that *RLT* met with complete and uniform praise when it was published in 2003; however, what minor criticism *RLT* received tended to be based on more superficial aspects of the book such as the extent to which it was (or was not) engaging. For instance, one reviewer describes the book as "dull," with "excruciatingly clichéd appreciations of her [Nafisi's] beloved literary works" from an author who comes across as "overly somber, arrogant, and irredeemably aloof" (Munson 73). This critic offers some support of this rather harsh criticism in that "one chapter consists almost in its entirety of her final lecture on *The Great Gatsby*" (Munson 73). Such portions of the text can be rather condescending to readers, who are put in the role of the student. Overall, in *RLT*, Nafisi may come across as a rather domineering, dogmatic, and in some ways, egocentric instructor, whose ultimate subject may be more herself than the students she teaches or the country in which she lives. Still, some critics may be unconsciously responding negatively to Nafisi's authorial assertiveness. Granted, a postmodern critic could argue that since there are no real truths beyond a person's perceptions (which themselves are subjective), there is nothing more Nafisi could do but honestly describe her perspective and passions. Other reviewers argue that "although she describes how her pupils dress, move and speak, it is often difficult to differentiate between them" (Stewart and Allardice 53). This, of course, is a matter of perspective, but even if it were a completely accurate statement, it could be part of Nafisi's argument: namely, that in the stifling Islamic Regime there are no real opportunities for women (or men) to become individuals.

The above details more immediate reviews of *RLT* when it was published in 2003; however, a shift occurred in the way critics began regarding *RLT* in 2004 and 2005. Whereas the 2003 reviews tended to be strongly positive, reviews published in late 2004 and afterwards tended to be mostly negative, if not downright hostile. Amy DePaul offers a compelling explanation for this dramatic critical shift, suggesting it could be attributed to how, by 2005, there existed "a different America than the one in which it [*RLT*] first appeared" (77). DePaul further explains: "Since 2003, a reformist president in Iran has been replaced by a more conservative leader, diplomatic scuffles over Iran's nuclear capabilities have ensued" (77). Further, as war in Iraq seemed to be a much costlier and lengthier endeavor than previously anticipated, revelations were made about missed opportunities and potential cover-ups by the Bush administration regarding terrorism, September 11, and reasons for invading in Iraq; consequently, the country grew more cynical about potentially manipulative portrayals of the Islamic Middle East.[6]

While it could be argued that Nafisi's book gives voice to often voiceless and oppressed Iranian women, these new critics (generally post–2004) suggest that Nafisi condemns Islamic men in a rather derogatory manner that contributes to Orientalist stereotypes of masculine barbarism. For instance, one reviewer suggests that *RLT* became especially popular because of the manner in which it reinforced "popular stereotypes of Muslims as backward and primitive" and helped "maintain a widespread (albeit factually erroneous) notion that Muslim women are victims of an inherent misogynism in Islamic tradition" (Bahramitash 222). This reviewer makes a fair general criticism, but because it is not directly supported through examples, it fails to be convincing. It is true that on more than one occasion Nafisi blames Iranian men as a whole for making "half the population invisible" (70). Yet, it is important to recognize that this is not just Nafisi's perspective; the other female students in her class also seem to harbor strongly negative feelings towards Iranian men to the extent that one suggests, not entirely in jest, "How about genitally mutilating men ... so as to curb their sexual appetites?" (70).

Still, Nafisi may portray most men as sexist and domineering in the sense that, in Nafisi's descriptions, Iranian men appear to want to control the lives of their wives and daughters, and they tend to look down upon educational opportunities for women. Is this a fair depiction of the majority of Iranian men? Presumably not, but in line with other writers already examined (Satrapi, Sofer, and Khakpour), Nafisi makes a strong case that on an objective level the Islamic Republic is mostly patriarchal and does not treat women as equal to men. Of course, one could argue that the United States remains a patriarchal country as well, but, if anything, Nafisi's portrayal of women in Iran seems to more clearly mirror the position of American women in the 1940s and 1950s. It is hard to imagine a compelling argument that American women have not gained more rights and have not made progress toward equity since then. In addition, Nafisi does not completely vilify all of the men in *RLT*. This is best exemplified in that one of Nafisi's best students, Nima, whom Nafisi calls a "born teacher" and who "writes brilliant and unfinished essays on James, Nabokov and his favorite Persian writers," is male (343).[7] In addition, even if it is Nafisi's aim to critique what she sees as an overwhelmingly patriarchal and sexist Islamic Republic, her choice to focus upon a close knit solidarity of women could be part of a purposeful and worthwhile attempt to counteract the perceived or actual Iranian patriarchal system. Similarly, one of Nafisi's students, Yassi, who stays with Nafisi's family from time to time, emphasizes the importance of this female bond, explaining that traditionally, in pre–1979 Iran, "The women were the backbone of the family, the ones on whom everyone depended. They worked at home and they worked outside the home" (62). However, in the atmosphere of the Islamic Republic, it is not the women, but "the men, the uncles, who always held the promise of the future for Yassi" (62).

Another heavily debated issue is whether Nafisi condemns Islam in *RLT* as some reviewers suggest[8] or if she portrays a perversion of Islam in Iran by a more radical fringe element that, at least in her view, oppresses women. No doubt, Nafisi would argue that she is doing more of the latter than the former. She would also point to the comments of some of her students, like Yassi, who tells Nafisi that her family "felt that the Islamic Republic was a betrayal of Islam rather than its assertion" (31). This question of whether the Islamic Republic really reflects or represents the real spirit of Islam can be seen in how Nafisi depicts the Islamic Republic. She writes: "We were all victims of the arbitrary nature of a totalitarian regime that constantly intruded into the most private corners of our lives and imposed its relentless fictions on us. Was this rule the rule of Islam?" (67). The answer to this rhetorical question, for Nafisi, is clearly no. In many ways, Nafisi's position is best expressed by her categorical rejection that Islam (or any religion for that matter) can be "a political entity" (103).[9] In essence, Nafisi defends the quintessentially American idea that there should be a division between church and state, and this is a legitimate point of view that does not necessarily express any disdain towards Islam. It is important to not implicate Nafisi in a supposed denigration of Islam without ample support because similar claims were made about Iraq war protesters in 2003, who were often deemed unpatriotic for not supporting their country. It is ironic that the presumably liberal critics who charge Nafisi with denigrating Islam and being in league with the neo-conservative movement also were probably against the Iraq war and were presumably labeled as unpatriotic.

Other criticisms of *RLT* take on a more deconstructive agenda, and attempt to undo what they perceive to be an unfair, inaccurate, and misleading dichotomy between the West and the East (Bahramitash 222). Borrowing from Edward Said, one reviewer suggests that *RLT* continues in the Western tradition of Orientalism by suggesting that "the Occident is progressive and the best place for women, while the Muslim Orient is backward, uncivilized, and the worst place for women" (Bahramitash 222). Indeed, *RLT* does suggest that the United States and the West are veritable beacons of freedom for oppressed Iranian women. As we will see from more contemporary memoirs and literature written by diasporic Iranians, the United States does not often turn out to be that place of jubilation and liberty for women (let alone any Iranian immigrants or exiles). Rather, recent immigrants can end up with new American lives that are in some ways worse (economically, culturally, and racially) than their previous lives in Iran. Still, Nafisi's choice to end *RLT* with her leaving Iran for the United States suggests that she believes in Gatsby's green light. This connection suggests that Nafisi clings to the boundless optimism of Gatsby in the potential for the transformation of the individual or self-made person in the United States.

Critics (at least post–2003) also tend to suggest that *RLT* leaves no real room for individual transformation or agency, but rather, that it denigrates Iranians and specifically, Iranian women by regarding them "as victims and not as agents of social transformation; thus it is blind to the ways in which women in the East resist and empower themselves" (Bahramitash 222). However, while it is true that Nafisi does not focus on empowering Iranian activists like Shirin Ebadi, is it fair that she should be criticized for this, when the focus of her book was an alternative class held at her home (as opposed to a sociological study of Iran during the Islamic Republic)? If we believe *RLT*, the women who attend Nafisi's classes may be more timid at first, but as the class progresses, they begin to find their voices. If *RLT* promotes the perception of the West as savior, which Bahramitash suggests,[10] then in this case it is doubly apparent in the sense that it is an Iranian woman (Nafisi) who is setting the groundwork of the Orientalist motif of the damsel-in-distress narrative. It is conceivable that Nafisi purposely set up a simplistic dichotomy and narrative in order to cater to Western readers, but it is more likely that she genuinely believes in the dichotomy. Some critics have also suggested that Nafisi is either a subscriber to neo-conservatism or an active agent in the neo-conservative movement.[11] Assuming Nafisi's suggestions in *RLT* are accurate (and there is some evidence supporting her views)—e.g., that women are denied the same legal rights as men, that they are subject to debasement and harassment by men, and that they are denied individuality and independence—is it really fair to condemn Nafisi for wanting to encourage her primarily Western audience to be disturbed and even outraged by some of the problems she perceives in Iran?

The problem with the Orientalist readings of *RLT* is that they deny any possibility that the most rich and powerful countries in the world (which are predominantly Western) cannot or should not involve themselves in the affairs of other countries like Iran in a beneficial manner, or that they should only do so in a completely objective manner. It is certainly possible that women who are currently working for change in Iran can manifest change on their own. However, suggesting that the depiction of potential oppression in an Islamic country is an act of Orientalism because there exist more empowered women who are not explored in a text does not negate an argument (Nafisi's) that there exists a significant oppression of women in Iran. Not content to stop with just Iran, other allied critics suggest that *RLT* contributes to larger stereotypes about Middle Eastern and Muslim women.[12] As *RLT* only covers Iran, it should not be asserted that the book makes any sort of implication or blanket statements about Muslim, Middle Eastern, or Asian societies or nations.

Though her students' stories often take a back seat to Nafisi's personal history, Nafisi does distinguish her students. For instance, there is Yassi, the most self-assured and youngest student in the class, the more reserved Manna, and the more outspoken Azin, "nicknamed the wild one" (5). While it is true that Nafisi sometimes generalizes about her students, this may not be her doing but rather, the aftereffects of a regime that may disallow or limit female independence. The problem with categorizing *RLT* as an Orientalist text is that critics can end up further silencing women who are already being silenced by the regime, and inadvertently defend problematic policies of the regime that can and often do infringe on basic human rights, especially for women.

To be sure, critics of *RLT* are more convincing when they criticize Western stereotypical, even racist perceptions of Muslims as well as people from predominantly Arabic and Persian countries. Even as late as the 2008 presidential election, anti–Muslim and anti–Arabic sentiment can be seen in the large percentage of the American electorate who feared Barack Obama and stated that they would not vote for him because they believed he was Muslim.[13] It has also been suggested that Nafisi has a "contempt for Islam" which can be seen through comments in *RLT* such as "It is a truth universally acknowledged that a Muslim man, regardless of his fortune must be in want of a nine-year-old virgin wife'" (Nafisi 261; Bahramitash 233). However, this allusion to Jane Austen's *Pride and Prejudice* is not from Nafisi but from one of her students, Yassi, who delivered it somewhat comically, in "that special tone of hers, deadpan and mildly ironic, which on rare occasions, and this was one of them, bordered on the burlesque" (257). In addition, Nafisi's claim that the Islamic Republic reduced the marrying age from thirteen to nine is accurate, as are her claims that "adultery and prostitution were to be punished by stoning to death; and women, under law, were considered to have half the worth of men" (261). While these policies were rarely, if ever, enacted or realized, it is hard to imagine how the policies could be defensible in any shape or form.

The question then is how best to navigate this difficult tightrope of wanting to critique an Islamic Regime (as Nafisi does), but not wanting to contribute to already rampant and damaging stereotypes of Muslims in the United States and Western world. One way to counteract these stereotypes of Muslims would be to clearly distinguish between a regime and its people; however, according to more recent critics, this is exactly what Nafisi failed to do in *RLT*. Instead, they argue, *RLT* contributes to stereotypes of and even racism towards Muslims and Iranians, as perhaps best exemplified by Nafisi's simile that compares life in the Islamic Republic (at least for women) to rape. She writes, "Living in the Islamic Republic is like having sex with a man you loathe.... If you're forced into having sex with someone you dislike, you make your mind black — you pretend to be somewhere else, you tend to forget your body, you hate your body" (329). Some critics have gone as far as to suggest that *RLT* is mere propaganda for the Bush administration that reinforces "the message that the political elite seeks to convey" (Bahramitash 223; Donadey and Ahmed-Ghosh 643).[14] However, no critics, as of yet, have provided solid evidence of any political connections between Nafisi and the Bush administration.

Still, it is true that Nafisi does often make somewhat simplistic binary oppositions between the perceived liberating West and the perceived oppressive Islamic Republic. However, in defense of Nafisi, it is not Nafisi herself, but rather, some of her students, like Manna, who suggest that due to the restrictions placed on women by the Islamic Regime, they gravitate more towards seemingly superficial Western style accoutrements, exemplified, for instance, through their desire "to wear outrageous colors, like shocking pink or tomato red" (14). Further, it is difficult to disagree with how color and clothing can accentuate individual differences and characteristics when those are so frequently muted in the Islamic Republic. In response to a scene in *RLT* in which Nafisi celebrates how her female students remove their ubiquitous dark clothing and veils to reveal colorful clothing, Anne Donadey and Huma Ahmed-Ghosh argue that Nafisi compares "their ability to wear bright clothing" to "capitalist consumerism," which, they believe, Nafisi presents as a primary means towards liberation (633). As an example, Nafisi couldn't have made a clearer contrast between the West and the Islamic Republic through two separate pictures of her class. In the first picture, "they [Nafisi's students] are, according to the law of the land, dressed in black robes and head scarves, covered except for the oval of their faces and their hands" (4). However, in the second photograph they "have taken off their coverings. Splashes of color separate one from the next. Each has become distinct through the color and style of her clothes, the color and the length of her hair; not even the two who are still wearing their head scarves look the same" (4). Through oppositions like this, Nafisi encourages the reader to morally judge both regimes and she provides further rationale for the perception of the Islamic Republic as part of the so-called Axis of Evil.

Still, it is relatively innocuous to suggest that Nafisi encourages a moral dichotomy between Iran and the West. In comparison, among the most extreme and only partially supported criticisms of *RLT* is that the book can be seen as not only contributing to Western disdain towards Iran but also as a supposed tool of the American neo-conservative movement to invade and colonize Iran (Dabashi and Keshavarz).[15] While there seems to be little to no direct support for the claim that *RLT* was a politically calculated text that "may, in effect, prepare the American public for a tough line against Iran," and makes "a harsh move against the culture seem justified, perhaps even necessary," *RLT* does portray the Islamic Republic as an oppressive, totalitarian regime (Keshavarz 29). As such, it may have contributed to further demonizations of Iran. However, the real issue is whether or not Nafisi's overtly negative portrayal of the Islamic Republic is sufficiently supported. Also, one could, of course, use the same logic presented in the quote above from Keshavarz (and some certainly have) to condemn leftist depictions of the United States by political dissidents like Michael Moore.

The amount of ire Nafisi's book has provoked in some critics can be seen through condemnations of *RLT* for enforcing "a harmful, widespread stereotype of Iranians so distorted as to make them seem subhuman" (Keshavarz 6). As established earlier, it is true that Nafisi does not focus upon native Persian or Iranian literature and there is definitely some truth to Keshavarz's assertion that that the text "suggests a total absence of interest in literature by the local culture" (7). It could be that Nafisi portrays women as "passive, even masochistic victims," (9) but the Regime is at least partially responsible for this passivity, even masochistic behavior, and thereby, writers who critique Nafisi for supposedly debasing women end up inadvertently defending the sexist and oppressive policies of the Islamic Regime through their assertions. It is generally accepted as fact that, prior to the 1960s or 1970s (even if not to the present day), women in the United States were oppressed by a patriarchal culture. Would we condemn female writers of this time for speaking out against this oppression, even if it meant portraying women as passive? While Nafisi may not display the full spectrum of Iranian women, the extent to which Nafisi misses the mark in terms of providing a holistic depiction of Iranian women cannot be objectively determined.

*RLT* has also been condemned for "its unfailing hatred of everything Iranian" and for being "reminiscent of the most pestiferous colonial projects of the British in India," with Nafisi as "native informer and colonial agent" (Dabashi, par. 11). However, a book that celebrates the power of literature is hardly analogous to any "pestiferous colonial projects," which might include physical abuse, maiming, and even murder. Also, a close reading of the text reveals that Nafisi most certainly does not hate everything Iranian (evident, for instance, through her incorporation of some Persian texts and culture into her classes). Rather, Nafisi is extremely distraught with what she would describe as Iran's political and cultural turn for the worse as the Islamic Republic. Nafisi's disdain for the Islamic Republic does dwarf what may very well be her intrinsic love for Persian literature and culture. Still, this does not mean that Nafisi has forsaken and condemned native culture and literature. As established earlier, *RLT* does not present itself as a historical or sociological text. Therefore, it is not entirely fair to condemn the text for failing to include or sufficiently discuss "surrounding successive US imperial moves for global domination" (Dabashi, par. 13).[16]

Criticism of *RLT* is more convincing in terms of how Western literature can, and may in this case, serve as a means of cultural subjugation.[17] In that, Nafisi does uphold the primarily white, Eurocentric canon through her choice of texts. However, it has also been suggested that Nafisi promotes "the racist cause of a singular literary canon in the United States and Europe," and that she is guilty of "denigrating, dismissing, or ignoring the existence of non–Euro-American literary and cultural traditions" (Dabashi, par. 22).[18] This serious criticism suggests the question: Should Nafisi be held responsible for educating her American readers about the significance, value, and importance of Iranian literature because she is Iranian in Iran teaching Iranian students? This argument sets up a problematic precedent for writers from other countries writing for an American audience or for minority American writers. Does Nafisi, as an Iranian-American who hails from the "non–Western world," really have the responsibility to fully and comprehensively represent "the culture of her origin" to her Western readers? (Keshavarz 29). Shouldn't Nafisi have the right to focus on what she feels is most important? Nafisi is, after all, not a history professor, but a literature professor, and an Americanist at that. Implicitly, Keshavarz holds Nafisi responsible for educating the American public, who she views as misguided and misinformed about Iran. It is hard to hold Nafisi to this standard, though, since she had not published anything commercially successful up until *RLT*, and presumably had no reason to believe that her readers would turn to her, if they indeed have, for a history lesson about Iran and the contemporary Middle East.

In addition, while critics of *RLT* may believe Iranian literature to be "second to none" (Dabashi, par. 22), this assertion could be considered a similar kind of ethnocentrism along lines of what Nafisi has been accused of doing by the same critics. While it is true that *RLT* does seem to uphold the Western white canon, this should not mean that American or European literature has no place at all in the curriculum of literature departments or curriculums at Iranian colleges and universities. Just as it is important for Iranian culture and literature to be studied at Western colleges and universities (along with other cultures and groups), it also important for Western culture and literature to be studied at Iranian colleges and universities (along with other cultures and groups).

Along similar lines, in her book *Jasmine and Stars: Reading More Than Lolita in Tehran* (2007), Fatemeh Keshavarz suggests that *RLT* can be seen as part of a "New Orientalist" genre or movement[19] in Iranian and Iranian diasporic literature which "simplifies" the subject matter and "explains almost all undesirable Middle Eastern incidents in terms of Muslim men's submission to God and Muslim women's submission to men" (Keshavarz 2–3).[20] Keshavarz suggests that *RLT* encourages a colonial sentiment, and she criticizes it for excluding Iranian writers. Yet, from the title of her book, *Jasmine and Stars*, one could argue that Keshavarz is also generalizing, essentializing, and even exoticizing Iranians in an Orientalist manner.[21] For instance, Keshavarz writes: "The jasmine and stars that I have collected for you in this book are unique in the sense that they belong to my personal story. I have picked the stars from midsummer nights in the Shiraz of my childhood and youth, and the jasmine blossoms from grandma's prayer rug where she kept them" (Keshavarz 12). Such a passage could encourage a kind of noble savage ethos of Iranians.[22] There may indeed be "jasmine flowers, skies full of stars, and passerby who sing about love," in the same country that Nafisi writes about, but stating this hardly paints a sophisticated picture of Iranians or Iranian culture, and its emphasis upon physicality and sensuality glosses over deeper political and social issues that someone like Nobel Prize winner Shirin Ebadi might convincingly argue are more serious and pressing issues facing Iranians (Keshavarz 12).

Still, the extent of Keshavarz's critique (which leaves virtually no room for any kind of praise of *RLT*) puts her in a position of potentially defending the literary censorship of the Islamic Regime, which has banned books like Nabokov's *Lolita* as well as *The Great Gatsby*[23] for being "morally harmful" (108). Indeed, Nafisi discusses this censorship in *RLT*, explaining her growing dissatisfaction with her academic position at the University of Tehran with the following: "Could one really concentrate on one's job when what preoccupied the faculty was how to excise the word wine from a Hemingway story, when they decided not to teach Bronte because she appeared to condone adultery?" (11).[24] Nafisi does celebrate the American and European canon, calling them the "great works," and she seems pleased that they are "celebrated by the young," in part because many of these works have been banned (39). In this sense, Nafisi is more in line with Shirin Ebadi, who suggests that the Islamic Republic has taken a turn for the worse in comparison to life under the Shah. Ebadi explains that the Islamic Republic, unlike SAVAK under the Shah, does "not draw the line at dissidents," but rather, "its mandate included the targeting of translators of French literature as well as organized political activists calling for a secular government" (131). Keshavarz rightly identifies that "readers other than pious Muslims have had difficulty dealing with what Nabokov allows to happen to *Lolita*" (37). However, having difficulty with a text is a completely different response than outright banning it, which is something I would hope that no writers would want to see done by any country or legislative bodies.

To be certain, Nabokov's *Lolita* is a text that details sexuality, and sexuality in its various forms or the muting of sexuality plays a significant role in *RLT*. According to Nafisi, "Our culture shunned sex because it was too involved with it. It had to suppress sex violently, for the same reason an impotent man will put his beautiful wife under lock and key" (304). Again, Nafisi does uses a metaphor that indicates her disdain focuses upon her perception of the Islamic Republic as a sexist and patriarchal nation. This is something which a critic like Keshavarz rejects, but such a position nearly appears to defend the sexual abuse of women in Iran who can be married as early as nine years old.[25] It may very well be that "recounting the horrors of Muslim sexuality is spreading," and indeed one can see "native voices who can testify to the true wickedness they have personally experienced" (Keshavarz 53). However, should authors merely ignore this? Should they balance their writing with accounts of "normal" sexuality? Perhaps one of the reasons that Keshavarz and other critics take such issue with *RLT* is that they take it personally. As Keshavarz tellingly explains, "Books like *RLT* confirm our suspicion that something *is* seriously wrong with us" (72).[26] However, such admissions reveal that critics evaluating *RLT* sometimes lack critical distance and objectivity.

For the most part, Nafisi has remained mostly silent about the criticism *RLT* has received in recent years. In a rare instance, Nafisi did speak to the criticism, and ironically, suggests that many of her most virulent critics are guilty of the exact same kind of one-dimensional, simplistic, dichotomic thinking of which she has been accused by them. In her own words, Nafisi tells an interviewer:

> It was truly amazing, the lies and slanders that were spread.... But it points to yet another problem — the way people want to segregate and categorize everything. Everything is reduced to a single figure: "all Americans are like George W. Bush," "all Iranians are Islamic fundamentalists." And the American people, the Iranian people, have no way of saying, "This is not who I am" [qtd. in Watts].

While Nafisi makes a valid rebuttal in rejecting the writers whose critical points about *RLT* often seem themselves to be motivated by a simplified dichotomy, there are still somewhat simplified dichotomies in *RLT*, the most important and overarching being between the supposedly liberating West and the supposedly oppressive Islamic Regime.

One of the most significant as well as the most praised and condemned aspects of *RLT* is Nafisi's depiction of women as well as her students. For instance, it has been suggested that *RLT* is devoid of requisite historical and sociological accounts of "the long and noble struggle of women all over the colonized world to ascertain their rights against both domestic patriarchy and colonial domination" (Dabashi, par. 13). Along similar lines, Keshavarz suggests that its "silence on women who had made an impact was among the most significant acts of erasure in the book" (21). This criticism is mirrored by Donadey and Ahmed-Ghosh, who suggest that Nafisi "does not discuss the attempts, and in some cases strides, made by Islamic feminists toward women's rights while she lived in Iran" (628).[27] While it is true that Nafisi might have focused on Shirin Ebadi and other women in her book fighting for "intellectual and artistic or social change" (Keshavarz 21), her book's focus was on a group of students, who, it could be argued, are much more representative of average Iranian women than Ebadi, a Nobel Prize–winning judge.[28]

In keeping with Orientalist theory, Nafisi could be accused of a preoccupation with the veil as symbol and image. For instance, Donadey and Ahmed-Josh suggest that Nafisi employs "a clear binary opposition between the enforced robe and head scarf as homogenizing symbols of women's oppression and the glorious individuality symbolized by diverse clothing and hairstyles" (633). However, Nafisi does not find the veil itself to be objectionable, but rather, the enforcement that the veil be used irrespective of a person's religious beliefs. It is important to recognize that Nafisi is not alone in this sentiment. One of her students, Mashid, describes wearing the veil before the revolution "as a testament to her faith. Her decision was a voluntary act. When the revolution forced the scarf on others, her action became meaningless" (13). Her act becomes meaningless because the Islamic Republic forces a religious symbol upon people who may not be authentic believers. Does a popular book like *RLT* "make it difficult for Muslim women, both in North America and Muslim countries, to defend their rights as citizens as well as their gender rights," as Bahramitash suggests (223)? There is no concrete evidence that it has. Rather, it could be at least equally argued that *RLT* may have helped Muslim women defend their rights through its portrayal, albeit not as complex as it could be, of not only the problems in the Islamic Regime, but its encouragement of social protest and political awakening.

In order to determine how Nafisi portrays women in *RLT*, it helps to return to the text. According to Nafisi, at her previous institution, the University of Allameh Tabatabai, women were unfairly targeted by the administration for simple things: "for running up the stairs when they were late for classes, for laughing in the hallways, for talking to members of the opposite sex" (9). While it could be argued that similar things may occur at especially strict schools, the fact that women were specifically targeted (as opposed to men) is a clear example of gender inequality. Similarly, Nafisi identifies how officials of the Islamic Regime, in this case a group that calls itself "the Blood of God," focuses upon women by patrolling "the streets to make sure that women like Sanaz wear their veils properly, do not wear makeup, do not walk in public with men who are not their fathers, brothers or husbands" (26). Other authors like Marjane Satrapi and Azadeh Moavani have also documented the use of this morality police squad in the same manner as Nafisi. In *RLT*, other Iranian woman also describe the sexist and abusive power of "the Blood of God" or the Revolutionary Guards. For instance, Nafisi's daughter describes how the morality police raided a classroom looking for Western-style contraband and inspecting the nails of the female students to see if they could discover any evidence of manicures (58). An even more dramatic depiction comes from another of Nafisi's students, Sanaz, who goes on a vacation to the Caspian Sea and, along with a few other young women, is accosted by the morality police who give the girls "virginity tests" twice to verify the results, even though they find no evidence of Western goods or illicit activities (73). Even though this group does not find any incriminating evidence, they force Sanaz and her friend to sign a confession and then give them twenty-five lashes each (73).

In her own way, Nafisi attempts to act as a catalyst promoting change in the lives of her female students, although whether or not she succeeds in doing so is uncertain. After all, Nafisi does leave Iran at the end of *RLT*, and she does not stay to help her students (although it is possible that she feels she can't help them anymore or that only they can only really help themselves). Nafisi does explain that she chooses students for "the peculiar mixture of fragility and courage I sensed in them. They were what you would call loners, who did not belong to any particular group or sect" (12). The implication here is that Nafisi will help her students learn how to be courageous and independent through their study of literature; however, Nafisi may choose students who will comprise a docile and largely non-challenging audience for her lectures.

Nafisi has also been heavily criticized (and praised) for her depiction of life in the Islamic Republic. The main question suggested by this criticism is whether her account is a justifiable and courageous description of a totalitarian regime or if it is more of an account of extended, unfair generalizations and stereotypes as well as debasement of a people and their religion. Nafisi does describe life in the Islamic Regime as both tragic and absurd (23). She also condemns the Islamic Republic as being driven by philistines, as indicated by her statement. She writes, "We lived in a culture that denied any merit to literary works, considering them important only when they were handmaidens to something seemingly more urgent — namely ideology" (25). Even though it may not be her intention, such comments can lead a reader to think of Islam as a primitive, intolerant religion and Muslims as barbaric. However, Nafisi's point about the Islamic Republic (not about Islam or Muslims) has been documented by other writers such as Azadeh Moavani, an Iranian-American journalist (to be explored in the next chapter), who lived in Iran during both the Khatami and Ahmadinejad administrations. Moavani explains, "Though books are inexpensive by any standard — generally costing no more than the price of a couple of sandwiches — little in public life encourages reading. There are few public libraries, no reading contests in schools and scarce promotion of any book apart from the Book. (Billboards inform Iranians that if they can memorize the Koran in its entirety, they will be awarded a formal university degree)" ("Letter from Tehran" par. 5). Still, it is true that Nafisi spends very little time in *RLT* discussing how, historically speaking, Iranian and Persian culture greatly value art and literature and have done so for centuries.

One lingering question brought up by Nafisi's general omission of Iranian and Persian literature from *RLT* is whether Nafisi promotes Western or American culture over Iranian culture or whether she more accurately reflects the desires of Iranians, especially Iranian youth, in the Islamic Republic to embrace Western or American culture. Nafisi has been accused of glorifying the West, and specifically the United States, in *RLT*. Instead, Nafisi suggests that her book mirrors post-revolutionary Iran's (or at least most Iranian citizens') fascination with the West and the United States. She suggests that at this time, "the myth of America started to take hold of Iran. Even those who wished its death were obsessed by it. America had become both the land of Satan and *Paradise Lost*. A sly curiosity of America had been kindled that in time would turn the hostage-takers into hostages" (106). Nafisi explains that in the late 1980s and 1990s there was an explosion in purchase and use of satellite television to the extent that "in the poorer, more religious sections of Tehran, the family with a dish would rent out certain programs to their neighbors" (67). This account is supported by Satrapi's works as well as Moaveni's (to be explored later). In addition, Nafisi describes her own children as embracing American rock bands like the Doors.[29]

As mentioned earlier, Nafisi does end *RLT* with her final act of leaving Iran for the United States, this time seemingly for good. In so doing, she does seem to reject the Islamic Republic and embrace the West and the United States. It is telling that while, initially, Nafisi's husband does not want to leave Iran because of his great love for his native country, Nafisi does not concur with him (at least as far as what Nafisi reveals in the text). This may very well be because she despises what Iran has become as the Islamic Republic and this disdain may overpower her love for Persian and Iranian culture. Even though Nafisi admits that some things improve towards the end of the Rafsanjani administration (and as Khatami prepares to take office in 1997), she continues to feel jaded and uninspired. Specifically, before she leaves Iran in 1997, Nafisi acknowledges that there has been progress for women but she feels this is tempered, if not counteracted, by "the raids and arrests and public executions," which "also persist" (341). Also, right before leaving Iran, Nafisi explains that she would like "to write a book in which I would thank the Islamic Republic for all the things it had taught me — to love Austen and James and ice cream and freedom" (338). In other words, the Islamic Republic's attempt to demonize the United States and the West has seemingly backfired, at least for Nafisi, who becomes even more pro–Western. Ultimately, there is little support for the claim that Nafisi portrays Islam as a "monster," since it is not Islam that Nafisi indicts, but a perceived vicious political totalitarianism she believes to exist in Iran. Rather, there is more evidence that authors like Kesharvaz conflate the Islamic Republic with Islam itself, when it was Nafisi's intention to demonstrate that the Islamic Republic should be seen as an extreme perversion of Islam.

# Next Generation
# Iranian-American
# Memoir Writers

*Azadeh Moaveni and Firoozeh Dumas*

As mentioned in the last chapter, Azar Nafisi, while the most commercially successful, is by no stretch of the imagination the only Iranian or diasporic Iranian memoir writer published in recent years. Nafisi (born in 1955) represents a different generation than the new, emerging generation of Iranian and diasporic Iranian memoir writers generally born in the 1960s and 1970s. This group of writers has published such works as Gelareh Asayesh's *Saffron Sky* (1999), Firoozeh Dumas's *Funny in Farsi* (2003), Roya Hakakian's *Journey from the Land of No* (2004), and Zarah Ghahramani's *My Life as a Traitor* (2008). The journalist and memoir writer I will next explore, Azadeh Moaveni, completed what could be seen as the exact opposite of Nafisi's journey. Instead of growing up in Iran as Nafisi did, Moaveni grew up in the United States. Instead of subsequently moving to the United States as Nafisi did, Moaveni moved to Iran and lived there on two separate occasions for years at a time, as documented in *Lipstick Jihad* (2005) and *Honeymoon in Tehran* (2009).[1]

Moaveni, born a generation after Nafisi (mid 1970s as opposed to mid 1950s), explains that when she went to Iran for the first time in 2000 as a journalist, she "aspired to belong to a literary circle not unlike that of the engaged women of Azar Nafisi's *Reading Lolita in Tehran*, who found relief from their authoritarian society in the imaginative world of novels" ("Letter from Tehran," par. 1). However, she finds, "that bookstores did not exist as such — there were only bookstore/stationery stores, or bookstore/toy stores — was the first sign my plan might not work" ("Letter from Tehran," par. 1). Instead, she "began to wonder why books figured so little in the lives of my otherwise intellectually curious friends" (par. 2). While critics like Fatemeh

Keshavarz praise the importance of Iranian literature, Moaveni discovered that most Iranians (not unlike most Americans) tend to be drawn towards "self-help books and their eclectic offshoots, on topics like Indian spirituality and feng shui" (par. 3). She also suggests, "When Iranians aren't reading about depression or the harmonious arrangement of furniture, they're drawn to soap-opera-ish novels about family life and chaste, unrequited love, bearing titles like *The Solitude of Lonely Nights* (par. 4).[2] First hand revelations like these, counteracting general Western presumptions of Iran, make Moaveni's works especially important and meaningful. In this chapter I will begin by exploring Moaveni's two memoirs, *Lipstick Jihad* and *Honeymoon in Tehran*, which depict an Iran in flux, whose citizens are being increasingly Americanized[3] while the Islamic Republic conversely becomes more politically anti–Western. Moaveni's books reveal a largely bifurcated Iran with a public, domineering political structure and with citizens who tend to lead more open, permissive lifestyles in private.

One of the most valuable aspects of *Lipstick Jihad* is Moaveni's comparative approach in which she examines American life in contrast to Iranian life. When asked in an interview as to "some of the biggest differences in your mind between American culture and Iranian culture," Moaveni stressed class differences as being preeminent (Lumsden, par. 7). Moaveni also sees a crucial difference between Iranian and American culture in terms of communication styles. In her words, "American culture is incredibly forthright. There's this premium on telling it like it is and being frank. Iranian culture, and Farsi, the language, is really evasive; it has all these rituals and cues and formalities in how people deal with one another" (qtd. in Lumsden, par. 12). To Moaveni, one of the ways the Iranian Revolution has failed or can be seen as hypocritical is that the Revolutionary Guard, who typically uphold traditional and conservative Islamic morals amongst the Iranian people, have become more Westernized in their lifestyle choices (Lumsden, par. 10). In an odd parallel, Moaveni also sees the younger generation (or Burnt Generation) of Iran as desiring "Western-style rights," in the sense that they, like the Revolutionary Guard, want "the right to individual choice in lifestyle, career choice, who you marry and who you don't" (qtd. in Lumsden, par. 30).[4] The difference between the Burnt Generation and the Revolutionary Guard is that the former is more upfront in their desires whereas the latter tends to conceal or mask their desires.

Unlike *Reading Lolita in Tehran* (*RLT*), both of Moaveni's accounts met with overwhelmingly strong praise and received no subsequent serious backlash from critics. This might, of course, be different if either *Lipstick Jihad* or *Honeymoon in Tehran* became as popular as *RLT*, for they would then have commanded greater attention (and scrutiny). However, there are other reasons for the different receptions of Moaveni's and Nafisi's memoirs. First, Moaveni's two books detail a time of greater reform (with the possible exception of the first two years of the Ahmadinejad administration). In fact, as late as 1999, when Moaveni visits Iran (before settling there in 2000), she describes the "atmosphere" as "decidedly Soviet. My female relatives and I wore dark veils and sandals with socks, wiped off our lipstick when we saw policemen in the distance. My aunt still came along for the ride, if a male cousin was dropping me off late at night, in case we were stopped at a checkpoint" (40). These Nafisi-like observations will change as the political and cultural atmosphere in Iran gradually lightens in 2000–1, after the 1999 student demonstrations. This new, more permissive atmosphere allows Moaveni to be less critical of contemporary Iran than Nafisi. Moaveni is also much less insular than Nafisi, who, by her own account, tends to use literature as a means of escape. Moaveni is also young and single (at least in *Lipstick Jihad*), whereas Nafisi is married with children. Much of the impetus for change in Iran comes from people of Moaveni's age or younger (the Burnt Generation), and Moaveni is able to infiltrate into their world. Lastly, Moaveni may be able to write more objectively about Iran because she is American-born, and doesn't have as visceral a connection to Iran as Iranian-born Nafisi seems to have.

As mentioned earlier, reviews of *Lipstick Jihad* tended to be quite positive. Malina Dunk of *Iranian Studies* describes *Lipstick Jihad* as shedding light "not only on post-revolutionary Iran and Moaveni's hyphenated exile community, but also on the risks and boundaries of identity and humanity itself" (251).[5] Along similar lines, Meline Toumani, writing for *Nation*, praises *Lipstick Jihad* for looking "critically at political and social problems in the country," and as "a kind of integration of nostalgia and reality" (28).[6] Only seldom did critics find flaws in *Lipstick Jihad* and those flaws tended to be focused more on the form rather than the content, Moaveni's use of satire,[7] and her inclusion of herself in the narrative.[8]

As *Lipstick Jihad* is an autobiography as well as a memoir, it is helpful to establish some background about Moaveni herself. Born in California in 1976, Moaveni attended the University of California at Santa Cruz, and, after graduating, she worked as the Iranian and Middle Eastern correspondent for *Time* magazine ("About Azadeh," par. 1). Subsequent to a brief time living in Egypt as a Fulbright Scholar, Moaveni decided to move to Iran (as detailed in *Lipstick Jihad*). She explains this decision as being driven by both personal and professional reasons:

> I was quite sick of being a partial American and a partial Iranian and I
> thought if I went back, I had a shot of becoming "really Iranian," whatever
> that means. I had the usual rootsy homeland bug, and all the identity neu-

roses of second-generation Middle Eastern kids. But more importantly, what made me stay there, is that I knew Iran would be absolutely central to Middle Eastern politics for my whole life, and I wanted to understand its internal dynamics ["A Q&A," par. 17].

In essence, Moaveni's first semi-permanent trip to Iran is personal in nature, but as Moaveni soon discovers, in Iran, the personal is the political. Along these lines, *Lipstick Jihad* is not just Moaveni's bildungsroman, but also an ongoing bildungsroman of Iran itself.

In many ways, the title "Lipstick Jihad" illustrates how the text is more multi-faceted than *RLT* and also how *Lipstick Jihad* is much more ironic and less polemic than *RLT*. Moaveni's title can be seen as trivializing jihad, and it could be argued that Moaveni's connection of lipstick with jihad debases the victims of jihad as well as, from another perspective, those who seek to perpetuate it. At the same time, the title can be seen as a more serious suggestion that not only more fundamentalist Middle Eastern Muslim groups like Hezbollah or al-Qaeda, but also the proponents of the Islamic Republic, have declared a jihad upon supposed signs of Western or American "immorality" or "atheism" such as the wearing of lipstick. On another level, the title can be seen as reflecting the growing youth movement in Iran, whereby young people, especially women, have learned to lead double lives, typically wearing traditional garb and the veil in public, but even when in public, staging small but significant protests (jihads of a sort) by using loose head scarves barely covering their hair or wearing lipstick or makeup (and abandoning all regulations upon appearance in private).

Indeed, the picture on the cover of *Lipstick Jihad* expresses the public/ restrictive and private/permissive duality. It portrays a young, presumably Iranian woman dressed in traditional black garb with a head covering. However, upon further scrutiny, one can see that the head covering is more of a loose scarf or small hood pushed back on her head, exposing a significant amount of her hair. This woman, who appears to be standing outside of a building (possibly a mosque) covered with ornate art work and something written in what appears to be Farsi calligraphy, talks on a mobile phone, wearing designer sunglasses and light lipstick. This woman, the cover suggests, seems to be more representative of contemporary Iran, which, to Moaveni, has become more dualistic. This can be seen in how most Iranians, especially younger Iranians, tend to ignore or try to find ways around the religious edicts of the Islamic Regime in often clever ways, while they gravitate increasingly towards Western and American culture. Lastly, it is also important to consider the subtitle of *Lipstick Jihad*, "A Memoir of Growing Up Iranian in America and American in Iran." Through this subtitle, Moaveni suggests that she is caught between her American and Iranian identities. While in the United States, Moaveni is labeled as Iranian and thereby excluded from the American mainstream, but when she is in Iran, Moaveni is labeled American and equally separated from the Iranian mainstream. While she cannot assimilate in either country, it is precisely this state of betwixt and between that allows Moaveni to objectively and analytically detail Iran in a non-unilateral manner that Nafisi was unable or unwilling to pursue.

*Lipstick Jihad* begins with an account of Moaveni's upbringing in the United States as an Iranian-American and details the challenges facing her and her Iranian-American peers. Like many American born Iranians, Moaveni comes to think of Iran in polarizing terms. On the one hand, her parents encourage her to think of Iran as "suffused with drama and magic," and as a once beautiful and mighty country, "a place of light, poetry, and nightingale" (ix, 6). However, the elder generation tempers their romanticization of Iran with their belief (reminiscent of Nafisi), passed on to Moaveni, that Iran has been subjugated "by a dark, evil force called the Revolution" (ix). Also, while growing up in California during the 1980s, Moaveni recalls the animosity directed towards Iranians by many Americans during and after the hostage crisis, which leads her to try to hide her ethnicity from her peers (9).[9] Indeed, Moaveni describes how "for many years my overriding objective in meeting new people was to avoid mention of my Iranianness" (9).

The post–hostage crisis (post–1980) climate in the United States, in other words, does not promote tolerance, let alone acceptance of Iran or of Iranian-Americans. According to Moaveni, this general anti-Iranian sentiment becomes consciously and subconsciously internalized by those in the Iranian-American community, who seem to wish to assimilate as quickly as possible. As Moaveni explains, "Often when Iranians encountered one another in public, they pretended not to recognize each other as fellow Iranians, speaking English to one another in identical accents" (11). At the same time that many Iranian-Americans seemingly deny their ethnic identity, other Iranian-Americans latch onto their ethnic identity as a means of feeling superior. As Moaveni explains, sometimes it is Iranian-Americans themselves who aggressively compete with one another by weighing "ancestry" (11). A contributing factor is that Westerners often marginalize and falsely categorize Iranians as being part and parcel of the Islamic, Arabian Middle East.[10] Seemingly disallowed or held back from assimilating, these factors help create a bifurcation in Moaveni between her Iranian identity, which she does not want to acknowledge for the most part, and her American identity, which cannot be fully developed as others (predominantly white, native-born Americans) directly or indirectly remind her that she is not like them. She explains, "As I teenager

I felt there was nowhere to turn, and I often felt invisible, along with my two irreconcilable halves" (26). Karim and Ramideh call this feeling of Iranian exiles "a double allegiance" to both Iran and the United States (10). However, what we see with Moaveni is not so much a double allegiance as a double exclusion from the mainstream white American world and the Iranian world. For Moaveni, this leads her to the conclusion that she "never felt American at all," let alone Iranian-American or "a hyphenated American" (28).

College does little to mitigate Moaveni's feelings of alienation and exclusion as a seemingly invisible minority because, in classes, academic discussions of ethnic identity largely marginalize and exclude Iranian-Americans. Despite the push towards multiculturalism and diversity in college curriculums during the late 1990s, Moaveni finds no real space to discover her ethnic roots at UC Santa Cruz. As such, she feels culturally compelled to continue turning her "back" on her ethnicity which she finds burdensome (26). This has the consequence of driving Moaveni further from her Iranian heritage, manifested by how she purposely dates non-Iranians (196). Adding to the confusion are the demarcated American ethnic categories, which, by and large, offer no space for Iranian-Americans. When contemplating whether she should consider herself a minority, Moaveni hesitates and states, "All the Iranians I knew seemed to consider themselves European with a tan" (26). Yet, such thinking might be a relic of life in pre–Islamic Republic Iran, when Iranians generally wanted to distinguish themselves from their Arabian neighbors and when the Shah tried to make Iran more Westernized or Europeanized. While living in the United States, though, most Iranians tend to not be regarded as White or Caucasian; rather, they are grouped with the larger Arabian and Islamic Middle Eastern community. According to Moaveni, the events of September 11 further encourage this categorization, which help foster a general anti–Iranian or anti–Islamic sentiment in the United States that in turn leads to a general state of "paranoia" and a general belief in a "conspiracy" (235).[11] Still, even before September 11 changes the cultural landscape of the United States (and possibly academia as well), Moaveni describes feeling a sense of alienation as an Iranian-American college student. Specifically, she finds herself growing envious of other minorities at UCSC, like a Chicano student whose classes and Chicano/a professors encourage him to find himself and learn more about his ethnic heritage. With no Iranian, Iranian diasporic, Persian or Persian diasporic classes or professors, it is only through Moaveni's own self-guided research that she discovers and learns about Iranian and Persian history and contemporary Iranian and Persian literature. In so doing, she begins "to feel, for the first time in my life that my Iranianness was not an obstacle to my independence" (28).

As mentioned earlier, Khatami-era Iran (1997 to 2005) as depicted by

Moaveni is a much more open and liberal environment than the one portrayed by Azar Nafisi in *RLT* circa 1994 to 1997 (Rafsanjani-era). In fact, this more liberal environment allows Moaveni to be less judgmental and condemning of the Islamic Republic (which was and continues to be a frequent criticism of *RLT*). Whereas during Nafisi's stay in Iran, there was widespread censorship of literary (especially Western) texts, Moaveni explains that during Khatami's administration, not only did Iran seem "to be undergoing a literary revival," but texts were also generally subject to less censorship (27). Consequently, Moaveni describes how she "would meet friends for coffee, browse magazines and take home a few books, which suddenly had elegant ornamental covers — the complete Barnes & Noble experience" (27). While it is possible that such activities might have occurred when Nafisi was in Iran, during Moaveni's time in Iran, the Islamic Republic appears more appreciative and accepting of literature.

At the same time, Moaveni is careful not to gloss over the censorship that Nafisi depicts in *RLT.* Moaveni explains that "if a novel has made it past the censors, most Iranians assume that it has been tampered with" (27). Still, unlike Nafisi, Moaveni gives Iranians agency by explaining how they learn to bypass censorship by "searching for the Shah-era edition or the bootleg film version" (27). This is where Moaveni's status as an investigative journalist (as compared to a literary critic) helps her provide the reader with a more accurate and comprehensive depiction of Iran. As a journalist, Moaveni is more objective than Nafisi. Instead of directly condemning the Islamic Republic as Nafisi might, Moaveni more typically states objective facts such as: "In the most recent vetted edition of *Madame Bovary*, for example, Emma's adultery is omitted. Characters in Western novels who drink Champagne or whiskey find themselves uniformly sipping doogh, an Iranian yogurt soda that has never made anyone tipsy" (27). Further, not having the same emotional and intellectual connection to literature that Nafisi has, Moaveni does not necessarily regard these changes as completely devastating the novel as Nafisi might. Rather, she sees ways that censorship has turned out to be beneficial (in a presumably unintentional manner) for other Iranian writers. With fiction still so heavily censored, Moaveni explains that there has been a corresponding increase in popularity of "literary journalism" or memoirs in Iran (27).[12] Despite the recent changes, Moaveni's view of the Islamic Republic is similar to Nafisi's in that both believe that it thrives upon fear and conditioning. Even though Moaveni believes that in a "national referendum, the vast majority of Iranians — men and women alike — would have voted to abolish the mandatory veil," she also believes that Iranians have "internalized the minding gaze of the regime, and turned it back outward" (84).

As depicted in *Lipstick Jihad*, Moaveni sees two general divisions in the larger Iranian populace. One is between the growing rich, who are often the clerics, and the growing middle-to-lower economic class. The other main division in contemporary Iran is between the younger and older generation. In both cases, religion plays a role in that one side appears to be considerably less religiously dogmatic than the other side (in this case the younger generation and the middle to lower class). Moaveni believes that most Iranians have come to the conclusion that the clerics have economically devastated, if not ruined, Iran "in the name of Islam," by focusing so single mindedly on religious edicts instead of developing sound economic policies (49). Younger Iranians, according to Moaveni, have also come to resent the clerics due to their controlling, religious edicts.

However, with the exception of the 1999 student demonstrations and the 2009 post-presidential election riots, neither group has put forth a significant effort to oust the religious regime. There are several reasons for this, the most significant one being that the Iranian Regime has grown so entrenched and powerful as to render any opposition to it comparatively impotent. Another reason is many in both groups are consumed by the struggle to economically survive. Also, younger Iranians have found ways to get around the rules and the morality police. As Moaveni suggests, "They had perfected the art of inventing and synchronizing stories on the spot, how to predict what sort of policeman would take a bribe, and what sort would respond to a convincing argument" (54–55). In many ways, this public/private dichotomy can be seen as similar to a DuBoisian double consciousness, an additional level of self-awareness and caution that Moaveni doesn't seem to have as a newly transplanted American.[13] Moaveni also suggests that her American identity, as well as her lack of familiarity with Iranian culture and customs, sexualizes her and makes her appear sexually willing to Iranian men, and indeed, she describes being propositioned when she allows a man to sit beside her (71, 73–4).

While the above may suggest that Iran is less than progressive about gender and remains especially oppressive for women, still, when Moaveni is in Iran, circa 2000–1, she sees hope for a burgeoning women's movement through the general reform movement, which, according to Moaveni, "had awakened in Iranians two sentiments rare in the Middle East: hope and high expectations" (61). Yet, the successes of the reform movement are questionable as exemplified by the opening of nightclubs and the increase of nightlife in Tehran (70). Ultimately, Moaveni comes to the conclusion that Iran has become "sick," as noted by one of her chapter titles, "My Country Is Sick." One consequence of the massive repression she perceives in Iran is, ironically, an overly sexualized country. In fact, Moaveni calls Tehran "one of the most sexualized milieus I had ever encountered," and notes that "people really, really wanted to talk about sex" (70). Animosity towards the clerics and the Islamic Republic also produces a general disdain for Islam, encouraged by reformists. According to Moaveni, had the reformists had a "wish list, at the top would have been to abolish the system of rule by the supreme religious leader" (75). Not only have most Iranians come to regard the clergy as corrupt, but, according to Moaveni, "a wide swath of Iranians" have become redirected "towards the esoteric and the mystical" (95).

While living in Iran, Moaveni goes through a somewhat slow but gradual transformation that illustrates key differences between Iranians and Americans. At first she is more like a typically enthusiastic and optimistic American, believing that she can not only discover the "real Iran" and thereby discover herself, but also that in some small way she can help forge change. Moaveni is overly naive in her initial, simplistic optimism which soon peters out as her political activism and social curiosity are gradually replaced by her own personal desires and needs. As Moaveni explains, "I gave up searching for myself, and for what constituted the real Iran, whatever that meant. Instead, I dedicated my days to one task alone: decorating my apartment.... The apartment soon became my world — a substitute for the world outside, to which I seemed not to belong, unfit to understand" (112). In essence, Moaveni becomes like most younger Iranians — extremely dissatisfied with the Iranian Regime, but feeling powerless to change anything except their own personal lives. Just as a person with body dysmorphia can wreak havoc on his or her body due to displaced animosity, the internalization of animosity towards the Islamic Regime can have damaging results for younger Iranians who may become more self-aggrandizing, cold, and calculating.

Ultimately what defeats Moaveni's desire for broader social change in Iran (and defeats most younger Iranian-Americans) is her perception that the Iranian political power structure is so firmly enmeshed that it is virtually impossible to change. She especially feels this way, as a doubly scrutinized American woman, when interviewing President Khatami's Chief of Staff. The Chief of Staff tells Moaveni that secular women like Moaveni will never be able to hold positions of political power in their lifetime, that she will "never be an Iranian ambassador," and that there may not be female ambassadors in their lifetime (121). Moaveni, perhaps feeling defeated or believing the Chief of Staff is accurate, becomes disillusioned and subsequently, like the majority of young Iranians, shifts her focus even more to immediate materialistic concerns and personal matters. To Moaveni and most Iranians, the Islamic Regime's general policy of don't ask, don't tell (at least in private) when it comes to things like alcohol, drugs, and sexuality placates them. However, the Iranian Regime is careful to not create too licentious an atmosphere, lest their authority begin to wane. Consequently, as Moaveni reports, "Every few months, a drug smuggler was hanged in public, a woman murdered for dressing immodestly" (125). Moaveni also describes how people are flogged for "possessing and selling alcohol" and "the lashings sparked an open debate about the role Islamic law should play in modern society" (127). Still, this doesn't faze many young Iranians, who, according to Moaveni, retreat "into the mountains to make out with boyfriends," while "numbing" themselves "with drugs because a chemical haze was more bearable than the stark reality of everyday life" (136). The longer she is in Iran, the more Moaveni discovers a kind of underworld or underground movement of Iranians who do illegal or unsanctioned things like drinking and taking drugs while others engage in even seemingly more innocuous but still rebellious behaviors such as, for women, exercising in gyms in shorts and tank tops without wearing any kind of headdress. Moaveni also witnesses how the religious edicts of wearing loose clothing and the veil have backfired, leading to a huge increase in cosmetic surgery, "particularly of the face" (164). In that sense, the further restrictions have inadvertently Westernized Iranians and promoted more self-aggrandizing, hedonistic, and superficial (in essence, overly Westernized) behavior counter to the ideology of the anti–Western Islamic Regime.

The chaos Moaveni sees around her is especially more pronounced for her as a woman, and *Lipstick Jihad* depicts an Iran not just oppressive towards women, but generally conflicted. As Moaveni explains, "The regime fed young people such contradictory messages — women were liberated but legally inferior; women should be educated but subservient; women should have careers but stick to traditional gender roles; women should play sports but ignore their dirty physical needs" (179). In essence, the Islamic Republic sets up impossible, paradoxical standards for women, in which they are typically educated but disallowed not only from having a genuine public identity, but even from having a genuine private identity. Consequently, Moaveni concludes that "for women, searching for relationship was, if not a search for self, a search to anchor a self adrift" (179). This can be a seen as a kind of triple-consciousness, "a total shrouding of a woman's real life and desires" (186). Ultimately, Moaveni is deeply affected by this triple-consciousness, which leads her to question her own identity as well as whether American relationships, as she has experienced and considered them, should actually be considered as superior to Iranian relationships (something that Nafisi might have taken for granted in *RLT*). While Moaveni sees "American-style-love" as more "tolerant, with a more gentle approach to the individual at its core," she also

finds the Western style pursuit of love and individual satisfaction to be potentially, if not actually, selfish and self-indulgent (137). Indeed, when Moaveni
returns to New York City after her time spent in Iran, she finds New York
(and with it, the United States) to be a much more isolating and alienating
place than she did before she left. On the other hand, Moaveni comes to
believe that Iran has more of a community, despite its "dysfunction and unruli-
ness" (137). In contrast to her life in New York City, which she comes to
describe as "a disconcerted, cold void.... In Tehran, at any given hour of the
day, at least four different people could have told you where I was, what sort
of mood I was in, and what my plans were for the evening" (232).

To some extent, the turning point in *Lipstick Jihad* seems to come after
the events of September 11 not just in the United States, but also in Iran,
where Moaveni was residing at the time. Soon after 9/11, Moaveni witnesses
"a candlelight vigil for the victims of the attack on the Twin Towers at a square
in north Tehran" (223). However, she is quick to mention that "the vigil,
with its undercurrent of sympathy and openness to America, was just one
strand of the Iranian reaction. It was only in the astounding indifference
around me that the depth of accumulated resentment of American foreign
policy in this region became apparent to me" (223).[14] One of the things that
ultimately pushes Moaveni to leave Iran is a crackdown on her journalism
after former president Bush gives his "Axis of Evil" speech. For Moaveni, Iran,
even at its worst, is never a caricature of evil, but rather an extremely complex
country "alive with ideas, a place of clumsy fashion shows and sophisticated
bloggers" (244). She concludes that she "eventually found that Iran ... was
elusive, that it defied being known. Its moods changed mercurially by the
day, the scope of its horizon seemed to expand and shrink by the season, and
even its past was a contested battle" (245). Indeed, part of Moaveni's main
purpose in *Lipstick Jihad* is to illustrate these complexities in Iran and to counteract the problematic, monolithic and often false image of Iran in the Western
media and in the minds of Westerners alike.

While Moaveni's *Honeymoon in Tehran* chronologically picks up where
*Lipstick Jihad* left off, the former is much more politically engaged than the
latter, in part because it is situated during the election and the beginning of
the Ahmadinejad regime, 2005–7. During this time Moaveni witnesses and
comments upon the ascendancy, election, and administration of Mahmoud
Ahmadinejad. In these two short years (2005–7), Moaveni suggests that the
Islamic Republic reverts to a more fundamentalist, repressive environment,
rolling back many of the reforms made by the Khatami administration, and
ultimately becomes more reminiscent of mid–1990s Iran as described by Nafisi
in *RLT*. When Moaveni first returns to Iran in 2005, before Ahmadinejad's

election, she finds that restrictions on the general public have eased up considerably in the past few years. Not only is it easier to get through the airport, Moaveni finds that she "gave little thought to what I should wear" whereas when she "first visited Iran as an adult, back in 1998, I spent the entire stay in a shapeless black manteau ... that reached my knees" (16).[15] However, these new advances or liberation would not last much past the election of Ahmadinejad.

By 2005, according to Moaveni, Iran seems to have opened up as well with a burgeoning "alternative music scene" and a growing film and photography industry, both of which produce works of some social critique and are generally tolerated by the Islamic Republic (25, 46). As Moaveni explains, "It seemed as though Iranians had reached a tacit accommodation with the government over which taboos might be reconsidered" (47). Specifically, Moaveni points to how "women novelists dominated the best-seller lists with personal tales of romance and sex, topics that a few years earlier they could not even broach" (47). At the same time, Moaveni acknowledges that "literary fiction" dealing with these matters or offering strong social critique can still be and is censored or banned. In 2005 Iran, Moaveni also sees young people becoming bolder in their resistance to the edicts of the Islamic Regime. Whereas, in *Lipstick Jihad*, young people tended to confront the Iranian Regime and its officials by lying, pleading ignorance and being circumspect, Iranians now tend to confront perceived unfair or restrictive authority figures "by shouting down [the Regime's] enforcers, daring them to engage in hostile, full-fledged confrontation" (95). Indeed, it isn't a large step from verbal confrontation to physical confrontation, which begins occurring in full-force during the 2009 demonstrations. Still, in Moaveni's account, contrary to the way in which Iran is typically portrayed by Western media, Iran appears more of a Western-style capitalist country with "bribery" being not only "a fact of daily life," but also intertwined with "everyday matters" (155–6).

One could argue that it is indeed the encroachment of Western style capitalism in Khatami-era Iran that helps give rise to the ascension and election of Ahmadenijad. This Western style capitalism helps spurn a growing disparity between the rich and the poor in Iran[16] with the younger generation (the Burnt Generation) being disproportionately poor, many of them, even through their thirties, living at home longer and marrying later due to financial necessity and consequently becoming increasingly dissatisfied (27). While such changes might seem cosmetic and trivial, it is important to recognize the importance of marriage in Iranian society. For both men and women following traditional Islamic edicts, marriage allows for the expression of sexuality, and for women who are not offered as many career choices (or a career at all), marriage offers personal and financial independence (at the very least, from their parents). With the rise of pre-marital sex and cohabitation, relations "between parents and children," according to Moaveni, become "strained" (51).

The economic problems in Iran extend far beyond young people to the general populace, and are exacerbated by conflicted economic policies which appear to encourage capitalism while limiting the free market. While, according to Moaveni, there are "a handful of affluent Iranians (ranging from the comfortably well-off to the obscenely wealthy)," the so-called middle-class, people like "college professors, engineers, graphic designers," are hardly middle-class from an American perspective. Rather, they lead a meager, almost hand-to-mouth existence, earning "only enough to cover expenses like rent and school tuition" (50).[17] In fact, it is the rather bleak and dire economic environment that, according to Moaveni, helps catapult Mahmoud Ahmadinejad to the presidency in 2005. Due to general political apathy and an overwhelming feeling of powerlessness, especially among young people who tend to be more concerned with their immediate financial or personal issues, many Iranians, including Moaveni herself, choose not to vote in the presidential election. As Moaveni explains, "By now, many Iranians had come to view elections as a ceremonial act, an empty practice that lent a veneer of democratic consent to the mullahs' absolutism. By boycotting the race altogether, many believed, Iranians could reject the entire system of Islamic rule" (14). This rather flawed logic or rather, this rationalization, for not participating in the political process[18] helps led to Ahmadinejad's victory, buttressed by most of Iran's religious leaders who eventually throw their support his way during the run-off election (54–5). At the same time, Moaveni uncovers Ahmadinejad's grass-roots appeal.[19] Ultimately, she credits Ahmadinejad for touching an emotional nerve in Iranian people; she writes, "I can't count the dinner parties I attended where otherwise sensible individuals breathlessly said things like, 'He says what is in my heart'" (108). In fact, when Ahmadinejad is elected,[20] it is largely viewed as "progress," and as Moaveni details, "For the first time in as long as I can remember, the somber sense of living in an irretrievably failed society lifted, and the future seemed specked with, of all things, opportunity" (195).

The "opportunity" Moaveni means is largely economical. However, not only does Iran's economy not improve during the Ahmadinejad administration, it worsens with "the prices of basic commodities from cigarettes to tomatoes to butter" rising "20 percent" (236). For Moaveni, though, the ultimate turning point in the Ahmadinejad administration comes in 2005 after "the Bush administration had launched a $75 million program tacitly aimed at changing the Iranian regime" (242). As she suggests, "Although its planners did not discuss the program in such explicit language, preferring vague terms such as 'advancement of democracy,' the end of the Islamic Regime (or its transformation into a moderate, normal state, which was pretty much the same thing) was quite clearly their goal" (242).[21] For Moaveni, this "democracy fund" was clearly "intended to foster resistance to the government" (242). As we will see in a subsequent chapter on Iranian prison narratives, the American "advancement of democracy" program increasingly worsened Iran-U.S. relations and helped lead to the imprisonment of Iranians and diasporic Iranians alike.

Even though the extent to which the goal of the American program was actual regime change is debatable, it is hard to deny that the Islamic Regime believed, at the very least, that the U.S. strongly desired and encouraged regime change in Iran. Not only did the policy end up encouraging the Islamic Regime to become increasingly skeptical of the intentions of the United States government, many Iranians also grew suspicious of the United States. As Moaveni explains, anti–American sentiment subsequently rose in Iran due to a growing belief that the United States had largely failed in Afghanistan and Iraq as well as a growing concern that the United States had developed too prominent and aggressive a presence in the Middle East (106). In turn, this led to a more heightened response on the Islamic Regime's part, which now set "out to systematically crush any tie, however legitimate, unthreatening, or frail, between Iranians and even its own officials," and also "began arresting scholars on trumped-up charges of plotting a 'velvet revolution,' rounding up activists for allegedly receiving money from abroad, and labeling writers (and even one sculptor) as subversive" (243). While she doesn't directly state it, Moaveni indirectly places at least part of the blame for the increased militancy of the Ahmadinejad administration on the United States.[22]

Still, surprisingly enough, in the bleak, Ahmadinejad-era environment, Moaveni meets, falls in love with, marries, and has a child with an Iranian man, Arash. This domestic narrative comprises the backbone of *Honeymoon in Tehran*. As mentioned earlier, marriages are extremely important occasions in Iranian society and culture. Consequently, Moaveni's exploration of her engagement, pregnancy, and subsequent marriage reveal much of importance about contemporary Iran. However, it is not Moaveni's intention to use her engagement and marriage to debunk the Iranian Regime as a wholly sexist and oppressive country. After all, when Moaveni decides to move in with Arash before they are married, it is Moaveni's parents, now living in the United States, who are more concerned for Moaveni's well-being than Moaveni herself, who knows ways (or believes she know ways) around the Regime's dictates

(76). Still, Moaveni has good reason to be concerned when she becomes pregnant before she is married, as the supposed punishment for premarital sex in the Islamic Republic is "lashings and a year of banishment" (126). While the Regime rarely ever enforces such punishments, they do so on rare occasions in order to demonstrate the power they hold and to inspire fear and submission.[23]

While it would seem that marriage might be freeing for women in Iran,[24] reminiscent of Marjane Satrapi's experiences ten years earlier, Moaveni reveals ingrained sexism in the marriage process in Iran. For instance, when she applies to get married, Moaveni discovers that, despite being twenty-nine years old, she needs her father's permission, whereas her husband does not (134). Also, the discrepancy between men and women can clearly be seen in the "generic" Iranian marriage contract, which "leaves space for a husband to accord his wife certain privileges which the law enabled Iranian women to secure from their husbands: typically the right to divorce under particular terms, to travel out of the country alone, to acquire a passport" (152–3). Even still, under this contract, Moaveni can only divorce Arash under certain circumstances. When Moaveni prepares to give birth in an Iranian hospital, she also discovers that hospitals traditionally bar husbands from the delivery room because they believe (or the Islamic Regime believes) that they aren't "prepared" to handle the experience of labor (225). Again, this is evidence of sexism as well as of persistent gender stereotypes. It is only through buying a more expensive delivery room at the hospital and having a more liberal, female doctor that Moaveni is able to smuggle Arash in.

All of these events ultimately push Moaveni to the same decision that Nafisi made in *RLT* and Satrapi made in *Persepolis 2*: to leave Iran. Further, as Moaveni learns that an increasing number of journalists are being jailed, she grows understandably concerned and fearful (308). The major breaking point, though, comes from a seemingly minor incident, but one that represents for Moaveni all that she has grown to despise about the Islamic Regime: how Iranian citizens are ultimately powerless (at least in public and subject to the potential and actual vindictive caprice of others). While on vacation with Arash and their baby, Moaveni is accosted and chastised by a "teenage enforcer" for not dressing properly. As Moaveni explains, "It was one thing having our security compromised by my work, which was deemed sensitive in the state's paranoid view. It was another thing entirely to come so close to arrest as an ordinary citizen, because a teenage enforcer took issue with the fabric of my headscarf" (312). For Moaveni, this illustrates how much she is and will continue to be subject to the whim of the local authorities (even teenaged "authorities"), who can chastise and potentially arrest her for the smallest of reasons.

Unlike Nafisi, though, Moaveni doesn't end her memoir with her leaving Iran for the promised shores of the West. While Moaveni and her family go to England, Moaveni briefly describes life in England in order to illustrate that Muslims in the West are not necessarily afforded a better, more inclusive life there. Instead, Moaveni and her husband notice a kind of ethnic segregation in London as they live in an area that they call "Little Riyadh," which Moaveni describes as "altogether more like a dour Muslim village than the charming London quarter I expected" (321–22). Even though the area is multiethnic, "the neighborhood's sizeable Muslim community seemed to exist in a separate sphere — it was as though everyone else came from a distinct country but they were from a besieged and borderless place called Islam" (322). In this seemingly segregated, monocultural environment, some Muslims become even more radical in their beliefs as a way to maintain their religious and cultural identity. While in England, Moaveni also witnesses racism directed towards Muslims, which makes her feel a greater solidarity with other Muslims, but it also creates a sense of further alienation among members of the Muslim community (324–5).

Ironically, while in London, in this Middle Eastern community, Moaveni experiences a kind of intercommunity sexism that she did not even experience in Iran, such as a grocer who won't take money from Moaveni's hand because he is (or at least believes himself to be) an ultra-devout Muslim who cannot touch women that are not part of his family (322). As Moaveni explains, "I found the Muslim presence to be so assertive that I once even forgot I was in England altogether" (323). For Moaveni, one of the culprits is the chimera of multiculturalism itself, which, in her view, drives England to become too accepting of "antediluvian Islam rather than push the faith into a healthy acceptance of modernity" (324).

Ultimately, Moaveni leaves the reader with a sense that neither the West nor the Islamic Republic views the other in a neutral or fair way. She concludes *Honeymoon in Tehran* with a trip back to Iran in April 2008.[25] Despite Ahmadinejad's anti–Western rhetoric, Moaveni finds that Iran has become even more capitalistic than it was before she left.[26] While the Western ideology of equality and multiculturalism appears more like a chimera, Iran's religious ideology and dictates also seem to mask a deeper political corruption and a rather schizophrenic capitalistic market system. In essence, as Moaveni demonstrates, the West is much more like Iran in its lack of ethnic and religious acceptance and integration, while Iran is much more like the West in its adoption (albeit not directly) of free-market capitalism. However, both countries publicly emphasize their differences from one another as a way to express their own superiority and often as a way to demonize the other.

While Moaveni's memoirs provide an important counterpart to Nafisi's as a more objective and balanced account of both the West and Iran, there is another form of more popularized Iranian memoir, which safely sanitizes Iran for popular consumption. Indeed, if there is an Iranian or diasporic Iranian memoir writer who might be second to Nafisi in terms of commercial success, it would probably be Firoozeh Dumas, the author of the commercially successful *Funny in Farsi* (2003) and *Laughing Without an Accent* (2008).[27]

*Funny in Farsi* has also been critically successful as well; it was a "finalist for the PEN/USA award in 2004," while Dumas herself "was also a finalist for the prestigious Thurber Prize for American Humor, the first Middle Eastern woman ever to receive this honor" ("About Firoozeh Dumas," par. 2). Whereas *Reading Lolita in Tehran* experienced a critical backlash, for the most part, Dumas has received strong critical praise for her writings (more so for *Funny in Farsi* than *Laughing Without an Accent*). While, unlike Nafisi, Dumas mainly focuses on the United States and Iranian immigrants, her work, like Nafisi's, could also be seen as championing the West or the United States over Iran. Dumas may not be as overly critical of the Islamic Regime, but her memoirs make it clear that she views the United States as morally, ethically, and even culturally superior to the Islamic Republic. Although Dumas may be successful in humanizing Iranians, she also simplifies them as well and glosses over more serious issues of social and ethnic stratification, discrimination, and racism. In short, Dumas's memoirs are easily digestible works that help solidify the Western reader's belief that Western culture is superior, while providing bland reassurance that Iranians are basically the same as everyone else.

One of the reasons for the success of *Funny in Farsi* may indeed be the way Dumas presents the United States in such flattering and idealistic ways, as a welcoming place for immigrants and as a place to liberate previously oppressed persons like Dumas's family. For instance, reviewers Susan Woodcock and Jackie Gropman praise *Funny in Farsi* for illustrating "the kindness of people and her [Dumas's] father's absolute love of this country" (172). While reviewers tend to concur that *Funny in Farsi* is "light," or an "easy read," they also suggest that there is a deeper purpose to Dumas's tone and choice of content (Woodcock and Gropman; Toosi; "Funny in Farsi"). Namely, as Woodcock and Gropman argue, "her humor allows natives and nonnatives alike to look at America with new insight" (173). Along similar lines, Kristine Huntley, writing for *Booklist*, believes that "the comedy of her family's misadventures" balances "the more serious prejudices they face" (1731). For critics and for Dumas herself, this light tone or humor allows readers to relate to Dumas's family and to understand and appreciate the universality of humanity. To some extent, this is a noble goal, but it is also overly idealistic and ultimately counter-productive at the same time, contributing to the general public perception that the United States is egalitarian and what minor problems Iranian-Americans (or other ethnic minority group) may have can either be laughed away or offset by the immigrant's devoted thanks at being allowed to live in this "great" democratic country. However, to date, no reviewer appears to have made this criticism of Dumas, perhaps because in many ways she is the perfect illustration of the literary American Dream at work. Indeed, this extends to Dumas's actual composition of *Funny in Farsi*. Reminiscent of J.K. Rowling, in 2001, Dumas, "with no prior writing experience ... decided to write her stories as a gift for her children" ("About Firoozeh Dumas," par. 2). It may not be a coincidence that Dumas began writing in 2001. While she has not directly suggested this in an interview,[28] she may have wanted to try to neutralize the hostility expressed towards Muslim Middle Eastern Americans that ran rampant in the weeks after 9/11.[29]

One of the most important developments involved with *Funny in Farsi* is how, more than any other work explored in this study (with the possible exception of *Reading Lolita in Tehran*), it has become a text so frequently used by educators and community leaders alike.[30] In that, both Dumas herself as well as *Funny in Farsi* alike have been used not only to purportedly help a large swath of Westerners/Americans better understand Iran and Iranians, but also to help them better understand the (Middle Eastern) immigrant experience. Augmenting the book's use is the fact that Dumas herself frequently lectures across the country. In these visits, according to her website, Dumas reminds "us that our commonalities far outweigh our differences," and she states that she does "so with humor" ("About Firoozeh Dumas," par. 5).[31] In essence, Dumas holds up the quintessential American ideal of racial egalitarianism and the mythology of the melting pot.

However, in so doing, Dumas, albeit inadvertently, helps maintain the implicit and subtle but still powerful racial and ethnic hierarchy in the United States. In fact, her publisher, Random House, attempted to market *Funny in Farsi* to as broad an audience as possible, certainly beyond an Iranian or even an Ethnic Studies audience. Instead, Julie Cooper, writing for Random House, suggests, "Her poignant descriptions of what it feels like to be a stranger in a strange land will resonate with anyone who has ever experienced social alienation at any stage of life. In her unflinching examination into the essence of the Iranian immigrant experience, Dumas exposes America as it has never before been seen" (par. 2). It is hard to see how Dumas could expose America as it has never been seen as her characterizations of the United States tend to be conventional and certainly not threatening to even extremely conservative readers who might be resistant to believing that certain minority groups experience anything worse in the contemporary United States than mainstream (white) Americans do. At the same time, while Random House's enticement may indeed broaden the audience base for *Funny in Farsi*, it also lessens any social importance the text could have for ethnic minorities or for Iranian-Americans. In essence, it encourages non-minority readers to believe that they too can experience what it is like to be a minority and that their own personal feelings of alienation and exclusion are no different from that of a historically oppressed, or in this case, a more recently targeted ethnic minority group.

While finding common ground and emphasizing the universal nature of humanity are admirable goals, in this case, they come at a cost of glossing over more serious issues of institutional discrimination and favoritism. Were *Funny in Farsi* only treated as a memoir, it would not be a significant as if it were (as it is) treated as a socio-historical text. Indeed, according to Random House:

> Given its expansive examination of everyday life and culture in Iran and America, *Funny in Farsi* would also be an ideal text for students of social studies and world cultures. Its depiction of life in the 1970s, and its focus on the political crises that developed between Iran and the United States at that time, would make it a useful text for courses in American and Middle Eastern history, and for classes that study the immigrant experience [Cooper, par. 5].

Dumas herself does little to nothing to dispel Random House's depiction of *Funny in Farsi*. In fact, Dumas suggests that she has been able to capture both diasporic Iranians and the mainstream audience.[32] She also corroborates Random House's description of *Funny in Farsi* by calling it "a universal tale of being an outsider," with the only real prerequisite being that one has gone through "adolescence" ("Funny in Farsi — Author Interview," par. 16). Also, when Dumas describes how many "teachers" tell her that "even their students who normally do not read loved reading *Funny in Farsi*," it is hard to not want to praise *Funny in Farsi* ("Funny in Farsi — Author Interview," par. 16). Indeed, Dumas makes a compelling point: "One of the biggest problems I have faced as an Iranian in America is that no one knows much about Iran except what is on the evening news. Politics has grossly overshadowed humanity in the Middle East and I wanted to write a book that would shine the light on humanity" ("Funny in Farsi — Author Interview," par. 22). In that sense, *Funny in Farsi* could be seen as working to counteract the imbalance of coverage of normal, everyday Iranians and diasporic Iranians.

At the same time, *Funny in Farsi* is largely one-sided and one-dimensional. In her quest to be a voice of equality and universal humanity, Dumas becomes apolitical, glosses over historical issues as well as social and ethnic stratification, and leads the reader to an overly idealistic conclusion that all humans are basically the same and that we all can not only get along but achieve equity if only we try and recognize each other's humanity. With humor, this compelling idea becomes almost irresistible to a reader who wants easy solutions to big problems or who wants confirmation of (either consciously or subconsciously) the moral supremacy and ideology of the United States. Unfortunately, this vision is not realistic. In an interview, Dumas describes how she received e-mails from readers which have "a common theme: "Your family is just like my family!" followed by "But 'I'm Mexican,' 'Chinese' or 'third generation American from Minnesota'" ("A Spoonful of Humor," par. 1). As a result of these e-mails, Dumas concludes, "I was thrilled to see that the theme of my book, shared humanity, was reaching such a diverse audience" ("A Spoonful of Humor," par. 1). Yet this common theme elides social and ethnic stratification. The presumably white, third generation American from Minnesota, while connecting with *Funny in Farsi* on some level, may also come to the conclusion that the lives of Iranian-Americans or any other ethnic minority are no more challenging or institutionally limited than the lives of mainstream white Americans. Not only is this not true, Dumas's stories prove otherwise, even though Dumas does not highlight this. It is tempting to want to believe in Dumas's ideal that "everyone has a story and everyone's story counts" (Dumas, "A Spoonful of Humor," par. 7). However, some stories count more than others. Stories or memoirs that are generally optimistic and non-critical like Dumas's tend to resonate more with the American public than other stories.

Still, one of the more surprising elements involved in *Funny in Farsi* is that, in 2006, it was "translated into Persian," and subsequently published in Iran (Benson E1). Further, "despite cuts from Iranian state censors (the chapter about ham was deleted, for example), it has gained a popular audience in that country, where it won a readers' choice award ... from a Tehran magazine for young adults called Forty Lights" (Benson E1). Dumas accepted these rather deep cuts made to *Funny in Farsi* so that it would be published in Iran, as there would have been no other legal way to get it published otherwise. At the beginning of her follow-up to *Funny in Farsi*, *Laughing Without an Accent*, Dumas describes the process of getting *Funny in Farsi* published in Iran. By and large, Dumas accepted the censor's requested wide and sweeping changes, including removing an entire chapter, "The Ham Amendment." As Dumas explains, "In that chapter, which I considered the soul of my book, I explained my father's philosophy that it does not matter what we eat or whether we are Muslim, Christian, or Jewish; it's how we treat our fellow man that counts.

The censor did not agree" (*Laughing Without an Accent* 9). In fact, Dumas's father makes a not so subtle dig at the censor, suggesting (perhaps accurately so) that "it was probably because the censor did not believe in our shared humanity, at least not with the Jews" (9). Still, Dumas accepts these changes, even though she feels the deleted portions are the "soul" of the book. She thereby privileges getting published over the content of the book. Perhaps because the content was watered down and the book doesn't really contain overt criticism of the Islamic Republic, when it was published in Iran, "it became an instant bestseller" (10).[33] Yet, *Funny in Farsi* creates a one-dimensional portrait of the United States, one that makes the country seem both enticing and superficial at the same time.

Indeed, we can see this at the very beginning of *Funny in Farsi*. As one critic argues, "nothing mars" Dumas's father's "love for his adopted country" ("Funny in Farsi" 654). Indeed, Dumas's father represents the good immigrant, or in this case, an Iranian-American who extols the virtues of the United States over his home country. As Dumas explains, her father firmly believes in the American Dream and that "America was a place where anyone, no matter how humble his background, could become an important person" (4). In essence, for Dumas's father, the United States is "the Promised Land," and it is in this country that Dumas (who moved to the United States when she was seven years old) learns to be a good American consumer. Indeed, for Dumas the major appeal of the United States is that there she "could buy more outfits for Barbie" (4). Again, keeping with Dumas's desire to not seem ungrateful or embittered, she does not mention that she presumably later found a painful discrepancy between how she perceives herself as an ethnic other in contrast to the presumably white and blonde Barbie. Careful as she is to rarely bring ethnicity up in her narrative, Dumas also mentions how she is embarrassed when her mother comes to her school to drop her off, but Dumas does not describe herself as being embarrassed due to their ethnicity or to her mother's difficulty speaking and understanding English. While it is conceivable that these things did not bother Dumas as a child, the more likely explanation is that Dumas chose not to mention it in *Funny in Farsi*, or that she repressed her own presumably conflicted feelings towards being Iranian-American. It may also be a calculated move on Dumas's part to de-emphasize ethnicity in order to build on her overarching theme of the universal connections we have as human beings which, she believes, largely transcend ethnicity.

Along similar lines, Dumas expresses no regret, sadness, or anger during her recollection of her grade school experiences, even when she was immediately marked and alienated by her teacher who, upon introducing Dumas to the class, wrote her [Dumas's] name on the board and spells out I-R-A-N underneath it (4–5). It is hard to believe that a child would have no real response to being immediately singled out as an ethnic other in front of the class. In all fairness, though, Dumas may gently rebuke her teacher who, upon introducing Dumas and her mother to the class, appears to debase Dumas's mother for not being able to find Iran on a class map (7). Still, Dumas's criticism of her teacher is mild at best (if it exists at all). Rather, Dumas portrays the entire situation as more lightly comic than potentially devastating as it might be to other children who are outed and implicitly marked or mocked as an ethnic other. While Dumas may be successful in drawing more readers in with this approach and helping them relate to the story, it does come at a cost of de-emphasizing the importance of how teachers can reinforce ethnic difference and consciously or unconsciously alienate students from others in the class. None of this, however, is enough to shake Dumas's (and her family's) seemingly unshakable belief in the intrinsic good nature of Americans, as noted by how Dumas and her mother get help from strangers after they have difficulty remembering where they live (soon after they moved to the United States). Dumas even concludes this chapter with, "After spending an entire day in America, surrounded by Americans, I realized that my father's description of America had been correct. The bathrooms were clean and the people were very, very kind" (7).

Unlike Nafisi, who did not hesitate to critique what she perceived as a patriarchal and sexist Islamic Regime as well as a largely patriarchal and sexist Iranian culture, Dumas offers no criticism of unequal gender relations, even when it comes to her own family. While it's possible that Dumas might be a feminist at heart who chooses not to promote her ideas to the general reading public for fear of losing a broad audience, it is more likely that she is not a feminist, and indeed, this might make her as well as *Funny in Farsi* more appealing to the general reading public. When Dumas writes about how her father met and decided to propose to her mother, she says the most important reason was "my mother fit my father's physical requirements for a wife" (5). Dumas states this matter-of-factly with no criticism or suggestion that her father should have chosen a partner on the basis of personality, character, or compatibility. As it turns out, her father, according to Dumas's account, merely gives his sister a picture of a woman he finds attractive and asks her "to find someone who resembled her" (5). That Dumas's aunt ends up doing this for Dumas's father is further evidence of Iran's patriarchal culture (in this case, pre–Revolutionary Iran). There are even prejudicial, if not racist, overtures to Dumas's father's search for a wife. In fact, Dumas goes on to explain, "Like most Iranians, my father preferred a fair-skinned woman with straight, light-colored hair" (5). When Dumas tells the reader that her mother ended up marrying her father when her mother was only seventeen, and that she "officially gave up her dreams, married my father, and had a child by the end of the year," there is no indication that Dumas feels that her mother had at all been oppressed or that she was part and parcel of what she inadvertently portrays as a rather sexist culture and country (5).

In a way, it makes sense that Dumas not take a critical tone here. For, after all, in a book entitled *Funny in Farsi*, one can surmise that there will not be much, if any, hard-hitting (or even soft-hitting) cultural and social analysis. Still, it is this light tone that may appeal not only to mainstream American readers who often bristle at the mere mention of the word "feminism," but also to conventional Iranian readers (and censors) who might not see anything problematic with Dumas's father's approach. In either or both cases, this is a good example of how, at least when it comes to gender issues, the mainstream American public and the mainstream Iranian public are not that dissimilar. In fact, Dumas appears to defend this seemingly indifferent manner of presenting unequal gender relations and sexism in Iran. Specifically, she argues, "Marriage, in my culture, has nothing to do with romance. It's a matter of logic. If Mr. and Mrs. Ahmadi like Mr. and Mrs. Nejati, then their children should get married. On the other hand if the parents don't like each other, but the children do, well, this is where sad poetry comes from" (24). Yet, there is nothing inherently logical about parents determining who their children marry, and it is not the case that this generally happens in Iran, especially not in contemporary Iran as described by Azadeh Moaveni or even Shahriar Mandanipour (whose novel *Censoring an Iranian Love Story* I will explore in a subsequent chapter). While Dumas may make a valid point in that the "success rate" of these more arranged marriages is "probably no worse" than Western style marriages determined by the partners themselves, she does not consider that it is more difficult to divorce in Iran, and there is a greater stigma for divorce in Iran that in the West (in addition, as Marjane Satrapi and Azadeh Moaveni point out, women do not have as much rights in marriage and divorce as men do) (24). Also Dumas does not consider that success in marriage may not be determined by whether a couple stays married, but by the content of their marriage.

For Dumas, the process of assimilating does not seem especially emotionally taxing for immigrants, nor does Dumas suggest that she and her family have at all been belittled by their attempt to acculturate. Rather, to Dumas, the American Dream is less of a dream and more of a reality for immigrants. Indeed, in order to learn English, Dumas's mother does not appear to have to take classes or work that hard. Instead, Dumas tells us that her mother learns English by watching game shows like *The Price Is Right* (and by using Dumas herself as a translator). When cultural and language misunderstandings occur, such as when Dumas and her mother go to a hardware store and ask to buy some "elbow grease" after being told that they would need to use elbow grease in order to clean something, Dumas presents the laughing employees as not mocking them (12). Rather, the older narrating Dumas presents herself as laughing with the employees at this misunderstanding. If there is any evidence that Dumas believes that the process of assimilation for diasporic Iranians (or immigrants in general) is challenging, it is when she tells us, "I no longer encourage my parents to learn English. I've given up" (12). While she never directly states it, it is possible that Dumas has come to this resigned position because of the difficulties that she and her parents have faced while trying to assimilate. If so, this is a portion of Dumas's memoir that she does not really focus upon in *Funny in Farsi*. Still, Dumas suggests that even if one is not able to assimilate completely, there are ways to join existing communities that help immigrants lead something close to their old lives in the United States. Towards that end, Dumas describes herself as being "grateful for the wave of immigration that has brought Iranian television, newspapers, and supermarkets to America" (12). Indeed, these opportunities and this community are especially available where Dumas grew up and where her parents continue to live, Southern California, which has the largest population of Iranian expatriates in the United States.

Perhaps another factor that helped *Funny in Farsi* get past the censors in Iran and also potentially helped reinforce the image of the United States as largely materialistic and superficial is Dumas's portrayal of both her family's pursuit of wealth and their allied pursuit of entertainment. In this manner, Dumas is able to connect to at least three distinct audiences simultaneously. First, her account resonates with American readers who believe in the American Dream and who prize material objects and entertainment. Secondly, her account resonates with Iranian clerics who may view the United States as amoral and superficial for the same reasons. Lastly, her account resonates with the general Iranian populace who may be enticed by the possibility of some measure of wealth and greater entertainment either in Iran or as Iranian-American expatriates. Towards these ends, Dumas describes her father as desirous of wealth.[34] In the United States, Dumas's family does have an opportunity to become wealthy when her father participates on the game show *Bowling for Dollars*. While her father does not perform well during the taping, the mere fact that he had this opportunity suggests, especially to readers not familiar with the United States, that wealth may be relatively accessible if only they immigrate to the United States. Furthermore, even though Dumas's father does not win, in a sense, he has already won since he has a good job and he is able to more than sufficiently support his family. Presumably because of this, Dumas portrays her father's loss during *Bowling for Dollars* as an amusing anecdote rather than a devastating experience.

Besides, according to Dumas's account, there is simply so much more to do of great enjoyment in the United States, and more specifically where they live in Southern California. Indeed, Dumas describes how in their first two years in California, she and her family make pilgrimages to amusement parks and fairs like Knott's Berry Farm, Marine World, the Date Festival, and the Garlic Festival. As further evidence that they believe in the idea and ideology of the United States (as opposed to the actual reality), Dumas and her family are particularly enamored by one of the quintessential idealistic representations of the United States: Disneyland.[35] Another place they gravitate towards is the ultimate place to pursue the American Dream: Las Vegas. Dumas describes Las Vegas as her "father's favorite spot on Planet Earth" (50). Even though he doesn't frequently win there (like most), Dumas does not portray him as being cheated, nor does Dumas's father feel this way as he believes he has been compensated in turn by the plentiful food at the cheap buffets. In essence, without realizing it, Dumas's family become the epitome of Vegas suckers.

At the same time, it is certainly conceivable that Dumas and her family had a different experience than contemporary Iranian immigrants since they first settled in the United States before the Iranian Revolution and subsequent hostage standoff of 1979–80. In fact, Dumas writes, "I was lucky to have come to America years before the political upheaval in Iran" (31). Prior to 1979, Dumas suggests that "the Americans we encountered were kind and curious, unafraid to ask questions and willing to listen" to the point that she felt like she was being "interviewed nonstop by children and adults alike" (31). What Dumas largely leaves out of *Funny in Farsi* is the animosity directed towards Iranian-Americans in the period after the Iranian Revolution. This may be because, even before the Iranian Revolution, Dumas felt that she needed "to be a worthy representative of my homeland" (33). In essence, Dumas assumes the role of a diplomat in her reluctance to critique the United States or Iran, but in doing so, she ends up glossing over more serious issues.

Even after the Iranian Revolution, when Dumas experiences a certain measure of prejudice, if not racism, from her peers, she chooses to not react. For instance, when she is asked by peers if she has camels, Dumas does not respond with any real measure of anger, but rather with sarcasm. While it may be true that Dumas's use of humor helps to defuse the situation more than if she responded with anger, her sarcasm is also a kind of capitulation to the treatment of ethnic minorities by the American mainstream.[36] While Dumas does acknowledge that Iranian immigrants who came to the United

States after the Iranian Revolution had a much more difficult time adjusting and being accepted than Dumas's family did, Dumas and her family choose to focus on the United States they experienced prior to the Iranian Revolution.[37] To a large extent then, the United States that Dumas and her family have chosen to accept as the real United States is the one they experienced before the Iranian Revolution as opposed to the more discriminatory United States they witnessed after the Iranian Revolution. However, a more realistic and contemporary account would address the latter more than the former. Indeed, leading non–Iranian readers to the conclusion that the United States is, at heart, a racially egalitarian country could further draw these readers into the illusion of a racial utopia.

When Dumas appears to be treated differently because of her ethnic appearance, she doesn't seem fazed by it, nor does she perceive it as being anything remotely prejudicial, when it very well might be so. Instead, Dumas states more matter-of-factly, "In America, I have an 'ethnic' face, a certain immigrant look that says, 'I'm not Scandinavian'" (37). Dumas seems unaware of or unwilling to acknowledge how minority groups can be stereotyped by the (white) mainstream. For instance, she mentions that when she was growing up in Southern California, she and her family were often mistaken for being Hispanic. Dumas doesn't realize the prejudice inherent in the comments made to her when others presume that she and her family are Hispanic, such as, "Could you please tell Lupe that she doesn't have to clean our house next week, since we're going to be on vacation?" (38). The implicit stereotype here is that most people of Hispanic descent engage in manual labor like cleaning houses. In a way, being classified as Hispanic might be preferable to Dumas than if she reveals her true ethnicity, as, post–1979, Americans generally were less welcoming to Iranian-Americans than Hispanic Americans.

Dumas, herself, wants to physically assimilate to the racial mainstream and appear more Caucasian, if not Nordic. As she explains, "People see me and think of hostages. This is why, in my next life, I am applying to come back as a Swede. I assume that as a Swede, I will be a leggy blonde. Should God get things confused and send me back as a Swede trapped in the body of a Middle Eastern woman, I'll just pretend to be French" (41). While she presents the above in a comic manner, the mere fact that she mentions it at all suggests there is an element of truth to it. In fact, Dumas does take on a mainstream (white) American identity by choosing and using an American name, Julie. While Dumas suggests that she does so because her real first name is difficult for most Americans to pronounce, it is probably at least partially due to her desire to whitewash her ethnic identity and to thereby more fully assimilate to the United States. Dumas uses her original name when she attends college, but afterwards reverts to "Julie" because she finds it difficult to get a job interview when she puts Firoozeh on her resume and cover letter (65). While it could be a coincidence, Dumas does get a flurry of interest after she uses the name "Julie." However, Dumas does not take this as an opportunity to demonstrate how ethnic minorities, and specifically Muslim Middle Eastern Americans, can be discriminated against in the United States. Rather, she objectively states what occurs with no real commentary, let alone criticism.

In many ways, Dumas continues to be even more neutral and harmless in her follow-up to *Funny in Farsi, Laughing Without an Accent.* The title alone, which, unlike *Funny in Farsi,* is largely divorced of ethnic implications, suggests that Dumas has moved more towards embracing a kind of post-ethnicity she perceives to be possible in the United States. It is through humor, ultimately, that Dumas feels that people can connect on deeper, universal levels. Hence, the title suggests that when we laugh, we transcend ethnicity and nationality. While this may be true, Dumas doesn't seem to want to recognize that there is little to no way to hide ethnicity and nationality (let alone accents) when we converse with one another.

By sacrificing the exploration of deeper concepts through her desire to find common ground, *Laughing Without an Accent* appears a much more strained work than *Funny in Farsi.* Whereas *Funny in Farsi* received a considerable amount of critical attention, there were very few book reviews of *Laughing Without an Accent,* and those reviews tended to be mixed. For instance, *Kirkus Reviews* describes several of the chapters as "nothing more than five-page campfire stories" and that Dumas "isn't about teaching," but rather "she's about entertaining the masses" ("Laughing Without an Accent," 228). This review ultimately concludes that *Laughing Without an Accent* "offers a few laughs, but little else" (228). While this might seem like an especially strong criticism, Dumas herself might not feel that this summation of her work completely debases it. In *Laughing Without an Accent,* she describes how, in *Funny in Farsi* (and presumably in *Laughing Without an Accent* as well), she was very careful "not to cross the line into anything embarrassing or insulting. My goal was to have the subjects of my story laugh with me, not cringe and want to move to Switzerland under assumed names" (4). Even when she describes the way Iranian officials censored *Funny in Farsi,* in *Laughing Without an Accent* she presents it as more amusing than a violation of her artistic freedom, and hence she agrees to the changes so that the book can published in Iran.

As with *Funny in Farsi, Laughing Without an Accent* continues to extol American culture and customs over Iranian culture and customs. What small criticisms Dumas may have had about the United States seem muted and mild. For instance, while on the one hand, Dumas portrays the United States, in particular its educational system, as more nurturing than its counterpart in Iran, she also gently and implicitly suggests that the American educational system is somewhat lackadaisical. As Dumas explains: "When I met my first teacher in America, Mrs. Sandberg, I was so confused. She was so nice. Her classroom was unlike anything I had ever seen — colorful posters on the walls, children's artwork hanging from the ceiling; it was like a party. Mrs. Sandberg never yelled, assigned homework, or even lost her temper, but she knew how to control the classroom" (42). The fact that Dumas describes this teacher as never assigning homework is troubling, yet in some ways, her approach works. At the same time, careful not to debase either side, Dumas also praises the stern treatment by teachers during pre–Revolutionary Iran (45). In so doing, she cleverly caters to both sides without really making a significant point.

Significantly, Dumas also does not address the nature of education in post–Revolutionary Iran. While this may be attributed to how she may have no direct knowledge of life in post–Revolutionary Iran, the more likely reason is that Dumas does not want to investigate the contemporary Iranian education system because doing so opens up the book to criticism from either American or Iranian readers. In fact, the only way she ends up addressing the educational system in Iran is through drawing a parallel in how both nations tend to cater too much to building up the self-confidence of children, as opposed to really teaching them. As Dumas explains, "Good old Iranian or American qualities such as aiming high and striving despite difficulties have been replaced with everyone receiving a trophy for participating" (52).

For each point of praise or criticism Dumas makes about either the United States or the Islamic Republic, she balances it out with an equivalent comment about the other country. Whereas *Funny in Farsi* was more of an open love letter to the United States, *Laughing Without an Accent* seems more intent on retaining a more neutral tone, and in doing so, retains the possibility of crossing over into Iran (and being published there). For instance, Dumas explains that she is "grateful" that her "twelve-year-old daughter does not have to wear an overcoat and a *hijab*," as she would in the Islamic Republic, whereas in the United States, "she can wear whatever she wants and dream of being whatever she wants to be" (200). At the same time, Dumas follows this clear praise of the United States with several pages critiquing how the American media tends to sexualize women, especially in music videos, and how female pre-teens and teenagers have been presented with American "role models" who seem to be not much more than overly sexualized automatons. In contrast, Dumas praises Iranian women who must submit to the seemingly oppressive dictates of the Islamic Regime and who are also "strong and smart, defying the strict rules set by the totalitarian government every chance they get" (204).

While Dumas's compare-and-contrast approach does lead the reader to some level of critical analysis beyond the simplistic dichotomy of the "good" West and the "evil" Islamic Republic, it also demonstrates how Dumas is reluctant to express any potentially contentious views for fear of insulting one culture or nation. The end result is an infrequent and underdeveloped analysis of both countries in favor of informational, neutral, and largely muted material. This can be seen clearly through one of the biggest contrasts Dumas outlines between the United States and the Islamic Republic. In her own words, "If there's one thing that separates Middle Easterners from Westerners, it's the way we mourn. We can out mourn anyone. For many in the Middle East, a highly emotional funeral is proof that the deceased is missed" (154). Once again, Dumas states this difference in a more informational manner, and in so doing, she is able to maintain neutrality or objectivity. Dumas further explains: "In the United States, the ability to 'move on' after a death is usually seen as a sign of inner strength and generally commended. A widow who starts dating is often called a survivor. In Middle Eastern culture, however, a widow who starts openly dating is looked upon with suspicion and disdain. A widow who mourns her husband for the rest of her life is viewed as devoted" (155). It is significant that Dumas focuses on widows, not widowers. The gender specific language leads the reader to conclude that Iranian women are not treated equally in Iran. However, Dumas makes no mention of this, either because she doesn't realize it or doesn't want her book to seem overly or at all contentious.

Ultimately, what comes out most clearly in *Laughing Without an Accent* (as well as in *Funny in Farsi*) is that Dumas strongly believes in illustrating the similarities between cultures and nations. In her own words, Dumas describes herself as "a bridge builder" (215). While she may indeed be this, the bridges that she builds do not seem to be stable or significant ones, nor do they lead to a place of great insight. Rather, Dumas is overly idealistic in her belief that conversation and personal meetings can transcend, if not completely diffuse, national and ethnic differences. For instance, in *Laughing Without an Accent*, Dumas recounts how she lived in an International House while attending the University of California at Berkeley. Dumas describes her experiences there: "It is the kind of place where one often sees an Israeli, a Palestinian, an Italian, and a student from Nebraska eating dinner together and discussing politics, soccer, and Bollywood" (72). Furthermore, she emphasizes, "If every world leader could spend one year living at an International House, there would be far fewer wars. Of that, I am absolutely certain" (72).

As much as it would be pleasant to believe that conversation and mutual interests can efface political, religious, and cultural differences and conflicts, living in an International House is not analogous to complex international relations between countries, cultures, and large groups of people.

As many of the chapters in *Laughing Without an Accent* appear to concern non-ethnically specific matters such as relationships, marriage, having children, and having a career, Dumas also promotes a post-ethnicity she perceives to be possible in the United States. Towards this end, when Dumas relates how one of her former Jewish high school friends describes one of the primary characteristics of a quintessential Jewish mother as causing others (mainly her children) to be guilty, Dumas tells her, "That's not a Jewish mother... That's my mother" (134). In essence, in Dumas's vision, ethnicity does not or should not matter much, and ethnic or national difference, when highlighted, should only be celebrated, never criticized or critically analyzed in a manner disrespectful to anyone involved. While these goals are noble and fit with mainstream American ideology, they fall short of shedding significant insight upon either country. The end result is two books which have been commercially successful (the first commercially successful in both Iran and the United States) mainly because of their non-threatening, appeasing, and sanitized accounts of both countries.

While it is commendable that Dumas wants to counteract the frequently negative manner in which both the United States and Iran often view one another, her books swing too far to the other side, and provide a rather cursory, overly positive account of both countries. Most tellingly, one of Dumas's editors tells her that *Funny in Farsi* became popular because Dumas largely stayed neutral in the book (10). Indeed, simplicity often sells, and while it could be said that Dumas went slightly beyond the simplistic moral distinctions of the "good" United States and the "evil" Islamic Republic, these distinctions were largely replaced by a vision in which both countries and people are more similar than different, and what differences they have are largely to be celebrated. It is an appealing vision, to be certain, but one that ultimately lacks depth and insight into either country. For more insightful and important accounts of life within the Islamic Republic itself, we will turn to a study of contemporary Iranian prison narratives in the next chapter.

# 6

# From Inside the
# Walls of Evin Prison

*Contemporary Iranian Prison Narratives*

In this chapter I will explore Iranian prison narratives not only as a microcosm through which to view power relations in the Islamic Republic, but also as vehicles promoting social justice, individual, and governmental change. The prison narratives I will explore, as they involve various kinds of torture, can also be considered trauma narratives. As Susan Brison argues, one goal of trauma narratives is to "gain memories" (46). Towards that end, the narratives I will explore also serve a key function not only by allowing the victim to manage (as opposed to repress) the traumatic experience, but also by turning the tables on the oppressor. These trauma/prison narratives are also important in terms of how they illustrate the transformation of the protagonist's identity due to the traumatic experience(s). Brison describes this as the "undoing of the self in trauma," and argues that it shatters "one's fundamental assumptions about the world and one's safety in it, but also severs the sustaining connection between the self and the rest of humanity" (40). In the case of Iranian prison narratives, as with many other prison narratives, it is the narrative itself which serves to reestablish the relationship between the self and the world. All of the prison/trauma narratives to be explored in this chapter do exactly this, but in different ways.

Further, as Tiffany Ana Lopez argues, "popular narratives of violence have a reductively common plot that significantly thwarts critical discourse: an evil perpetuator commits a monstrous act that leaves his victims traumatized forever, beyond all repair. He must be punished, preferably by a long prison sentence imposed by a tough on crime leader" (62–3). Iranian prison narratives intentionally or unintentionally upset and deconstruct the easy dichotomy between good and evil, as well as between the West and Iran. In the first trauma/prison narrative to be explored, *My Life as a Traitor* (2007), the damage caused by the vicious circle of violence and torture perpetuated upon the inmates of Evin prison during the time of the Shah is perpetuated in turn upon the twenty-year-old narrator, Zarah Ghahramani, a suspected political dissident. The cycle of violence can be seen as a microcosm of the forces that threaten to tear Iran apart as well as a microcosm of the main conflicts between the West and Iran. With *My Prison, My Home* (2009), Haleh Esfandiari demonstrates how the attempts to bridge the gulf between these two cultures and political systems largely fail as Iranian paranoia, beget by Western actions, leads to the imprisonment of the sixty-seven-year-old academic narrator. The narrative also demonstrates the power of the contemporary global media in effecting change, or in this case, Esfandiari's release. Last, we see how Iran's attempts to respond to and control global media lead to the imprisonment, torture, and eventual release of Maziar Bahari and Ahmed Batebi, as well as further politically distance the West and the Islamic Republic from one another. Still, one of the most powerful messages that comes through Iranian prison narratives is the power of diplomacy through the global media, not through any direct political means.

Having taught courses in Iranian and Iranian diasporic literature and culture, I can attest to how students tend to be more drawn to prison narratives than other forms of Iranian or Iranian diasporic literature. Similar to Holocaust narratives, Iranian prison narratives can pique the interest of readers (especially students) with their shocking, often outrageous details. Also, it is difficult to think of anything more suspenseful than the account of a narrator who describes navigating the thin line between life and death in a potentially and sometimes literally fatal prison environment. Writing in 2005, D. Quentin Miller argues that "prison literature has gained a wider audience in recent years,"[1] and while this indeed may be due to the suspense and drama of the narrative, it may also be due to a greater desire on the reader's part to stand witness and address, if not attempt to correct, human rights violations (1). Tiffany Ana Lopez suggests that one of the reasons for the interest in prison literature is "as a culture, we long to understand what motivates violence" (62). If, indeed, as Lopez suggests, "like many literary works about trauma and violence, prison narratives ask the reader to move beyond the page or stage and step into the larger arena of personal transformation and community building," it is hard to imagine a better candidate than Iranian prison narratives to help forge social change as well as a deeper understanding of contemporary Iranian government and culture (75). Yet, it would be remiss to suggest that Iranian prison narratives only encourage personal transformation and community building within Iran, as they also encourage transformation and community building in the West.

As established in a previous chapter, Azar Nafisi's *Reading Lolita in Tehran*

(*RLT*) has been strongly criticized for supposedly being overtly pro–Western, demeaning to Iran and to Muslims alike while purportedly being aligned with the neo-conservative movement. Yet, as we shall see, the first memoir to be explored in this chapter, *My Life as a Traitor*, could be seen as even more pro–Western and anti–Islamic Republic than *RLT*. Ghahramani's account of how students are trained in Iranian schools to consider Americans as "demons" and as "faithless, perfidious creatures" can lead the reader to demonize Iranians in turn (10). While it may be the case that Iranian students are taught this rhetoric in school, Ghahramani also explains that "at home, Americans were not such demons" (10). In fact, Ghahramani dates some of the trouble that she would later have with the Iranian administration to her love of "under-the-counter Western pop music," and suggests that her "predilection was bound to make trouble for me in a country where a very stern version of Islam had been imposed" (18). For Ghahramani, like Nafisi before her, the Islamic Republic has largely hijacked Islam for its own purposes and uses it to uphold a mostly totalitarian state in which virtually anything deemed to be Western (especially American) is to be condemned and avoided (18). Again, while such a view is certainly defensible, it can have the aftereffect of leading the readers into exactly the kind of demonization (of the Islamic Republic, in this case) that Ghahramani suggests her teachers encouraged of the United States when she was in school. However, critics have not suggested this, nor have they indicted Ghahramani for potentially debasing Iranians and glorifying Westerners. As with Azadeh Moaveni, one reason this may not have occurred is that neither Moaveni nor Ghahramani became nearly as popular as Nafisi. Had either achieved a similar level of commercial success, it is quite possible that either (especially Ghahramani's) might become the target of criticism. In addition, both Moaveni and Ghahramani are young women in their twenties, not established literary professors in their forties (like Nafisi), and thereby not held to the same literary standards as Nafisi is by the literary community.

At the same time, one key aspect that separates Ghahramani's memoir from those of Moaveni and Nafisi is that Ghahramani's is a trauma narrative, in which Ghahramani recounts her thirty day incarceration at Iran's notorious Evin prison where she is physically and emotionally tortured. It can be challenging to be critical about trauma narratives as doing so risks being labeled as an oppressor. If, indeed, as Susan Brison argues, it is "currently accepted as uncontroversial" that trauma narratives "contribute significantly" to "recovery," or that they serve as a form of emotional catharsis, as Sigmund Freud would argue, then it is indisputable that the actual composition of *My Life as a Traitor* was helpful in Ghahramani's recovery or healing process (Brison 40; Kaminer 484). Further, it is difficult not to acknowledge Ghahramani's memoir, for as Carol Burke argues, "because the penal machine has historically been more successful in silencing women than men, the stories that women have to tell are more difficult to retrieve" (xi).

Still, another important device separates Ghahramani's memoir from Nafisi's *RLT*. Whereas Nafisi tended to be assertive and academic, possessing a level of self-importance, Ghahramani portrays herself in a self-critical and unassuming manner as a traitor who cannot withstand torture and not only becomes an informant but also lies in order to protect herself. Of course, Ghahramani's response is understandable since she is tortured, and to some extent Ghahramani's self-critical portrayal can lead readers to regard her as even more heroic in her honesty or through her seeming self-effacement. Indeed, we can see shades of this in book reviews. For instance, Caroline Leavitt, writing for *People* magazine, describes *My Life as a Traitor* as "graceful" and says that "in this searingly honest, brave book, she's nothing short of heroic" (58). Along similar lines, *Kirkus Reviews* describes *My Life as a Traitor* as "shockingly honest" (1140). Yet these reviews raise the question of how we, as readers, can know that Ghahramani is being completely forthright in her details, especially since she has a co-writer, Robert Hillman. Rather, the reviewers tend to assume that Ghahramani is being honest because she frequently portrays herself and her behavior in less than flattering terms. Not only is she, after all, a traitor (although it is doubtful that any readers really would regard her as such), but, also, Ghahramani by her own account is rather superficial and weak.[2] However, these confessions do not necessarily mean that the narrative is completely accurate or comprehensive.

At the same time, what resonates most in the book reviews of *My Life as a Traitor* is the manner in which most reviewers readily accept the abysmal portrayal of the Islamic Republic and Evin prison, while praising Ghahramani's self-admitted Western inclinations. For instance, Dave Hickey, writing for *Art in America*, describes the depiction of the Islamic Republic in *My Life as a Traitor* as "a world where evil seeks us out on the street" (37). Hickey's use of the word "evil" certainly seems to be aligned with the Bush administration's description of Iran as being part of an Axis of Evil. Instead of considering that Ghahramani's self-critical overtures may be somewhat of a device (or a device from the co-author, Robert Hillman), he concludes: "Ghahramani's candor in *My Life as a Traitor* is so disarming and feels so right" (Hickey 37). For Hickey, *My Life as a Traitor* contains "a dream of Eden that illuminates her book without sacrificing its modesty" (37). While he does not specify what that "dream of Eden" refers to, it can be safely assumed that, for Hickey, Eden is synonymous with the West and he appears to have no qualms making this analogy. Along similar lines, other critics also suggest that *My Life as a*

*Traitor* is not only an "astonishing, relentlessly honest account" but also "a strong reminder of the privileges of democracy" (Block 118). Patrick Clawson, writing for the *Middle East Quarterly*, takes it as a given that the Islamic Republic is a "totalitarian country," without considering that Ghahramani's portrayal may only be one person's perspective (or the perspective of two, depending on how much Hillman was involved in the writing) and that this perspective displays the Islamic Republic in the worst possible light.[3] Clawson compares Iran not only to the formerly Communist Soviet Union, but also to fascist Germany (89).[4] While there have been some important developments for women in Iran, especially during the Khatami administration, *Kirkus Reviews* suggest that the memoir reminds "us how little has changed for women in Iran" (1140). Thereby *My Life as a Traitor* may reinforce generalizations and stereotypes of Iranian women as passive victims.

It is important to consider the genesis of *My Life as a Traitor*, as it can be seen as a text purposely constructed for Western consumption. It is extremely doubtful that the book would ever have been written, let alone published, were it not for Ghahramani's co-writer, Robert Hillman. It is unclear to what extent Hillman contributed to *My Life as a Traitor*, but Hillman's own account of how he met Ghahramani as well as the genesis of her memoir appears like a form of neo-colonialism, in which, borrowing from Gayatri Spivak, a white man attempts to save a brown woman from brown men. Specifically, Hillman describes meeting Ghahramani in 2003, a couple of years after she is imprisoned. His account emphasizes the dangers he believes her to be in as well as her fragile state of mind. He writes:

> Her days and nights were vexed by the need to take care: any infringement of Iran's rigid dress code would be harshly punished, any expression of political dissent would see her returned to Evin for a very long time, or until her interrogators judged her so cowed by certain refinements of the torture she had already endured that she could no longer imagine rebuking her government [Hillman, par. 4].

While it is possible that Ghahramani might be under additional scrutiny since she was previously imprisoned,[5] as we have seen in Moaveni's memoirs, it is not the case that all or even the vast majority of Iranian women are "harshly punished" by "any infringement" of the dress code, and it is quite rare for someone to be strongly accosted or arrested for violating a dress code.

There is also some evidence that Hillman himself may have increased Ghahramani's paranoia and convinced her to leave. By Ghahramani's own account, "After they [Hillman and his wife] learned about my story, Robert kept telling me, 'They're going to take you again.' I wasn't planning to leave Iran, but it just became clear that it's not possible to live a normal life, so I decided to do it" (Butler, par. 16). Hillman also claims, "Her [Ghahramani's] story could have been told with variation by thousands of young Iranian men, and without variation by a few young Iranian women. She was 20 and studying languages at university when first detained by state security agents late in 2001" (par. 5). While there may be some truth to this, we will see when exploring other prison/trauma narratives that the experiences of inmates vary. Actually, Ghahramani's story could have been much worse (false executions, permanent physical damage, rape, or actual execution); possibly it might have been better had she not resisted and purposely insulted certain guards.[6]

In many ways, Ghahramani presents herself as rather superficial, in an odd way analogous to common Middle Eastern perceptions of the United States or the West.[7] She explains how, as a child, she first fell in love with "pink shoes" which "expressed more about the world in which I wanted to live than anything I could have possibly have put into words. In a strange way, those pink shoes and my appetite for the places I might go in them led me, after many twists and turns, to a cell in Evin Prison" (13). In other words, Ghahramani suggests that her predilection for Western consumer items and traditional (at least in a Western sense) feminine items targets her. This characterization helps lead (Western) readers more towards an us (West) vs. them (Iran) mentality. Hardly a feminist, Ghahramani concludes: "This is the truth about me. I am a simple, middle-class girl full of middle-class silliness. I want a husband and babies and a nice kitchen with a food processor and a pop-up toaster and a rotisserie and one of those special kettles designed by some genius all made of stainless steel and looking like it belongs in an art gallery" (169). By not presenting herself as being politically minded or even all that socially cognizant,[8] Ghahramani (with her co-writer Hillman) is able to depict herself as even more of an innocent victim (which she might honestly be). This is also aided by her depiction of herself as weak and initially unable to stand up to the techniques of her interrogators. Indeed, it doesn't take much more than a few hours of blindfolding, threatening, and slapping to get Ghahramani to "name" her "friends" (41). Still, even though she describes herself as "weak and cowardly," the vast majority of readers, unfamiliar as they presumably are with torture, would certainly forgive Ghahramani's supposed lack of courage, and view her even more as a vulnerable young (brown) woman to be rescued from vicious (brown) Iranian men.

Along these lines, Ghahramani tends to depict the guards and interrogators at Evin as monstrous, evil sadists who take pleasure in hurting the prisoners. To some extent she may be justified in her perspective, for if we accept her account (and we have no reason not to), she has been savagely beaten. However, how can we be certain her account is entirely accurate? Can we know for sure, for instance, that the guards that interrogate Ghahramani really take pleasure in Ghahramani's fear and enjoy seeing her suffer, as she suggests (3–4)? For Ghahramani, the interrogators exist in a "brutal, primitive" manner, but even if they do, it is possible that their own vicious behavior was sparked by their own vicious punishments at the hands of the SAVAK (as Dalia Sofer details in *The Septembers of Shiraz*), or they might have been traumatized by first-hand experiences in the Iran-Iraq war (4).

Ghahramani suggests that she is completely innocent of the charges eventually brought against her, and while this seems accurate, and while Ghahramani is denied due process, she does not acknowledge that her guards have a rationale for interrogating her in the sense that she seemed to be involved in student demonstrations that challenged the Iranian government. Ghahramani wonders, "What had I done to deserve this? Voiced a few opinions, handed out petitions, gathered in street protests with my friends. I had never hurt anyone, never fired a gun, never thrown a stone" (4). While her statement may be true, Ghahramani has also had many meetings with student protesters. While she wouldn't be imprisoned for doing this were she living in the United States (or in the West), her behavior and actions could be sufficient grounds for an investigation under the Patriot Act. Yet, Ghahramani doesn't acknowledge that what may drive her interrogators is the connections her father had with the Shah (as well as his possible SAVAK connection), which leads them to be more suspicious of her.[9] While such grounds are not legally defensible in American courts, it is not completely irrational or illogical to suspect Ghahramani more than other student protesters of her age on this basis of her familial background. Further, by Ghahramani's own account, she does lie to protect herself and her friends who have also been imprisoned or who are in danger of being imprisoned. When the interrogators present intimidating evidence of Ghahramani with another person arrested, Arash, and ask her what she did with him, she thinks to herself: "I can't say what I did at Arash's house. Can I? No, I can't. I don't know what the interrogator's response would be. He already considers me depraved for having gone alone to a house of a man who is not my husband. If I tell him what happened, he may use it against Arash. Or he may use it against me" (41). While Ghahramani never directly states what happened between the two, it can be assumed that there was some kind of romantic or sexual relationship, which would not be allowed under the edicts of the Islamic Republic.

As mentioned earlier, in many ways Ghahramani positions herself as being akin to an American teenager. To be sure, this may not have been calculating on her part, but rather an honest reflection of who she really is or was. At the same time, it may encourage her presumably Western readers to want to rescue her (and others like her) and to demonize Iran. After all, Ghahramani positions herself as a rather simplistic person without significant political beliefs, let alone a political agenda. Rather, she reports that, as a girl, all she wanted to do was "sparkle in the sunlight" (19). She also describes herself as not being "interested in making cosmic claims; I wanted to be free to walk down the street with the wind in my hair. I wanted to go to the movies all by myself if I felt like it. I wanted to choose my occupation from as extensive a list as could the boys I knew" (76). The latter sentence is as close to a feminist statement as Ghahramani makes in *My Life as a Traitor*. That her audience is mainly Westerners becomes even more clear when she addresses stereotypes of Iranians she believes to be held by Westerners, such as, "The depth of our [Iranians'] grieving has to do with the importance of love in our culture. This may sound very strange to Westerners who have been encouraged to adopt a cartoon-version of Iranians — suicide bombers, warmongers, religious zealots. But love is the more important thing to grasp when you study Iranians" (29). Ghahramani would not have felt the need to state this had her intended or expected audience been primarily Iranian.[10] While her account does work to counteract generalizations or stereotypes of Iranians, it does so by making them seem rather simplistic in her emphasis on "love."

Further, in contrast to the West, Ghahramani portrays her childhood and teenage years in the Islamic Republic as largely restrictive and dissatisfying. For instance, she focuses on a seemingly absurd edict made when she was in the fourth grade. This edict states that children are not allowed to wear white socks anymore because doing so would be akin to "mocking the blood of martyrs who gave up their lives fighting the Iraqis" (97). Ghahramani also recounts how administrators and teachers traumatized students who wore white socks by suggesting that their actions have extremely displeased the "martyrs." Still, Ghahramani herself is hardly politically aware, nor is she a feminist crusader, and her generalizations about men are oddly reminiscent of and possibly in tune with the stereotype of the Islamic Republic. For instance, she writes, "It is almost an occupational hazard of being female, this profound conviction that love will bring about desired change. Perhaps it is a form of egocentricity. Perhaps there is a type of arrogance in women which compels them to believe that love is so vital that even a benighted fool will eventually give up his appalling habits" (57). Ghahramani also suggests, "Women (but certainly not men) are capable of loving to distraction without surrounding completely to the erotic" (159). The seemingly conservative-minded Ghahramani gets involved in the student movement because of her gathering feelings that the Islamic Republic is hypocritical and that it "awarded all sorts of treats to the people who endorsed its ideology, whether or not the endorsement was sincere, and withheld favors from those who voiced even the mildest criticism of those in power" (47). While this perspective may certainly have some validity, if we believe Ghahramani's account of herself as being largely apolitical, then it would seem that she gets involved with the demonstrations mainly because she is swept up by their rhetoric.

The end result of Ghahramani's being swept up by the rhetoric of the student movement is her subsequent incarceration, imprisonment, and torture. Indeed, a central portion of *My Life as a Traitor* is Ghahramani's experiences being tortured. As Michel Foucault argues, torture can be seen a "ritual" which aims to "mark the victim" by "either the scar it leaves on the body or by the spectacle that accompanies it, to brand the victim with infamy" (34). Ghahramani experiences both kinds of torture (scarring and spectacle) when incarcerated in Evin Prison. Both techniques serve to break Ghahramani down, but they also produce an understandable anger, hatred, and ultimately, a murderous rage in Ghahramani. This fits with Foucault's analogy of "interrogative based torture" being similar to "a duel" (41).

While it may be understandable that Ghahramani ultimately ends up demonizing her guards, doing so puts her in a position similar to various Islamic Regime officials who likewise stereotype and demonize Americans and pro–Western Iranians. For Ghahramani, not only are her guards and interrogators "evil," but she also describes them as not being in the "same moral and ethical category as normal people" (67). Again, Ghahramani's response is understandable since she has been tortured, but disallowing the interrogators' humanity or considering them to be sub-human may be more of a response to how she is treated by them, which to her is essentially akin to "an animal," with guards "who could shear me or cut my throat with equal inconcern" (71). This demonization disallows Ghahramani from considering that there could be at least a partial explanation (not to be confused with a convincing rationale) for the guards' and interrogators' behavior and actions towards her and others. In fact, under the Shah and the SAVAK, they may have gone through physical trauma similar or worse to what Ghahramani goes through at Evin. Ghahramani also admits that she does not always tell her interrogators the truth for fear of the possible consequences. The interrogators, for their part, do have some potentially incriminating evidence against Ghahramani and it stands to reason that they may be treating her worse and torturing her because they believe she is withholding information (which she is). This is certainly not to condone the techniques of the interrogators but, rather, to provide an explanation. From their perspective, the interrogators presumably feel that they are acting in the best interest of the Islamic Republic.

In her account, Ghahramani does provide some glimpses of humanity in the guards and interrogators, but these are merely glimpses because Ghahramani resists acknowledging their humanity, just as she perceives (in this duel-like situation) that they are not acknowledging her humanity. For instance, a female guard repeatedly makes sexual advances to Ghahramani, which Ghahramani tries to rebuff until a climactic moment in which the guard corners Ghahramani while Ghahramani is in the bathroom. After Ghahramani knocks the guard down and runs away, other guards catch Ghahramani and savagely beat her. Further, when the female guard, who has been facially disfigured, asks Ghahramani if she'd rebuff her advances if the guard was pretty, the guard tells her, "I was prettier than you before they bombed the street. I got burned then. My family died. I have no friends" (224). Ghahramani is ultimately unsympathetic to the guard and makes no attempt to try to fathom her behavior. As Ghahramani has just been tortured, this is understandable, but what she does not realize is that she is becoming part of a vicious circle of violence that has at least partially helped beget the behavior of her torturers.

Indeed, one of the most significant portions of *My Life as a Traitor* is a depiction of how Ghahramani changes while she is imprisoned, interrogated, and tortured. Ghahramani's transformation can be seen as comparable to what may indeed have happened to her guards themselves. After being repeatedly terrified and beaten by her guards, Ghahramani starts to give in and wonders: "What is true and what is a lie are merging in my mind, but worse than that, it all seems hopelessly unimportant. Where is my conviction? Have I ceased to believe in anything? I haven't even got a firm sense of myself as a human being" (90). This state is not that dissimilar to the desperate straits many find themselves in when they embrace fundamentalist religion, or in this case, Islam. Without clear beliefs or even a stable identity, it is easy to surrender to all-encompassing beliefs and allow those beliefs to subsume or become one's primary identity. Further, Ghahramani gradually gets paranoid while imprisoned, believing that a cellmate above her, Ali, who she knew before entering prison and who she talks to while in prison, may be a "spy" (92). As we will see with the other prison/trauma narratives, this paranoia is a definite hallmark of the current Islamic Republic, and has led to a number of unwarranted arrests, imprisonments, and presumably, deaths.

Ghahramani also goes through waves of masochistic behavior, suicidal tendencies, and finally begins thinking obsessively of "murder" (138). First, she feels that she wants "to die," and then she provokes a beating from the guard in order to feel something (136). Then Ghahramani seeks revenge on those who tortured her, which may be exactly what drove many who currently torture and abuse Ghahramani and others at Evin prison. In Raskolnikov-like reasoning, Ghahramani concludes: "I think I have the right to murder the man I despise. What will he ever contribute to the human race? He exists to make misery. I can kill a person like that" (146). Thus, we can see a damaging vicious circle of violence perpetuated and maintained by suffering, punishment, and torture. Indeed, Ghahramani concludes that suffering "corrupts you…. It will consume what little courage you have, and then you are left with nothing" (162). However, she does not seem to be able to apply this same idea to her torturers.

Ultimately, in keeping with the trajectory of prison/trauma narratives, which typically display how the self can be undone, when Ghahramani is finally released, she appears to be a different person than she was when she entered Evin about a month earlier (Brison 41). When the guards give Ghahramani the dress in which she was arrested, Ghahramani sobs, thinking, "Oh, Zarah, you silly thing; you poor, stupid, lovely girl" (235). *My Life as a Traitor* concludes when Ghahramani is dropped off outside the outskirts of Tehran. As she walks to the perimeter of the city, Ghahramani calls her parents and, in a kind of post-traumatic communion, eats bread that a stranger gave her. While doing so, she concludes, "If I were in Paradise, this is what I would wish it to be: fresh bread, tears of joy, and my mother and father hurrying to me" (242). However, Ghahramani concludes *My Life as a Traitor* with, "I clutch my blindfold tightly in my free hand" (242). This indicates that her traumatic prison experience has understandably had a profound effect on Ghahramani, whose clutching of the blindfold indicates her continuing animosity towards those who imprisoned and tortured her. Also, the fact that she writes "my free hand," indicates that the experience has not completely broken her, and that merely by being released, she has triumphed in some way. The triumph may ultimately lie in the writing of the narrative itself, for as Brison argues, "In telling a first-person trauma narrative to a suitable listener, the survivor is, at the same time and once again, a second person, dependent on the listener in order to return to personhood" (41). "Free hand" may also allude to Ghahramani's future emigration to the West (Australia), where she may feel that she subsequently discovers this "freedom" not allowed in what she no doubt now perceives to be a wholly vicious and oppressive Iran.

To some degree, the next prison/trauma narrative, Haleh Esfandiari's *My Prison, My Home* (2009), can be seen as the polar opposite of *My Life as a Traitor*. Whereas the latter was written by a largely apolitical twenty-year-old Iranian college student, the former was written by a sixty-seven-year-old Iranian expatriate academic who was working "as the director of the Middle East

Program at the Woodrow Wilson Center in Washington D.C." (Esfandiari 3). Esfandiari's account details how she appears to be entrapped in Iran (while visiting her ailing mother), kept from leaving through a seemingly staged theft of her passport, and imprisoned for supposedly being a spy and an informer, but more probably because she is a means through which the Iranian administration attempts to extract information about the United States and its intentions in or with Iran. Whereas Ghahramani depicts her treatment in Evin Prison as largely inhumane, Esfandiari's account is more complex and nuanced. Other than being unjustly imprisoned and kept in solitary confinement against her will, Esfandiari is not really tortured,[11] certainly not to the extent Ghahramani was, as depicted in *My Life as a Traitor*. In fact, Esfandiari depicts most of her guards in rather flattering terms and she does not completely demonize her interrogator, Ja'fari, as Ghahramani did. In all fairness, though, Esfandiari, as a high ranking and older academic, seems to have received better treatment than Ghahramani, but at the same time, she doesn't resort to the same kind of retaliatory name calling and insulting that Ghahramani does.

Still, there are important similarities in the two narratives, not the least of which being that both are accounts of female imprisonment. This fact alone appears to have helped market their respective memoirs. Just as Ghahramani seems to encourage a kind of Spivakian neo-colonialism, so does Esfandiari. Even though Esfandiari proves herself to be an extremely strong, intelligent, and prepossessing woman, reviews of her memoir often point out her age (67), her petite stature, and the fact that she is both a mother and, more importantly, a grandmother. For instance, in Trudy Rubin's review, she describes Esfandiari as "a 69 year old grandmother standing barely 5 feet tall and weighing 105 pounds" ("Iran Cannot Silence").[12] Along similar lines, Christina Lamb, writing for *The Sunday Times*, argues, "It is hard to imagine how anyone could have thought that this then 67-year-old grandmother visiting her frail 93-year-old mother in Tehran was a threat. But to the Iranian authorities she was the key figure in an American plot to bring down the regime" (6). Even Esfandiari's colleagues at the Wilson Center focused on her appearance, calling her "small-framed," and "a diminutive, soft-spoken woman, a mother, and a grandmother" (Lagerfeld 2; Gildenhorn and Hamilton 6). The false implication of these writers is that Esfandiari, given her gender, her age, her stature, and her status as a grandmother, could not possibly be a threat.

While it may be understandable that members of the Wilson Center used this rather patronizing and demeaning language to appeal to the more conservative segment of the Islamic Republic when Esfandiari was imprisoned, such language also helps market Esfandiari's memoir as another account of a vulnerable, victimized woman at the hands of the brutal, sexist Islamic Regime, positioning the United States to be, once again, in the role of the proverbial Spivakian white man saving a brown woman from brown men. Whereas Ghahramani's account is more akin to a damsel-in-distress narrative, Esfandiari's account is more akin to a grandmother-in-distress narrative — except that the memoir Esfandiari actually provides for the reader turns out to be more of an account of an extremely strong, intelligent, prepossessing woman, who despite her age and her stature is able to stand up to the Islamic Regime. At the same time, there is only so much power Esfandiari can exert as a prisoner in Evin. Hence, Carl Brown's description of *My Prison, My Home* as being part and parcel of "prisoner-as-pawn literature" is appropriate (169). It is through Esfandiari's imprisonment that we can see the outlines of the complex framework of Iranian-American relations. It is telling that reviewers are mostly drawn to the portions of Esfandiari's account that most resemble a traditional trauma or prison narrative, as this is the form with which readers are most familiar.[13]

Ironically, in her position as Director of the Middle East Program at the Woodrow Wilson Center in Washington, D.C., Esfandiari, by her own account, sought to promote a better understanding between Iran and the United States by "organizing talks and conferences on Middle Eastern issues," yet she finds herself caught in the crosshairs of both countries and ensnared in the tumultuous bureaucracy of a country (Iran) that has grown incredibly paranoid and suspicious of the West (24). Whereas in the case of Ghahramani, the Islamic Republic seemed more concerned with homegrown threats, now, in the Ahmadinejad era, the major concern is the perceived influence of the West (notably, the United States). For Esfandiari at least, it is not as smooth a bureaucracy as it was for Ghahramani just a few years earlier. No doubt, things proceed slower for Esfandiari and government officials are less apt to help her because she is an expatriate Iranian who resides in the United States. Like Ghahramani, it is also more difficult for Esfandiari because of her gender, and she is forced to enlist the help of a male friend to try to expedite the laborious process of procuring a replacement passport for the one that was stolen from her. Also, in Esfandiari's account, the bureaucrats she must deal with seem more unmotivated and blasé than religiously or nationalistically devoted, as they tended to be in Ghahramani's memoir. This can be seen in Esfandiari's description: "Unhurried, sloppy in dress and in the performance of their duties, these men demanded as little of themselves as the bureaucracy demanded of them" (10).

Part of the reason why Esfandiari may also be heavily scrutinized in Iran can be attributed to lingering anti–Semitism in Iran, encouraged by Ahmadinejad and his administration. Indeed, Esfandiari argues that "the repressive apparatus of the state ... was in full resurgence" after Ahmadinejad's election in 2005 (140).[14] Esfandiari becomes the unwitting recipient of this anti–Semitism since her husband is a Jewish academic who teaches and lives in the United States. As mentioned earlier when examining Sofer's *The Septembers of Shiraz*, Iran has an almost paradoxical relationship with its Jewish population, tolerating and granting rights to certain Iranian Jews, but acting more with disdain towards those deemed to be Western "Zionist" Jews. It is very possible that the Iranian administration believed Esfandiari was in cahoots with Israel because of her perceived familial connections. At times, Esfandiari, somewhat reminiscent of Azar Nafisi, appears at least partially nostalgic for the pre–Islamic Revolution, Shah era, when there seemed to be more rights for women, which were subsequently, according to Esfandiari, rolled back by post–Islamic Revolution era clerics (41, 43). Still, true to her more objective nature, Esfandiari recognizes that the "political stability" seemingly engendered by the Shah was "purchased at a price — repression" (45). The repression, in turn, helped produce dissatisfied Iranian citizens and a subsequent political administration (after the Revolution) that gravitated more towards fundamentalist religion, which provided previously silenced individuals a means of expression (45).

A good deal of the suspicion that the Iranian administration harbors towards Esfandiari is due to her work for the Wilson Center. To a large degree, their suspicion is understandable, since Iran, by and large, does not have politically non-affiliated academic centers as the Wilson Center purports to be. In addition, it is not unreasonable to suspect that such centers could be fronts for partisan, domestic or international agencies affiliated with the American government. Indeed, the lead story on the Friday, April 2, 2010, Wilson Center website seems extremely political and even military in nature: "Counterterrorism in the Obama Administration: Tactics and Strategy" (par. 1). While it becomes evident upon reading the article that the Wilson Center was simply the site where Coordinator for Counterterrorism Daniel Benjamin outlined President Obama's counterterrorism plans, one might wonder why Benjamin is presenting this plan at the Wilson Center and what input the Center might have had or will have upon Obama's plans. Also, according to Global Sponsors, one of the Wilson Center's leading contributors, the mission of the center is "knowledge in the public service" ("Development: Global Sponsors," par. 1). This mission suggests a certain commitment to the practical application of ideas. In other words, the Center could be construed as being a rather politically active entity.

In terms of the Wilson Center's Middle East Program, for which Esfandiari worked (and continued to work for after her release), their mission is largely non-partisan, but portions of it could be construed as partisan and activist. For example, they describe the Middle East Program on their website as paying "special attention to the role of women, youth, civil society institutions, Islam, and democratic and autocratic tendencies" ("Middle East Program," par. 1). The implication here is that portions of the Middle East are autocratic whereas the United States is not only democratic but in a better position to judge the governments of other countries. Still, there are more innocuous descriptions of the program such as that it "hosts programs on cultural issues, including contemporary art and literature in the region" ("Middle East Program," par. 1). The website also offers some implicit criticism of Middle Eastern countries as being patriarchal and sexist, as they describe themselves as devoting "considerable attention" to "the role of women in advancing civil society, the problem of trafficking in women, and the attitudes of governments and the clerical community toward women's rights" ("Middle East Program," par. 3). The Wilson Center also appears interested in potential regime change as noted by their statement that "the Middle East Program monitors the growing demand of people in the region for democratization, accountable government, the rule of law, and adherence to international conventions on topics such as human rights and women's rights" ("Middle East Program," par. 4). In terms of Iran, the Middle East Center also describes themselves as devoting "considerable attention to the analysis of internal domestic and social developments in Iran; the aspiration of the younger generation for reform and expansion of individual liberties" ("Middle East Program," par. 5). While the Center does describe itself as being invested with "potential avenues for reconciliation with the United States," this point is made last and comes right after the points "foreign policy priorities," and "Iran's nuclear program" ("Middle East Program," par. 5).

Considering these self-described goals, it is generally understandable that Esfandiari's interrogator, Ja'fari, believes that the Wilson Center had a secret agenda and that it is "an agency of the American government, that we were implicated in some nefarious plot against the Islamic Republic, and that we routinely held secret meetings to plan strategy to this end" (58). Esfandiari may know better since she works at the Wilson Center, but given the way the Center describes itself on its website, it is not unreasonable to suspect that the Center could be a political arm of the United States government or military, which has a history of involvement in the Middle East. According to Esfandiari, the Wilson Center is "a nonpartisan think tank" and serves "a forum" to hear a wide variety of views about Iran, including those from the

Islamic Republic itself (60). However, this appears to be only part of its goals, and while the Center may be nonpartisan, it does not appear to be a completely neutral arbitrator or evaluator of the Middle East, for its very mission suggests that there are serious political problems in the Middle East that need to be ameliorated, and the Center's perspective on these problems is much closer to that of the United States than Iran or other predominantly Muslim Middle Eastern countries.

While imprisoned, Esfandiari encounters difficulties due to differing interpretations, semantics, and differing cultures. For instance, the Middle East Program was initially titled the Middle East Project and Esfandiari's role as initially to be a "consultant" (63). Esfandiari's interrogator, Ja'fari, responds strongly to both words because to him, "'consultant' had sinister implications, and 'project' implied an elaborate plan, entrusted to me and designed to subvert the Iranian government" (63). In his somewhat paranoid (but not unreasonably so due to how the American government had recently approved funds to supposedly promote democracy in Iran) mindset, Ja'fari also believes that Esfandiari cooperated with the George Soros founded and headed Open Society Initiative (OSI), which helped promote regime change in certain countries (65). In essence, Ja'fari chooses to distrust the United States and Esfandiari, while presuming the worst of both, rather than giving either the benefit of the doubt. Given that the United States did engage in Iranian regime change during the early 1950s with the fall of Mossedegh and the rise of the Shah, Ja'fari's response is not irrational. Also, as an interrogator, Ja'fari may want to take a harder line with Esfandiari because he may believe that she will be more likely to confess that way.

At the same time, one of the newer developments in Iran (since Ghahramani's incarceration in 2001 or 2002) as noted by the response to Esfandiari's imprisonment is what appears to be fissures in its own political structure, mainly between moderates (who were more in control during Khatami's administration) and hard-liners (who re-take power during Ahmadinejad's administration). Esfandiari describes herself as caught "in a tug-of-war over policy — and over me" (71). Whereas "the more moderate group argued that holding and interrogating me was of no benefit to the Islamic Republic and would only damage Iran's image abroad ... a hard-line faction believed they caught the "big fish," a mastermind in the plot to overthrow the Islamic Republic" (71). In a way, this battle over what to do with Esfandiari foreshadows the deep divisions between more moderate supporters of Mir-Hossein Mousavi and the harder-line, conservative supporters of Mahmoud Ahmadinejad, which erupts into chaos and violence after the June 2009 presidential elections, and continues to divide Iran.

To her credit, despite her unjust incarceration, Esfandiari manages to keep relatively detached and objective about Iran, and unlike Ghahramani, Esfandiari never resorts to demonizing Iran (although, in all fairness to Ghahramani, Esfandiari is never physically tortured). While Esfandiari does identify and implicitly critique the sizeable economic differences between the rich and poor in Tehran, and she also seems to suggest that there was more gender equality during the time of the Shah, she is not content to vilify the Islamic Regime or the Ahmadinejad administration. Instead, she suggests that recent Iranian efforts to talk with the U.S. have been counter-productively thwarted by the Bush administration (118). Even more significantly, she heavily criticizes the Bush administration's funding for the supposed promotion of democracy in Iran as well its eventual approval by Congress (120). She criticizes it as being "ill conceived from its inception," and ultimately doing more harm than good (120). Ultimately, she concludes that this "harmful program of democracy promotion" not only "contributed to my detention," but also helped resolve "an iron determination by Iran's security services to squash all American plans regarding the Islamic Republic" (121).

It may be that Esfandiari's ability to view politics and the conflicts between the United States and Iran more objectively helps her maintain her composure and strength while in Evin Prison. If, as Michel Foucault suggests, an interrogation can be akin to a duel, then Esfandiari's interrogators try to wear her down with repeated questions as well as questions that cover seemingly trivial and personal incidentals like who Esfandiari sees in Washington, D.C., and the names of her grandchildren. The latter seems more like an attempt to scare Esfandiari, and indeed, this kind of informational warfare helps the interrogator (Ja'fari), for the more he knows about the subject, the more power he can try to exert over her.

Unlike Ghahramani, Esfandiari depicts her interrogator as more of a mundane, banal bureaucrat, who may also be a teacher in a second job,[15] rather than a sadistic and violent sub-human. He, in her account, appears more like an overworked and high-strung American detective. While Esfandiari largely critiques Ja'fari's attempts to obtain more information, his techniques are not completely unreasonable. She describes him as typically arriving "in the morning with downloaded information, which he then expected me to explain to him" (62). Since, as established earlier in this chapter, the mission and goals of the Wilson Center and its Middle East Program are somewhat nebulous, it makes sense that Ja'fari, who according to Esfandiari believes that the Wilson Center is involved in "a plot aimed at the Islamic Republic," would grill Esfandiari for more information (62). While he never physically threatens Esfandiari, Ja'fari does try "intimidation," by telling Esfandiari, "We will keep you in Iran," and "We can make life difficult for you," or that they might put her in a less comfortable area of Evin Prison (77–78). However, these are things that a Western detective might tell the interrogated in a heated session.

In a way, Ja'fari's methods can be seen as somewhat akin to a literary critic, in how he attempts to interpret the implications and semantics of Esfandiari's words as well as that of the Wilson Center. For instance, to confront Esfandiari, he uses a sentence included in the cover of her book, *Reconstructed Lives: Women and Iran's Islamic Revolution*: "She and her informants describe strategies by which women try and sometimes succeed in subverting the state's agenda" (78). In particular, Ja'fari responds strongly to the words "subverting the state's agenda." While Esfandiari didn't write that sentence herself, and the sentence is taken out of context, it shows the extent to which Ja'fari searches for what will corroborate his position and perspective — that Esfandiari and the Wilson Center are involved in an effort to promote regime change in Iran.

While Esfandiari becomes understandably agitated from Ja'fari's techniques in her memoir, she takes steps to ensure that she does not portray him and other interrogators as monstrous. While this may be part of Ja'fari's attempt to win Esfandiari's trust, he does allow Esfandiari to call her ailing mother on occasion and alerts her, when she is blindfolded, to obstacles close to her so she doesn't hurt herself (143). Also, Esfandiari describes her second interrogator, Hajj Agha, as "almost always courteous," responsive, and generally honest. At the same time, she also describes him as "threatening," "intimidating," and accusing her "of endangering national security" (144). Hajj Agha also accuses Esfandiari of being "parsimonious with words" and not being "forthcoming," both of which are at least partially true (145). For her own part, Esfandiari understandably does not want to implicate anyone else, but this makes her seem to be less than cooperative. Even Esfandiari admits that there was a "logic to Hajj Agha's theory," although Esfandiari calls it "mad," mainly because she views it to be extremely paranoid to think that the United States would spread its wealth to "think tanks and foundation," in order to help produce regime change in countries like Iran (150). Yet, Ja'fari's reasoning, while possibly lacking some support, hardly seems "mad" or completely "divorced from reality," as Esfandiari argues, since by her own account, the United States has already "allocated funds" for Iranian regime change during the George W. Bush administration (150).[16]

While the tenor of Esfandiari's interrogations is certainly friendlier than Ghahramani's, like Ghahramani, Esfandiari also views her interrogations as a kind of duel or battle of wills. Like Ghahramani, Esfandiari learns to relish the opportunities to parry back an interrogation, and she begins to lash back (although not as severely as Ghahramani) during her interrogations. In Esfandiari's own words, "In my blackest moods, the unwelcome interrogations provided me with a form of healing. In the face of bullying and false accusations, I grew angry and defiant. I knew I must not let them break me" (154). If her interrogations can be seen as a kind of duel, it is Esfandiari who ultimately wins, for after she is released, presumably due to how public opinion so strongly turned against Iran for incarcerating Esfandiari, it is her main interrogator, Ja'fari, who gives Esfandiari a gift from the Intelligence Ministry — "a book of poetry by Hafez — almost as a repentant gesture" (215).

At the same time, this act of Ja'fari's, supposedly on behalf of the Intelligence Ministry, should not be misconstrued as a genuine transformative act on his or Iran's part. While Esfandiari does not experience a transformation as large as that of Ghahramani (who is younger and also physically abused while in prison), her experiences, before, during, and after her incarceration, do change Esfandiari. Even before she is incarcerated, Esfandiari uses extremely strong language to describe how it felt when an Iranian police officer searched and ransacked her mother's home when Esfandiari was staying there while trying to obtain a replacement passport (for the one that was stolen). Esfandiari writes, "I viscerally felt the violation of my privacy, almost physically, as if I had been raped. I felt a hatred for the men who were doing this to us, with an intensity that astonished me" (70). In response to this act, we can begin to see a transference of hostility onto Iran as well as a growing paranoia, which ironically, mirrors that of Iranian officials towards the United States. Esfandiari writes, "I had loved Iran with a passion.... Yet these horrible people had made me feel alien in my own homeland" (74). It is telling that Esfandiari uses the past tense with "I had loved Iran," as it suggests that her nationalistic love has begun to dissipate due to the actions of those Iranian officials who searched her mother's home and seem to be preventing her from leaving (and who subsequently incarcerate her). Esfandiari also describes her growing, but possibly justified, paranoia, which also mirrors that of the Islamic Regime, that they (Islamic Regime) are following her every move. Esfandiari writes, "My entanglement with the Intelligence Ministry meant I would never again feel safe in Iran, even at home. I could no longer carry out an unguarded conversation over the telephone. I believed the intelligence people were reading my e-mail. My nerves were always on edge" (101). In many ways, the state Esfandiari now finds herself in is exactly the state in which her captors exist continually, and it is this paranoid state that ultimately led to Esfandiari's arrest.

While Esfandiari may have difficulty understanding or feeling sympathy towards the seemingly paranoid behavior of her captures, she portrays her guards in largely flattering terms. Whereas, quite possibly for compelling reasons,

Ghahramani depicts her guards as monstrous, Esfandiari strongly praises the vast majority of her guards. She describes one guard, Hajj Khanum, as being "genuinely concerned about my well-being" (162). When Khanum gives her a rose, Esfandiari states, "The gesture, in the unkind world of Evin, moved me" (162). Along similar lines, another of Esfandiari's guards, whom she nicknames "Sunny Face," keeps Esfandiari optimistic and purchases items for the inmates at "the local market" (163). As Esfandiari would have nothing to gain by depicting her guards in this manner, it is a further testament to her ability to maintain her objectivity in the worst of situations. Whereas Ghahramani's guards tended to be embittered war veterans, disfigured war casualties, or just generally sadistic (at least according to Ghaharamani's narrative), Esfandiari's are, by and large,[17] intelligent, religious, and sympathetic. While they tend to come from the lower to lower-middle class, her guards are generally well-educated, and according to Esfandiari, not only do they take pride in their appearance, but also they possess the hope that their families will be able to economically advance (165). Esfandiari even explains, "At least one aspired to go to America" (165). Again, while Esfandiari may be kept in a much nicer part of Evin Prison than Ghahramani,[18] it is also possible that Esfandiari is able to keep her objectivity while being incarcerated, whereas the tortured Ghahramani is not. In addition, the difference in the attitudes of the guards could also be due to a slowly shifting momentum in Iran (or at least in Evin Prison) towards a greater open-mindedness.

As mentioned above, Esfandiari's actual imprisonment is nowhere near the ordeal that Ghahramani experienced. Esfandiari is never physically tortured; she is consistently given food and water, even if the former is not to her liking, and allowed the opportunity to purchase items through a local market (with help from "Sunny Face"). At the same time, Esfandiari doesn't merely acquiesce to the expectations placed upon her. Despite the regulations, she doesn't agree to wear the chador even when in front of the prosecuting magistrate (130). In response, the magistrate says it is not permissible to be married to a Jew and that doing so is analogous to having "committed adultery" (130) and that "the punishment is death by stoning" (130). This, though, seems more aimed to intimidate Esfandiari as opposed to an actual threat. Like Ghahramani, Esfandiari is also largely denied due process, and is initially kept without any kind of substantive legal proceedings. When Iranian officials try to get Esfandiari to sign a paper waiving her right to a lawyer, Esfandiari refuses, and attempts, through her contacts, to obtain the services of Nobel Prize–winning lawyer and human rights activist Shirin Ebadi (131). One of the ways Esfandiari keeps strong is by almost continually exercising in her cell (walking and doing exercises) and she keeps mentally alert by composing books in her head (158).[19] Unlike Ghahramani, who is allowed no outside contact, Esfandiari is also allowed to call her ailing mother two to three times a week.

As a diplomat with connections, Esfandiari's case also illuminates the extent to which the media, both Western and Iranian, can play a significant role in the lives of prisoners, and also has become the primary way through which many Western (or even Iranian) prisoners can get released.[20] Indeed, if Ghahramani had the global or even local media strongly on her side as Esfandiari did, Ghahramani's imprisonment would have presumably been much easier and shorter in length. To a large extent, the fight for Esfandiari's release is one built upon public relations and the use of the global media. On the one hand, the Islamic Regime wants to use Esfandiari to provide evidence that the United States is plotting to overthrow the Islamic Regime in a kind of Velvet Revolution reminiscent of those in late 1980s and early 1990s Eastern Europe. Indeed, according to Esfandiari, her interrogators are not subtle about wanting her to play this role. She explains, "On my very first day at Evin, Hajj Agha had hinted that my release would be expedited if I gave 'an interview' explaining what I knew of the American agenda for regime change in Iran" (172–3). Possibly because she feels that it will help get her released, Esfandiari does agree to do this interview, and feels she can do it and still be truthful. However, even though after completing the interview, Esfandiari feels that she "had spoken no untruths," and "implicated no one," she also feels "soiled and tainted by the whole affair" (176). Further, according to Esfandiari, the Iranian editors end up splicing her footage to make it seem that she was involved in a domestic (within Iran) Velvet Revolution attempt (along with the United States).[21]

Yet, it is not Iran that ultimately wins the media battle for public relations over Esfandiari, but rather Esfandiari's relatives and friends in the United States (and to a lesser degree, in Iran) prove victorious (victory being her release).[22] Not only does the staged Velvet Revolution program largely fail to resonate with the Iranian public, Esfandiari's own appearance (diminutive), age (67), gender (female), position (largely non-partisan academic) and familial status (grandmother) all work against the Iranian Regime, who, in contrast, appears cruel and heartless.[23] According to Esfandiari, "The story of a sixty-seven-year-old grandmother held in solitary confinement in a notorious prison simply for having organized conferences on Iranian and Middle Eastern issues was in itself compelling. The Iranian government fueled press attention by the extraordinary allegations it made against me" (200). Part of the reason the allegations seem so "extraordinary" is the difficulty the general public has believing that a sixty-seven-year-old grandmother could be a kind of spy or the impetus for a Velvet Revolution. Also, in large part due to the extraordinary efforts of Esfandiari's husband as well as members of the Wilson Center, a grassroots effort, organized and led on the Internet, also helps to spur on Esfandiari's release.[24] Further, the press battle doesn't end when Esfandiari is released. Due to stress and her own almost incessant exercising while in prison, Esfandiari loses a considerable amount of weight in prison, and appears especially frail (and potentially abused) when she is released from prison. While, even by her account, Esfandiari is not denied food nor is she physically tortured, it appears that she has been. Consequently, while Esfandiari is still in Iran, waiting to go to back to the United States, her main interrogator pays her a courtesy call to make sure she is healthy and is receiving her appropriate medications.

While, like Ghahramani, after her incarceration in Evin, Esfandiari leaves Iran, presumably never to come back,[25] Esfandiari is more objective about the Islamic Regime than Ghahramani, although for both, the experience has clearly tarnished their opinion of their homeland. In both cases this comes through in the memoir, although Ghahramani depicts Iran in much bleaker terms than Esfandiari. Esfandiari's seeming disdain for Iran is more political in nature and mainly can be seen after she returns home to the United States, when, in September 2008, Esfandiari discovers that she has been invited to a reception for Mahmoud Ahmadinejad when he is in New York City for a United Nations session (219). It is hard to disagree with Esfandiari that "the irony was overwhelming" (219). In her own words, "The very government that a year earlier had branded me a spy, an agent of Mossad and the CIA, an enabler of 'soft revolution,' and a threat to national security was inviting me to appear in the same room with the Iranian president and perhaps to engage with him in idle chatter as he circulated among his guests" (219). For Esfandiari, this is merely more evidence of the despotic behavior she perceives in the Iranian government.[26] However, she is able to distinguish between the government and the people in a manner that Ghahramani seems largely unable or unwilling to do.

If indeed the "scars of prison never really heal," as Esfandiari suggests, those scars can manifest into a greater animosity towards the injurious party — namely Iran (221). Towards that end, Esfandiari explains that she is still "devoted" to Iran, but does not approve of the government because she believes that it does not treat its citizens "with decency" (222). However, true to her ability to maintain objectivity as an academic and activist, Esfandiari chooses to not give up on Iran. Instead she concludes, "I continue to believe that the governments of Iran and the United States should sit at the same table and talk to each other. Thirty years of estrangement have yielded nothing of value, and I believe that change is more likely to come of an Iran that is engaged with the rest of the world rather than isolated from it" (222). Perhaps most tellingly, after her release, Esfandiari went back to her prior position as Director of the Middle East Project for the Wilson Center where she continues to this date (2011). If her experience did indeed help solidify her beliefs in "human freedom and individual rights" as well as her commitment that more needs to be done to help other prisoners who "have no one to speak for them," Esfandiari is now in a position to function as an excellent arbitrator between the two countries (222).

If it is accurate that Iranian prison narratives capture readers by subscribing to the neo-colonialist desire to save brown women from brown men, it would follow that more Iranian prison narratives would be published by women, which indeed appears to be the case. Also, if the success of Iranian prison narratives can be said to hinge somewhat on the damsel (Ghahramani) or grandmother (Esfandiari) in distress archetypes, it would also follow that more Iranian prison narratives would be published by women. While this is the case, there are other important Iranian prison narratives written by men. To begin, I will explore the case of Maziar Bahari, an Iranian-Canadian journalist. *Newsweek* published Bahari's prison narrative in 2009. To a large degree, Bahari's incarceration can be traced back to his appearance on the comedic *The Daily Show with Jon Stewart* during an account by Jason Jones (a reporter for *The Daily Show*) of life in Iran in June 2009. As Bahari explains:

> Jason interviewed me in a Tehran coffee shop, pretending to be a thick-skulled American. He dressed like some character out of a B movie about mercenaries in the Middle East — with a checkered Palestinian kaffiyeh around his neck and dark sunglasses. The "interview" was very short. Jason asked me why Iran was evil. I answered that Iran was not evil. I added that, as a matter of fact, Iran and America shared many enemies and interests in common [par. 47].

This interview with *The Daily Show*, while comedic in nature, according to Bahari was enough to make the Iranian government and law enforcement suspicious of his supposed Western connections to the point that they arrested him while he was in Iran.[27] Instead of realizing that the skit was mostly falsified or exaggerated, Bahari's interrogator, whom he calls Mr. Rosewater, takes it seriously, asking Bahari why Jones was "dressed like a spy" (par. 48). One reason Mr. Rosewater may not see (or refuses to recognize) the humor in the episode is because it occurs during the time of the June 2009 presidential riots, following the re-election of Ahmadinejad. The organization that arrests Bahari, the IRGC or Islamic Revolutionary Guard Corps, which reports to Iran's Supreme Leader Khamenei, had become more powerful of late, and according to Bahari "many suspect that the Guards rigged the election. Certainly they led the crackdown that followed" (par. 9). It doesn't help that Bahari is an expatriate Iranian[28] and a Western (Canadian) journalist, thereby perceived to be biased and a possible spy.

In many ways, Bahari's prison narrative can be seen as combination of Ghahramani's and Esfandiari's. Like Ghahramani, Bahari is physically tortured (although perhaps not as severely as she is). However, like Esfandiari, Bahari is able to maintain his objectivity and does not purposely provoke his guards or interrogators. While Bahari does portray his primary interrogator, Mr. Rosewater, as vicious and sadistic, he does not completely demonize him as Ghahramani tends to do in her prison narrative. Again, in keeping with Michel Foucault's analogy of the interrogation to a duel, when Bahari is interrogated, he is immediately put in a demeaning position by being forced to sit at a desk similar to "primary school," while he is blindfolded and instructed "to look down" (par. 1). Mr. Rosewater wastes no time letting Bahari know that his life is on the line. As Bahari explains, "'This prison can be the end of the line for you if you don't cooperate' were his welcoming words" (par. 12). These fear tactics continue throughout Bahari's incarceration; even right after Bahari is freed, Mr. Rosewater tells him "never to speak of what had happened to me in jail," or he "would be hunted down," where he could be put "in a bag" (par. 12).

Similar to Esfandiari, Bahari is accused of being a spy, and his seemingly paranoid interrogators are determined to find political connections between Bahari and others. Mr. Rosewater tells him that Bahari is "in charge of a secret American network" (par. 29). Like Ghahramani, Bahari appears to give in after the relentless questioning,[29] and even confesses to things that he may not have done (although the extent to which he does this remains unclear). However, Bahari's confession is not enough to save him from the "beatings" he subsequently receives from Mr. Rosewater,[30] whom Bahari portrays as deriving a rather sadistic pleasure from hurting Bahari, especially when Bahari experiences migraine headaches.[31] Coupled with Bahari's physical torture are Mr. Rosewater's threats that Bahari may be executed in the not so distant future.[32] To combat his interrogators, like Esfandiari, Bahari begins to almost relentlessly exercise in his tiny "20-square foot cell," which he describes as akin to a tomb (par. 23). While Ghahramani goes through waves of anger, suicidal tendencies, and murderous rage, Bahari generally stays stronger (like Esfandiari), although he reports, "Twice I seriously considered suicide by breaking my glasses and slitting my wrists with the shards. I wondered how long it would take to bleed to death" (par. 98).

As mentioned earlier, one similarity in the three prison narratives is the Islamic Republic's relentless belief that the inmates have been involved in a kind of conspiracy, especially if they are from the West.[33] To some extent, as we saw with Esfandiari, this is understandable in the sense that the Bush administration did sponsor a rather nefarious bill presumably aimed at regime change in Iran. Also, in their quest for information, the interrogators might purposely want to maintain an aura of certainty so they can wear the interrogated down. It is telling that Bahari's interrogators do not distinguish between Western media and Western governments, believing them to be part and parcel of one another, presumably because they are in Iran. Consequently, when Bahari is accused of being an "agent of foreign intelligence organizations," and Bahari asks which organizations, he is told "CIA, MI6, Mossad, and NEWSWEEK" (par. 7). His interrogator, at least, does not distinguish between the free press (*Newsweek*) and the American government (CIA), presumably because the Islamic Republic does not really have a free press.

Similar to Esfandiari, Iranian officials also accuse Bahari of participating in a plot to help stage a Velvet Revolution, which illustrates the extent to which they want to have evidence with which to implicate the United States and the West. Nearly identical to Esfandiari, Bahari's captors also want him to explain, on video, "how a velvet revolution was staged — by foreigners and corrupt elites, using the Western media — and how only the wisdom and munificence of the Supreme Leader had thwarted this latest attempt" (par. 66). Specifically, Mr. Rosewater "insisted that I'd masterminded the coverage of the election by the agents of the Western media in Iran" (par. 64). Given the turmoil and violence in June 2009 Iran, it appears that his captors were trying to come up with any reason to blame the West (especially the United States) for the ensuing political chaos, as accepting it as a legitimate internal rebellion could give additional power to the demonstrations. Hence, Bahari's captors are especially harsh towards him, accusing him of destroying "people" and provoking "people against the Leader" (par. 64). Also, to be freed, like Esfandiari, Bahari agrees to answer questions on television about a Velvet Revolution in Iran, and he also feels, like her, that he can do so without confessing to anything specific. In his own words, "I tried to keep my answers as vague as possible, with what I hoped would come across as ironic detachment. (A source in the old Intelligence Ministry told me later that my soliloquy was 'a case study in saying nothing')" (par. 67).[34] Just as Esfandiari reported how the Bush administration's attempt to surreptitiously fund regime change in Iran not only failed, but also helped lead to increasing paranoia and suspicion of the West by Iran, Bahari's experiences indicate that the United States' more extreme interrogation techniques at facilities like Abu Ghraib have helped justify similar techniques practiced upon incarcerated Westerners in

Iran like Bahari, who, once admitted to prison, is greeted with the following from a guard: "Welcome to Abu Ghraib, Guantánamo, or whatever it is you Americans build" (par. 20).[35]

Indeed, Bahari's captors seem very aware and cognizant of the United States, in particular. For instance, Bahari's main interrogator, Mr. Rosewater, appears to be obsessed by New Jersey, which he seems to think of as representing all that he and and others have come to despise about American culture: materialism, atheism, immorality.[36] Indeed, Mr. Rosewater calls New Jersey "godless" and a soulless façade; hence, he accuses Bahari of "planning to eradicate the pure religion of Muhammad in this country and replace it with 'American' Islam. A New Jersey Islam" (par. 34–35).[37] Given how many Iranians have access to satellite television, it is certainly possible that Mr. Rosewater's perceptions of a shadowy, amoral, even criminal New Jersey could be shaped from numerous crime dramas and gangster movies.

In Bahari's case, then, even more so than for Ghahramani or Esfandiari, the media plays a primary role not only in helping to get Bahari arrested, but also, like Esfandiari, in shaping the impressions of his interrogators as well as ultimately helping to free him. As a journalist himself, Bahari seems well aware of the power of the media. Hence, when a "friendly guard," calls Bahari "Mr. Hillary Clinton" because Clinton had mentioned Bahari and was working to help free him, Bahari is ecstatic to the point that he "wanted to hug the guard," because he knows this will be his best chance to be freed (par. 100). Indeed, as it turns out, just as the Wilson Center and Esfandiari's husband worked tirelessly to help get her released with help from the media, so had *Newsweek* and Bahari's wife, Paola, who relentlessly kept giving interviews (par. 101–102).[38] It seems that Bahari's interrogators are media-savvy as well, and as they notice the tide is shifting against them, especially with its focus upon Bahari's expecting wife (which Bahari calls "a key part of the publicity campaign on my behalf"), they tactically try to use the media to save face, with Mr. Rosewater "claiming he wanted to free me before our baby was born at the end of October" (par. 101). Almost identical to Esfandiari's experience, not only is there external pressure to release Bahari, there is also internal pressure to release him as well. According to Bahari, "there were Iranian officials who also disagreed with my detention" (par. 102). Both incarcerations and releases reveal a growing fissure in Iranian politics and within the Iranian populace made ever so apparent during the June 2009 demonstrations. Ultimately, with officials feeling that Bahari is "more of a liability than an asset in jail," he is released after nearly four months in prison (par. 102).

While, like Esfandiari, Bahari's interrogators and guards try to intimidate and coerce him to be silent,[39] they are even more stern with Bahari (possibly because he is younger and male), as represented best by Mr. Rosewater's last words to Bahari, that not only can the Revolutionary Guards find Bahari "anywhere in the world," but that he should "remember the [body] bag" (par. 107). However, like Esfandiari, who went back to work at the Wilson Center after she was released from prison, Bahari rebels against his captors most publicly by reappearing on *The Daily Show* in late November 2009 after his release. In this way, Bahari snubbed his nose at his captors and suggested that he will not be cowed into submission. However, this may have only resulted in the additional ire of the Iranian government, who subsequently (in Spring 2010) sentenced Bahari to "13 and a half years in prison and 74 lashes for six charges ranging from propagating against the state to insulting President Mahmoud Ahmadinejad" (Mobasherat, par. 2).[40] While it might seem odd that the Iranian government specified the exact number of lashes Bahari would receive, doing so serves several purposes. First, it makes the barbaric act of whipping someone seem ordered and exact, alluding to some sort of formula whereby certain acts equal a certain number of lashes. Also, it illustrates how, as Foucault has argued, torture "forms part of a ritual," subject to "detailed rules," and which aims to "mark the victim," either physically or psychologically (34). In this case, the Iranian government, clearly displeased with Bahari, attempts to mark him in both these ways.

The next and last prison narrative to be explored, written by Ahmad Batebi, is more of a transcribed (and often translated) oral history, possibly in part because Farsi is the author's native language and he does not appear to be completely adept with English. Whereas Bahari, unless he decides to go back to Iran (which is highly unlikely to say the least), can only imagine what it would be like to be imprisoned for years at a time, Batebi experienced all this and more during his lengthy incarceration in Evin Prison. Batebi, a University of Tehran student in the mid– to late 1990s, was studying photojournalism when he became involved in the student protests and demonstrations in the late 1990s, which reached a fever pitch in 1999.[41] Batebi was unwittingly involved in a demonstration[42] that took an especially violent turn, when Iranian soldiers began firing upon the crowd, injuring and killing several students. Batebi and others were arrested, but Batebi stood out due to a picture taken of him, which became famous worldwide, with him "holding the bloody T-shirt of a fellow student demonstrator" (Shane and Gordon, par. 6).[43] Despite the fact that he had nothing to do with the taking and subsequent distribution of the picture and did not even see it until he was on trial, Batebi was held responsible for the damage that the picture appears to have done to Iran's reputation. In fact, Batebi reports being first shown the picture by the judge at his trial, who subsequently told him, "You have signed your own death sentence" (Shane and Gordon, par. 6). This judge also told Batebi, "You have defaced the face of the Islamic Republic that is a representative of God on earth. You have defaced it around the world. And therefore you have to be sentenced to death" ("How Ahmad Batebi," par. 13).

Once again, we see with the case of Batebi how aware and concerned the Islamic Regime is about how their image can be tarnished or embellished by the global media. Towards that end, to try to manage Iran's global image, the Iranian government attempts to "force" Batebi "to say on television that the famous T-shirt was stained with paint or animal blood" (Shane and Gordon, par. 26). When Batebi refuses to do this, his captors torture him, beginning with "17 months in solitary confinement,"[44] and continuing by beating Batebi with "a metal cable," breaking his teeth, simulating drowning in "a pool of excrement," sleep deprivation, mock executions, and finally, cutting him and then putting salt in his wounds (Shane and Gordon, par. 26–9; "How Ahmad Batebi," par. 19, 20, 27, 34). Similar to Ghahramani and Bahari, Batebi also reports that "several times during his torture he wished he would die, and a few times he thought he was going to," most specifically during his mock executions ("How Ahmad Batebi," par. 34). This is a legitimate fear on Batebi's part, for not only does Iran execute some of its prisoners, during Batebi's mock executions, the prison officials literally executed inmates right next to Batebi ("How Ahmad Batebi," par. 38). While these are clear human rights violations and morally indefensible, assuming their accuracy, they illustrate the extent to which the Iranian government will go to prevent negative caricatures of them in the global media, for they have realized that once these caricatures have been sufficiently distributed (which doesn't take very long with the Internet), there is little to mitigate the damage already wrought.

As mentioned previously, Batebi's incarceration and torture can clearly be traced back to the worldwide attention that the photo taken of him during the 1999 student demonstrations received. From that, it would seem that Western media inadvertently condemns Batebi to his fate in prison; however, it also appears that Western media helps save his life, "as advocates around the world took up his cause. Consequently, his death sentence, for 'agitating people to create unrest,' was commuted, first to 15 years and then to 10" (Shane and Gordon, par. 30). Again, similar to Esfandiari and Bahari, Batebi benefits from lobbying efforts on his behalf due primarily to the popularity of the picture taken of him. Also, unintentionally, Batebi also ends up benefiting from his subsequent medical problems. Released and then rearrested in 2006, Batebi subsequently "suffered what was probably a stroke and several seizures," and was then "released for medical treatment" (Shane and Gordon, par. 32).[45] However, instead of returning to prison, as he was ordered to do,

Batebi, with help from some Kurdish volunteers, fled Iran for Iraq "with no passport and little identification to a new land" (Shane and Gordon, par. 41). While the Iranian media has "suggested that he [Batebi] has long been in league with the United States and Israel," Batebi insists that "the United States played no role in his departure from Iran, a fact American officials confirmed" (Shane and Gordon, par. 7, 11). However, as a spokesperson for the National Security Council, Gordon D. Johndroe, explains, "The United States did give him permission to enter this country 'out of concern for his safety'" (qtd. in Shane and Gordon, par. 11). Indeed, recent reports suggest that Batebi resides in the Washington, D.C., area and works for Voice of America[46] ("How Ahmad Batebi," par. 56).

Similar to that of Ghahramani, Batebi's narrative may have sparked interest in the United States because while it vilifies Iran, it also glorifies the United States and the West. Indeed, Batebi's feelings towards the United States are immediately apparent right after he lands in the United States. He reports being "enthralled" when seeing "the airport worker waving the jet into the gate was a Muslim woman wearing a tight head scarf" (Shane and Gordon, par. 45). In his own words, Batebi explains, "It seems to me that people here are free to live their lives, as long as they do no harm to anyone else" (qtd. in Shane and Gordon, par. 46). Still, as much as Batebi seems to embrace the seeming freedoms he discovers in the United States, he still holds some allegiance to Iran, and in that sense he mirrors Esfandiari's objective diplomacy. Both are able to successfully separate the government from the people. Indeed, "when asked about the possibility of American military action against Iran," Batebi responds, "I might go back and fight for my country myself" (qtd. in Shane and Gordon, par. 52). At the same time, Batebi's narrative illustrates the primary ideals of the American Dream: that with hard work and commitment, anyone can achieve at least a modest level of success and happiness. As Shane and Gordon explain:

> He has some ordinary goals, the dreams of a man who spent most of his 20s in a prison cell. He wants to study politics and sociology, he said, and work as a photojournalist. He wants to play guitar. He thought for a moment, then he remembered one more modest ambition. "I want to fish!" Mr. Batebi said, his face relaxing into a smile. "I'm going to go fishing!" [par. 53].

In an interview, Batebi also explains that he wants Iranians to "reach democracy" but he believes that to get there, Iranians would have to "follow a long cultural process" (qtd. in "Iran Has No Capacity," par. 35). It is uncertain whether or not Iran will ever want to become a Western style democracy, but Batebi's and the other Iranian and Iranian diasporic prison narratives demonstrate the wide gulf that separates the West from Iran.

While these prison narratives can be seen as testifying to human rights violations, they also illustrate the deep fissures and fractures within Iranian government and society. As Shirin Ebadi has suggested, Iran seems most vulnerable to documented human rights violations as well as to the influence and power of global media in general. However, these narratives also illustrate the extent to which Iran has become media savvy as well, counteracting their own negative image by the West with their portrayal of an amoral, colonialist, and corrupt West. Caught between the rhetoric of the two countries, Iranian political prisoners like these four explored in this chapter become almost akin to pawns moved by both governments. As Susan Brison argues, "working through, or remastering, traumatic memory (in the case of human-inflicted trauma) involves a shift from being the object or medium of someone else's (the perpetrator's) speech (or other expressive behavior) to being the subject of one's own" (39). Thereby, it is the pawns that ultimately have the last and most lasting words — through their prison narratives, thus giving the form even more importance and significance as a way for the author to illustrate the inner workings of the Islamic Regime from deep within one of its most notorious areas: Evin Prison.

# Censorship in Iran
## *Shahriar Mandanipour's*
## Censoring an Iranian Love Story

Ever since Ayatollah Khomeini issued a fatwa against Salman Rushdie in 1989 for the supposedly blasphemous content of Rushdie's novel *The Satanic Verses* (1989), Iran, and more generally, the Islamic world, has been thought (at least from a Western perspective) to be an oppressive, stifling, and controlling environment for any would-be writer intent on either tackling serious subject matter or offering cultural, political, or religious critique.[1] To be sure, this point of view has some validity, and it is objectively accurate to state that Iran does not have the freedom of the press that Western countries possess, nor do writers or publishers in Iran have the freedom to print what they choose. However, the issue of censorship in Iran and in Islamic countries in a wider sense[2] is significantly more complex than it might initially appear. First, in the case of Iran, there have been developments in what artworks can and cannot be published or shown there since the 1989 fatwa against Rushdie. As Trevor Mostyn explains, in 1990s and early 2000s Iran, especially with the more reformist Khatami administration (1997–2005), there was a gradual loosening of censorship as noted by the release of certain Iranian films as well as certain Western art.[3] However, there have also been continued examples of imprisonment and executions of writers deemed to be blasphemous or threatening.[4]

The gradual opening up of the Iranian press may seem at odds with the continued crackdown upon Iranian writers and intellectuals, but it reveals a growing fissure in Iranian society between a more liberal segment of the population (which tends to be more numerous but holds less power) and a more conservative religious segment of the population (which tends to be less numerous but holds more power). It also reveals the vagueness and ambiguity involved in Iranian laws about publication and censorship. As Mostyn explains, "Technically, the Iranian Constitution guarantees freedom of publication and the press, but that freedom is not unconditional. Article 24 states that: 'Publications and the press are free to publish their ideas unless they are injurious to the fundamentals of Islam or public rights. Details will be provided by legislation'" (53). This law allows officials extremely wide latitude to define what is "injurious to the fundamentals of Islam or public rights," and what is not. Injury, just like obscenity, is in the eye of the beholder, and the beholder in this case tends to be more religious and conservative minded than the general Iranian public.

Still, the issue of censorship in Iran becomes even more complex when investigating the causes. A common automatic response to Iranian censorship would be outright condemnation, along with a general debasement of those in the Iranian government who sanction censorship. However, this argument fails to consider the different cultural beliefs and practices of Iran and the West, specifically the United States. First, as established in previous chapters, the Iranian government often acts upon a premise of suspicion and paranoia, although, as previously established, this suspicion and general paranoia is not completely irrational given that Western countries like the United States have a substantial history of meddling in or attempting to meddle in Iranian politics. Towards this end, in his book *Giving Offense*, J.M. Coetzee argues that paranoia helps give rise to censorship because the same logic paranoids use, namely that "the air is filled with coded messages deriding them or plotting their destruction," extends to the review of literature (34). Literature can then be seen as being either a political tool for the author or something that can have significant political importance. In this sense, Iranian officials can be seen as emphasizing, in ways they hardly intended, the importance of literature as a powerful art form with the ability to shape readers. For these officials, censorship allows the government an element "of control" in helping to determine the thoughts and beliefs of the populace (Coetzee 34). In Iran's case, the government wishes to exclude the discussion and coverage of perceived taboo subject matter, such as sexuality or critique of the government or religion, which could, in turn, they believe, lead to rebellion and a loss of power for those currently in power.

For Coetzee, censorship and paranoia are part and parcel of a "dictatorship" and while it could be argued that Iran is a dictatorship run mainly by the Supreme Leader (Khamenei) and to a lesser extent by the President (Ahmadinejad), there is more involved in Iranian censorship than just the political structure of the country.[5] In this case, it is the combination of an uncertain political regime attempting to protect itself from potential (and possibly actual) threats coupled with an emphasis on community over the individual that can drive countries like Iran to censorship. To a lesser extent, some Muslims in censoring countries also argue that the freedom of the press in the West is somewhat of a chimera.[6] Towards that end, some "Muslim writers even believe that freedom of speech is permitted in the West on condition that it does not target Israel" (Mostyn 19). While such claims may not be substantiated, Western countries do censor in times of war (e.g., during the Bush administration, the media was not allowed to show pictures of the coffins of American soldiers who had been killed in Afghanistan or Iraq), and the United States had its own literary censorship trials all the way through the 1950s and 1960s.[7]

While most Western writers and critics would presumably agree with J.M. Coetzee's claim that state censorship of writing is "an inherently bad thing," even Coetzee himself suggests that while "writing does not flourish under censorship ... there may even be cases where external censorship challenges the writer in interesting ways or spurs creativity" (9, 11). If indeed, writers in a repressive, censoring country feel that "their minds have been invaded," their writing can be seen as a vigilant response to this perceived invasion as well as a way "that they express their outrage" (Coetzee 36). Similarly, Michael Levine calls censorship "an impediment whose very resistance makes another, more equivocal and double-edged style of writing possible" (2).[8] In this chapter, we will explore an example of this double-edged style of writing in a novel by Shahriar Mandanipour, *Censoring an Iranian Love Story* (2009).

Due to Iranian censorship of certain forms and portions of literature and the arts, there is a dearth of younger, politically and socially conscious Iranian literary writers. As we will see in a later chapter, the vast majority of young politically conscious Iranians have taken to the Internet, primarily though their use of blogs, but also, mainly for organizational purposes, to Twitter as well. To determine the particular difficulties facing contemporary Iranian literary writers still living in Iran, it is helpful to examine Mandanipour's *Censoring an Iranian Love Story* (which will subsequently be referred to in abbreviated form as *CILS*), translated and published in the United States, but not yet legally published in Iran. Born in 1957 and having served as a former solider during the Iran-Iraq War during the 1980s, Mandanipour is not technically a part of the Iranian "Burnt Generation" (who were generally born in the late 1960s and 1970s and who comprise the majority of this study). However, his generation is not vastly dissimilar to the Burnt Generation, especially since, after initially fighting for the Iranian Revolution in 1979, Mandanipour has since changed his views and grown more cynical about politics. As he explains in an interview, "My generation sacrificed, but didn't know what democracy was. To get killed was an honor.... We got rid of the Shah, but didn't know what we wanted" (Lydon, par. 1). In addition, the main characters in *CILS* are also younger (in their twenties and thirties), and hence, could be considered to be members of the Burnt Generation.

After Iran became more of a theocracy in the early 1980s, Mandanipour and others of his generation grew disillusioned, but in many ways, they also grew complacent as the Islamic Regime gathered strength and punished those who spoke out against it. Mandanipour himself seems to hold more faith in the younger Iranian generation, who, as he describes in an interview, "wants freedom to walk together, and the future right now" (Lyons, par. 1). Still, we will see through his multifaceted narrative how difficult it is for a romantic relationship to blossom in Iran and how even more difficult it is to effectively write about romance in the Islamic Republic.

As mentioned earlier, Mandanipour participated in the Iranian Revolution and subsequently fought in the Iran-Iraq war, although reportedly more for literary than nationalistic or moral reasons.[9] Unfortunately, Mandanipour would initially not be able to use these or any of his experiences in the Iran-Iraq war in his work since "his work faced a complete ban from 1992 to 1998, which was lifted in 1998" (Baghramian, par. 2). With the reforms brought about by the Khatami administration, however, Mandanipour was finally able to publish his work in 1998. As Baghramian explains, in that same year, "almost perversely, he was awarded Iran's most prestigious literary prize for contributions to literature in the previous two decades" (Baghramian, par. 2).[10] Subsequently, Mandanipour has published (in Iran) a number of books of fiction and nonfiction as well as scores of essays.[11] Still, this is not to suggest that Mandanipour's recent publications have come easy or without great peril. Reportedly, during this time Mandanipour "has been subjected to harassment, threats, censorship, and intimidation by Iran's Ministry of Culture and Islamic Guidance" ("Shahriar Mandanipour," par 4). Presumably tired of having to self-censor, abridge or cloak his work in dense, possibly clunky figurative language to escape censorship, Mandanipour moved to the United States in 2006 "on Brown University's International Writers Project Fellowship" (Baghramian, par. 3). Subsequently, Mandanipour became a Writer in Residence at Harvard University and Boston College as well as a Visiting Professor of Literary Arts at Brown University (Baghramian, par. 3; Eisenmenger, par. 1).[12]

Similar to previous works already explored in this study such as *My Life as a Traitor* and *Reading Lolita in Tehran*, *CILS* provides a rather critical portrayal of contemporary Iran, while reviews of *CILS* have been largely positive, possibly because the critics reviewing *CILS* write for Western journals whose editors and readers may be more apt to perceive Iran as a totalitarian and oppressive country. Critics praised Mandanipour for his metafictional techniques as shedding important light into censorship, the Islamic Republic, and the role that literature can and cannot play in the Islamic Republic (Wood 74; Hoffert 85).[13] Other critics suggest that the novel provides "a timely glimpse of the complex and infuriatingly paradoxical society that is today's Iran" (Baghramian, par. 11). Along similar lines, Michiko Kakutani, writing for *The New York Times*, suggests that *CILS* "leaves the reader with a harrowing sense of what it is like to live in Tehran under the mullahs' rule, and the myriad ways in which the Islamic government's strict edicts on everything from clothing to relationships between the sexes permeate daily life" ("Where Romance," par. 2). These critics assume that Mandanipour authentically portrays the "real" Iran, possibly because he has lived there virtually his whole life and he has directly experienced censorship, whereas they have presumably not. In that regard, Mandanipour may receive a much gentler reception than Azar Nafisi who also painted a bleak portrait of Iran,[14] but who many critics subsequently labeled a neo-colonizer colluding with the neo-conservative movement in the United States. Yet, whereas Nafisi championed Western writers in *Reading Lolita in Tehran*, Mandanipour is an Iranian fiction writer, not an academic, and hence, cannot be accused of the same kind of literary and social colonialism as Nafisi. Should that mean that Mandanipour's critical portrayals of a largely irrational Islamic Republic are to be trusted more? Practically speaking, they probably should not be, but realistically, they are, by Western critics and the Western reading audience. In fact, James Wood, writing for *The New Yorker*, suggests that "the text is veiled, but the author lifts the veil for his non–Iranian audience" (73). Such language may cater to the Western public's fascination with the veil and the assumption that there is a reality or truth hidden underneath the veil, when this might not be the case at all.

*CILS*, in fact, is not critiqued for its depiction of Iran (which seems to be essentially accepted by critics as accurate),[15] but for some of its plot devices.[16] For instance, Baghramian and Wood critique *CILS* for what they perceive to be the "uninteresting" or "stilted and dull" love story (par. 9; par. 74). While such a criticism is understandable, both writers miss the point that Mandanipour is making, which is, among other things, that the ultra repressive codes of the Islamic Republic take away meaning, depth, and intrigue from romantic relationships; rather, the intrigue and suspense revolve all around the logistics of meeting. In essence, ironically, the depth is in the prelude since the edicts of the Islamic Republic stymie romantic relationships (at least pre-marital ones) from progressing. Coupled with this is the fact that the protagonists, despite being in their 20s and 30s, are both inexperienced virgins and their first attempted foray into a relationship is understandably awkward and uncomfortable, especially since to merely spend any time together they must go against the Islamic Republic's law that stipulates that unmarried men and women not related to one another should not be left alone in the same room together and should not be seen together in public. Unless one accepts pre-arranged or hastily constructed marriages, this creates a conundrum and seeming paradox that Mandanipour explores at greater lengths in the novel — namely, how can Iranians begin relationships with one another when they are not supposed to be alone together in the first place?

This conundrum or paradox faces an Iranian writer who wants to write a love story because the substance of the novel (meeting and courting) should not technically occur if the Iranian populace were strictly following the edicts of the Islamic Regime. Further, were Mandanipour to write about more clandestine romantic relationships, he could be accused of contributing to the delinquency of the public, and hence, his novel would never be published in Iran. As it turns out, this actually did occur as *CILS* "cannot be read in Iran," while it can be read in the West (Wood 72). Perhaps realizing this, Mandanipour appears to write for an American or Western audience. For his part, the narrator of *CILS* acknowledges the difficulties involved in trying to publish a love story in Iran, but he defends his decision because he considers himself "an experienced writer" who "may be able to write my story in such a way that it survives the blade of censorship" (11). However, while the narrator uses various Iranian and Islamic symbols and metaphors as well as other tricks and techniques, it is not enough to escape censorship and ultimately it is the censor who bests the narrator (although it is not a fair fight since the censor has the power of the state behind him). Still, the censor does not best Mandanipour himself who ultimately is able to get the novel published (albeit not in Iran).

In *CILS*, Mandanipour illustrates the manifold challenges facing a contemporary Iranian writer who, in many ways, is disallowed from writing about most things of social or personal importance. For Baghramian, though, "the received impression that censorship stifles artistic creativity is not always true," because to her, Mandanipour and other authors have been able to circumvent censorship through their use of "a unique literary language with thousands of symbols, metaphors, and similes that in addition to their mystical meanings and interpretations also whisper of amorous and sexual" (par. 9). Yet, Mandanipour does not suggest that censorship stifles creativity as much as it stifles the ability of the author to tell a coherent and realistic story (if the subject matter is something that the Islamic Republic has deemed illicit) and it also can prevent the author from communicating what she or he might want to convey to the audience. Even simple things like describing Sara lying down "on her bed" to read a book cannot be included because the mere mention of lying on a bed is perceived to be sexual in nature (17). The narrator also has to omit descriptions of prison and politics. For instance, the narrator cannot write about how Dara used to be in prison and how he has to check in with a law enforcement official at periodic intervals. The censor also will not accept any political critiques of the Islamic Regime, however vague, such as Dara's suggestion that "the more I swear I am no longer involved in politics, the more they suspect me" (31). Consequently, the narrator crosses out such language (31).

Unfortunately, for the narrator, much of what he feels compelled to self-censor (or is directly told by the censor to omit) is details that help paint a more complex and realistic portrait of life in contemporary Iran. For his part, the censor aims to portray an idealistic Islamic Republic mostly free of strife and immorality. The censored material includes everything from simple profanity to the basic demeanor and actions of the characters. For instance, the narrator finds that he cannot write about amoral or questionable characters who try to bribe Sara into removing her headscarf because, the censor would argue, such a scene would either encourage immoral behavior or be insulting to the Iranian people. Thus, the censor and the Islamic Regime regard literature as either didactic or reflective. Despite the fact that the narrator hardly glorifies the character who removes Sara's headscarf, he realizes that the scene could be viewed "as provoking and injurious to public chastity," or that he could "be found guilty of showing support for the anti-hijab measures" (108). Thus the censor prevents Iranian authors from portraying questionable characters, even if the author has no intention of glorifying their behavior. The mere mention of the behavior or action is enough to invite censorship. Without the ability to portray such characters, the author cannot effectively or realistically depict contemporary Iran.

Iranian censorship prevents Western readers from perceiving Iran and Iranians as normal, complex human beings who are interested in and discuss sexuality and politics. The censorship also can make the content of the story appear unrealistic to Iranian readers who would know from their first-hand experience what has been generally or specifically omitted. Through his deletions, the narrator suggests to the reader that there is a hidden, subterranean Iran that the Islamic Regime does not want its readers (both in Iran and in the West) to know about (or to encourage). For instance, later in the novel, the narrator blots out a discussion by a salesclerk at a bridal shop with Dara about whether or not he knows what to do on their wedding night, and her offer to give him Viagra (187). The suggestion here is that these surreptitious discussions and activities occur frequently in Iran, but the Islamic Regime wants neither to acknowledge nor encourage it. Instead, they want to, as much as possible, project an image of an overtly religious and chaste Iran, as signified by how many Iranian television shows, at least according to Dara, display Iranian women wearing the hijab in all circumstances, even at home, which Dara suggests is not realistic or accurate (199).[17] Rather, what the narrator, Dara, and Mandanipour believe to be realistic is a bifurcation between behavior in public and behavior in private.

Also, the narrator and Mandanipour himself are both prevented by the censor and the Islamic Regime from displaying private Iranian lives, behaviors, and thoughts. For Mandanipour, part of the bifurcation involves public paranoia, encouraged by the Islamic Regime in their promotion of Western conspiracies and private pragmatism, which places the individual first. However, as writers, neither the narrator nor Mandanipour can portray the public pragmatism (e.g., individual solutions) of the Iranian people as doing so would involve discussing matters (e.g., sexuality, politics, and so on) deemed taboo by the Islamic Regime, which believes the mere mention of such subject matter could encourage Iranians to further resist the government through their increasing quest to find individual solutions.

As mentioned previously, the intended audience for *CILS* is the West, and whether or not Mandanipour intended it or not, the cover of *CILS* indicates once again that Islamic, Middle Eastern women are being used to sell literature from the region to a Western audience. The cover displays only a woman's eyes (no other part of her face or body) encircled by crossed out language with dark markers obscuring but not completely covering over the text. In that sense, the censored text mirrors a veil that surrounds the woman, and just as the reader may want to see what is literally and figuratively underneath a woman's veil, they likewise want to see what is underneath the censored text. As there are two main protagonists in *CILS*, both male and female (Dara and Sara), there is no compelling reason why the figure on the cover has to be female other than a marketing ploy to sell the text or to make the censorship-veil connection. The cover effectively feminizes the text and suggests that the uncensored text, like the unveiled woman, needs to be saved from oppression by the presumably Western "liberated" audience.

Yet, the novel goes far beyond this colonialist mentality to provide the reader with a postmodern exploration of the nature of fiction writing itself as well as an extended study of the causes and effects of censorship. It is not merely Mandanipour's intention to portray censorship as completely deleterious to the author, the reader, and the community, but to show, within the novel, the manifold ways in which censorship delimits, perverts, and changes the very nature of fiction writing. By showing the reader what sections the narrator, who may be Mandanipour himself, has cut, we are allowed both a window into the forces behind censorship and a look at how it functions. Mandanipour also provides first-hand access to the mind of the author who tries to bend his way around these rules without compromising the integrity of the narrative.

One technique that can be used and which this narrator certainly employs to bypass censorship is the use of euphemisms and figurative language.[18] For instance, while the narrator cannot directly write about dancing, he can use (or at least try to use and get past the censor) words like "rhythmic movement" to more vaguely indicate dancing (10). We also learn from what the narrator deletes (or self-censors) that he cannot write about drinking (which is not allowed according to Islamic law); nor can he do anything as seemingly innocuous as describing Sara in a dress. The only way to circumvent the rules is to try to make a description of Sara as asexual as possible, with no or very few references to her body. As an example, the narrator writes: "Dara sees the beautiful Sara. He sees the projection of her two crystalline collarbones that curve and end as handles of two crystal goblets. Sara's arms are like icicles against which the moonlight shines as they dangle beside two curved impressions" (273). However, the narrator is dissatisfied with this description, which conveys neither Sara's warmth nor her beauty. Another technique the narrator tries is to tell the reader about all the things he won't write about Sara, like that she's taken off her headscarf, that she continues undressing, and about her "sheer and low-cut camisole" (286). Of course, he has just written about these things, and stating that he will not write about it is a way for the narrator to try to get around censorship. It is extremely doubtful that such techniques would pass the censor's scrutiny and therefore these attempts may either be intended for the Western reader or are a manifestation of the narrator's overconfidence in his belief that he can hoodwink the censor.

The other technique authors like the narrator of *CILS* can use to bypass censorship is the use of ellipsis marks. Through the use of ellipsis marks, authors can lead readers towards certain thoughts or actions without actually stating them. For instance, when writing about a sexual encounter, which technically could not be written about under Iranian censorship laws, one could more indirectly write, "They went into the bedroom, and she turned off the light...." While, in this case, it seems pretty clear what occurs after the ellipsis marks, Mandanipour suggests that preventing authors from writing about sexuality actually produces the exact opposite of the intended result: namely more sexualization. In Mandanipour's own words, the use of ellipsis marks allows the reader's "imagination" to go "farther" and become "more naked than the words the writer had in mind" (14). Mandanipour also compares the experience of readers ("especially" Iranian readers) seeing ellipsis marks to "nuclear fission," resulting in the reader taking over the narrative from the author or the censor (147). Mandanipour concludes that these restrictions themselves encourage seemingly contradictory tendencies between romance and pornography, realism (in the text) and postmodernism (implied), and politicization and apoliticization. Thus, the censorship and restrictions placed upon Iranian writers actually backfire in the sense that by omitting certain subject matter deemed to be provocative, readers can become even more desirous of anything provocative and think even more about what has been omitted.

This tricky situation, Mandanipour suggests, presents a nearly impossible dilemma for an Iranian fiction writer, especially a fiction writer who would like to portray the seemingly most simple of all literary conventions — a love story. It should go without saying that an author wanting to publish his work in Iran (or Mandanipour in this case) would need to censor or heavily cloak virtually anything sexual or sensual. This already limits the author's ability to write a realistic and insightful adult love story. However, Mandanipour suggests that even censors can find hidden sexual meanings intended or not intended by the author in various parts of the narrative. This makes sense, because, after all, in a way, censors are no different than the general Iranian reading public, who, in part due to cultural prohibitions against the display and discussion of sexuality, tend to oversexualize literature due to censorship. One example of this occurs at the beginning of *CILS*, in which the author crosses out "sway on top of each other," even though it refers to "the scent of spring blossoms, carbon monoxide, and the perfumes and poisons of the tales of *One Thousand and One Nights*" (3). Further, the narrator points out how many things can be interpreted as having sexual undertones, even things that may be completely innocuous. For instance, the narrator writes, "Sara wants to stir her hot chocolate, but drops her spoon on the floor. Dara takes his spoon out of his teacup and offers it to her..." (57). In this case, the use of ellipses as well as a reader's active imagination can create a scene in which a spoon might be seen as vaguely phallic, the hot chocolate vaguely vaginal, and the act of stirring someone's hot chocolate to be a general metaphor for intercourse. In essence, the paranoia that censorship engenders tends to encourage the reader to look for and decipher figurative language, codes, and hidden meaning in virtually everything, even when none were really intended by the writer.

To be certain, the paranoia involved with believing that there is nearly always more to language than its actual meaning is a hallmark of contemporary Iran. Along these lines, one of Mandanipour's intentions in *CILS* is to demonstrate the complexities of censorship and how those complexities reflect the complexity of Iran itself. Mandanipour points out that while the Iranian constitution "strictly prohibits censorship and inspection," it also "makes no mention of these books and publications being allowed to freely leave the print shop" (8). Consequently, what occurs is that both authors and publishers feel the need to self-censor and to submit the manuscript to the Ministry of Culture and Islamic Guidance prior to publication. Otherwise, a publisher could be nearly or completely ruined financially since the Ministry might not allow the printed books to be sold. This rather ingenious method allows the Iranian government to absolve itself of much of the responsibility of censorship while still censoring the works themselves. It also serves to place the onus of responsibility on the shoulders of the author and publisher, who learn to internalize these taboos and, it is presumably hoped, act and write accordingly. In the case of *CILS*, it is important to recognize that it is the narrator (or Mandanipour if he is the narrator) crossing out sections of the narrative rather than the censor. The author who has had years of experience with censorship is self-censoring portions of his writing that he believes the censor would most object to. Such self-censorship can and does affect the writing itself. With so much attention placed upon what can and cannot be written, the writer's energy can be dissolved merely in the act of writing a scene. Self-censorship can also disallow a writer from writing what she or he wants to convey to the reader.

As we have seen through fiction and nonfiction explored in previous chapters, another technique of the Islamic Republic is to personalize matters by assigning a single inspector or interrogator to a suspected or imprisoned person. This technique of developing a personal relationship between the accused and the interrogator helps to manipulate the accused and can increase specific fears and a sense of powerlessness (as opposed to a more generalized sense of fear and powerlessness). Indeed, the most powerful fears are specific ones. For instance, on some level, we all know that one day we will die; however, this fear can become much more powerful if we are diagnosed with a terminal cancer. At the same time, specificity can give the accused an illusory sense of control. Continuing with the example above, a person suffering from terminal cancer might actually feel a sense of relief at getting a diagnosis, knowing what will happen, and might believe somewhat irrationally that she or he can beat the cancer, just as the accused might believe that she or he can beat the single interrogator. However, this may indeed only be an illusory empowerment, not an actual empowerment.

In *CILS*, and in general, within countries that employ censorship, authors often have to deal with a single person — a censor. It is the censor who holds the ultimate power as far as whether or not a literary work will be published.

Mandanipour makes it clear that if the narrator does not work with the censor and does not compromise or acquiesce at least somewhat, then his work will simply not be published. As an example, Mandanipour describes the narrator meeting an author named Golshiri, who refuses to change anything in his stories to get published, and consequently, is not published (248). This, Mandanipour suggests, will be the narrator's fate if he is too overly idealistic or does not compromise with the censor. At the same time, as Coetzee suggests, the censor sees himself as part of a larger group or "in the interest of a community," and subsequently "imagines its outrage and acts it out" (9). In the case of the narrator of *CILS*, this rather self-important censor who acts out the supposed outrage of the Iranian people (or more generally the Islamic Regime) is a Ministry reader whom, in a reference to Dostoevsky, Mandanipour calls Porfiry Petrovich, possibly because the censor feels his job may be akin in importance to a detective inspecting a murder (which was Petrovich's role in *Crime and Punishment*). Along these lines, Mandanipour sarcastically describes Petrovich as underlining "every word, every sentence, every paragraph, or even every page that is indecent and that endangers public morality and the time-honored values of society" (9).

For Petrovich and much of the Islamic Regime, literature is didactic. Any subject matter deemed to be illicit according to the Islamic Republic cannot be included in a literary work because Petrovich (and the Iranian government whom he serves) believes this is equivalent to either sanctioning the behavior or promoting the behavior. Essentially, censors view their jobs as "holy" because they believe that they are keeping sinful ideas and expressions away from "the pure minds" of simple and innocent people. The irony of Mr. Petrovich's self-importance is that, as Mandanipour suggests, literary writing is not commonly valued by the Iranian populace and is generally not thought of as being a lucrative or even rational career to pursue. As Mandanipour (or the narrator) describes, when he tells other Iranians that he is "a writer," they typically act befuddled and ask him what his real job is. For Mandanipour (or the narrator), this is because "ninety-nine point nine percent of Iranians do not perceive literature as serious work" (64–5).

Further, we can see the extent to which Mr. Petrovich views literature as essentially didactic in function when the narrator imagines Petrovich criticizing the female protagonist, Sara, for purportedly acting disrespectful to her parents, which he believes to be a by-product of "Sara's forbidden and clandestine love affair" (138). Petrovich admonishes the narrator for his story, claiming that if the plot progresses in this fashion, "this ignorant girl will wreck and ruin her life" (138). He even goes a step further by commanding the narrator to "give her [Sara] a stern warning" (138). For Mr. Petrovich, authors should create morally upstanding characters that serve as role models to readers, as questionable characters could help contribute to delinquency or rebellion. This point of view, according to Mandanipour, even extends to universities in Iran. For instance, the narrator of *CILS* includes a scene in which Sara attends a literature class at Tehran University in which the instructor interprets all works as devotional in nature, and condemns contemporary Iranian literature like *The Blind Owl* as violating this supposed sacred trust between writer and reader (217).[19]

Another of Mandanipour's intentions is also to ridicule the process of literary censorship in Iran. One way he does this is through describing his (potentially autobiographical) first meetings with Mr. Petrovich. He first meets Mr. Petrovich when a collection of his short stories, already printed and about to be released by the publisher, supposedly receives complaints from the Ministry of Culture and Islamic Guidance. Specifically, the Ministry charges that there are thirteen places in the narrator's book where the author purportedly used "sexy words and phrases" (33). Essentially, any "sexy" word or phrase is the mere mention of virtually any or every portion of the female body beyond the face. Even when the author's intention is clearly not to express lust, the text can be censored merely on the basis of mentioning parts of a woman's body. As an example, Petrovich objects to a story about a "wounded war veteran," who looks at his fiancée but reports being "disgusted by the feelings her breasts do not awaken in me" (36). In this case, it is the mere mention of breasts that the censor deems problematic,[20] even though it could be argued that the Islamic Regime might want to associate a feeling of disgust with the contemplation of breasts. The irony of this totalitarian dictate lies in the supposition that were authors not to use words like breasts it would eliminate or reduce sexual desire, when, if anything, it is more likely to do the opposite. In another story, a dehydrated woman in her sixties rips her clothes off and pours water on her body. Despite the age of the woman and the non-sexual nature of the scene, Mr. Petrovich insists that the narrator delete it, with no regard for the content and trajectory of the story at all. In the end, though, Mandanipour does not completely demonize the censor, as in this case he can be reasoned with to some degree. In this case, the narrator is able to talk Mr. Petrovich out of cutting some of the material in his short story collection.[21]

While the narrator's relationship with the censor is certainly tumultuous, it is not quite in line with Coetzee's comparison of the relationship a writer has with a censor to that of a potential rape victim with a potential rapist.[22] While this is an extreme analogy, in *CILS*, the relationship between the narrator and the censor threatens to (and ultimately does) impinge and ultimately overshadow the love story between Sara and Dara. In a figurative sense, it could be argued that the censor rapes the narrator's story; however, such an argument rests on a rather hyperbolic claim and lessens the significance of actual rape. Still, while the narrator does not have anything remotely approaching a romantic relationship with Mr. Petrovich, their relationship becomes pivotal and nearly all-consuming to the narrator to the point that it crowds out the narrator's ability to invest himself in the narrative and in the characters. Not only can this compulsive but understandable obsession about Mr. Petrovich, which in a way mirrors an obsessive love for another, be seen in the many crossed out lines throughout the novel, it is also apparent in the manner in which the narrator keeps considering what Mr. Petrovich's potential and actual reaction will be to the plot, the characters, and their actions. The narrator also worries about capitulating too much to Mr. Petrovich and how doing so or being perceived as doing so might affect his integrity in the eyes of Iranian readers (in a sense, he feels that Mr. Petrovich threatens to destroy his literary integrity).[23]

To demonstrate the dilemma that can face a contemporary Iranian writer who wishes to be published in Iran, Mandanipour has Sara and Dara discuss a story written by Mandanipour himself. They both describe it as "a cowardly story," because the couple in the story does not rebel against the Regime's dictates when they can (by talking to one another when no government officials are nearby). Indeed, Mandanipour would agree; however, this "cowardly," watered-down story might very well be the only version that Mandanipour could publish in Iran. Sara and Dara also discuss the metaphors Mandanipour may be using and what he suggests (e.g., a sexual symbol through his use of wells). In that way, reading becomes rather like decoding, but the reader cannot effectively interpret the author's intent as the author may have been censored or the language modified, cut, or changed by the censor (63). In other words, to interpret literature in Iran, one has to consider two parties, the censor and the writer, both typically at odds with one another. In addition, it is nearly impossible, if not completely impossible, to ascertain who is responsible for the omissions and the language itself: the censor or the author.

Mandanipour also portrays how censorship extends beyond literature to other aspects of everyday life in a seemingly totalitarian Iran (at least as suggested by *CILS*). As an example, the narrator discusses how he wanted to name his daughter Baran but the General Register Office does not allow it because they do not think the name Baran is Islamic enough (47). The narrator learns that the only way to get around these rules is to be surreptitious. He does this by tricking an administrator to agree to the name Roja, which is Russian for "Red Star" (48). Naming his children becomes a way of rebelling against the Islamic Republic. The Register Office also prevents the narrator from naming his second child Mahan (49). Surprisingly, the narrator gets the Registrar to agree to let him name his child Daniel. It is a name that the narrator purposely chose because it is traditionally Jewish, and getting the Registrar (who represents the Islamic Regime) to agree to its use allows the narrator to feel that he is rebelling against the Islamic Republic. That he uses his children as pawns of a sort (though it is only a name) illustrates the extent to which the Iranian Regime and its policies have come to consume the narrator, who feels he is stuck playing a perpetual chess game with them in order to gain any kind of leverage or power.

Just as the Registrar's instance that Iranians use Islamic names illustrates a lack of imagination and a stubborn insistence on interpreting everything literally or in a one-dimensional manner, one of Mandanipour's criticisms of the Islamic Republic's approach to censorship is their complete unwillingness to distinguish the intention of the author from the plot, the characters, and the characters' actions. While the censors do look for figurative language, they are not open to the idea that different readers can interpret figurative language in different ways or that figurative language can be purposely ambiguous. Therefore, the mere mention of a portion of a woman's body or any reference to something vaguely sexual typically results in the material being censored or banned, regardless of the context. Towards this end, Mandanipour describes how, earlier in his life, Dara was arrested for buying and selling banned cinematic masterpieces (77–8). Dara agrees with the person who arrests him that helping to spread vile films is not good, but he argues that these films are great artworks, and hence, should be distributed. However, claiming a work of art is superior to other works of art is not sufficient, since Iranian censors do not consider aesthetics as being independent from politics. The only possible way to salvage a censored work, if it is deemed to have illicit material in it, it seems, is by making a case that it espouses a strong anti–Western or anti–American point of view. This is made apparent in a discussion of whether or not to abridge or ban the American film *Dances with Wolves* (1990). Beyond the depiction of exposed skin and the intimate scenes between men and women, the censoring board even objects to the title of the film since it has the word "dance" in it (94). However, they are encouraged by how the film shows "how savage the Americans were" (94). In the end, they decide to cut many romantic and vaguely sexual scenes, but they still release the film as a whole for its supposedly anti–Western (or anti–U.S.) overtures (97).

As mentioned earlier, Mandanipour wrote *CILS* seemingly knowing that it would be censored and banned in Iran (which it was and continues to be). This is apparent in his asides to Western readers, such as the questions

Mandanipour poses in response to social customs in contemporary Iran (e.g., preventing boys and girls in classes from communicating with one another). For instance, Mandanipour writes, "Now you probably want to ask, what are boys and girls supposed to do if they need to discuss a school assignment or exchange ideas?" (15). Further, Mandanipour uses sarcasm to half-heartedly nudge his Western writers with the following: "If you ask one more question like this, I will be forced to say: Madam! Sir! Why can't you imagine any culture other than your own? What kind of a question is that? Clearly girls and boys have no school-related discussions and no need to exchange educational information" (15). The sarcasm then is ultimately directed towards the Islamic Regime and not towards Western readers (who would be in on the joke), and it is through comments like this that it becomes apparent that Mandanipour's sympathies lie mainly with the West. At the same time, Mandanipour does not completely glorify his Western readers while denigrating Iranians as noted by his technique of having a rather ignorant Western reader pose questions that Mandanipour then answers. In this way, Mandanipour is able to discuss political and social customs and events in Iran while portraying Westerners as unenlightened, which is something that the Iranian censor or censors would presumably appreciate (although it's not clear if he's doing this for their behalf or whether it more accurately expresses his true beliefs).

Still, for Mandanipour, trying to escape literary censorship in the Islamic Republic is nearly impossible if not completely impossible to do while maintaining the integrity and clarity of the text. For instance, what if Mandanipour wants to describe a character's hair? He cannot do it under the dictates of the Islamic Regime, for he shouldn't know what a woman's hair really looks like unless he has been intimate with her, and even if he has, censors might not want him to include this level of intimacy as they would argue that it could or would contribute to the supposed delinquency of Iranian readers. Mandanipour would have to write something ambiguous and rather clunky like: "Rippling nightlike strands that flow from the living marble and that the black wind ushers toward the light…" (64). Without being told that Mandanipour is writing about black hair, the reader might have no idea what he really means by "nightlike strands" (black hair) flowing "from the living marble" (the human body). In addition, this example illustrates that Iranian authors may have to use words with undesirable connotations (e.g., marble being related to death), just to get past the scrutinizing eyes of the censor(s). Mandanipour also faces the paradoxical problem of trying to write realistically when, in reality, so many Iranians do not follow all or even most of the dictates of the Islamic Regime (especially in private). If any of his characters have been sinful according to the tenets of the Islamic Regime, the only way he can describe their "sinful" behavior in the text would be to have them repent and change their ways, which they probably would not do in real life.

Still, in order to manipulate the text into something closer to what he intends it to be, Mandanipour also uses ambiguity if not purposeful confusion in order to get past the censor (Mr. Petrovich). This is apparent at the very beginning of the novel, which depicts a political protest outside Tehran University. It is significant that Mandanipour begins the novel with a political protest outside this university, which was the focal point for the June 1999 student demonstrations "against the banning of several liberal pro–Khatami newspapers" that resulted in the death of several students and the arrests of hundreds of students like Ahmad Batebi, who was explored in a previous chapter (Mostyn 55). Our first introduction to the female protagonist (Sara) is when she is carrying a sign that reads "Death to Freedom, Death to Captivity," which confuses the other demonstrators to the point of inaction (5). In a similar way, Mandanipour hopes to confuse the censor by creating a character, Sara, who seems to be neither an agitator nor a supporter of the Islamic Regime. Specifically, it is not clear whose captivity she means on the sign: that of the West or that of the Islamic Republic? Does she want an end to the illusory "freedom" supposedly provided by Western culture, which most proponents of the Islamic Regime would argue is a sham, or does the sign argue that the Iranian Regime effectively killed freedom? Also, how can a person want an end to both freedom and captivity (if this is indeed what Sara means)? Yet, only through this confusion and ambiguity can Mandanipour possibly have characters involved in political activities other than blind allegiance to the Islamic Republic.

Another way that Mandanipour or the narrator seems to try to escape censorship is by presenting himself as a redeemed writer, one who has seemingly reformed from his previous rebellious ways, and no longer wants to write anything political or bleak, but rather, now wants to write a simple, non-political love story. At the same time, the narrator's rationale seems somewhat half-hearted. He suggests that he wants to compose "the love story of a girl who has never seen the man who has been in love with her for a year and whom she loves very much" (8). In a way, this is the only kind of love story Mandanipour could write and still be published in Iran, as it fits with the social regulations of the Islamic Regime. At the same time, the narrator knows that this is not the way that most people fall in love in Iran, or anywhere else for that matter, but he knows the censors will demand that he adhere to the social regulations of the Iranian Regime. Specifically, he is hampered by the Islamic Regime's stipulation that "any discourse between a man and a woman who are neither married nor related is a prologue to deadly sin" (10). Further, he is aware that, if he is found guilty of depicting this in his fiction, he could, even as a writer, "be sentenced by Islamic courts to such punishments as imprisonment, whiplashing, and even death" (10). These regulations make it difficult, if not impossible, to write an Iranian love story other than one that depicts an arranged marriage between two strangers.

Still, even though it seems like his plot fits nicely into the dictates of the Islamic Regime, the narrator finds himself hampered by cultural stipulations, just as unmarried men and women must feel hampered in their attempt to meet one another. Specifically, the narrator is challenged by the Islamic Regime's dictate that unmarried men and women like Sara and Dara "cannot walk together for very long" (53). Doing so could result in them both being accosted and arrested (53). In fact, the narrator's dilemma is even worse than it would be for real-life lovers in Iran. Were they real people, at least Sara and Dara could more often surreptitiously meet or communicate, but since this is a story subject to censorship, the narrator has to be even more careful of what he writes, for everything in his story will be exposed to the censor. In a way, it is akin to living one's life with a Revolutionary Guard constantly looking over one's shoulder.

Another issue that Mandanipour and the narrator face is that if the dictates of the Islamic Regime are to be followed, the characters must not only be virgins, but romantically inexperienced. To satirize this stipulation, Mandanipour's makes one of his characters (Dara) a thirty-something-year-old virgin while his female character (Sara) is a twenty-two-year-old virgin. Mandanipour explains that, to write a love story according to the values espoused by the Islamic Regime, he must make Sara a virgin because "a girl who is neither married nor a virgin cannot possibly fall in love; she has been deceived by false love, has lost her virginity, and must therefore become a woman of ill repute" (58). Mandanipour explains Dara's virginity as due to how, according to the Islamic Regime, "he cannot even make contact with a vulnerable lady" (58).[24] While there are, no doubt, twenty- or thirty-something virgins in Iran (as in any other country), to suggest that this is the rule more than the exception is doubtful. Still, the biggest problem Mandanipour faces is that he cannot even include a direct mention of his characters' virginity as doing so would, ironically, be fodder for the censor since the mere mention of sexuality is enough to censor or ban a work of literature, even though their collective virginity could be used to promote values aligned with the Islamic Regime.

Still, in order to write a realistic love story, Mandanipour must have the two characters meet somehow, even though virtually all dictates of the Islamic Regime stymie this. Their relationship begins with Dara, who is selling books at this point, surreptitiously noticing Sara and putting secret notes in books for her, declaring that he has been "in love" with her "for a very long time" (19). As their relationship progresses, or at least attempts to progress, Sara and Dara try to circumvent the dictates of the Islamic Regime by meeting in places like mosques and emergency rooms and pretending that they are related to one another (111, 113, 180). While Mandanipour never directly states this, it is probable that an Iranian censor would strongly object to the narrator's depiction of such illicit activities because doing so, a censor would argue, could promote social deviance. Mandanipour also details what a complex endeavor it is for Sara to enter Dara's home on her own. Dara must sneak Sara into his house over the surveilling glances of his neighbor, Mr. Atta,[25] of the Volunteer Militia, who spies on "suspicious" people in community. Specifically, Mr. Atta terrifies them by brandishing firearms and searching their possessions at will (211). With Mr. Atta, Mandanipour reveals how the Islamic Regime encourages Iranians to internalize repressions and repress one another. Mandanipour suggests that Sara and Dara would, ironically, have been more likely to remain virtuous were the Islamic Republic more accepting of unmarried couples being together in public. Mandanipour writes, "Of course, to get to know each other better and to protect their pure and chaste love, they would have preferred to go for a walk in a beautiful park in northern Tehran" (283). However, the dictates of the Islamic Regime force them to seek shelter in private as well as in public spaces, and as they break rule after rule, undoubtedly rules in general begin to lose their meaning.

With what might seem to be a hackneyed plot device, Mandanipour also illustrates how the economic and cultural landscape of contemporary Iran has changed through his introduction of a third major character, Sinbad, who becomes Dara's rival for Sara's affections. To some extent, Sinbad is the polar opposite of Dara; he is a wealthy merchant whereas Dara is relatively impoverished (120). Yet, like Dara, Sinbad has also rebelled against the edicts of the Islamic Republic after the Revolution, by shaving and wearing Western clothes. However, unlike Dara, Sinbad has not stayed true to his rebellious ideology, and instead makes money largely by obtaining non–Western foreign imports (like Chinese pencils) so as to avoid trading with Westerners, a stance no doubt encouraged by the Islamic Regime (195). With this, Mandanipour illustrates not only the economic disparity in Iran, but also how Iran is not all that economically dissimilar to the West. As we have seen previously, despite its self-preservation as anti–Western, Iran is still largely a capitalistic country, and this capitalist mentality can be seen with Sara's mother, who tells Sara that she "will never forgive" Sara if she falls "in love with a penniless man" (195). Sinbad himself seems to hold no allegiance to anyone but himself, and the narrator describes him as having "pilfered this country's oil money" (232). Mandanipour also utilizes Sinbad to illustrate how Mr. Petrovich becomes so obsessively focused on appearance that he ultimately champions the more problematic Sinbad over Dara. In fact, Mr. Petrovich grows unhappy with the narrator as it seems increasingly likely that Sara will choose Dara, whom Mr. Petrovich views as a "good-for-nothing former Communist and film peddler," over Sinbad, whom he views as "far stronger," despite the fact that Sinbad appears much more Western, amoral, and corrupt than Dara (262).[26]

As further evidence of Mr. Petrovich's completely myopic behavior and inability to distinguish between fantasy and reality, Mandanipour ultimately suggests that Mr. Petrovich suffers from a kind of psychosis. Specifically, Mr. Petrovich cannot perceive the difference between Sara and a real person. As the narrative progresses, Mandanipour suggests that Mr. Petrovich is falling in love with Sara, as noted by Mr. Petrovich's comments, "Please take Sara out of this womanizer's home," and "I forbid you to allow Dara's hand to touch her" (292). Mr. Petrovich even goes as far as to tell the narrator that not only does he want to meet Sara and marry her, but he also wants the narrator to write him into the story so he can have Sara for himself. It is this selfishness that Mandanipour ultimately suggests motivates the censor as well as the entire censorship process: a general personal and cultural insecurity (about something like sexuality, for instance), which is then projected onto others.

By the end of the novel, it becomes clear that what Mandanipour is illustrating is that a contemporary Iranian writer simply cannot write an effective and realistic love story, and that it has become increasingly difficult to establish normal and satisfying relationships under the dictates of the Islamic Regime. To some extent, Mandanipour also illustrates how he, himself, has been nearly defeated by years of censorship by the Islamic Regime. Mandanipour (or the narrator) writes, "Perhaps I too, as a writer who for years has written under governmental censorship and cultural censorship of the people of my land, will subconsciously arrange a dark ending full of repentance and shame for my protagonist and antagonist so that my story receives a publishing permit" (284). In other words, Mandanipour (or the narrator) may have internalized the dictates of the Islamic Regime and learned to self-censor. Indeed, in response to Mr. Petrovich, who keeps censoring the narrator and influencing the direction in which the narrative proceeds, the narrator writes, "Every single bone in this story is broken. Every single one of its chapters has gone to a wasteland around Tehran, those same places where they burn garbage" (293).

For Mr. Petrovich, who can only conceive of literature as didactic, a novel is "good" if it promotes moral behavior (according to the dictates of the Islamic Regime). Consequently, for Mr. Petrovich (and for the Iranian administration), "a nice educational story" is one in which "Sara ends up loathing Dara" or one in which "the guilty characters will suffer such remorse, misery, and ruin" that the narrator's "story will at least take on a morally educational aspect and that it becomes a lesson to boys and girls who, according to an old Iranian proverb, are like cotton and fire, and if left alone they will destroy not only themselves but their house and home as well" (284, 294). Didactic fiction, though, that is forced upon an author only backfires and in this case, the narrator eventually tells Mr. Petrovich that he has given up on writing his story, and that "writing a love story with a happy ending is not in the destiny of writers of my generation" (294). Proceeding from this, Mandanipour suggests that, in real life, the Islamic Regime stifles romantic relationships in its attempt to exert complete control over its citizens. Along similar lines, the narrator comes to the conclusion that he "no longer" has "any control over it or its characters" and that he has "been completely scissored out of this story" (294).

Yet, even if this is not entirely true, stating it allows Mandanipour to get some veiled references or potentially objectionable language past the censor because he has effectively absolved himself of the responsibility of anything his writing might imply (or not imply). He can, in other words, blame some of the content of his novel upon the censor himself (Mr. Petrovich). Still, with the conclusion of the novel, the narrator has Sara discuss a jasmine bush that has been allowed "the freedom to spread throughout the garden," which she describes as "beautiful" (294). If this "freedom" represents the West, then it is immediately counteracted when Sara subsequently believes that "a pair of terrifying eyes were looking at me from inside the bush," corroborated by Dara who believes he sees someone in the bush as well (294). The novel concludes with an allusion to *A Thousand and One Nights*: "And all I know is that before it is too late, as fast as possible, even with a flying carpet, I must get to my house and lock the door from the inside..." (295). With this final line, Mandanipour suggests that the only way to adequately deal with the dictates of the Islamic Regime is to withdraw and isolate one's self (which, according to authors like Azadeh Moaveni, is exactly what many Iranians have been doing—bifurcating their public and private selves). This is not necessarily as defeatist as it might seem. For, as Coetzee has suggested, "No matter what the state does, writers always seem to get the last word.... And those who write the books, in an important sense, make history" (44). Ultimately, it is Mandanipour who has the final word and who is able to reveal what is or would be censored, and how the rampant paranoia of the Islamic

Regime has infiltrated virtually all aspects of life in Iran. Still, self-imposed isolation can prove fruitful, for what better environment for engaged writing is there than seclusion, a time to barricade one's self in a room of one's own? The difficulty, albeit a large one, is disseminating this writing to the general public.

# Contemporary Iranian and Iranian Diasporic Poetry

It would be difficult to dispute that in the West, of the various forms of literature, poetry has lost more of its power and influence as compared to fiction and drama (excepting poetry set to music). Whereas there continues to be a market as well as both popular and critical interest in fiction and, to a lesser extent, in drama, contemporary poetry struggles to find a sizeable audience and market. This championing of prose and drama over poetry occurs in the United States, but according to Nahid Mozaffari and Ahmad Karimi-Hakkak (editors of the anthology *Strange Times in Persia*), in Iran, the situation is reversed. Indeed, to the present day, Iranians tend to value poetry over all other forms of literary writing (Mozaffari and Karimi-Hakkak xvi; Karim 11). Poetry has a long, centuries old tradition in ancient Persia and Iran, dating back to the origins of Islam and the Sufi tradition,[1] over a thousand years ago,[2] with an especially rich period being the eleventh through thirteenth century as exemplified by the writings of Omar Khayyám, Rumi, and Hafez. This cultural valuing of poetry, though, according to critics, waned from the fourteenth to the nineteenth century, at which point a new group of less traditional poets,[3] influenced by European modernism, helped reinvigorate poetry.[4]

Considering the centuries long history of the importance of poetry in ancient Persia and Iran, it might be surprising that diasporic Iranian poetry has not been published much in the West, let alone become commercially successful (certainly not in comparison to memoirs like *Reading Lolita in Tehran*).[5] While this lack of marketability and commercial success can be attributed to how the American public tends to prefer prose over poetry, Mozaffari and Karimi-Hakkak suggest that there are "difficulties of rendering the complexity and beauty of Persian poetry into other languages," difficulties that have "permitted only a few brave souls to attempt the translation of literature" (xvi). Indeed, this is a common problem in poetry translations as poetry tends to be extremely dense with meaning sometimes hinging upon the figurative interpretation of certain words that can be culturally and linguistically specific.

Another difficulty facing Iranian poetry is that, like fiction and nonfiction, it has been subject to censorship. Similar to the situation depicted in Shariar Mandanipour's *Censoring an Iranian Love Story*, in order to get their work published in Iran, Iranian poets typically have to cloud their work in dense figurative language while downplaying or cutting any actual or potential political implications and anything that could be deemed insulting or injurious to the Islamic Regime or to Islam. While it has been suggested by critics that Iranian poetry publications have increased in recent years,[6] this appears more like temporary progress accomplished by the Khatami administration and subsequently rolled back during the Ahmadinejad administration. Indeed, as Mozaffari and Karimi-Hakkak suggest themselves in their anthology *Strange Times in Persia* (2009), "Gone are noisy incantations of revolutionary marches, replaced by quiet meditations on youthful love" (368).

Still, this does not mean that there has not been any socially, politically, and culturally rich poetry published in Iran or by Iranian diasporic poets in other countries. While there may be a relative dearth of socially, politically, and culturally engaged Iranian poetry because of censorship, there exists a body of socially, politically, and culturally important Iranian diasporic poetry. As Persis Karim argues, Iranian diasporic poetry can be seen as not only "an important source of continuity, connecting Iranians to the voice of their past, and to a nation that was dramatically disrupted by the events of the 1979 revolution," but also as "a medium to articulate and express an Iranian American identity and 'presence' in North America" (111).[7] As one might expect, the poetry of the Iranian diaspora tends to be more political and socially charged than its Iranian counterpart. While some of this could be attributed to how there is no significant censorship of writing in countries such as the United States, it could also be due to Western editors and publishers being drawn to more socially and politically invested poetry from Iran (or the Middle Eastern region) rather than domestic or love poems. When most Westerners or Americans think of Iran (and the Middle East for that matter), they do not think of love or nature poems; rather, they tend to be more interested in Iran politically as an Islamic nation, in its supposed quest for nuclear weapons as well as in its supposed subjugation of women. Consequently, there is more of a Western market for Iranian poetry that engages with politically and socially charged subject matter.

As we have previously seen (for instance, in Porochista Khakpour's *Sons and Other Flammable Objects*), young expatriate Iranian writers often express in their poetry a feeling of being torn between dual allegiances to their native country and their adopted country. This sense of being divided or conflicted is especially exacerbated for Iranian expatriates given the extent to which Iran has been demonized in the Western media since the Iranian Revolution of 1979 and after the attacks of September 11. Poems by young expatriate Iranian writers indicate that they feel unable to really assimilate or adjust to life in the West due to their ethnicity, which is often misunderstood. For instance, in Leyla Momeny's poem "Persian Princess Insania," the speaker describes herself as sheltered in "tehrangeles," and not able to break out of her cocoon (line 42). She writes, "two decades of shy smiling / have gotten me far —/ my feet planted firmly / in waters of ambiguity" (16–19). This "ambiguity" may indeed be a manifestation of how the speaker, due to her ethnicity, is not fully accepted by the general American public outside of her immediate Iranian community. She also sees this community as somewhat delimited, as noted when she suggests that "the men in my family / never learned how to cry," and how she calls them "nihilist-hedonist patriarchs" (22–23; 27). Momeny concludes the poem with "I, misplaced among arabs, Latinas, *I-am-half* italians / no longer believe in *us*" (54–55). The "us," in this case, seems to refer to the Iranian-American community. The speaker has grown tired of being misperceived and disallowed a viable individual identity, both by her family and by non–Iranians. She has also grown weary of fighting against the perspectives of both groups to the point that she has abandoned or is trying to abandon her own ethnic group.

Many of the poems written by diasporic Iranians can be found in anthologies, which offer readers a wide variety of voices and perspectives about Iran and about the diasporic Iranian condition in different (predominantly Western) countries. One such an anthology is entitled *The Poetry of Iranian Women*, edited by poet Sheema Kalbasi.[8] As with Iranian memoirs, one way publishers market this collection is through the perception that Iranian women are heavily oppressed by Iranian men and need to be heard (and saved). We can see this in the foreword to the collection, written by Desi Di Nardo, in which she suggests that "Kalbasi enthralls us with an album of writing that glimmers underneath a veil of repression and intolerance and gives us a glimpse into the experiences and lives of women who are our sisters, daughters, mothers, neighbors, and friends" (viii). Using the loaded word "veil," Di Nardo preys upon the Western public's fascination with the veil as not only a supposed symbol of oppression but also a point of interest and intrigue in terms of what may be underneath the veil.

Another probable selling point of the poetry of Iranian expatriate writers (similar to memoirs and fiction) is how so many of them include Western-style condemnation of the Islamic Regime and its supposed oppression of women. This can be seen, for instance, in Sholeh Wolpe's poem "It's a Man's World to the End of the End," which is a condemnation of perceived sexism and oppression in the Islamic Regime. The poem begins, "I am a woman. Simply / To look at me is a sin —/" (lines 1–2). However, it is not accurate that merely to look at a woman in Iran is "a sin." Rather, the Islamic Republic often projects so-called sins onto the women if they are not sufficiently or adequately dressed. While it is true, as the poem asserts, that women "must be veiled," it is hyperbolic to claim that, "To hear my voice is a temptation / that must be hushed" (3–5). Even though Iranian women may not be offered as many occupational opportunities as Iranian men,[9] Iranian women do comprise a majority of students at Iranian universities (Harrison, par. 7). Therefore, the assertion that, "For me [an Iranian woman] to think is a crime / so I must not be schooled" (6–7) is not substantiated. Still, the poem may be purposely hyperbolic for effect as it concludes, with biting satire, that, even in the perceived afterlife, women will continue to be oppressed according to the dogma of the Islamic Regime. Wolpe writes: "I [an Iranian woman] am able to bear it all / and die quietly, without complaint. / Only then can I be admitted to the court of God / where I must repose naked on a marble cloud / feed virtuous men succulent grapes / pour them wine from golden vats / and murmur songs of love" (8–14). Here we can see how Wolfe criticizes the perceived sexism in the Iranian Regime through an updated Greco-Roman allusion.

Along similar lines, several poems in the collection *The Poetry of Iranian Women* allude not only to a generalized sexism in the Islamic Regime, but also to its violent and potentially deadly nature. Specifically, we can see this in several poems written about stoning women. While it is true that, legally speaking, Iranian women can be stoned for committing adultery and for other supposed transgressive crimes, this is a law that is rarely utilized[10] (in comparison to predominantly Islamic countries such as Sudan and Somalia).[11] This is not to lessen the importance of the poems that indict Iran for inhumane and barbaric methods of torture and execution, which the Islamic Republic uses, albeit rarely. At the same time, some of the poems about stoning make the Islamic Regime seem like evil incarnate, ready to employ this vicious act for the most minor of infractions. For instance, in the poem "Stoning," Mehrangiz Rassapour provides a virtual litany of outlawed behaviors that can supposedly result in a stoning (when in actuality stoning is reserved for adultery and murder), from kissing or drinking, to merely being a woman or any person. She writes: "Seeing is forbidden / stone me / Kissing is forbidden / stone me / Drinking is forbidden / stone me / Sobriety is forbidden / stone me / The past is forbidden / stone me / The future is forbidden / stone me /

I'm a woman/ stone me / I have eyes / stone me/ I have a tongue / stone me / I have a brain / stone me" (lines 25–44). While, in this case, Rassapour may use stoning in a figurative manner to represent the unjust restrictions and abuse inflicted upon Iranian women, it is difficult to ignore the literal implications of stoning itself because the image of stoning is so powerful that it can crowd out any possible figurative intention by the writer. While Rassapour may not have intended this, her poem does contribute to the inaccurate assumption that the Islamic Regime will stone any woman, or possibly any Iranian, for any cause whatsoever.

Along similar lines, in Lobat Vala's poem entitled "The Epic of Stoning," not only does the Islamic Regime appear incredibly barbaric, vicious, and bloodthirsty in their desire to enact and display a stoning, but so does the Iranian audience (which appears like a Roman audience enjoying an execution in the Coliseum). In this poem, the author describes the execution of a woman as a "show" and depicts "the crowd" as "excited for the entertainment, stoning a young girl to death / Scavengers thirsty for blood / In their eyes' madness / Passion and lust ... orgy" (Vala lines 2–6). This poem further encourages Western readers to cement widely held impressions that Iran is a legitimate part of the fictional Axis of Evil by presenting the Iranian populace as largely atavistic, violent, and misogynistic.

Other poems in collections written by Iranian expatriates also indict Iran and thereby contribute to the Western perception of Iran as, if not part of the Axis of Evil, then a generally morally repugnant and culturally backwards nation. For instance, Iranian-American Zara Houshmand's "Invitation to the Hungry Ghosts" describes the political system in Iran as a natural abomination "with Fascism digging in like gangrene, the earth abused, / Rolling over to die, the work laid out like a feast" (lines 2–3). The imagery of disease, decay, and death contribute to the poem's general dichotomy between the natural world, represented by the Iranian people, and the unnatural world, which symbolizes the Islamic Regime itself. It is the Regime itself that champions death and martyrdom, exemplified by how, according to Houshmand, the only real poetry championed by the government is one that celebrates the martial victories of the Regime. Hence, "Only war gets poets in the door here" (10).

Similarly, other poems in collections written by Iranian expatriates focus on the violence or, more specifically, they are elegies recounting the unnecessary and unjustified deaths of young Iranians at the hands of the government. For instance, Anglo-Iranian Shirin Razavain's poem "Dying Young" indicts the Islamic Regime for cutting short the lives of younger Iranians, presumably dissidents, who spoke out against the Regime. The poem begins, "My friends

/ Are all dead" (lines 1–2). In her poem "Kaddish," editor and poet Sheema Kalbasi also alludes to Iranian deaths and directly condemns what she perceives to be a violent and monomaniacal environment (the Middle East). The fact that Kalbasi entitled the poem "Kaddish" (alluding as it does to a Jewish, not Islamic, prayer for the dead) illustrates that Kalbasi's allegiances are not for Islamic Republic, but then again, nor are they necessarily for Israel and the West. This can be seen how, in this poem, Kalbasi describes the entire "Middle East" as a "bloody sore…. / where only the streets / silently / speak of the dead, / where the buttercups / cups, cups are red / from blood, / where bodies are tossed / in oil, oil, / hot hot oil" (lines 2–12). The last image of bodies being tossed in oil mirrors the act of cooking, and through these images, Kalbasi suggests that human life has lost its general meaning in most areas of the Middle East, in which nations consume or destroy bodies (or humans) for gain or profit, or in the name of a larger, dubious cause.

Additionally, many of the poems written by Iranian expatriates decry prior and still existing violence in Iran and the Iran-Iraq war, as well as the devastating price that some Iranians have paid in the name of supposed religious or political justice. For instance, in the poem "The State of Red," Mandana Zandian, after recounting the terror of the Iran-Iraq war, concludes the poem by stating that "God always yawned" (line 42). The suggestion, then, of this and other similar poems is that the brutal Iran-Iraq war was a sham in which religious officials of the Iranian Regime manipulated the Iranian populace into believing that they were fighting a holy war when they were actually fighting to satisfy the greed of the corrupt mullahs and the Iranian government. For other Iranian expatriate poets, this hypocrisy, greed, and dishonesty can be traced all the way to the time prior to the 1979 Revolution. For instance, Nazanin Afshin-Jam's "Someday" indicts the late 1970s revolutionaries for inciting the nation under false pretenses. She describes the revolutionaries as being "on the march then / In 1978 / They filled our minds with hate / They deceived the nation / In the name of religion" (lines 1–5). Afshin-Jam ultimately describes the 1979 Islamic Revolution as a "Regressive Revolution," and in this poem, ultimately promotes a counter-revolution that would "redeem our rightful place" (11, 26). Throughout the poem, Afshin-Jam further encourages the Iranian reader to revolt with the repeated chorus "Someday / We will find a way" (13–14, 27–28, 39–40, 48–49). She also concludes, "And someday is right now" (57–58). This poem could not be more direct in its encouragement of political revolt; Afshin-Jam may be more like an armchair warrior suggesting that her Iranian brethren rebel (with presumably violent results) while she is safely ensconced in the West. Indeed, it is not difficult to see how poems like this one could be used to help rally Westerners (or even neo-conservatives) to support and encourage a new Iranian Revolution (if not indirectly or directly participate in it).

In contrast to the political poems mentioned above, *The Poetry of Iranian Women* includes a number of poems that are generally apolitical. As established earlier, older and celebrated Persian poets like Hafez are renowned for their love poems, and these poems, predominantly written by Iranian women still living in Iran, may be in that style.[12] This is not to suggest that such love poems might not have any political or social criticism to them all, but if they do, such implications tend to be subtle and ambiguous. For instance, in "If the Earth was a Farm," Roshanak Bigonah writes "If the earth was a sunny farm / it would be possible to run / through the shanks of maize / become deaf, be blind, not breathe, / run to the wooden hand-rails / and behind the oak trees / interlace with you" (lines 8–14). This poem may express Bigonah's sorrow at not being able to express affection towards an unmarried beloved in public. In order to avoid censorship, Bigonah may have changed the title and tone and made the poem more universal ("the Earth") and less sensual ("interlace with you"). If there is any subtle social criticism in these more domestic love poems, it is generally subverted and ambiguous. For instance, in the poem "Matrimony," Farideh Hassanzadeh writes, "We pass one another / I walk to the kitchen / You depart for the office / I walk to the mountain of plates and clothes / And you are off to the forest of desks or files" (lines 1–5). In this poem, we can see the clearly designated gender roles of female homemaker and male breadwinner as well as the speaker's despondency in how she must attend to the "mountain of plates and clothes." However, the male office worker hardly seems better off in that he goes to a "forest of desks or files." Presumably, anything more significant than this (e.g., the female speaker blaming her husband for their unequal gender roles or for having a career at the cost of her own prospects) would not make it through the Iranian censorship process. This is not to suggest that the poem has been robbed of all of its social and cultural implications. However, it certainly appears, as one might expect, that it is much more challenging for an Iranian poet to write more direct, socially engaged and culturally critical poetry than it is for an Iranian expatriate.

Towards that end, the Iranian poets that appear most politically engaged and the ones that tend to receive the most attention in the West are diasporic Iranian poets rather than Iranian poets. The first Iranian American expatriate poet I will look at in greater lengths is the editor of *The Poetry of Iranian Women*, Sheema Kalbasi. Specifically, I will look at Kalbasi's poetry collection *Echoes in Exile*, which was published in 2006. Kalbasi "was born in Iran, but also resided in Denmark, Pakistan, and now the United States" (Kalbasi, *The Poetry of Iranian Women* v). Similar to the collection she edited, *The Poetry of*

*Iranian Women, Echoes in Exile* is dichotomously organized with politically and socially engaged poetry separated from more domestic, predominantly love poetry. The first section of *Echoes in Exile* is entitled "The Warrior" and mainly focuses upon Iran and the Iranian diasporic experience. The second section of *Echoes in Exile* is entitled "Silent Sensuality," and the poems in this section are predominantly personal, emotional, and apolitical. In a way, this organization perfectly reflects the often-dichotomous lives Iranians often lead in Iran (with a division between their public and private selves) as well as the dichotomous lives Iranian expatriates often live (with a division between their Iranian and Western identities).

Indeed, the organization of *Echoes in Exile* can be seen as illustrating Kalbasi's own dual identities (if not somewhat conflicting allegiances) as both Iranian and Western. As a diasporic Iranian, she has to address questions and suppositions about her ethnicity and home country; yet, presumably in the privacy of her own home, Kalbasi is able to lead a life mostly divorced of nationality and ethnicity. From this position, her more private, apolitical, and emotional poems in "Silent Sensuality" emerge. In fact, it is significant that she equates sensuality with "silent," as in this private, protected space, Kalbasi appears to seek a post-ethnic identity but finds that in order to approach anything close to this state she must progress beyond language, as vocalizing her desires or feelings (just through the sound of her presumably accented voice) could codify her identity as an Iranian-American.

Kalbasi's dedication of the collection not to a single person or group of people, but rather, "To Humanity," reflects a desire to stay objective if not a general belief in post-ethnicity (or post-nationality). At the same time, the quote that she uses in her dedication, from Kahlil Gibran, "He who does not prefer exile to slavery is not free by any measure of freedom, truth and duty," demonstrates that *Echoes in Exile* will be socially and politically charged, which indeed, it is. Since Kalbasi herself is an exile, the quote also suggests that Kalbasi's belief is that the essential choice that faced her and her family when they lived in Iran (and by extension, most Iranian families of this time) was whether to pick exile (in the West) or slavery (a life in Iran). This does not necessarily mean that Kalbasi equates the West with freedom as the quote from Gibran only suggests that a person who chooses slavery over exile cannot be considered free in any way; it does not necessarily suggest the converse, that is, that a person who chooses exile will necessarily experience freedom. Rather, the quote suggests that "freedom" itself (as well as "truth," and "duty") is subjective and not easily defined. Indeed, in *Echoes of Exile*, Kalbasi does not present the Iranian expatriate experience as completely liberating, but rather, only partially so.

For Kalbasi, one of the main causes of the individual and collective problems in Iran (and among Iranians and diasporic Iranians) is the aftermath of what appears like a relentless war fought among various countries both in and around Iran (in the Middle East) since the Iranian Revolution. Towards that end, the "Warrior" section of *Echoes in Exile* depicts the devastating psychological and sociological effects of warfare upon individuals. For instance, in the poem, "Nothing," the speaker laments: "Nothing is all I am, / Nothing overloading nothing," while she recounts, "The bombs, lights that blind and Damascus, / Burning after Tehran" (13). This numbing, brutal, and violent environment appears to affect virtually everyone in the Middle East, not just residents but also foreign visitors as noted by how "Children die, and journalists are filming for a / deadline" (13). Ironically, "nothing" can suggest peace and calm, the antithesis of what one would except in a war zone where "bullets shoot and blood drops" (13). In fact, the shell-shocked speaker may aspire to a kind of numbing nothingness. In this poem, Kalbasi refers to "the Central Park" (13). While there is certainly more than one Central Park (and one in Tehran), it is possible that she refers to New York City's Central Park. If so, the poem can then be read as an expatriate's account of how troubling the seemingly peaceful West is to the exile who has experienced war. Instead of feeling peaceful, the speaker experiences an overwhelming sense of absence and meaninglessness, concluding that "Here nothing happens / But I write to keep nothing from overloading nothing" (13). Since it is technically impossible for "nothing" to overload nothing, it can be presumed that what the speaker refers to is not really a complete nothingness, but a painful emptiness she feels as a result of the trauma of war.

Whereas the speaker's location and home cannot be precisely determined from the poem "Nothing," Kalbasi clearly addresses the dislocating effects of being an Iranian expatriate in the poem "Exile." In this poem, Kalbasi depicts the presumably Iranian expatriate speaker as "dripping, dripping, not marking my existence" (35). Without a clear sense of identity and without a "reminder of my roots / yours," the speaker finds that she leads more of a fragmented existence marked by "moments of loves, family, home" (36). Similarly to the previous poem analyzed, "Nothing," this speaker, despite living in the supposedly liberated West, concludes, "I am one of the nobodies of the world," and that most people regard her as a "refugee" despite her "womanhood," her "skills," and her "Ph.D." (37). Ultimately, others exoticize the speaker's experiences based on stereotypes (presumably war-torn or despotic) surrounding her home country (also presumably Iran). Not feeling at home in her new country as an exile and being exiled (or self-exiled) from her native country, the speaker finds herself "dipping in blood-freed-memory waves" (37). In other words, the speaker turns inward and withdraws, unable to form a lasting connection or home within her native or adopted countries. Still, Kalbasi portrays the West with ambiguity and ambivalence. While she seems to laud the way the West offers a kind of personal liberation and peace for recent immigrants, she also portrays it as hardly a welcoming promised land for them. On the one hand, Kalbasi depicts the West (especially in contrast to the violent content in the poems in the "Warrior" section, mainly taking place in Iran or other areas of the Middle East) as almost Edenic in the more pastoral poem "New England." In this poem, the speaker describes children playing on a beach (presumably in New England) and how she revels in the innocence and joy her daughter experiences while near "the white waters and dancing waves" (17). In this poem, unlike the poems discussed earlier in the "Warrior" section, there is no mention of violence or warfare.

Still, in Kalbasi's poems, recent immigrants tend to view the plentiful and beckoning West with some measure of caution or hesitance, if not resistance. For instance, in the poem "My Sublime Divine," the narrator once again describes being with her daughter (as she did in the poem "New England"). This time, however, her daughter is older, and the divisions between first- and second-generation immigrants seem clearer and better defined. Whereas the first generation speaker describes herself as seemingly overwhelmed and stumbling "between the coastal isles," at the Mall, her daughter "toddles" nearby, and plays the role of a good Western consumer, drawn to flashy, colorful items and motivated by advertisements. Sounding reminiscent of a commercial, her daughter "asks / if her skirt is tropical enough, / spotless, and bright" (18). Her daughter is also transfixed by the other consumer items, telling her mother, *"I want that, Please Mom / that one I want"* (18). In addition, despite being "a little girl" with "little feet," the speaker's daughter wears "a pair of women's shoes," and "tries on a vintage styled ladies' hat" (19–20). This alludes to the more conventional Western pressures (which can be seen as forms of oppression) placed upon young women and even young girls to present themselves as older and more sophisticated. Still, the poem remains ambiguous as noted by how it ends with the first-generation immigrant reveling in the joy her daughter experiences, calling her "my sublime divine" (20). Realizing the joy that shopping seems to provide for her daughter, the speaker, despite her reservations about the ways Western consumerism can affect young girls, ultimately is reminded of how much she loves her daughter and wants her to provide for her happiness.

In many ways, the key opposition Kalbasi sets up in her poems between the West and Iran (or the general Middle East) is between blissful peace (the West) and violent destructiveness and uncertainty (Iran or the Middle East).

This is poignantly illustrated, for instance, in the poem "Drawings." In this poem, Kalbasi contrasts a second-generation immigrant child's drawing of her "walking / with her father / hand in hand / in a Halloween costume... / and a rabbit / the Sun, / a white home," with the first-generation immigrant mother's drawing, "showing her dad, dead / behind prison walls, / the soldiers with guns, / the war, / the cluster bombs" (20). At the same time, Kalbasi complicates this opposition or dichotomy between by illustrating how the blissful peace of the West can be more like a chimera, which, when examined further, encourages a kind of ignorance.

Another way Kalbasi complicates the oppositions between the West and Iran or the Middle East is through contrasting the seeming bliss of the West with more somber subject matter concerning reality for immigrants in the West. This can be seen in the poem "Let's Dance Cha, Cha Oil," which, despite its seemingly upbeat and celebratory title, is more an account of the challenges that immigrants to the West experience, if not an outright lament about life in the West. In this poem, the speaker begins by describing how an "institution's personnel" dehumanize the "suffering" of "a mother at birth" (40). While Kalbasi does not define the "institution," it is presumably related to Western governments or legislative bodies or it may be "the agents of socialization" that the speaker mentions in the next line (40). The speaker, an Iranian immigrant, is amazed at how, in the West, her identity becomes a confusing and frustrating mish-mash of contradictions. This is apparent when she claims, "Ironically I am a Caucasian; who knew a Caucasian is a colored girl" (40). In other words, the speaker learns that despite its ideology, in the West, race still not only matters but is especially vexing for expatriate Iranians considered ethnic others despite their race (Caucasian). In a sense, the West ends up being hardly more nurturing (if at all) for recent Iranian immigrants than their native country as evidenced by the following lines from the speaker: "*When I was born an Iranian / My identity got lost / At the immigration line / Where I stood nameless / For three years without a mother to nurture the girl / and a shaky refugee status that kept me from / remembering what my home looked like when I left*" (40). Further, in the new Western environment, the speaker loses touch with her native culture as noted by how "*When I left, father never sat by my bed and never told the / stories of the Persian kings again*" (40). Later, the speaker concludes, "The relationships tend to fail / between the immigrant and the host country" (42).

One reason that these relationships may fail, the speaker suggests, is the manner in which the West categorizes and separates ideas, individuals, and groups. This is what the speaker describes as "Segregating the segregation / Shi'ism, Bahaism, Communism, Capitalism, Monarchy / Tribalism" (42). In other words, in its quest to categorize and explicate groups and ideas (e.g., monarchy, capitalism, and communism), the West simplifies ideas, nations, or people (that a nation is entirely capitalist or communist, for instance). Ultimately, the speaker, an Iranian expatriate, finds herself balanced precipitously between both cultures and nations (Western and Iranian), "in the middle, just around the corner / of an identity crisis between the arrestee, exile, refugee / and human" (43). It is this state of being betwixt and between rather than the actual perceived oppression from the native or host country that the speaker ultimately identifies as being "the most stressful experience!" (43). She feels dissatisfied in consumer-based Western cultures where "the European business-government sales men," are "Testing Cha Cha oil," which she also calls "black gold," presumably for its marketing potential (43). Ultimately, Kalbasi makes it purposely ambiguous as to which country or style of government she implicates, which illustrates how Iranians expatriates can perceive a general lack of difference between life in the native and host country. In response to the supposed liberation of the West (presumably the United States given her reference to "freedom" and "democracy") Kalbasi writes, "Sponging on the brimful prejudice / Symbolic formulation of freedom, democracy, / Images flying in the blood-red air" (44). The "blood-red air" indicates the price or consequences of "freedom," violence, and death. That Kalbasi describes freedom as "symbolic" and "sponging on the brimful prejudice" indicates her resistance to simplistic Western ideology.

Kalbasi also critiques the West for not fully accepting or wanting to accept the traumatic feelings experienced by immigrants, as exemplified by the speaker's own description of her upbringing in Iran, where she was "kicked in the face by a revolution and anti- / human rights regime" (46). Instead of accepting, confronting, and helping to heal the immigrant's trauma, the West instead, as suggested by the poem, focuses on achieving a rather superficial happiness, exemplified by "the pharmaceutical drug companies / That sell anti-depression pills / To the refugee," who "was unable to / control the fear from bombs" (46). These quick-fire attempts to achieve happiness ultimately fail because they ignore the root cause of the trauma; hence, the speaker concludes, "all I remember is that kick in the face!" (46). If, indeed, it is as the speaker suggests, "Life concentrates in one side of the world; heavy, / Light on the other," this dichotomy between the overly tragic and serious Middle East (Iran) and the more frivolous and superficial West (United States) contributes to how both countries ultimately fail their citizens, but in different ways (46). While Iran may fail in limiting, debasing, or destroying basic and intrinsic pleasures of life, the United States fails by amplifying the importance of those pleasures so that they crowd out virtually everything else and leave no significant room to address, let alone acknowledge, more serious and tragic individual, collective, and world-wide issues.

Just as Kalbasi criticized the Middle East in her poem previously explored, "Kaddish," she also personifies and castigates the region in her poem "Middle East" (27). In this poem, the speaker dreams that she "was innocent," and describes herself searching "to hear your worldly murmur: Peace" (27). However, the "murmur" of "peace" the narrator believes she hears from the Middle East is literally nothing but a dream, when in reality she suggests that the entire region is responsible for its own seemingly never-ending vicious cycle of violence. The speaker suggests that she "offered you my love / wrapped in honesty," but she finds herself "shrunk with disbelief," when this gift was either rejected or treated with disdain. Towards the end, the poem turns more macabre, with the speaker posthumously stating that the peace that she longed for led to her death, leaving her "longing in my grave / to receive the flowers / with your handwritten note: *Rest in Peace*" (27). That she has not received either the flowers or the note indicates that her death was not celebrated, commemorated, or appreciated, but rather that in her struggle for peace, her death turned out to be in vain.

While the poem "Middle East" criticizes the entire region, the poem "Hezbollah" criticizes fundamentalist Islam and relates it to Iran. While most Hezbollah members tend to be from Lebanon, Kalbasi wants readers to see the Iranian origins of the movement as well as how Hezbollah has played a key role in Iran.[13] Towards that end, she writes in the footnotes to the poem that Hezbollah was "developed by Ayatollah Ruhollah Khomeini, leader of the Islamic Revolution in Iran" (28). She criticizes the Iranian branch of Hezbollah for being hypocritical in their supposed defense of Islam as evidenced by their treatment and disdain of those of the Baha'i faith, hundreds of whom, according to Kalbasi, "have been killed and hundreds more imprisoned" (28).[14] She also criticizes them for their disdain of the Kurds who are treated as "just part of a game" (28).[15] Instead of concentrating on their country, the Iranian Hezbollah branch commemorates and concentrates on demonizing Israel and glorifying Palestinians as noted by their "mourning over the tassels of demolished / homes of the homeless in a country / not even close to my land, sitting on tinplates / of power while announcing another castration" (28). Indeed, this anti–Israel and pro–Palestinian rhetoric can be heard in President Ahmadinejad's rhetoric, in part because it is a way to rally neighboring predominantly Arabic and Islamic countries to Iran's side in their shared celebration of a common cause.

Despite the seemingly pessimistic nature of Kalbasi's poetry about the Middle East, similar to Marjane Satrapi, Kalbasi champions the power of the individual and family, which can and often does trump any government and nationality. One of Kalbasi's most powerful poems, "Mama in the War," not only displays the importance of the individual and of family, but also serves as a testament to the strength of the Iranian people, who display great courage and resilience even during traumatic, potentially deadly events. In this poem, the speaker addresses her mother: "You took us, / your children, / under you hands, mama, / beneath the steps of our home's first floor, / to protect us from the bombs" (38). For the speaker, her mother's "only mission / was our safety" (38). In this poem, Kalbasi does not mention the Islamic Regime; all is drowned out by the grace and courage of women like the speaker's mother. Towards that end, the speaker writes: "You are my president, mama, / you and all those women / who protected / and still defend their children / against the blinded-with-hatred / soldiers of death / all around the world" (38). In essence, just as with Satrapi, the personal supplants the political, with the speaker's mother making "a new reform of solidarity / and election of bravery / in our home" (39). The speaker concludes the poem with "My vote goes to you, Mama," and through this concluding line, Kalbasi suggests that any real hope for change needs to come from the family and the individual as opposed to any political system (39).

The next poet to be explored in detail, Roger Sedarat, also tends to champion the family and the individual over any political system or nation. Sedarat holds a Ph.D. in English from Tufts University, and is currently an Assistant Professor in the MFA program at Queens College ("Roger Sedarat," par. 2). *Dear Regime* (2007) "won the 2007 Ohio University Hollis Summers Poetry Prize" ("Roger Sedarat," par. 4). Unlike the vast majority of the poets explored in this chapter as well as the vast majority of diasporic Iranian writers explored in this study (with the exception of Azadeh Moaveni), Sedarat was born and raised in the United States; however, he grew up in San Antonio, Texas, far from the Iranian-American community in Southern California. Perhaps because there were so few Iranian-Americans in the area, Sedarat reports that he and his family experienced a good deal of hostility from some in the San Antonio community. As he explains, "During the time of the Iranian Revolution and the hostage crisis, I was repeatedly warned by my father not to tell people we were Iranian. I'd answer the phone and hear death threats, our home and family car were vandalized, etc." (qtd. in Gonzales, par. 9).

Indeed, perhaps due to the nature of his rather fraught childhood, Sedarat may have developed, as many writers and artists who deal with racism, discrimination, and bullying do, a technique of using humor to diffuse aggression and prejudice. For Sedarat, humor, which he describes as an "affirming method," is one way to break down stereotypes and to connect with his readers. Further, he also wants to humanize Iranians and Iranian-Americans through a kind of comedy (sometimes tragic-comic). In his own words, "As grave as the situation appears in the Middle East, I want my American audience to understand that Iranians especially have a tremendous sense of humor, as well as deep sense of the poetic tradition" (qtd. in Gonzales, par. 17). Along similar lines, Sedarat seeks to depict Iran (and the Middle East) in more realistic terms as opposed to dichotomous and oppositional terms such as "over-romanticized" or barbaric (qtd. in Gonzales, par. 5).

The title of Sedarat's collection (*Dear Regime*) indicates that, in a way, his intended audience is the Islamic Regime itself. While *Dear Regime* is a collection of poetry, the book also makes *Dear Regime* appear almost like an epistolary collection (which it is not). As *Dear Regime* has not been published in Iran (which Sedarat must have anticipated), it is hard to conclude anything but that the intended audience is Westerners (more specifically, Americans). Still, if there is an epistolary quality to *Dear Regime*, it is that the collection as a whole can be seen as a litany of indictments and criticisms of Iran for what Sedarat perceives as the megalomania of the ruling clerics and administrators, their reckless disregard for human rights, and the general debasement of the Iranian people (although Sedarat takes caution not to implicate the Iranian people themselves).[16] This, of course, is not significantly different from the American government's general attitude towards Iran.

However, as the first poem, "Ghost Story," illustrates, we can see some differences in Sedarat's approach to and attitude towards (as opposed to that of the American government) Iran. Instead of, for instance, challenging Iran's ambition to possess nuclear weapons, Sedarat is more resigned to this occurring in the future, as noted by the lines: "By the time said country gets the bomb / my infant son will read the news" (3). Still, in this poem, one way that Sedarat's son, or children in general, help save the speaker "from terrifying thoughts of the future" is through their reinforcement of the idea that what appears permanent or unchanging actually is transitory (3). The Iran of the present time may become an entirely different country (even though they may get "the bomb," this does not necessarily mean that Iran will be anything close to a totalitarian country) by the time Sedarat's son comes of age. Just as the speaker sees his son "enshrouding himself in a white cotton sheet / for his mock–Muslim burial," the speaker also gives his son, or children, the agency to bridge differences through the creativity involved in covering or modifying "that which becomes too scary to see" (3). In that case, it appears that Iran is the entity "too scary to see," but that does not mean that this frightening entity (or nation) will never be confronted or changed. In this poem, it is the younger generation that has the most potential to change and forge meaningful connections between Iran and the West.

Still, in *Dear Regime*, Sedarat illustrates some of the more devastating aspects of life in the Islamic Regime, and he illustrates the manner in which the Regime can violently dehumanize Iranians. For instance, in the poem "Body Cleaner," Sedarat examines not only the gruesome act of executions, but also more importantly, the procedures preceding executions in Iran, namely the job that the Body Cleaner or executioner has to do: literally cleaning and grooming people before they are executed. To Sedarat, Iranian executioners do not recognize or do not allow themselves to recognize the futility of these acts and these preparations allow the executioners and those that decree the executions a certain measure of self-denial. Instead of realizing that they are about to kill other human beings, the executioners believe they are preparing them for the afterlife. Sedarat, in a macabre tone, describes the executioners "washing bodies and brushing hair / on the last night of their lives" (5). The place of execution, meanwhile, smells of "rosemary-scented olive oil" (5). These seemingly gentle and sensitive acts, though, only make the upcoming execution seem even more barbaric. Also, implicitly, Sedarat suggests that the executioners' use of Islam to justify executions is blasphemous as noted by the lines that indicate "the hands" of the soon to be executed "reaching for God / coming up empty" (5). Thereby, the setting of the executions appears as a Godless environment.

Further, Sedarat suggests that he wants this and other poems that detail violence in the Islamic Regime to serve as agents of change. Towards that end he writes that he "wanted to send copies" of pictures taken of the executed "to the New York Times, / but it would put certain people in danger, / so instead, I put it in this poem / hoping that at least one reader / stops long enough / to think about the burden / of living in a world / with death sentences" (6). That Sedarat does not qualify the kind of death sentences makes these last lines more generalizable, especially given that executions are still legal in the United States and other Western countries. Indeed, the body cleaning process that precedes an execution is not that dissimilar to the more Western tradition of offering a condemned person a last meal of their choosing.

Still, for Sedarat, the scope of the damage Iran has done to its people goes well beyond executions and includes those who were so psychologically (or physically) damaged during and after their previous lives in Iran to the extent that they are essentially deadened when they become exiles. For example, the poem "Dear Regime" takes the form of a letter from a family that essentially implicates the Islamic Regime in the death of their expatriate father who "returned from Iran with everything but his bones. / He said customs claimed them as government property" (4). The use of the word "bones" indicates how the father has been robbed of his essential self. Too traumatized by his experiences in his home country (presumably Iran), the speaker's father cannot be resuscitated by life with his family as an exile and he dies soon after, the speaker suggests, because of the trauma he endured while living in Iran. The speaker's mother, in an act mirroring a military funeral, ends up "folding him [the father] into a rectangle," just as one might do with a flag (4). Towards that end, the father can be viewed as a kind of casualty of war, albeit, in this case, more of an invisible war perpetuated upon Iranians and Iranian expatriates. The dehumanization of the father seems complete as the speaker's mother (the deceased's widow) also puts him "in a white shoebox," as one might a small bird or animal, which is probably all that the father was to the Islamic Republic (at least according to the speaker). The family also asks the Islamic Regime to grind "*him* [the father] *into powder,*" and to "*burn this to a fine ash*" (4). In other words, the family wants the Islamic Republic to take responsibility for his death. The speaker, quite possibly Sedarat himself, also writes that "*his family would be better off with nothing,*" because they believe that the Islamic Republic had already essentially destroyed his father before he even left Iran (4).

In *Dear Regime*, Sedarat depicts Iranian citizens as largely victims of the Islamic Regime itself, and these implications can be seen in Sedarat's ten-part poem entitled "In Praise of Moths." As moths are generally considered a mild nuisance that can damage crops or clothing, it may be somewhat difficult to discern why Sedarat might write a poem in which he praises moths. While moths are also drawn to bright lights, and can essentially destroy themselves through this deathly attraction, the poem uses moths as a symbol that can somehow transcend human life. In the first part of the poem, the speaker recounts the death of his father-in-law right after the birth of his son. However, the moths immediately represent a re-birth evident by how the speaker's now crawling child, while in his deceased grandfather's house, opens "the closet door / to a blizzard of moths / and he gasped in delight / at insects capable of devouring / his favorite wool blanket" (7).

At the same time, in the second part of the poem, the moths seem more parasitical, feeding on the Iranian populace, and upon Iran itself "where mullah's beards breed moths by the hour" (8). In this case, the moths can be seen as the mullah's followers who blindly follow him (or the Regime itself) potentially to their deaths, just as moths circle a light. Also, we can see the connection Sedarat makes between moths and blind, misguided followers of presumably fundamentalist Islam with the line, "Moths circle moonlight mosques' gold minarets," which then leads to anti–Western sentiment, noted by how "an anti–U.S. speech hangs in the air" (8). In this case, the gold represents the presumed materialistic corruption of Islam as well as that of the mullahs and the Islamic Regime. At the same time, as this is a poem that seems to praise moths, the moths do not only represent the blind or seemingly hypnotized followers of fundamentalist Islam. Rather, Sedarat praises the moths that devour clothing as a representation of eating away or exposing the artifice in the Islamic Republic, leaving it naked and exposing its "record / Of personal atrocities" (10). Whereas the moths (Iranian citizens) had been revolving around the corrupt leaders of the Islamic Regime, the speaker envisions them driving them towards a nobler goal. Namely, he suggests that he will "shine a light / On the chador to help hungry moths find / Thick fabric that keeps women locked inside. / The truth will surface from the suffering; / We'll walk naked with God (who's all seeing)" (10). In this case, Sedarat's hopes seem to lie with the seemingly blind followers of fundamentalist Islam in Iran, and hinge on the belief that their orientation can be rearranged and that they can ultimately work as agents of change, uncovering the truth, rather than obscuring it by blindly following Iranian mullahs and the Islamic Regime.

For Sedarat, moths represent a duality in Iran between blind allegiance to fundamentalist Islam (as in a moth circling a light) and as a liberating force (as in moths devouring oppressive clothing and stripping down to the core). While parts of "In Praise of Moths" seemingly have no direct connection with moths, these parts still illustrate the complexities and dualities Sedarat sees in Iranian culture. One on the one hand, several parts of the poem seemingly mock traditional forms of Persian poetry like a ghazal[17] (a poem composed of rhyming couplets with the same meter) and a qasida (a poem in which every line contains an identical end-rhyme, typically used to commemorate a regal figure). In this case, the speaker is like a moth consuming an old form, but he does so in order to produce something more authentic and truthful by "turning over forms," as Sedarat describes it (11). Sedarat also employs humor to illustrate hidden truths, for instance, "the 'glug glug' of booze in Muslim countries / Echoes through most mosques (the devil's ghazal)" (11), despite the fact that alcohol is traditionally banned in Muslim countries like Iran. While Sedarat's humor may, on the surface, appear trivial or insubstantial in places, such as with the seemingly insignificant lines, "My Father's Buick, a real gas guzzler, / Backfired, and wrote its own kind of ghazal" (11), these lines work to humanize an elite poetic form (the ghazal), making it more accessible to general readers. For Sedarat or the speaker, this is an important task since this poem (like many of the other poems in Dear Regime) envisions a more equitable and egalitarian Iran as opposed to contemporary Iran, which the speaker depicts as an "empire of decay" (15).

This depiction of contemporary Iran as decayed continues as the speaker decries what he perceives Iran has become in the poem: a violent and largely corrupt country. His repetition of the word "Qasida" also calls upon an important traditional poetic form as a method to re-connect with Iran's pre-revolutionary (and pre–Shah) Persian past. Sedarat writes: "'Qasida!' / Scream poets from unmarked graves. 'Qasida!' / I saw my uncle murdered. Qasida. / They beat a girl for Lipstick. 'Qasida' / Blood drops on the walls of the mosque. 'Qasida'" (15–16). Ultimately, the poem becomes a call for action against the current Islamic Regime. While Sedarat admits that the poem "will not redeem you," he hopes that it will "push you past the threshold," and concludes, "This poem will never stop: qasida / Until people start chanting "Qasida! / Qasida qasida qasida q—'" (16). However, the fact that Sedarat ends the poem in the middle of the word "qasida" does undercut the seemingly optimistic strength of the poem as it suggests that the poet or chanter is cut off, possibly by force or even by an assassin.

Ultimately, one of the reasons that Sedarat may praise moths is that they are not considered a truly threatening or frightening insect (despite the destruction they could potentially inflict upon crops, for instance). Consequently, in the last part of the poem, composed as a letter to the Islamic Regime, Sedarat begins by writing, "The trick to reading this book / is to stop taking yourself so seriously / just because you find yourself the butt of a joke" (18). Moths may also symbolize transformation, since they undergo a metamorphosis from caterpillar to winged creature. In this case, the moths are the Iranian people whom he addresses in his letter to the Regime to take his "hand" and to join him a metaphorical "dinner / after your twenty-five-plus-year fast," because even if they were to metaphorically or literally cut off his hand so he could not write, "Like the severed tail of the desert lizard / it can move on its own" (18). In other words, after the poem has been written and has been disseminated, it takes on its own life beyond that of the writer.

In keeping with this division between the citizens and the governments, for Sedarat, one of the main divisions remaining in Iran is between intellectuals or artists and the governing, typically educated, often overtly religious body. In a country that censors artistic expression, especially that of a political nature, artists and writers are often forced to become self-isolates, rebels, or exiles. In this topsy-turvy environment, those who might otherwise be among the country's most respected intellectual leaders are forced to abandon much of their life's work. For instance, in the poem "Agha D," the speaker describes meeting "the literary historian of a nation" (19). However, the speaker describes him "writing a book in his underwear," which suggests that the Agha D may have become isolated (living by himself) or may be economically disadvantaged. The speaker also describes Agha D as "cutting and pasting the faces of poets / into ruler-drawn boxes" (19). These poets, Agha D suggests, have been killed by the administration, presumably because of their political and socially charged ideas and writings, as evident by how "As he holds each black-and-white face before me, / he slices his throat with his index finger" (19).

Similarly, Sedarat details executions in Iran within the poem "At the Firing Squad" (which is reminiscent of "The Body Cleaner"), although he never states why people are being executed in the first place. This may be because, according to Sedarat, the supposed reason will inherently not justify the execution (e.g., protesting against or denouncing the Islamic Republic). Thereby, his portrayal of an execution seems more like a murder with the executed "unable to return the studied gaze / of squinted soldiers" (25). Sedarat makes it clear that his real desire is to "save people," but he also realizes that literature can do nothing specific as evident by the line, "the writer knows it will not change a thing" (25). This leads to Sedarat essentially abandoning his depiction of the executioners and asking that the poem be transformed into something at least more comforting to the executed such as "somebody's last cigarette / before the inevitable fall into the grave" (25).

Beyond the actual, unjustified executions that Sedarat believes occur in Iran (and actually do occur in Iran), he also paints a picture of a largely corrupt, totalitarian, and disingenuous Islamic Regime. For instance, even during what should be the most private and blissful of occasions, a wedding, Sedarat portrays the Islamic Republic as greedily interruptive. In the poem "Cousin Farzad's Wedding," Sedarat writes, "Soldiers show up uninvited, opening / presents before it gets started, keeping / silver platters for their wives" (23). Not only do they effectively steal items during the wedding, they also seem hypocritical in their enjoyment of Persian music and their subsequent dancing before "confiscating" the Persian music that plays, which is behavior contrary to edicts set by the Islamic Republic (23). Further, they also charge the family "a fine of three thousand U.S. dollars," which they subsequently use "for vacation on the Caspian Sea" (23). If this were not enough, they also invite more of their fellow soldiers to crash the wedding after they leave. While such incidents probably do occur in Iran, this poem does effectively demonize the Iranian soldiers in a way that could lead one to regard them as monstrous and sub-human.

At the same time, Sedarat's intent is not to just demonize the Islamic Regime and its officials. Rather, some of Sedarat's poems do seek to answer the larger question of how Iranian soldiers might end up as he portrays them in "Cousin Farzad's Wedding," namely greedy, selfish, and inhumane. For instance, while in the poem "At the Hezbollah Recruiting Station," Sedarat details how young Iranians can be drawn into a radical terrorist group, his depiction appears not that dissimilar to how many Western military organizations try to entice potential members to join. In this poem, Sedarat describes the recruiting process as akin to the recruiting of potential Cub Scouts (34). Sedarat makes this analogy not only because of the number of "preteenaged boys who hand out leaflets and little candies," but also because they entice young Iranians to join through the rhetoric of national and religious service (34). This rhetoric, though, is not that dissimilar from that used by the American military or most Western military organizations.

Those who enlisted in the Iranian military (or its youth groups), Sedarat suggests, if they are lucky enough to survive their adolescence, often grow despondent and cynical as they age. We can see this in the poem "Revolutionary Reflections," which Sedarat dedicates to one of the former American hostages held by Iran (from 1979 to 1981): Barry Rosen. In this poem, Sedarat describes how "The young idealists who stormed the embassy / now fear their twenty-something children / will fight some useless war" (36). However, Sedarat also takes aim at the West as well, specifically the former Western hostages held by Iran after the Revolution. He writes, somewhat tongue-in-cheek, "Better to progress in the Western world / represented by the ideal of a free country" (36). The fact that Sedarat uses the words "represented by the ideal of a free country" indicates that he does not entirely believe that the West embodies freedom, however one might define it. Further, he describes the former hostages as "the blindfolded teaching the veiled to see" (36). While the hostages were literally blindfolded through portions of their incarceration, in this poem, they serve as the metaphorical blindness of the West, whose people simplistically tend to believe that they can lead the oppressed "veiled" to liberation. Similar to the "young idealists" who imprisoned them, the "Ex-hostages, once unshaven for 444 days / look at the bathroom mirror in their latter years / much like the smooth-faced ex-revolutionaries / who, from time to time, reflect on their youth. / 'What were we thinking?' they ask" (36). For Sedarat, in this poem, neither side ultimately helps either the West or the current Islamic Republic, which he describes as heading "in a meaningless direction / where few really want to go" (36).

As mentioned earlier by Sedarat himself, one technique he uses in this collection to combat what he perceives to be hypocrisy and corruption in Iran is humor or satire. For instance, he satirizes Iran's ultra conservative policies on sexuality within the poem "Athletes Make the Best Persian Pornography." It has been well established in psychoanalytical theory from its beginnings with Sigmund Freud[18] that sexual repression can lead to a host of problems including transference, projection, and self-loathing. In this poem, Sedarat suggests that the Iranian Regime's obsessive focus upon censoring or banning anything perceived to be remotely sexual actually backfires and ends up sexualizing the most pedestrian of activities. For instance, in the first stanza, entitled "Reza Goes Bowling," Sedarat describes bowling, somewhat satirically, as having been "banned," in Iran "for its obvious sexual suggestions" (26). While Sedarat does not specifically state what these "sexual suggestions" could be, the last line, "putting three fingers in a red ball" (26), alludes to a sexual act. However, that analogy between sex and bowling would presumably not have been made were it not for the restrictions of the Islamic Regime as well as its own designation of bowling as sexually suggestive.

Even basic physical activity from swimming to biking (which Sedarat describes as "a no-no" for women) becomes sexualized and in turn is condemned or outlawed in Iran by the Islamic Regime (26). To Sedarat, these activities become ultra-sexualized due to how the Islamic Regime wants women to be heavily dressed, so that virtually none of their body (other than their face) is exposed or even vaguely so through the outline of their clothes. In the stanza "Shirin Takes Up Swimming," for instance, while Shirin wears "a blue bathing suit and polka-dotted / swimming cap" when she goes swimming, Sedarat mocks the restrictions of the Islamic Republic by writing, "Check out the skin that chadors / have kept you missing. Her kneecaps are beautiful!" (26). Traditionally, knees are not sexualized, but they can become so when the vast majority of a person's entire body is covered up to supposedly prevent any form of sexual objectification. Even the seemingly simplest of sports related contact such as the brief touching of hands during a "co-ed relay race" becomes fraught with sexuality in a country where unrelated men and women are not supposed to touch in public. Again, Sedarat uses satire by writing, "You haven't seen anything this sexy since / the Shah and his wife played baseball" (26). Of course, the implication is that this activity is not sexy at all, but in a highly repressive environment, so much more has become sexualized, which effectively counteracts the intention of the repression.

Such activities can also, Sedarat suggests (in keeping with basic psychoanalytical theory), lead to private sexual oddities (if not perversities) as well as an additional attraction to more sexually open Western media. For instance, in "Satellite of Love," Sedarat describes an Iranian husband dressing his "300-pound wife" as Pamela Anderson while making her "pour last night's *fesenjan* and rice over her body" (27). To be sure, it could be argued that it is the fault of the overly sexualized Western media, which emphasizes sexual expression, but what Sedarat demonstrates here is how what the Islamic Regime would no doubt describe as corrupt behavior is generally innocuous.

Still, similar to the writers previously examined in this study, Sedarat acknowledges the importance of the media and marketing in contemporary Iran. In "Prelude to a Blackout," he writes, "the greatest revolutions / are fought via satellite" (32). Even in the most seemingly impoverished and primitive of locations, such as "homes made of mud," we can see the presence of television (32). For Sedarat, this is neither specific to the West nor to Iran or the Middle East, but rather, it is more of a global phenomenon which should not be downplayed, as he notes when he writes, "Perhaps Mohammad, a man sick of the world / selling the soul through illusion, could see beyond / commercial hypocrisy, and into the nature of things" (32). The fact that Sedarat uses the word "perhaps" indicates that he is not sure that even a contemporary Mohammad could compete with the lures of media and technology ("illusion" and "commercial hypocrisy"). Yet, Sedarat also raises the question of whether it is the medium to blame or those who condemn it, or even the "falsely bearded men / who come with scissors to cut the wires" (32). While Sedarat offers no answer to this (although given his previous poems, it can be safely assumed that the mullahs he refers to, those "falsely bearded men," bear a significant amount of the responsibility), he poses a hypothetical situation in which "Allah / (all praise and glory to his name) appears to people / in the medium that best captures the spirit of age," namely television, and inspires the viewer who then becomes "a channel for the divine" (32). While religious figures do use media and technology to transmit their messages (as does the Iranian clergy, al Qaeda, as well as a host of Western religious figures and groups), Sedarat suggests that the ones who do are not truly religiously or nobly inspired.

Along similar lines, several of the poems in *Dear Regime* also take aim at the noble titles bestowed by Islam, which Sedarat suggests have been perverted by the Islamic Regime. For instance, whereas, typically, the name "Haji" is an honorable title given to someone who has made the pilgrimage to Mecca, demonstrating his or her religious devotion, in "Haji as Stick Figure," Sedarat overturns this correlation. What appears as sacred and estimable is actually spiritually empty and insubstantial. Instead of becoming more spiritually enlightened, Sedarat's Haji is a "shadow of a man," who fills a "void" with "pain" and "impending doom" (50). While Sedarat never states exactly why, he implies that any enlightenment the Haji has experienced only has made him aware of the spiritual bankruptcy of the Islamic Regime. Hence, the Haji is "a savior / without a spirit, a ghost haunting / every conceivable catastrophe," due to the vampiric nature of the Islamic Regime (50). It would seem that "the darkness he is forced to inhabit," and which causes him to be fearful, is Iran itself. Without a genuine religious environment, the Haji lives in a kind of purgatory in which there is "Always the longing to fill himself in, / to brush light into his being and feel his own gravity. / Only then might he find himself able to run / from his eternally recurring danger" (50). In this case, the "eternally recurring danger" can be seen as the Islamic Regime itself, which effectively nullifies any substantive spiritualism and genuine religious beliefs through its oppressive, if not totalitarian, dogma.

In this topsy-turvy environment, there is no real space for a true Haji, and in subsequent poems, Sedarat describe Hajis in comic terms or as overly disillusioned. For instance, in the poem "Permissible Grapes, Forbidden Wine," Sedarat blends a traditional Western children's song ("If You're Happy and You Know It") with his depiction of the Haji to illustrate how the dominant religious forces in the Islamic Regime lack maturity and how religious figures themselves in the Islamic Regime are not generally allowed to be anything but subservient children. On the one hand, Sedarat criticizes those hypocritical mullahs who call themselves Hajis but who more accurately are frauds seeking power. On the other hand, Sedarat depicts authentic Hajis who have become isolated and debased by what Sedarat perceives as the falsely religious environment in Iran. In this environment, Sedarat suggests, the only way for the Haji to recover that sense of true piety is to, ironically, go against the dictates of the Islamic Regime — in this case, by resuscitating Iran's historically rich wine-making region of Shiraz, as a way to reconnect with traditional Persian culture. Consequently, Sedarat writes, "Stomp your feet and store the red / in rows of barrels in your head arranged by ancestors / who ask if you're their true inheritor" (51).

Similarly, in the poem "This Little Haji," Sedarat uses the traditional Western nursery rhyme "This Little Piggy" to illustrate the plight of the Haji in the poem. While it is true that the word "little" in the title may suggest that the Hajis are insignificant or small, this does not necessarily mean that Sedarat is debasing them; rather, they may be so because of the debilitating environment in Iran. This can be seen in the lines "This little Haji cried, 'We little Haji are all of us alone,'" as well as the line, "These little Hajis, for all their crying of 'We,' are destined to remain single" (52). Still, Sedarat does not portray the Hajis as doing anything substantively religious in the poem; rather, they go to the "market," and stay "home," chewing "kebab" while "gnawing" on bones (52). However, the Hajis persist because they believe they "will last," while Sedarat suggests that they "will end up in the past" (52).

We can also see the powerlessness and ignorance of the Haji, who cannot or does not want to prevent anything truly inhumane and sacrilegious, such as the unjust execution of a political prisoner in the poem "When Haji Comes to Town." In this poem, the Haji can or actually chooses to do nothing to stop the imminent execution of a prisoner named Ali; rather, he lets the "city speak for itself," and, according to Sedarat, the city is completely indifferent and champions self-absorbed, Western-style consumerism, represented by the "glory of neon kebob signs, / gold Allah medallions flashing on teenagers" (58). In this case, it is the combination of the religiously dogmatic Islamic Regime along with hollow Western consumerism that ultimately produces a kind of nihilistic ennui. Still, this is not to suggest that Sedarat views religion or Hajis themselves as completely corrupt or without the possibility of redemption. For instance, in the interview-poem "The Hysterical as the Historical: An Interview with the Haji," the Haji describes himself as "a four-leaf clover who's been mown over" (60). However, not all hope is lost in that Sedarat imagines the Haji turning "himself into a mirror / to show those looking how to see" (58).

While the previous poems generally deal with life in Iran, in Sedarat's poem "Flying to Persia," a clever inversion of Yeats's well-known poem "Sailing to Byzantium," in which Yeats portrays the importance of transcendence in later life, the speaker, an exile, imagines himself heading to the Middle Eastern equivalent to Byzantium, in this case Persia, whose cultural heights occurred close to the same time as those of ancient Greece. By using the word "Persia," as opposed to "Iran," Sedarat also invokes a pre–Islamic and pre-colonized Iran, when it was both a military and artistic power. The poem begins similarly to Yeats's poem with the lines: "This is no nation for an activist. / Burned effigies of the colonizer / Assimilate into the incensed air" (41). Sedarat's use of the word "colonizer" presumably alludes to not only the Western (U.S.) establishment of the Shah, but given his previous poems examined, also to the spread of more contemporary Western consumerism and culture. At the same time, the first lines of the poem suggest that Sedarat believes that change in Iran is extremely difficult, if not virtually impossible, since without activists a country cannot substantively change. Still, the poem is not wholly pessimistic, suggesting that "The native language, having existed / through centuries of invasions, survives" (41). One way it survives is through "classic poems," that "have been memorized / By generations" (41). While Sedarat does not specify the poems, it can be safely assumed that he refers to classic Persian poets like Hafez.

Indeed, it is within art, poetry, or even the liberation of language itself that Sedarat ultimately sees the greatest hope for Iran. This can be seen in the last poem in the collection, "Reinstatement of the Rose," in which Sedarat suggests that rampant censorship in Iran has stultified the imagination, destroyed beauty, and betrayed quintessential ideals and tenets of Persian culture. He begins the poem with: "It's time to reinstate the rose, / banned too long for its multiple meanings" (71). "Rose" in this case may symbolize love, something romantic and heart-felt, but it may also represent violence and the blood of misguided martyrs, especially during the Iran-Iraq war. By using the word "reinstatement," Sedarat wants the reader to know that free expression was once an essentially part of Iranian or Persian culture, perhaps best illustrated through classic Persian poetry.

Indeed, for Sedarat, the "divine" can be found in language and meditation, which Sedarat presents as oppositions to violence and warfare, which he sees based on narrow interpretations and stunted imaginations, exactly the things that art helps counteract. Alluding to Iraq, Sedarat demonstrates what is to be overcome: "In streets of Karballah, believers' blood / runs like ink for the divine" (71). To combat this seemingly endless cycle of religiously motivated violence, Sedarat calls for the reinstatement of language (or figurative language) itself, and along with it the end of censorship. Hence, Sedarat writes, "If only to adorn graves / It's time to reinstate the rose" (71). Not only has censorship or blind dogmatism caused a limiting of the imagination (which, in turn, can lead to violence), according to Sedarat, it also metaphorically or literally destroys love itself. Indeed, Sedarat poses the question "How else can lovers signify / in gardens of broken glass?" (72).

For Sedarat, the time is right for the Islamic Regime to begin the process of reinstating the rose, or reinstating the importance of language and art, while allowing its widespread dissemination in all its forms. Alluding to the Iranian Revolution, Sedarat writes, "The once stormed embassy is now a museum. / Students of the revolution are professors / of a thorny past" (71). In other words, the fires that stoked the initial revolution have subsequently cooled to the point that the time has become ripe for change. Finally, Sedarat calls for this opening of language in order to "return the world to poetry" (71). In essence, he concludes — especially in a country like Iran, which has a long history of respecting art and poetry — that poetry can matter and can change people, and that "the language that governs the heart / at long last needs relearning" (71). "Relearning" poetry and reinstating it in complete freedom, to Sedarat, and no doubt, to most if not all Iranian and Iranian diasporic poets, would bring Iran (and perhaps the West as well) one step closer to the beginning of a personal, spiritual, and possibly even national transformation.

# Alternative Means
# of Communication
## *Iranian Blogs*

As Scott Rosenberg suggests in his book length study about blogs, *Say Anything*, "the rise of blogs has gone a long way toward making good on the promise of the Web's first inventors: that their creation would welcome contributions from every corner of the globe and open a floodgate of human creativity" (11). While Westerners may think of blogs as mainly composed by Americans for Americans, they truly have become a globalized phenomenon. Whereas blogs in the United States tend to be more personal and less serious, in a country like Iran, blogs are akin to underground electronic newspapers and diaries, which often rebel against the political administration as well as the cultural and religious mandates of the Islamic Regime. As Iranian bloggers can be and have been arrested, incarcerated, and even executed for their writings, blogging itself has become a political act in Iran, one potentially fraught with deadly consequences.

It may come as no surprise that in a country that practices artistic and literary censorship, would-be literary writers and activists have sought out and utilized alternatives to printed text. In the case of Iran, the main alternative to the printed word is the electronic word, primarily in the form of blogs. As this is primarily a study of printed literature, my exploration of Iranian and Iranian-American blogs will not be comprehensive or particularly in-depth.[1] (In addition, I have not corrected any grammatical and spelling errors in the quoted blog excerpts.) However, any study of contemporary Iranian and diasporic Iranian literature would be incomplete without at least a general exploration of the growing importance of electronic media as a vehicle for social protest and cultural change. This is especially the case since, according to most sources, Iran has become one of the most wired countries in the Islamic Middle East.[2] In particular, blogs have seen almost exponential growth in Iran as a means of communication and a method of expression. Possibly because of the difficulties involved in defining what is or what is not a blog, or the often transitory nature of blogs themselves, there are widely disparate estimates as to the number of active blogs in Iran. Harvard University's Berkman Center for Internet & Society is on one end of the spectrum, estimating "60,000 regularly updated blogs of virtually every political stripe" (Dayem 42), while a report on the other end of the spectrum suggests there are upwards of 700,000 Iranian bloggers (Sreberny and Khiabany 272). Indeed, despite the government's attempts to crack down on bloggers, as we shall see later, Iran is now considered to be third in the world in terms of the number of weblogs produced by a single country (Moaveni, *Honeymoon in Tehran* 128; Baer 8).[3]

One might wonder why the Islamic Republic has not made a concerted effort to crack down on the Iranian blogosphere, as it is often called. One reason this has not been done is the Iranian government itself has embraced blogging for its own purposes. This is best illustrated in how Iranian President Mahmoud Ahmadinejad composes his own online blog. While the Islamic Republic may have not initially scrutinized and censored blogs (most of which were initially personal or religious in nature), when bloggers began to cover more "political, social, religious and cultural" issues, Iran made more of a concerted effort to regulate the Internet and blogging (Dayem 42).[4] Still, despite what might be suggested by the media, Iranian blogs are not homogenous activist and anti–Islamic Republic rants. According to the Berkman Center, Iranian blogs, if they are political, may also be conservative and religious as well as secular and liberal (Ludtke 45).[5] However, one reason that Iranian blogs may seem more secular and liberal to Westerners is that it is probable that more of this kind of blog has been translated from Farsi (while some Iranian bloggers do write in English or translate their own work into English, the majority do not).[6]

Censorship and the banning of certain viewpoints, subject matter, and language has led many would-be fiction writers, poets, playwrights, or journalists in Iran to seek out and utilize the actual or perceived freedoms of cyberspace. Indeed, in her book *We Are Iran*, Nasrin Alavi suggests that since the late 1990s, "as many as 100 print publications, including 41 daily newspapers, have been closed by Iran's hardline judiciary" (2). Without the print or tele-visual media functioning in a free, unbiased manner, young Iranians have few or no options other than the Internet to express their views freely and to try to obtain relatively unbiased information.[7] Blogs also provide a free space for Iranians to court one another romantically (Alavi 16–17). This is especially important for young people in a country as socially conservative as Iran, where unmarried and unrelated men and women are not supposed to be seen in public together, which, as Mandanipour demonstrates in *Censoring an Iranian Love Story*, makes it especially difficult for relationships to blossom.

Still, blogging, while seemingly a safer medium than printed journalism or literature, has proved to be just as dangerous (if not more so) for writers. Whereas print writers who might have published something deemed blasphemous would presumably be stopped by a censor who would refuse to publish the work as is, bloggers may be able to (at least for a short time) post content later deemed to be blasphemous or problematic by the Islamic Regime. Since their content may end up being seen by the public before being censored, bloggers can be seen as much more potentially more dangerous to the Islamic Republic than traditional authors, and the blogs themselves can be extremely dangerous to a blogger who could be accused of blasphemy, arrested, incarcerated, and even, in some circumstances, executed. Indeed, according to Alavi, "It doesn't take much to be officially accused of 'blasphemy' in Iran — a crime punishable by death" (16–17). Realizing the potential for blogs to disrupt the government and spark unrest, the Islamic Regime began a crackdown in 2003 by blocking "sites and blogs that clashed with official state policy" (Amini 35). When that failed to work, the Islamic Regime tried to comprehensively block potentially problematic blogs by filtering and censoring any blogs with the terms "woman" or "gender" in them (Amini 35). Further, to inspire more fear, the Islamic Regime began arresting bloggers such as Arash Sigarchi and Mojtaba Saminejad, who were thought to have "criticized government policies online" (Amini 35; Cohen 57; Alavi 2).[8] When that still did not produce the desired end result of quelling dissent, in 2007, the Islamic Regime started a new policy to make blog owners "register their website or blog within two months" and thereby reveal their identity and contact information (Alavi 276).[9]

All indications are that the Islamic Regime has continued to arrest and imprison bloggers deemed to have written blasphemous material or deemed to be a threat to the state. Still, the potential dangers inherent in blogging have not dissuaded many to stop as it has become the primary means of expression for many (especially younger) Iranians.[10] While they might not enforce it, reports suggest that the Islamic Republic wishes to crack down further on blog activity by "passing a law imposing capital punishment on blogs that promote 'corruption, prostitution and apostasy,' ill-defined and highly elastic concepts that could place a death sentence on all of Iran's voices for change" ("Death to Bloggers" 16).

Perhaps because of the recent governmental crackdown on blogs, other methods of communication have become more popular in contemporary Iran, such as Facebook, text messaging, and especially, Twitter. During the summer 2009 protests in Iran, Twitter and YouTube were instrumental in galvanizing protests as well as spreading images of the revolt. In particular, the pictures and video footage of the death of Neda Agha-Soltan resonated deeply not only with Iranians but with the global community to the point that journalist Michael Baumann described Neda as becoming "the silent martyr of the Iranian election protests, much the way 'Tank Man' was to Tiananmen Square in 1989" (Baumann 51). While the use of these technological forms during the 2009 demonstrations did not amount to a "Twitter Revolution," which would spread "hope that the internet (and social networking in particular) would bring democracy to autocratic states the world over," it is hard to deny the importance these technologies have had and could still have in contemporary Iran (Baumann 51).[11]

Indeed, since 2009, Twitter has proved to be one of the most important means of communication, not only for Iranians to talk to one another, but for people to organize demonstrations and provide almost instantaneous reports to the outside world. Despite the Islamic Regime's attempts, it has proven difficult to dismantle these new technologies (Hosenball 14). To some extent, the United States has helped Twitter and other technologies stay online in Iran, especially during the 2009 protests.[12] At the same time, some have suggested that the Islamic Regime purposely held back dismantling the technologies in order to better identify problematic individuals.[13] As Lev Grossman explains:

> The day after the election, when protests against President Mahmoud Ahmadinejad began escalating and the Iranian government moved to suppress dissent, the Twitterverse exploded with tweets in both English and Farsi. While the front pages of Iranian newspapers were full of blank space where censors had whited out news stories, Twitter was delivering information from street level in real time: Woman says ppl knocking on her door 2 AM saying they were intelligence agents, took her daughter and we hear 1 dead in shiraz, livefire used in other cities [9].

In addition, major American news networks like CNN used Twitter reports as primary sources for their respective program (Flanigen 14). Still, reports on Twitter may not always be accurate or reliable as they are typically not verified or verifiable. In addition, one can imagine that the Iranian government may begin to (if they haven't already done so) plant false messages in Twitter in order to ensnare those they might believe to be a threat.

It is hard to determine what long-lasting effects these new media forms and technologies will ultimately have upon Iran. While Baumann argues that "ultimately, all of the protests, tweets, and YouTube videos did not lead to any substantive political revolution," it is certainly possible that these technological platforms helped generate a more substantial rebellion during 2009 and that they could help foment further rebellions or even revolutions (54).

Other critics suggest that new media technologies like Twitter might be a sign of "the looming age of cheap and effective Internet-powered protests that will soon extirpate all forms of authoritarianism" (Morozov 11). In fact, this appears to be exactly what has recently occurred in North African and Middle Eastern countries like Tunisia and Egypt during early 2011.

While it has been suggested that "learning from foreign blogs is a long and tedious process," not only is it possible to learn from foreign and domestic blogs by Iranians and diasporic Iranians, but it is also possible to get what appears to be more of an unvarnished account of life in the Islamic Republic as well as in the West (for diasporic Iranians) (Morozov 13). In addition, the Internet has also come to play and continues to play a significant role in the lives of diasporic Iranians in building a virtual community.[14] In particular, Jahanshah Javid's site www.Iranian.com has been cited by multiple critics as among the most popular and influential with one estimate suggesting upwards of half a million unique viewings monthly.[15] Some blogs also allow authors an opportunity to self-publish their own memoirs, poetry, or prose, and again, as such expression is limited in Iran, the blogs serve an important function.

Still, bloggers themselves have attested to the importance of as well as the inherent dangers of using the Internet for wider communication of topics and commentary that question or challenge the Islamic Regime. For instance, one blogger writes that he has "used my blog to openly discuss issues such as stoning and the execution of women and minors, areas rarely covered by even the most daring of reformist publications. But these posts have put me in danger" (Amini 34). Specifically, he explains that not only did he spend "four days in prison" in 2007, he and other "activists ... were charged with actions against national security" and "some ... received prison sentences" (Amini 34). For many younger and female Iranians, social media forms have become their primary means of expression in a culture that often denies them public, and at times even private, agency.[16]

One of the largest compendiums of Iranian blogs in English (and the primary source for this chapter) can be found at http://www.iraniansblogs.com.[17] However, most of the blogs are only active for a short period of time (e.g., from 2003 to 2005, 2006 to 2007, etc). This could be due to an author's own desire to discontinue blog writing, but it also could be due to fear of retaliation by the Islamic Regime or even actual retaliation by the Regime in terms of threats or an arrest. While some blogs appear almost entirely personal and non-political[18] (more like their American or Western counterparts), other blogs serve as alternative news sources with the writers sometimes describing themselves as journalists and suggesting to the reader that their blogs will provide a more unvarnished account of life in contemporary Iran.[19] Some blogs are unabashedly political,[20] like "Stop Torturing Us" (http://stop.tortur ing.us/), whose description or mission statement could not be clearer: "This is about systematic torture in Iran. Mental torture with horrible savage events like stoning, mass executions and so on while we are not being detained; and physical and mental torture while we are in detention" (par. 1). The author of the blog, for understandable reasons, never reveals his or her identity (there is only an e-mail address for inquiries). While it is impossible to determine with certainty if the author lives in Iran or in the West, given the pictures the author uses that are clearly from Iran, the former is more likely than the latter. "Stop Torturing Us" contains multimedia blogs with pictures, video clips, text, news reports and discussions such as "Iranian Teacher on Death Row" for purportedly "endangering national security" and "enmity against God" (par. 1). The blogger's pictures are purposely gruesome and graphic, including various stages of what appear to be Iranian executions and, in one case, a completely lacerated back, presumably after a lashing. "Stop Torturing Us," along with other blogs, also helps establish a community and promote activism with their use of links to Human Rights organizations and to other websites that describe the deaths of Iranian bloggers and political prisoners.

In the journal entries, "Stop Torturing Us" directly challenges its readers to witness and act upon human rights violations. For instance, in the June 23, 2010, entry the author begins, "I want you to watch following photos and think for a minute. Do you see anything wrong on these photos?" (par. 1). The photos are before and after pictures of the hangings of several male and female Middle Easterners in public spaces. The author does not specify whether the executions have occurred in Iran (as opposed to in a neighboring Middle Eastern country), nor identify the crimes purportedly committed by the victims. Even though the blog is from June 2010, there is no indication of when the executions occurred. In fact, as the blogger used one of the pictures in the 2008 entry, it can be safely assumed that at least some of the executions are not current. While this does not lessen the importance of the pictures or the executions themselves, it does suggest that the blogger is less of an objective news reporter (not subject to peer or editor review) and more of an activist. Still, other entries do include more specific material, such as one from April 26, 2010, which refers to a death sentence and a double amputation sentence for two supposedly convicted criminals, enacted on April 14, 2010 (par. 1).[21] "Stop Torturing Us" also includes writing that attests to unjust incarcerations, sentences, and executions. One such entry comes from May 8, 2009, and details the experiences of Farzad Kamangar, who was sentenced to death in 2008[22] for supposedly plotting against the Islamic Regime and engaging in terrorist-like activities (par. 1–3).[23] Other sources corroborate that Kamanger and others were indeed unjustly convicted, sentenced, and executed.[24] In that sense, "Stop Torturing Us" doesn't function as a definitive news source but rather as a compendium of various already published news accounts.

While "Stop Torturing Us" is a serious, politically active blog aimed at bringing attention to human rights violations in Iran, other Iranian blogs blend the personal, the literary, and the political, and like many of the authors examined in this study, utilize humor and sarcasm to critique the Islamic Regime. One example is the blog "Bingala" (like "Stop Torturing Us," "Bingala" does not reveal its author's identity, though it does reveal that he is male and lives in Tehran, and lists his favorite books, movies, and music). The author of "Bingala" sarcastically pokes fun at the Islamic Regime with the following poem in his June 28th entry: "USA, England, France & Italy all disgracefully / got knocked out of the world cup, God willing, / since they all voted for sanctions against Iran. / They shall soon witness our holy strength / when God helps Brazil who supported us win the Cup!!" (par. 1). "Bingala's" writings also reveal a way to, at least temporarily, get past Iranian filters — namely, by substituting symbols for letters. For instance, instead of writing the word "sexually," which would presumably be blocked by Iranian filters (in turn, probably resulting in the entire blog being blocked), the author writes, "$exually." Along similar lines, to discuss the movie *Inglourious Basterds*, the author blocks out the "a" in Basterds by writing "B@sterds." Bingala also critiques the Islamic Republic by using Western popular culture references, such as one entry (June 20, 2010) that suggests that Voldemort (a Harry Potter allusion) lives in the "Dictatorship Palace" in Tehran (and therefore would be either Mahmoud Ahmadenijad or the Supreme Leader Ali Khamenei). To be sure, not all of "Bingala's" brief (typically Twitter-length two to three line entries) revolve around political issues, as some vaguely detail his personal and romantic life, and indeed, there seem to be more of these entries before the June 2009 demonstrations.[25]

Still, it does seem that "Bingala" took greater aim at the Islamic Regime after the 2009 demonstrations as evident by his continued sarcastic critiques. For instance, in his short February 23, 2010, entry, "Bingala" writes, "Heaven is filled with prophets, saints & the filtered blogs" (par. 1). Here, "Bingala" seems to take aim at fundamentalist Islam, whose prophets and saints may be as falsely purified as filtered blogs themselves. Along similar lines, "Bingala" provides a list, in an entry from February 11, 2010, of Iran's "Most Dangerous Jobs." This list includes: "3) Astronaut Worms, Mice & Turtles; 2) University students & Journalists; 1) Iranian citizens" (par. 1). That "Bingala" chooses "Iranian citizens" as the most dangerous job indicates that he feels that no one is safe in Iran and that he believes being an Iranian citizen, perhaps due to the repressive and potentially deadly policies of the Islamic Regime, is a job in itself.

To be sure, there are not a large number of economic opportunities, especially for young people in Iran, a fact that "Bingala" mocks in a poem entitled "Iran's Government's Forced Marriage Policy," included in his January 20, 2010, entry. The poem reads:

> I can't get a job coz I got education
> I got education coz I couldn't grow a beard
> I don't grow a beard coz I don't have a job
> So I am looking for a girl with a job with a beard [lines 1–4].

The poem, as a whole, is set up in a cause and effect structure. The first line suggests not only that there are a paucity of jobs for educated people in Iran, but such jobs may be reserved for presumably less intellectually inclined or less politically threatening individuals who are generally not well-educated. The second line mocks the dogma of the Islamic Regime, which shuns clean shaven men as emblems of Western culture, while championing beards as emblems of religious (Islamic) piety. The speaker suggests that Iranian society (or at least the governing body) would have accepted him more had he the visual accoutrements (the beard) of the supposedly devout. However, with the third line, the speaker suggests his disdain not only for the Islamic Regime but also for even making the attempt to appear devout, which has all but petered out due to his unemployment. Finally, the last line satirically indicates that the speaker desires the impossible: "a girl with a job with a beard." In other words, he has come to believe that his plight is basically hopeless in the Islamic Regime.

The indictment of the Islamic Regime continues in another of "Bingala's" poems, "When Police Murders" (*sic*), included in his January 3, 2010, entry. In this poem, the narrator, representing the police, tries to rationalize the death of Iranian citizens, presumably during the June 2009 demonstrations. First, the narrator blames the death on a "soldier," but justifies the soldier's actions with the line, "He had the right coz they were all so green" (lines 2, 4). In this case, "green" refers to the Green movement, which supported Mir-Hossein Mousavi and helped lead the 2009 demonstrations. The narrator also ends up blaming the opposition or the Green movement itself by claiming that Mousavi "drove the car!" (6). Indeed, the Islamic Regime did blame both the West and the opposition party for fabricating and orchestrating Iranian deaths to promote their cause. In this atmosphere, "Bingala" suggests, there really is no such thing as law enforcement. This can also be seen in his tragic-comedic entry of December 5, 2009, entitled "110 (Aka 911)," which is reproduced in full below:

> For Baton attack press 1
> For Tear gas press 2
> For r@pe in detention press 3
> For Cardiac Arrest in detention press 4
> For Foreign Countries to kill you press 5
> For Police assistance if you are being robbed or killed please press the OFF
> button [lines 1–6].

Not only does this poem suggest that these horrific crimes are so commonplace in Iran that emergency system has created a separate dial-in entry for each, but Bingala also alludes to (in the last line) an essential ineffectiveness of the Iranian police themselves, who appear completely unconcerned if someone is being robbed or might be killed.

In one entry (from May 13, 2009), "Bingala" alludes to what he perceives to be an inherent corruption in Iran, by comparing elections to the Islamic Regime to George Orwell's vision of totalitarianism in his novel *1984*. Yet in another entry, from November 10, 2009, "Bingala" also implicates the West and the United States. He writes, "Bullsh!t Bullcrap Bullsh!t / They make it seem they are victimized. / If they have September 11, / we have June 12! / Which one is worse? ha America?" (par. 1). Bingala indicates at the end of this entry that June 12 is the date of "Ahmadinejad's coup d'etat." He implicates the West not only in a failure to fully recognize the devastation wrought by the post–presidential election demonstrations (which did result in the deaths of many Iranians), but also in an essential selfishness in how the West tends to gloss over the tragedies of other countries.

This entry is similar to that of another Iranian blogger, "Mr. Behi" (in his blog, "The Adventures of Mr. Behi"). In his February 16, 2010, entry entitled "Disproportionate Delusion," after "Mr. Behi" criticizes President Ahmadenijad, he also critiques the United States with the following: "The US government is now worried about Iran becoming a military dictatorship. Dahhhhhh! wake up! it is been a while since that happened and please remind me, what do you call your best pals in the government of Pakistan!" (par. 1). He concludes: "I think both policies (of Iran and the US) are suffering from this hallucination that 'whoever agrees with them is right'" (par. 2). Through these examples, we can see how both bloggers retain their independence, while challenging both the West and the Islamic Regime for their respective failings.

As mentioned earlier, various technological platforms such as blogs and Twitter took on a newfound importance during the summer 2009 Iranian demonstrations as a means to report on ongoing events and as a means to help organize the protests. When examining Iranian blogs, it is helpful to look at the entries during this time not only as a way to witness what appears to be an unvarnished account (although only one person's perspective) of the demonstrations, but also as an insider's account of what these demonstrations meant or still mean to at least one Iranian citizen. "Mr. Behi's" blog is especially pertinent and applicable in part because he is a quintessential member of the Burnt Generation. In his February 6, 2009, entry, "Mr. Behi" describes himself as being "only one when Iran revolted in hope for change" (par. 1). Given that the Revolution occurred in 1978 and 1979, this would mean that Mr. Behi would have been born anywhere from 1976 to 1978, and more importantly, it would mean that he would have no direct recollections of life (or barely any) in Iran before the Revolution. In this same entry, "Mr. Behi" suggests that he cannot relate to the Revolutionaries of 1978 and 1979 because his "world is very different from theirs" (par. 2). He continues: "Chanting 'No East, No West' is no longer valid for me. I am neither ready to change my life for an ideology. If they wanted Iran to change the world with revolution, I now want it to embrace the world with open arms" (par. 2). Still, he doesn't condemn the Revolutionaries, whom he regards as people who "had a dream and went for it fiercely" (par. 3). "Mr. Behi" claims that many of his peers still "dream about change," with some wanting to improve Iran, while others think of leaving, but "no one seem to really know why and how" (par. 3). At this point, "Mr. Behi" suggests, "We are Iranians and we dream. We write poetry, sing sad songs and dream, each in our own individual island" (par. 3).

However, "Mr. Behi's" somewhat defeatist attitude changes with the upcoming June 2009 presidential elections. This is immediately evident from the title of his June 8, 2009, entry: "Ding Ding! Mahmoud is done!" While it's impossible to determine if he's generally accurate, Mr. Behi claims that "Iran is all excited" and that "the atmosphere is so fresh" with the hope and expectation that Ahmadinejad would be leaving the presidency soon (par. 1). In many ways, "Mr. Behi's" entry anticipates the absolute and complete frustration and anger that would soon come after the election, since not only does Mr. Behi hope "for a very big turnout," he suggests that this turnout would counteract any possible "cheating" (par. 1). Further, "Mr. Behi" is very aware, as many Iranians perhaps were, of the symbolism of the rejection of Ahmadinejad (in a similar way to how Americans were aware of the symbolism of electing Barack Obama as president in 2008). Towards that end, "Mr. Behi" writes that the upcoming election (assuming Ahmadinejad lost) "would show how ashamed Iran is for her current president and how determined she is to send him back to his own little world of delusion and deception" (par. 2).

"Mr. Behi's" optimism (and presumably the optimism of many Iranians) is quickly dashed as the election results reveal that Ahmadinejad appears to have won the election. In his June 14, 2009, entry, "Mr. Behi" immediately and clearly critiques the election results as "fabricated" (par. 1). As support, "Mr. Behi" suggests:

> On the night of the election, someone was smart enough to plot incremental votes counts of Ahmadinejad and Mousavi as they were being reported. If you plot them in a simple XY graph, you can easily fit a line to the points! This is completely impossible considering the demographics of the country. Rival candidates lost to Ahmadinejad even in their home towns and one of the candidates got a ridiculous number of votes that is less than a number of people working for his campaign organization [par. 2].

The tenor of "Mr. Behi's" entries becomes understandably more intense towards the end of June 2009, after the majority of the demonstrations occur. The title of his June 29, 2009, entry is "You won't get away with this," with the "you" presumably referring to the Islamic Regime or at least those who helped maintain Ahmadinejad's power. "Mr. Behi" implicates "Iranian leadership" for "brutality and deception," while condemning the Guardian Council's approval of the election results as a mere capitulation to Iran's Supreme Leader, Khamani, who had recently approved the presidential results (par. 1). In response to the bloodshed and violence during the demonstrations, which "Mr. Behi" blames on the Islamic Regime, he passionately writes: "You may burn us to our ashes but the flame stays alive inside us. Freedom is our right and you, the dictator, the supreme leader who inflated yourself with this much agony and false merits ... will not be able to cage it forever" (par. 1). Even in his entries towards the end of July 2009 (such as one from July 21) "Mr. Behi" suggests that "the struggle in Iran is far from over and it is about to unleash yet another unpredictable chapter in the country's history. The Islamic system has already failed to contain the movement and is discovering an ever widening rift in its own trusted hierarchy" (par. 1). He describes the current system as one of "religious totalitarianism" and implicates the Islamic Republic for its rampant paranoia towards Westerners (par. 2). At the same time, "Mr. Behi" stops short of extolling the West. While his more recent critiques are centered on Iran, he does not suggest that the West is necessarily much or any better.

Similar to "Mr. Behi," the blogger whose site is titled "Tehran Post" (http://ord-per.blogspot.com/) also strives to maintain a level of objectivity between the West and Iran in his blogs. While we do not know this blogger's name, he does reveal his age (27) and that he is a student and works as a translator ("User Profile," par. 1). We can see from "Tehran Post's" earlier entries in 2007 that he has enmity towards both the West and the Islamic Republic, as clearly evident by the title of his August 28, 2007, entry: "Fuck You Bush," in which "Tehran Post" accuses the Bush administration of falsely accusing "Iran on Iraq,"[26] and he also implicates "the Saudis" who "are playing a destructive role in Iraq" (par. 2).[27] Similarly, in his April 1, 2008, entry, "Tehran Post" critiques the policies of the United States in the Middle East as being counterproductive, with the evidence being a "general trend" that he observes "in Middle East countries that the more the country is in good terms with West (something they call 'moderate'), the more radical people become" (par. 1). "Tehran Post" effectively identifies how many of the most radical fringe element of fundamentalist Islamic groups reside in countries that have generally positive relationships with the United States (e.g., Saudi Arabia). In reference to Hamas and the Palestinians, many of whom reside in Egypt, "Tehran Post" writes "If I lived in Egypt, I believed that Jews must be taught a good lesson and Islamic rules must be carried out in the society" (par. 2). In reference to how many al-Qaeda members hail from or reside in Pakistan or Saudi Arabia (again, both of whom have generally positive relationships with the United States, although the U.S.-Pakistan relationship has proven more tumultuous), "Tehran Post" writes, "If I lived in Pakistan, I would study in one of those religious schools, trained to become a suicide bomber and kill Shiites" (par. 3). Finally, he writes, "If I lived in Saudi Arabia, I would leave my well-to-do family, form a terrorist cell in the name of bin-Laden and attack Americans" (par. 4). Ultimately, "Tehran Post" ends up defending Iran: "So I thank god that I live in Iran, I don't believe in theocracy, I believe in women's rights, I don't hate other religious sects, and I understand that having relations with US is necessary, although the country has never done any good to us" (par. 5).

However, in his October 9, 2007, entry, "Tehran Post" seems as critical of the Ahmadinejad administration as he was of the United States. This entry, which was written in reference to Ahmadinejad's trip to the United Nations, critiques Ahmadinejad for his hypocrisy, exemplified by how he supposedly tolerated insults from the Columbia University president and student body, whereas "dissident students in Iran will be scattered by pepper gas if they want to protest against imprisonment of their classmates" (par. 6). "Tehran Post" concludes that Ahmadinejad is "the living posterchild of how a politician can lie flagrantly and disembowel concepts" (par. 6). In his June 1, 2008, entry, "Tehran Post" explains his attempt to be neutral and objective when writing about the West and Iran. He writes:

I don't want to be a spindoctor here, trying to whitewash everything Iranian action, whether by the government or people. i see all the deficits the iranian society has, and i'm always sad about the big problems of iranian culture.... However, the way western media treat iran is unfair i believe, we may not be a benevolent country, but definitely we're not the demon we are pictured. that's why i focus mainly on iran's bright side. i promise to shift the agenda if things become O.K. (will the day come? :-o )" [par. 2].

Indeed, we can see "Tehran Post's" support of Iran in his December 29, 2008, blog which strongly rebukes Israel (and the West) for its general treatment and dismissal of Palestinians to the point that, according to "Tehran Post," they (the Palestinians) are treated worse than animals (par. 5–9).[28]

However, when the Iranian Presidential elections begin to heat up in spring 2009, "Tehran Post" shifts his focus, as many Iranians did, towards domestic concerns. In keeping with his objective to remain impartial, "Tehran Post" appears determined to view both candidates (Mousavi and Ahmadinejad) in a neutral, objective manner. In his June 4, 2009, entry, for instance, "Tehran Post" claims that "Ahmadinejad attacked all his critiques in this debate, including some influential figures of the Islamic Republic" (par. 1). These claims generally run contrary to the West's perception of Ahmadinejad as being a puppet of the clerics or of religious extremists. Further, "Tehran Post" describes Ahmadinejad as being "far more eloquent," and generally more "confident" and "combative" than the more gentlemanly Mousavi (par. 2). "Tehran Post" concludes that "Ahmadinejad stole the show from Musavi [sic] with his combative style," with the only exception being "the last ten minutes of the show," in which, according to "Tehran Post," "Musavi [sic] was at his best: clear, calm, and articulate" (par. 7). Still, "Tehran Post" makes it clear that he is not an Ahmadinejad supporter, as he offers ways that Ahmadinejad could be more easily critiqued, namely "his mishandling of governmental affairs, rumors about financial corruption of his team and himself during his gubernatorial term in Ardebil and mayoralty in Tehran, and the whole string of his blatant lies that have become truly endless" (par. 8).

As further evidence of "Tehran Post's" attempt to stay neutral and objective, he, unlike the other bloggers explored in this chapter, does not include any writing during the June–July 2009 demonstrations other than the following June 20, 2009, entry: "no posts 'til everything calms down. sorry folks!" (par. 1). While "Tehran Post" makes it clear, when he returns blogging in mid–July (July 11, 2009), that he became disgusted with pro–Ahmadinejad articles and websites,[29] he generally glosses over the entire June–July demonstrations. When "Tehran Post" finally discusses the demonstrations, as he does in a December 19, 2009, entry, he reveals how the battles between the pro–Ahmadinejad groups and the Green movement groups have moved underground, mainly exemplified by graffiti messages scrawled along the walls and bathrooms of Tehran (par. 1). This has occurred, "Tehran Post" suggests, because "since the July presidential poll there have been few opportunities for protestors to gather without the fear of being tear gassed, beaten and arrested (and raped and murdered) by the crackdown apparatus" (par. 1). Indeed, in "Tehran Post's" more recent entries from December 2009 and January 2010, he condemns the deaths on the day of Ashura[30] to the point that he writes in his December 29 entry: "Islamic Republic, tell us that there are principles you believe in" (par. 1).[31] While "Tehran Post" may be uncertain of the guiding principles of the Islamic Republic, he remains equally skeptical of the motivations of the West (especially the United States) in the Middle East.

Along similar lines, the next blogger (http://yaserb.blogspot.com) to be explored also attempts to provide a neutral and objective account of life in Iran. Whereas "Tehran Post" had more political objectives, the blogger in "Under Underground" says one of his "goals for writing here is improving my English" ("User Profile," par. 1). He also describes himself as a graduate from Azad University, which he describes as the "worst university in the world" ("User Profile," par. 1). From "Under Underground's" June 2005 entries during the first election of Mahmoud Ahmadinejad, we can see, as Azadeh Moaveni illustrated in *Honeymoon in Tehran*, how Ahmadinejad's ascension took many Iranians by surprise. In his June 18, 2005, entry, "Under Underground" describes Ahmadinejad as an "extremist conservative" and says his potential election would be "a nightmare" and would produce an Iran like a "prison" (par. 1–4). However, "Under Underground's" attitude towards Ahmadinejad changes somewhat in the coming months. For instance, in his January 4, 2006, entry, while "Under Underground" criticizes Ahmadinejad for beginning "a new holy war" by denying the Holocaust, he not only also defends Ahmadinejad's freedom of speech, but also admits that "I really don't have any idea about holocaust (I don't deny or confirm it)," and concludes this entry by asking why is it a crime to deny or question the Holocaust (par. 1–5). It seems, then, that to some degree, he remains sympathetic to Ahmadinejad. "Under Underground" also provides a first-hand account of how the Islamic Regime depicts the United States as a largely incompetent, immoral country. For instance, in his September 9, 2005, entry, "Under Underground" describes how the Iranian media rushed to cover the mishaps surrounding Hurricane Katrina, and how Iranian rescue efforts have generally been better than American rescue efforts (par. 1–4).[32] Along similar lines, in his entry from February 5, 2007, "Under Underground" sharply criticizes the Persian service of Voice of America which he describes as "full of lies," and more of a "comedy instead of a real political program," composed mainly of previous Shah-supporting expatriates (par. 2).

Despite the increasingly hard-line rhetoric of "Under Underground" and how he seems to have gravitated more towards Ahmadinejad, by the time of the June 2009 demonstrations, he is firmly in Mousavi's camp. In his June 24, 2009, entry, "Under Underground" describes how he voted for and supported Mousavi, despite how so many Iranians (especially the poor) view Ahmadinejad as their "hero" for his supposed stance against "corruption" (par. 2). "Under Underground," who admits in this entry that his blog has been "filtered," does not directly state that Ahmadinejad's election was suspect, but rather, that his victory "was predictable," with only the margin of Ahmadinejad's victory in question (par. 3). Rather than condemning Mousavi's supporters and demonstrators, "Under Underground" describes them as "educated" and desirous of "a modern life," but largely terrorized by the Basji youth who, "Under Underground" suggests, "are trying to spread hate among people in Iran" (par. 4). "Under Underground" turns even more strongly against the Ahmadinejad administration by his September 10, 2009, entry, which has the subtitle "Green Miracle Is Alive." The fact that "Under Underground" describes the Green movement as a "miracle" indicates the extent to which he favorably views the movement. While "Under Underground" more objectively states that "many people are in prison including ordinary people and leaders of oppositions and many journalists," and that "opposition newspapers" have been "shut down" or censored, he does not directly condemn the Islamic Regime (par. 1).

"Under Underground's" skepticism, perhaps because of the way his blog is filtered, comes through in a largely indirect manner. For instance, in his September 10 entry, he writes, "every night they shows special reports that try to convince people that there were not any fraud in election, there were not any systematic torture or rape!!!! in prison, they were not shooting to people in demonstrations !!!!" (par. 3). In this case, "Under Underground's" use of exclamation points indicates his incredulous attitude towards the assertions made by the Islamic Regime (that they did not torture, rape, or kill demonstrators). Still, "Under Underground" reverts to criticizing the West for its sanctions against Iran, which he claims, in his September 30, 2009, entry, will not help establish a more "open society for Iranians," and which would not, in turn, lead to "democracy for Iran" (par. 3). For "Under Underground," the sanctions hurt the Iranian people the most. In his April 9, 2010, entry, he claims that if they were lifted, it would "allow Iran to buy new civil planes to reduce air crash in Iran" and, through new technologies like smart phones and laptops, younger Iranians will be less apt to "absorb ... fundamental thoughts" (par. 4–5).

Unlike the last two blogs explored, the author of the blog "Rotten Gods" reveals what appears to be his real name: Fariborz Shamshiri (although this may be a pseudonym). Given how "Rotten Gods" repeatedly indicts the Islamic Republic in his blog, the writer's act of revealing his identity is courageous and fraught with danger. In fact, in a March 20, 2010, entry, Shamshiri alludes to the death threats he has received since starting his blog and attributes his previous several month absence from blog-writing to another death threat.[33] Still, this may be Shamshiri's way to rebel against the Islamic Regime, to assert his independence and to demonstrate his unwillingness to be cowed into submission. Indeed, Shamshiri's entires are unabashedly critical of the Islamic Regime and he appears unwilling to water down his perspective or the news he provides for readers to protect himself. For instance, in his June 29, 2010, entry, Shamshiri writes: "In Iran we do not have Human Rights, we only have Islamic limitations so if anyone dares to speak up, criticize Islam and Islamic laws, as Secretary General of Iran's High Council for Human Rights put it, he will be destroyed" (par. 3). Shamshiri continues with: "Second, if we had a little freedom and there were no death threats for leaving Islam, I can say at least 30 to 40 percent of Iranians would leave Islam in no time. Even now that it is very risky to criticize Islam, anytime people feel comfortable enough, they will ridicule Islam, Islamic laws and specially mullahs. Without a slightest doubt, mullahs definitely are the most hated group in Iran" (par. 5). There is little doubt that such rhetoric could get Shamshiri into a considerable amount of trouble with the Islamic Regime, who could (and presumably might like to) charge him with blasphemy or a similar charge, like encouraging political rebellion. Still, for whatever reason, Shamshiri has been able to post over 750 entries in approximately three years (from mid–2007 to mid–2010).

Shamshiri's entries tend to combine editorial responses to news stories from Western and Iranian media with more objective news reporting from Iran. For example, Shamshiri includes a general news story from June 23, 2010, of how blogger Hossein Derakhshan had his first court appearance (par 4–7). Shamshiri also includes an accompanying video from June 6, 2010, which he recommends "for anyone who might be interested to figure out current political atmosphere in Iran" (par. 1). Like "Stop Torturing Us," "Rotten Gods" also utilizes a wide mix of multimedia forms in the entries (mainly YouTube videos, but also a number of pictures). In that sense both blogs function as testimonials to various perceived human rights violations in Iran. Along these lines, Shamshiri writes about police brutality and injustice through entries like one from June 3, 2010: "Iranian police throw suspects into the trunk of police car." This blog is accompanied by a video detailing exactly this activity accompanied with an explanation from Shamshiri, "During arrest Iranian police usually throw suspect into the trunk of car to humiliate and so crush their confidence. Then suspects would be held in temporary custody and during that moment usually will be tortured to confess. This is the process that suspects usually go through since they get arrested" (par. 2). Another entry (May 7, 2010) details prostitution in Iran and brings attention to a documentary made on this subject by "two underground filmmakers" (par. 1). Shamshiri also, in other entries like one from April 20, 2010, and one from April 13, 2010, details the various restrictions the Islamic Regime places upon the Internet, such as blocking "access to google image search section" (par. 1) and how the Regime seemingly retaliates against e-mail and online chatting through the following banners: "Warning! chat is enemy trap and email is a bullet fired by enemy in dark!" (par. 1). In this manner, the Islamic Regime attempts to demonize the Internet and electronic media, which they clearly view as significant threats to their political administration and culture.[34]

In their article "Blogs as Stealth Dissent," Wei Zha and David Perlmutter argue that whereas blogs in the West tend to be more personal, champion the citizen, and purposely "bypass the normal channels of the elite media," in other, more restrictive countries, blogs have the potential to effect political change, most notably by helping to usher in a more democratic system of government (277). While there is no shortage of Iranian blogs written by Western Iranian expatriates that promote regime change and democratization in Iran,[35] the blogs written by Iranians themselves have the most potential to effect change. Blogs, though, rarely can have the long-lasting staying power that works of literature can have, in large part because most blogs are nonfiction, are not always well-crafted, and are ultimately closer to journalism and diaries than artworks. Still, it is hard to dispute the pragmatic importance of Iranian blogs and other media platforms as methods to communicate and to establish virtual communities (particularly important in a country that tends to thwart free expression). However, especially in a country which has such a rich history and appreciation of literature, it is hard to imagine that blogs could ever supplant literature. What they can achieve through language and narrative is immediate and significant, but art and literature have repeatedly proven to have more lasting significance and meaning.

# Conclusion

On October 23, 2010, the lead story in *The New York Times* was, "Iran Said to Give Top Aid to Karzai Cash by the Bagful." This article claims that, as a way to counter Western power and presence in the Middle East and Central Asia, Iran has been trying to buy its way towards influencing the Afghani government. However, buried deeper within the article is the admission that "the Western and Afghan officials interviewed for this article spoke on the condition of anonymity" (Filkings par. 7). While it is understandable that these officials may have wanted to keep their identity private for fear of retaliation, anonymity does also increase the possibility that the information supplied may not be accurate or comprehensive. The article also claims that, to upset Western influence in Afghanistan, Iran has been providing the Taliban with financial and military assistance. As expected, the Islamic Regime, represented by Feda Hussein Maliki, the Iranian ambassador to Afghanistan, has denied these claims. Maliki's office "called the allegations 'devilish gossip by the West and foreign media'" (qtd. in Filkings par 8). With heated rhetoric like this from both the West and the Islamic Republic, it is clear that the demonization of both sides persists, and that, if anything, it has only increased since the 2009 Iranian demonstrations.

Further, the above is only one example of how much negative coverage Iran receives in respected Western newspapers. As another example, on the previous day, October 22, 2010, *The New York Times* published an article in their Middle East section, entitled, "Leaked Reports Detail Iran's Aid for Iraqi Militias." This article suggested that Iran's Revolutionary Guards have helped train Shi'ite militias in Iraq, which have, in turn, antagonized and attacked Western and allied Iraqi groups (Gordon and Lehran, par. 12). However, similar to the article from October 23, this article also suggests, "The reports are written entirely from the perspective of the American-led coalition. No similar Iraqi or Iranian reports have been made available. Nor do the American reports include the more comprehensive assessments that are typically prepared by American intelligence agencies after incidents in the field" (par. 13). If, indeed, these reports lack "comprehensive assessments" more typical of "American intelligence agencies," it is surprising that *The New York Times* published this story at all, considering the potentially questionable source(s). It is not unreasonable to consider that this story may have been published because Western editors and readers tend to be more apt to believe the worst about Iran.

Similarly, also on October 22, 2010, the *New York Times* reported (from Wikileaks.com) that the three young hikers recently jailed in Iran (who were subsequently released in 2011) were arrested while they were still safely within Iraq's borders as opposed to in or near Iran's borders. This story's claims are important in the sense that, if they are accurate, then Iran arrested the hikers on completely trumped up charges. Still, the source is admittedly dubious as the article suggests, "Although the documents appear to be authentic, their origin could not be independently confirmed, and WikiLeaks declined to offer any details about them" ("US: Iran Took Hikers," par. 5). Ironically, in a *New York Times* article published just one day later, entitled, "WikiLeaks Founder on the Run, Trailed by Notoriety," authors John F. Burns and Ravi Somaiya suggest that "WikiLeaks has been met with new doubts" (par. 32). These doubts include questioning the validity of the claims posted on the site as well as concerns for not protecting the safety of those endangered by the information released on the site.

While the above relate mainly to international issues, in this same period of time (October 2010), the *New York Times* also published an article criticizing the educational system in Iran as well as the ability of its citizens to practice freedom of expression. This article, from October 16, 2010, is entitled, "In Iran, Future of University Is in Flux." The author, William Yong, writes, "The supreme leader, Ayatollah Ali Khamenei, issued a ruling this week that Mr. Rafsanjani could not place the vast financial assets of the Islamic Azad University — which some estimates put at $250 billion — into a public religious trust. Doing so would have effectively prevented Mr. Ahmadinejad from seizing control of the institution" (par. 2). While this ruling does not mean that Ahmadinejad will effectively take control of the university, it does offer more opportunities for the government and religious institutions to shape the university in a manner befitting to them. Therefore, Yong suggests, the ruling demonstrates that the Islamic Regime has assaulted higher education and muted, if not strangled, independent thought and academic freedom, the hallmarks of universities and colleges.

This is not to suggest that the heated and often times demonizing rhetoric only comes from the West, directed at the Islamic Regime, as it works both ways, with the Islamic Regime continuing to critique and demonize the West. For instance, in an article published by Reuters, Robin Pomeroy details Ahmadinejad's meeting with Venezuela's president, Hugo Chavez. During this meeting, Ahmadinejad reportedly told Chavez that "they would defeat their common foes, the latest defiant salvo against Western countries that he says are failing in their attempts to isolate Iran" (par. 1). Pomeroy also interprets Ahmadinejad as threatening Israel with the following statement: "The enemies of our nations will go one day. This is the promise of God and the promise of God will definitely be fulfilled" (qtd. in par. 10). While it is true Ahmadinejad has stated that "the Jewish state will one day cease to exist," the quotation above could refer to Western countries like the United States (not just Israel) (par. 10). Also, the quotation does not necessarily mean that Ahmadinejad wants the Western countries to be obliterated or that he is promoting a military confrontation with the West. He may, instead, be suggesting that these Western countries will radically change their ways or, in the case of Israel, develop more of a division between church and state. Similarly, in a news release published October 18, 2010, the Associated Press suggests that Ahmadinejad "claims the United States will one day apologize and 'beg' Tehran that the two countries resume diplomatic relations," and that "the U.S. administration has allegedly become so weakened that it can't harm Iran in any way" (Associated Press, par. 1). This bellicose rhetoric (if it is indeed translated correctly) only serves to worsen Western-Iranian relations, as does the news release itself, by suggesting that Ahmadinejad is both hypocritical and untrustworthy as noted by how "Ahmadinejad has made a slew of different statements, at times urging U.S.-Iranian friendship while at other times predicting America's demise" (par. 2).

If this weren't enough, the Islamic Regime has accused the United States of engaging in terrorist attacks, as noted by Press TV's news release entitled, quite to the point, "US Behind Terror Acts in Iran." According to the release, "A senior Iranian commander [Mohammad-Reza Naqdi] says certain terrorist acts and the killing of defenseless people in Iran are the handiwork of Washington's lackeys" (par. 1). Further, the article suggests that "it is easy for the United States, which has equipment, power and wealth to find a handful of mercenaries from among tens of millions of Iranians to carry out its operations, the commander added" (par. 4). While this may be an accurate (or partially accurate) statement, and it is true that the United States has aided mercenaries like the Mujahadeen during the Soviet occupation of Afghanistan in the 1980s, the news release offers no support for the senior commander's claims (nor do we have any indication of how the commander supported his claims, if at all).

With both the West and the Islamic Regime ramping up their heated, oppositional rhetoric, it is hard to see how the United States will be able to engage in meaningful dialogue with Iran. However, it is my hope that this study has demonstrated that deeper understanding and communication is not as likely to come from political means as it can through literature and technology. Similar to the leaders and participants of the Arab Spring, Iranian and Iranian diasporic authors, especially Generation Xers (in the West) and Burnt Generationers (in Iran), have taken great strides towards bridging the chasm between the West and Iran. While both Western and Iranian governments continue to engage in a war of increasing heated and polarized rhetoric, Iranian and diasporic Iranian writers uncover the complexities and universal nature of both Westerners and Iranians. Their work moves readers far beyond the simplistic and problematic moral categorization towards uncovering political, cultural, and religious complexities. In this nuanced framework, Western democracies are not categorically superior to an Islamic Regime, nor is the West or the United States simply an opportunistic, greedy, colonizing force in the Middle East and around the world.

The literature of Iranian and diasporic Iranians asks readers to consider challenging but essential questions about other countries and cultures as well as their own. How welcoming is the United States to Middle Eastern Muslims in comparison to Iran and how open is Iran to the free expression of ideas through writing? Sadly, Western colleges and universities rarely devote academic resources (research and teaching) to the study of Iran, Iranians, diasporic Iranians, and their collective literature. It is my hope that this book will bring new attention to these various issues and illustrates that, through its various forms (fiction, poetry, memoirs, and blogs), Iranian and Iranian diasporic literature serve a crucial and necessary role of providing complexity and insight into a much maligned and marginalized people and country (not only Iran in the West, but also the West in Iran).

Over seventy years ago, in his poem "In Memory of W.B. Yeats," W.H. Auden wrote that "poetry makes nothing happen." While it may be true that poetry and literature rarely, if ever, produce direct change, they can both be agents of change, in that they help produce empathy and understanding, which are the very antithesis of demonization and polarization, those twin techniques that have led to the current situation whereby neither the West nor Iran can see much (or at all) beyond the categorization of the other as evil or demonic. It is my hope that this study has demonstrated that neither cultures nor countries should be considered in such stark judgmental terms, but rather, both Iran and the West should be seen as extremely complex and multi-dimensional. Literature is in a prime place to uncover those complexities, to produce understanding and to help bridge chasms. Marjane Satrapi, Dalia Sofer, Porochista Khakpour, Azar Nafisi, Azadeh Moaveni, Shariar Mandanipour, Sheema Kalbasi, Roger Sedarat, Haleh Esfandiari, and a host of other fiction and memoir writers, poets, and bloggers have done exactly this by providing historical perspective, cultural context, and perhaps more than anything else, a space for personal and intellectual empathy as well as understanding. For one cannot truly understand what initially appears foreign until one can place one's self in the position of others. This is precisely the opportunity that literature can and does provide for its audience. More than any words spoken by a politician, Iranian or Western, the works of Iranian and diasporic Iranian writers provide the most hope for improved relations between the disparate cultures and nations because they invite emotional and intellectual engagement, while pushing us, as readers, to go beyond thinking of any one country or culture as the epitome of morality or as part and parcel of a nebulous and, ultimately, completely fictional axis of evil.

# Chapter Notes

## Introduction

1. Egypt is more populous than Iran, but it does not have a state-sponsored religion like Iran does, and hence is not, strictly speaking, an Islamic country. It is also debatable whether Egypt should be considered part of the Middle East (or North Africa).

2. Ebadi further explains that this "divine clerical right to rule," was "invented and established by Ayatollah Khomeini" (*Iran Awakening* 153). While there are elections in Iran in which both men and women are allowed to participate, "any parliamentary motion or presidential decree may be unilaterally vetoed by either the Council of Guardians or the supreme religious leader (both of them unelected)" (Zanganeh xii). For Zanganeh, this has had the result of "turning the system into a sham of democracy" (xii).

3. Furthermore, Aslan distinguishes Iran from these other countries as expressed in the following: "In a theocracy, particularly an Islamic theocracy like Saudi Arabia or Afghanistan under the Taliban, the Quran is the only constitution. Yet the Islamic Republic is constructed upon a remarkably modern and surprisingly enlightened constitutional framework in which are enshrined fundamental freedoms of speech, religion, education, and peaceful assembly" ("From Here" 29). Along similar lines, Robert Baer explains, "In Iran, unlike in Saudi Arabia, religious police aren't on every corner to enforce the 'moral order.' And unlike in The Sudan, there are no arrests in Iran for the grave offense of naming a teddy bear 'Mohammed'" (9).

4. As Azar Nafisi explains, "The original settlers of the Persian plateau were Aryan tribes—the root of the word "Iran." Iranians consider themselves kin to those orderly Germans and therefore white" ("The Stuff" 5).

5. As Alavi further argues, "In Iran poets have an iconic status that is uncommon in the West, because throughout history our poets have given us the symbolic language of resistance" (93).

6. In an extensive search, I could find only a handful of classes offered at United States universities and colleges that included or focused upon Iranian or diasporic Iranian literature and culture. Some examples of these classes include Persian Fiction in Translation (Spring 2009, University of Minnesota); Topics in Modern Persian Literature and Iranian Culture (Fall 2008, Arizona State University); Introduction to Iranian Studies (Fall 2007, Rutgers University); Introduction to Persian Literature (Fall 2006, University of Maryland), Contemporary Persian Literature in Translation (Fall 2006, National University); Selected Topics in Iranian Literature and Culture (Fall 2006, University of Texas); Persian Literature and Thought (Spring 2003, Columbia University); Studies in Modern Iran (no date specified, Princeton University). Even one of the most preeminent scholars in Iranian and Iranian diasporic literature, Persis Karim, who teaches at San Jose State University, does not list that she has taught a single Iranian or Iranian diasporic literature class on her C.V., but rather, she teaches courses such as "Literature of the Middle East and North Africa" and "Ethnicity in American Literature." Typically, if Iranian or Iranian diasporic literature is assigned, it is in classes on world or postcolonial literature or in Islamic or Middle Eastern Studies courses.

7. Specifically, Kaye and Wehrey suggest, "Certainly, the regional shakeup will give Iran and its allies much to prey on. The Arab world's secular, liberal youth movements, often hobbled by a lack of organization and leadership, will compete with long-established parties with starkly different views of the future, be they remnants of the old regimes or Islamist forces" (183). They also suggest that "the United States' inconsistent policies toward the Arab revolts (for example, the varying U.S. responses to Bahrain and Libya) offer more fodder for Iran's resistance narrative" (183). At the same time, they acknowledge that "the region's pro-democracy youth see through the hypocrisy of Tehran's attempts to spin the Arab uprisings as a variation of its own Islamic revolution—even more so after Iran's violent suppression of its own opposition Green Movement and its support for Bashar al-Assad's brutal crackdown in Syria" (184).

8. As Shirin Ebadi explains, "For better or

worse, the United States is the sole superpower in the world today, and Iran is the most strategic country in a restive region vital to U.S. interests" (*Iran Awakening* 213).

9. This first Iranian-American novel is Rachlin's *Foreigner* (1978). I have chosen not to focus on Rachlin in this study because she is not a part of the new, emerging younger generation of Iranian and diasporic Iranian writers, who were generally born in the 1960s and 1970s, and whose work generally engages with life in post–Revolutionary Iran and as contemporary Iranian expatriates in the West. This should not be taken as any indication that Rachlin's work is not as worthy of academic study as the authors explored in this study; rather, she is more of a foundational Iranian diasporic writer whose writings help lay the groundwork for the authors to be explored in this study.

10. As Gelareh Asayesh argues, "If Iran was a color-blind society, it was because almost everyone was the same color" (13).

11. This is to say that, in Iranian-American literature, there remains "the dominance of Iran — its history as well as its contemporary culture and policies — in the exploration and articulation of Iranian-American identity. This is a striking departure from many other US ethnic literatures, where issues of homeland and heritage have tended to give way to representations of the everyday lives of immigrants in America" (Darznik 56).

12. Again, Darznik's point about the dominance of Iran (see note 11 above) is well taken.

13. As evidence of the general American suspicion towards Muslims, consider not only the large number of Americans, estimated to be about 13 percent, who, during the 2008 presidential elections, believed Barack Obama to be Muslim. Many among that group stated that Obama's presumed status as a Muslim would be a reason that they would not vote for him (Ruether 12). A quintessential example of this anti–Muslim sentiment occurred in a 2008 town hall meeting with Republican presidential candidate John McCain in which an elderly woman explained that she did not trust Obama nor did she want to vote for him because she believed him to be Arabic.

14. As Darznik argues, "The events of 9/11 and subsequent US-led attacks on Afghanistan and Iraq have created an intense curiosity about Middle Eastern culture," which has produced "far-ranging consequences for Iranian immigrant writing" (69). Yet, at the same time, as Lila Zanganeh claims, it is surprising that "at a time when there is ample talk and trepidation about Iran's military arsenal, at a time when the fears aroused by the September 11 attacks have opened doors to blatant expressions of hostility and racism, Iranians have gained a paradoxical gleam of pop-

ularity in this country — and around the world" (xiv).

15. *Reading Lolita in Tehran* was met with a good deal of critical resistance, as I will explore later.

16. In her Nobel Prize Speech, Ebadi suggests, "My selection will be an inspiration to the masses of women who are striving to realize their rights, not only in Iran but throughout the region — rights taken away from them through the passage of history. This selection will make women in Iran, and much further afield, believe in themselves" ("Shirin Ebadi's Nobel Prize Speech," par. 6).

17. To some extent, there seems to have developed a widespread youth movement throughout the Islamic Middle East, which tends to embrace popular American culture as well as the more conservative aspects of fundamentalist Islam. While this might seem like a contradiction, it actually can be attributed to the ability of younger Islamic Middle Easterners to separate citizens and culture from the government. This is apparent in Jared Cohen's *Children of Jihad*, which details his travels throughout the Middle East as a young Jewish male. When Cohen reveals to Hezbollah members of his own age in Lebanon that he is Jewish, they do not seem bothered, and explain that they have no problems with Jewish or American people but with the U.S. and Israeli governments (5). Further, Cohen describes them as appearing quite Westernized, evident by how they whistle at girls and wear preppy American clothes (1). Ultimately, Cohen concludes that "youth, the majority demographic in the region, share more similarities with their American peers than most of the world realizes" (272). I would argue that one of the ways that has happened is through how American culture has largely come to dominate worldwide culture. If that is the case then Cohen may indeed be right in saying, "Young people in the Middle East are reachable — and they could be waiting to hear from us" (275).

18. One Iranian blogger claims, "My generation is the damaged generation. We were constantly chastised that we were duty-bound to safeguard and uphold the sacred blood that was shed for us during a revolution and war. Any kind of happiness was forbidden for us" (Alavi 8).

19. As Nasrin Alavi explains, "In July 1999, Iran saw the largest student riots since the beginning of the Revolution" (53). Alavi further explains that student protests continued after the 1999 demonstrations. For instance, "In 2002 student protests in Tehran soon spread to half a dozen major cities, including Isfahan, Tabriz, Hamadan and Oromiyeh. The students were protesting against a death sentence handed down to Hashem Aghajari, a history professor who

dared to question the Islamic credentials of the state clerics and their unaccountability to the people" (138).

20. As Cohen explains, "Unemployment is rampant, with many experts estimating that close to 40 percent of the population is unemployed" (54).

21. For instance, Jared Cohen suggests, "opium, heroin, and cocaine are tearing away at the social fabric of Iran by seeping into wealthy communities and trickling down into the most impoverished" (80).

22. This economic decline and disparity can be traced back to the Iranian Revolution and subsequent Iran-Iraq war in the 1980s. Specifically, Iran's middle class continued to experience the fallout from the unequal structure that came about after the war. As Ebadi explains, "Real per capita income declined after the revolution, and the majority of Iranians had to work two or more jobs just to make ends meet. Meanwhile, the clerics in power established themselves and their families in luxurious homes in the fresh-aired upper reaches of north Tehran" (*Iran Awakening* 145).

23. Iranian clerics argue almost the complete opposite: that the Iranian Revolution of 1979 provides the true inspiration for the Arab Spring (Alfoneh 35). While it is true that the Iranian Revolution did respond to perceived inequalities, unemployment, and corruption in Iran (which does have some parallels to the movement behind the Arab Spring), the Iranian Revolution was much more non-secular and less youth driven.

24. According to a member of the Burnt Generation, one of the reasons for their anger and despair is that this generation "has never known security, or, for that matter, real happiness" (Afshan, par. 3).

25. Similarly, Nafisi argues that "at present, the most powerful forces for change in Iran's social landscape are emanating from women as well as from the younger generation of Iranians, the very children who, the Islamists had hoped, would in time rekindle their parents' long-lost political fervor" ("The Stuff" 8). She also explains: "These youths are well aware of how much their political freedoms are contingent on the preservation of their individual rights and personal spaces" ("The Stuff" 9).

26. This awareness comes in contrast to what many were indoctrinated with as children growing up in Iran. As Afshan explains: "We started our political lives early. As tiny children in kindergarten, we learned to march and beat our fists, shouting: 'Down to America!' 'Down to Israel!' (or from time to time, depending on the politics of the day, Britain or Russia). No one else bothered telling us anything about why we were supposed to harbor such ill-will towards the 'satan-of-the-day'" (par. 7).

27. Along these lines, Afshan argues, "Today, however, despite our despair, we have found hope. Hope among ourselves. Hope in numbers. Hope in the fact that the world seems to finally be caring. Hope in the fact that we may at last have a chance against the mullahs' rule" (par. 16).

28. However, there has arisen a bifurcation between a political, public Iran and a personal, private Iran, and young people have become adept at living a dual existence. While publicly, some Iranians may condemn Americans, privately they tend to be drawn to American culture. This love-hate relationship may be explained by repression. Trained to be conservative and self-denying, some Iranians may generally despise American culture to prevent themselves from giving in to their desires while all the more being drawn to those same desires.

29. In many ways, the history of modern Iran begins with the administration of President Mohammed Mossadegh. Mossadegh was viewed "as the father figure of Iranian independence," even though he was president for only two years, from 1951 to 1953 (Ebadi *Iran Awakening* 4). He also promoted "the freedom of the press" and democratic ideals (Ebadi *Iran Awakening* 4). Despite the advances Mossadegh made, it has been suggested that the main Western powers felt that Mossadegh sought too much independence, if not power. This was manifest in his attempt to take control of the production of Iranian oil. According to Shirin Ebadi, it was Kermit Roosevelt, Jr., who helped engineer a revolt against Mossadegh and the subsequent coup that led to the reign of the Shah (*Iran Awakening* 5).

30. While the Shah's reign meant better relations with Western powers like the United States, it caused a great deal of resentment in the Iranian people as well as fear. In order to maintain his authority and quell any potential uprisings against him, the Shah established his secret police organization, SAVAK, in the 1960s (Ebadi *Iran Awakening* 16). SAVAK put surveillance on institutes of higher education as well as "the streets of most of Iran's cities" (Ebadi *Iran Awakening* 16). As time went on and SAVAK grew, so did the Iranian people's resentment and disenchantment.

31. This reached such a point that even Iran's well-educated and often secular elite came to oppose the Shah and support the growing swell of the Islamic revolution. From her own personal perspective as a well-educated lawyer, Ebadi explains, "Who did I have more in common with, in the end: an opposition led by mullahs who spoke in the tones familiar to ordinary Iranians or the guilded court of the shah, whose officials cavorted with American starlets at parties soaked in expensive French champagne?" (*Iran Awakening* 33).

32. Many Iranians, especially secular Iranians, came to regret their decision to support the Is-

lamic Revolution, or rather, to support the deposing of the Shah. This became apparent with one of the first post-revolutionary edicts, or rather post-revolutionary suggestions, from the newly established Ayatollah and his administration. This was an "invitation" for women to wear head scarves. As Ebadi explains, "The head-scarf 'invitation' was the first warning that this revolution might eat its sisters, which was what women called one another while agitating for the shah's overthrow" (*Iran Awakening* 39). Along similar lines, other suggestions or edicts were passed in the early 1980s, such as the outlawing of Western clothes like ties (*Iran Awakening* 41). As Ebadi explains, "In the new atmosphere, everyone aspired to appear poor, and the wearing of dirty clothes had become a mark of political integrity, a sign of one's sympathy with the dispossessed" (*Iran Awakening* 42).

33. Gradually it became clear to many Iranians that "the revolution of 1979 was hijacked by the country's own clerical establishment, who used their moral authority to gain absolute power. This counterrevolution, however, despite the brutally intransigent response it has thus far received from Iran's clerical oligarchy, must not be quelled. This is because the fight for Islamic democracy in Iran is merely one front in a worldwide battle taking place in the Muslim world — a jihad, if you will — to strip the Traditionalist Ulama of their monopoly over the meaning and message of Islam and pave the way for the realization of the long-awaited and hard-fought Islamic Reformation" (Aslan 254).

34. One cannot overestimate the extent of the devastation brought on by the Iran-Iraq war. It has been estimated that "more than one million Iranians and Iraqis were killed or wounded. More than one hundred thousand soldiers were taken as prisoners of war, and the fighting produced about 2.5 million refugees" (Ebadi 92).

35. Indeed, Ebadi claims the war has significantly contributed to "Iranian attitudes about our future and our place in the world. First, the skepticism and mistrust it reinforced in us about America's motives in the region" (92).

36. As Ebadi explains, "Some of the hostage takers reformed their ways and tried to bring more freedoms to Iran in the late 1990s" (48)

37. According to Ebadi, whereas SAVAK tended to utilize "cruder physical torture," the current Islamic Regime tends to use more varied techniques to extract information from its inmates. Some of those techniques are eerily similar to the techniques used by the U.S. military at Guantánamo Bay and Abu Ghraib. These techniques include "sleep deprivation, mock executions, foot lashings, mind games played with fake newspapers that told of mass arrests or coups d'état, solitary confinement in cells the size of fox-holes" (134).

38. Furthermore, as she explains, the "West can keep Iran's human rights record in the spotlight, for the Islamic system has shown itself to be sensitive to such criticism. The Islamic Republic may hold firm to its right to nuclear power, even if it means suffering sanctions at the hands of the international community. But its more rational policy makers see a tainted human rights record as a self-inflicted wound that weakens Iran's bargaining power" (*Iran Awakening* 215).

39. As Nafisi argues, "The extent of the country's ruling elite's animosity towards American culture can be seen in how they have flogged and jailed Iranians for wearing nail polish, Reebok shoes, or lipstick" ("The Stuff" 6).

40. Shohreh Aghdashloo was nominated for her role in the 2003 film *House of Sand and Fog*.

41. While Abbas Kiarostami received global attention before September 11, 2001, especially in how his film *A Taste of Cherry* won the prestigious Palme d'Or Prize at the 1997 Cannes Film Festival, his reputation and visibility have increased in recent years.

42. Furthermore, she explains, "In Iranian culture, it was considered natural for fathers to love their sons more; the sons were the repository for the family's future ambitions; affection for a son was an investment" (Ebadi *Iran Awakening* 11).

43. According to Ebadi, the Islamic Republic also tends to favor men over women in a legal sense, providing many more rights to men in cases of divorce, and generally acting indifferent when men commit adultery, but not when women do so (*Iran Awakening* 123).

44. For instance, as Alavi points out, "in the courts ... a woman is legally worth half a man" (179).

45. As Shirin Ebadi explains, "This was no small achievement for a Middle Eastern country with a culture still patriarchal to its core. In neighboring Afghanistan, the Taliban forbade women to read; across the water in Saudi Arabia, women were banned from driving. Even countries that were making some progress, such as Egypt and Turkey, were unable to extend educational opportunities beyond a sliver of the secular privileged, to society at large" (*Iran Awakening* 107).

46. This is not to suggest that there wasn't any progress towards gender equality during the time of the Shah. As Asar Nafisi explains, "By 1979, at the time of the revolution, women were active in all areas of life in Iran. The number of girls attending schools was on the rise. The number of female candidates for universities had increased sevenfold during the first half of the 1970s. Women were encouraged to participate in areas previously closed to them through a quota system that offered preferential treatment to eli-

gible girls. Women were scholars, police officers, judges, pilots, and engineers — present in every field except the clergy" ("The Stuff" 4).

47. This would be similar to the core value of American second wave feminism which tended to reject the sexual objectification of women, whereas many third wave feminist critics have reconsidered the very nature of sexual objectification when it comes to, for instance, previously vilified forms such as pornography.

48. She writes, "To be a young woman in the Iran of the Islamic Republic involved a certain degree of uncertainty over one's identity, or at the very least, over one's romantic priorities. Most of my girlfriends had no idea whether they had a 'type.' In contrast to California, no one fretted much about being unready for commitment, or the passage from dating to dating exclusively" (*Lipstick Jihad* 179).

49. As Persis Karim explains, "Until the second half of the twentieth century, Iranian women were actively discouraged from and/or criticized for writing" (xxi).

50. As Jared Cohen argues, "Because of increased access to diverse perspectives and an enhanced ability to interact through digital, audio, and visual media, the current generation of young people enjoy an independence that their parents and grandparents could not have imagined. Such autonomy has never before existed in these police-state societies or tension-ridden environments, but it has become impossible for the watchful eye of government or the vigilance of their own parents to be everywhere without the complete banning of technology that has already become intertwined with Middle Eastern society" (273).

51. Robert Baer also suggests that "today Persian is the most common language on the Internet after English and Mandarin Chinese" (8). The extent to which Iran seems to be engaged in a kind of internal war of informational spin on the Internet can be seen in how President Mahmoud Ahmadinejad himself has a blog.

52. Jared Cohen estimates that "there are more than seventy-five thousand bloggers in Iran, with the majority under the age of thirty" (57). Nasrin Alavi estimates that there were 64,000 Iranian blogs in 2004 (1).

## Chapter 1

1. *Persepolis* "sold 20,000 copies in a single year and won the 2001 Alph'Art Coup de Coeur Prize in Angouleme as well as the Prix du Lion in Belgium." Both works have not only "been translated into many languages," they have also sold "over a million copies worldwide" (Costantino 431). Subsequently, Satrapi co-directed a film version of *Persepolis* (2007) with Vincent

Parronaud. The animated film included narration by celebrities such as Catherine Deneuve and Sean Penn. The film "won a Camera d'Or jury prize for best film by a new director at the 2007 Cannes Film Festival" (Costantino 432–33).

2. Given the increasing cultural emphasis placed upon visual as opposed to textual forms, it should come as no surprise that graphic novels have increased in popularity in recent years. According to a 2007 *Publishers Weekly* article, Scholastic Book Fairs have sold four million graphic novels since 2004 ("Graphic Novel by the Numbers," 9). Sales of graphic novels have also increased from about $75 million in 2001 to $220 million in 2006 (9). However, there is no indication that Satrapi began writing graphic works because she thought they would be lucrative. Rather, influenced by Art Spiegelman's graphic work about the Holocaust, *Maus*, Satrapi, who had interests in both visual art and writing, decided to write graphic works because it allowed her to combine her main interests.

3. As a case in point, one should consider the success of *Reading Lolita in Tehran* (2003), which stayed on the *New York Times* best-seller list for multiple weeks and has sold hundreds of thousands of copies.

4. There is certainly truth to these claims. For example, not only did the Shah host elaborate celebrations and parties, he also helped erect statues of himself (and he put up portraits of himself and his wife as well) throughout Iran during his reign. Also, in the 1970s, it was reported that "shrubbery in public parks is clipped in the shape of the Persian script spelling out his name; over 75 different sets of Iranian postage stamps show the royal portrait; and millions of colored lights are strung throughout the country every year as a reminder of the Shah's birthday" (Bill 326; Rahmim 40).

5. Satrapi herself identifies *Maus* as a primary influence upon her decision to write graphic novels. As Hattenstone explains, "Her identity as an artist was shaped in 1995 when she was given Art Spiegelman's classic Holocaust comic book, *Maus*, as a birthday present. She had no idea art could tell stories in such a way. Satrapi decided the comic book would be her chosen form. She was rejected time and again" (par. 22).

6. Satrapi herself seems to encourage a kind of poststructural reading of *Persepolis* and *Persepolis 2* through her desire to deconstruct conventional views of Iran. In Satrapi's words, "From the time I came to France in 1994, I was always telling stories about life in Iran to my friends. We'd see pieces about Iran on television, but they didn't represent my experience at all. I had to keep saying, "No, it's not like that there." I've been justifying why it isn't negative to be Iranian for almost twenty years. How strange when it

isn't something I did or chose to be?" ("Why I Wrote *Persepolis*" 9).

7. As Peter Schjeldahl explains, "Graphic novels — pumped-up comics — are to many in their teens and twenties what poetry once was, before bare words lost their cachet.... Like life-changing poetry of yore, graphic novels are a young person's art, demanding and rewarding mental flexibility and nervous stamina" (163).

8. Another probable reason for the success of *Persepolis* and *Persepolis 2* is that the works seem to transcend politics, ethnicity, and nationality. This was apparently one of Satrapi's goals, for, as Simon Hattenstone explains, "What has delighted her [Satrapi] is the story's universal appeal — it's not just about Iran; it's about growing up in any place with problems" (Hattenstone par. 25). Further, as Manuela Costantino explains, "Readers of all ages can identify with the child, feel for her, and learn with her about the complexities of national and international politics" (433).

9. Satrapi further explains that "Iranian women are not downtrodden weeds: my mother's maid has kicked our her husband, and I myself have slapped several men who behaved inappropriately in the street. And even during the worst period of the Iranian Revolution, women were carrying weapons" (qtd. in Kutschera 49).

10. Satrapi's timing turned out to be fortuitous in another sense. As Costantino explains, *Persepolis* and *Persepolis 2* really "started to gather popular momentum in 2003–4, a time when France was struggling with the debate over veiled Muslim girls in secular public schools and when the US expanded its 'War on Terror' against the Taliban in Afghanistan to Iraq" (434).

11. At the same time, later in *Persepolis*, immediately after the Islamic Revolution, Satrapi not so subtly critiques the new requirement to use the veil. On television, one member of the religious administration claims that it is required in order "to protect women from all the potential rapists" and that "women's hair emanates rays that excite men. That's why they should cover their hair" (74). When Satrapi goes back to Iran in *Persepolis 2*, she must, of course, wear the veil again. Her resistance towards the veil can be seen in the picture in which she looks extremely saddened and downcast while looking at herself in the mirror. The caption reads, "And so much for my individual and social liberties" (91). However, these so-called liberties hardly did Satrapi much good while she was in Austria.

12. For instance, Satrapi reads books about Fidel Castro and "about the young Vietnamese killed by the Americans" (12).

13. There is some historical debate as to who was ultimately responsible for the fire and subsequent deaths at the movie theater. Massoud Mehrabi suggests, "In the months before the 1979 revolution, about one-fourth of the movie theaters in Iran were set on fire by angry demonstrators who demanded the Shah's downfall. They saw the movie houses — where vulgar and misleading films, which were against Shariah, the body of Islamic laws, were shown — as a manifestation of the corruption of Iran's monarchy. These attacks on cinemas took such a chaotic shape that, according to the leaders of the revolution, the Shah's agents set fire to the Cinema Rex in Abadan in southern Iran in order to distort the image of Muslim revolutionaries. This fire claimed some 400 lives" (43).

14. Also, according to Satrapi, the school pushes reverence for the Iranian dead in the Iran-Iraq war by having them beat their breasts and having them line "up twice a day to mourn the war dead" (95).

15. Another sign of this mullah's sensitivity and wisdom is that he also asks Satrapi to design a new uniform that will please both the religious authorities and the student body (144).

16. This is not to suggest that Satrapi believes her family to be perfect by any stretch of the imagination. It is not Satrapi's intention to hold her family up as a beacon of excellence in an otherwise tainted or corrupt country. It has been said that one of the biggest issues facing Iran before the Islamic Revolution and even in contemporary times is the discrepancy between social classes. Satrapi portrays her family as wealthy, which becomes a source of some shame to Satrapi when she is a child. She grows up with servants who are largely illiterate and impoverished (25). Her parents, of more of an elite class, are satisfied with social hierarchy in Iran.

17. Satrapi counteracts this by including two pictures of so-called Communists and writing brief biographical sketches of both. In appearance, both Communists resemble harmless and meek academics with glasses and simple black clothing. The crime of one is that he supposedly "wrote subversive articles in the Kingdom" (47).

18. One of the guards suggests, "Our torturers received special training from the C.I.A." (50), thereby implicating the United States.

19. Naghibi and O'Malley suggest that *Persepolis* and *Persepolis 2* play "the increasingly mobilized stereotypes of the Islamic Republic as oppressive and backward against the Western conviction over its progressive liberalism in ways that contest both of those scripts" (224).

20. See Cohen's *Children of Jihad*, as well as Moaveni's *Lipstick Jihad* and *Honeymoon in Tehran*.

21. One should not condemn Satrapi too much for this, as she is a young adolescent.

22. Still, Satrapi, who is not immune to the lure of violent war stories, does something similar when she meets her future husband, Reza, at a party in Iran. There, she seems impressed by his

stories as a tank gunner in the Iran-Iraq war, concluding to herself, "What a man!" (124).

23. In an interview, Satrapi explains some of what motivated her: "At the time, Iran was the epitome of evil and to be Iranian was a heavy burden to bear" (41).

24. She also feels guilty for not staying in Iran during the difficult times, and wants her fellow Iranians who lived through the war to know that "I too had suffered" (113).

25. Keeping the people perpetually afraid disallows them from thinking of the more important issues. As Satrapi explains, "When we're afraid, we lose all sense of analysis and reflection. Our fear paralyzes us. Besides, fear has always been the driving force behind a dictators' repression" (148).

26. Satrapi suggests that "the Western Media also fights against us. That's where our reputation as fundamentalists and terrorists come from!" (168). In addition, Satrapi's mother displays her political ambivalence with the following: "Personally, I hate Saddam and I have no sympathy for the Kuwaitis, but I hate just as much the cynicism of the allies who call themselves 'liberators' while they're there for the oil" (168). Satrapi's father also appears quite cynical about Western/American motivates as noted by his comment: "The worst is that the intervention in Kuwait is done in the name of human rights!!! Which rights? Which humans?" (168)

27. In fact, her mother tells Satrapi, "This time, you're leaving for good. You are a free woman. The Iran of today is not for you. I forbid you to come back!" (187).

## *Chapter 2*

1. Ahmadinejad has also said: "It is quite clear that a bunch of Zionist racists are the problem the modern world is facing today" (qtd. in Peterson 3). Recently, Ahmadinejad organized a "conference" that was intended to investigate whether or not the Holocaust occurred. This "conference" met almost universal disdain from world nations as many believe it to be a manifestation of Ahmadinejad's anti-Semitism (Peterson 3).

2. In addition, "Iranian Jews are the oldest inhabitants of Iran and even under the present constitution have a right to choose a Jewish representative in Parliament" (Alavi 272).

3. Along these lines, Theodoulou also explains that there have been complaints "about discrimination, much of it of a social or bureaucratic nature" against Iranian Jews (6). Also, as Scott Peterson explains, "In 1999, charges of spying for Israel were brought against 13 Jews in Shiraz and Isfahan, sparking a new exodus and widespread fear" (2).

4. As Sofer explains, "It's loosely based on my family's experiences. When I was 8, my father was arrested for being a Zionist spy. We didn't know where he was. My mom would go out looking for him. And then he just reappeared one day, about a month later" (qtd. in Solomon, par 2–3).

5. Sofer recalls that in Iranian grade school, "Every morning before classes the entire school would line up in the schoolyard and sing revolutionary songs. Afterward we would chant: 'Marg bar America! Marg bar Israel!— Death to America! Death to Israel!'" (qtd. in Solomon, par. 5).

6. According to Masilyah, "The Shahs always tried to protect the Jews from mob attacks" (398).

7. We can also see that in how Leila, the friend of the Amins' daughter, Shirin, tells Shirin that her father, a Revolutionary Guard, "says that the people who are being taken to prison are sinners" (92). Leila's father seems to be hypocritical, as both Shirin and Leila find alcohol in Leila's father's basement (94).

8. Of course, there is much more that the SAVAK did, including torturing and even killing those they felt to be hostile to the Regime.

9. Evin Prison and its reputation will be covered in more detail in Chapter 6.

10. This became especially evident in comments President Ahmadinejad made during his September 2008 visit to the United States as well as during what many people believe was a staged media event in which President Ahmadinejad met with a group of Jews who claimed to be anti-Zionist and praised Ahmadinejad for his supposed ability to distinguish between Zionism and Judaism (Parsons). This is also evident in how Iranian Jews themselves seem to want to strive "to separate politics from religion" (Peterson 1)

11. Since Israel compels both men and women to serve in its armed forces, the fact that Isaac has relatives in the Israeli Army is not significant.

12. It is doubtful that the Amins, even if they wanted to do so, could easily convert to Islam, as the Revolutionary Guard would doubt their intentions.

13. In fact, what seems to have been a pivotal experience akin to a religious experience is when Isaac lost his virginity to an Anglo-American woman, Irene. Here we can see that being Iranian and Jewish has affected Isaac's self-esteem as an adolescent. As Isaac explains, "From that night on he had come to see himself differently, as someone to whom exciting things could happen.... It is to her that he even attributed the fact that, years later, he was able to win over Farnaz" (35).

14. Granted, Sofer doesn't portray secular Judaism in Iran to be especially empowering to

women either. For instance, Farnaz has mainly sacrificed her career for Isaac and she places blame on "their marriage contract" itself (135).

15. This is not to say that Isaac has fully abandoned his materialistic tendencies, for he experiences some regret after losing the money, which he describes as "his life's hard work" (257).

## Chapter 3

1. I know that this presumption was made because of my presentation, as I had never been presumed to be Iranian before I began researching and presenting about the subject matter.

2. Born in 1961 and most recently a professor of creative writing at the University of Southern California, Nahai is the author of four commercially successful and critically acclaimed novels: *Cry of the Peacock* (1991), *Moonlight on the Avenue of Faith* (1999), *Sunday's Silence* (2001), and *Caspian Rain* (2007). My decision not to focus on Nahai should not be seen as a denigration of her work. Her novels tend to focus on a pre-revolutionary Iran whereas this study tends to focus on a more contemporary, post-revolutionary Iran.

3. I would also put Dalia Sofer, Azadeh Moavani, and Roger Sederat, among others, in this group.

4. *Sons and Other Flammable Objects* "won the 2007 California Book Award 'First Fiction' medal" and it was "also a New York Times 'Editor's Choice' and Chicago Tribune 'Fall's Best' selection" ("New Faculty," par. 2). Reviews have generally been quite positive including praise for the novel for refusing "to oversimplify" issues of "racial and cultural identity" and for acknowledging "that navigating the demands of multiple cultures is anything but a tidy process" (Pusateri 70). *Publishers Weekly* suggests that Khakpour "imparts a perfect sense of the ironies of being Persian in America, where the blurry collective image of the Middle East alternates between blonde genies in bottles and furrow-browed terrorists in cockpits" ("*Sons and Other*" 33). In other words, Khakpour's novel debunks many common stereotypes of Middle Eastern Arabs, Persians, and Muslims.

5. Indeed, she recalls longing for the life she perceived other Iranian-Americans living in Westwood, Brentwood, and Beverly Hills, where she believes they "easily fit in" (Khakpour, "What I Saw," par. 19).

6. For instance, see the *Economist*'s article "Shorn of Dignity and Equality," *Off Our Backs*' article "Iran: Over 400 Women Protest Constitutional Sexism," Clark Forbes's article "Girls Score Over Sexism," or Geoff Pevere's article "Stark Study of Oppression Banned in Iran."

7. While over 60 percent of Iranian univer-

sity students are women, and it has been reported that they comprise a majority of students who "seek the basic sciences, especially physics," it has also been reported that "after the bachelor's level the rates of women studying decreases for physics" and other physical sciences (Izadi et al. 122). Still, there has been some progress for women in the field of medicine. While, in the early 1990s, only "12.5% of Iranian medical students were women," that number increased to approximately one-third in the early 2000s. However, the increase was mainly due to dictates that women be treated by female as opposed to male doctors (Azarmina 645).

8. Some examples are Mark Twain's *The Adventures of Huckleberry Finn*, Ernest Hemingway's *In Our Time*, F. Scott's Fitzgerald's *The Great Gatsby*, Jack Kerouac's *On the Road*, J.D. Salinger's *The Catcher in the Rye*, Ralph Ellison's *The Invisible Man*, Thomas Pynchon's *The Crying of Lot 49*, amongst others. At the same time, Armengol-Carrera argues, while "fatherhood" is a primary theme in American literature, "most canonical authors appear to avoid dealing with the issue of fatherhood, which thus remains largely absent from American literature" (211). He also argues that "paternal absence is a recurrent theme in twentieth-century American literature as well," but that this lack of father figure is not ethnically or non-ethnically specific (212).

9. While Hout mainly credits this to the importance and centrality of the family "in most Arab societies," Iran is not an Arabic society, but one in which family still plays a key and crucial role (287).

10. While it is not clear who names Xerxes, given Darius's dominance over his wife, Lala, it can be surmised that Darius played a significant role in the naming.

11. A useful parallel for Iranian Americans would be Turkish Americans, who are also predominantly Muslim, generally Middle Eastern, but, by and large, indistinguishable to most Americans. In a study of Turkish Americans, Ilhan Kaya discovered that "whereas the first generation is more isolated in America no matter the degree of their acculturation, second-generation Turkish Americans are much more integrated, as linguistic proficiency and cultural adaptation are less significant barriers to their participation in larger American society" (617). Like Iranian Americans, second generation Turkish Americans have also felt discriminated against because of their religion (Muslim); however, they have had a somewhat easier time adjusting to life in the United States (618). One reason second generation Turkish Americans may have had an easier time acculturating to the United States is that they do not have the stigmas associated with being Iranian (e.g., the hostage crisis, the nuclear debate, and Ahmadenijad's assertive and at times offensive rhetoric).

12. In truth, Darius is in this group and his demeaning behavior towards ethnic others is more of an act of misdirected aggression due to his own conflicted feelings about being Iranian American.

13. This may be encouraged by the mainstream U.S. media as well as negative news coverage about Iran.

14. In their seminal 1972 essay entitled "Racist Love," Chin and Chan argued that Asian Americans, specifically Chinese Americans, have been subject to negative as well as supposedly positive stereotypes by white Americans. They describe the latter as "racist love" and suggest that Asian Americans have been stunted and kept subjugated by patronizing whites who praise their supposed docility.

15. Specifically, Khakpour mentions an Iranian flag, "Arabic script" on books, "Persian carpets and old Eastern china," as well as an old picture of the Adam family at Disneyland that clearly marks them as immigrants and foreigners (138).

16. Xerxes claims otherwise and says that Darius frequently details unhappy or unpleasant stories of his upbringing in Iran, but this may be unfounded hyperbole on Xerxes's part.

17. Instead, he plays coy with the woman by suggesting that he would imagine that someone might put bells on the cats to alert the birds to their presence (and save them). By indirectly letting her know that he did it, but not directly admitting it, Darius is also able to maintain a level of power over his white neighbor.

18. She also describes Islamic Republic–era Iran as having attacked "every area of women's private and social life" (545).

19. Conventional wisdom aside, women in Iran were not necessarily in a better position before the Iranian Revolution in 1979. As Robert Baer explains, "The average age of marriage for an Iranian woman today is twenty-five; during the Shah's last year in power, it was thirteen. And doctors reportedly perform more sex-change operations in Iran than in any other country except Thailand, with the Iranian government even paying up to half the cost for some transsexuals" (Baer 9). Also, unlike most predominantly Islamic countries, "more than half of those graduating from university in Iran today are women" (Alavi 10). Still, women in both pre- and postrevolutionary Iran have certainly not been afforded as many rights as men, and contemporary post-revolutionary Iranian women in Iran are compelled to wear the veil, as well as being subject to a number of other requirements and restrictions not placed upon men.

20. More typical of a woman in Iran, for Lala: "Darius had been her only lover, her one partner, and while there had been a few suitors, she really had no experience with romantic unions. She barely had a chance with herself" (58).

21. Even Lala's walking is act of independence and rebellion, especially since the novel is set in Southern California, a region stereotyped as one in which people do not walk.

22. I realize that certain theories of third-wave feminism might dispute this in the sense of so-called superficial frivolities being politicized or leading to greater agency; however, in Lala's case, embracing these frivolities achieves neither political or personal agency.

23. Again, this runs largely counter to third-wave feminist ideology.

24. Specifically, she mockingly suggests that Darius could be a terrorist, calls Lala a "bitch" and describes them condescendingly as "those people," meaning those of Middle Eastern decent (228).

25. Still, the isolation and alienation may not be confined to just the Adam family, for Khakpour alludes to how this state accounts for most recent immigrants in the Adams' apartment complex, ironically named Eden Gardens, which may be an allusion to Barbara Eden of *I Dream of Jeannie* or to the United States as a perceived Eden for immigrants. Even though there are many immigrants who live nearby, they do not bond (with the exception of Lala's relationship with Gigi, which ends up failing), but rather, they tend to keep to themselves. As Khakpour explains, "The foreigners lived their old lives, each family thinking they were the only odd one out" (87). Still, Khakpour does not portray other, more assimilated Iranian-Americans as much better. Xerxes's future girlfriend, Suzanne, who is part Iranian and who has a more assimilated Iranian father and a white mother, seems to equivocate Arabs with all Muslims from the Middle East and September 11 hijackers (247).

26. Some examples are Robert Allen's *Channels of Discourse, Reassembled: Television and Contemporary Criticism*, Glyn Davis's *Teen TV: Genre, Consumption, and Identity* (2004), Victoria O'Donnell's *Television Criticism* (2007), and Charlotte Brunson's and Lynn Spigel's *Feminist Television Criticism: A Reader* (2007).

27. For more on Wallace's essay, see his collection, *A Supposedly Fun Thing I'll Never Do Again* (1998).

28. To some extent, there is nothing new to this. As Anny Bakalian and Mehdi Bozorgmehr argue, "During times of war or political crisis such as the terrorist attacks of 11 September 2001 in the United States, minorities that share the same ethnic or religious background as the 'enemy' of the state are subject to backlash" (7).

29. Pena also reports that "according to a study released by the CAIR, in a 2005 Cornell University poll of 715 respondents to a telephone interview on Muslim civil rights, almost half of respondents polled nationally said they believe the U.S. government should—in some way—

curtail civil liberties for Muslim Americans" (205). Along similar lines, "according to a recent Los Angeles Times poll, 68% of those surveyed favored the ethnic profiling of Middle Easterners. In other words, they favor treating all Middle Easterners as inherently suspect, despite the fact that only a tiny percentage of Middle Easterners are terrorists" (Williams 13). According to a July 2006 *USA Today*/Gallup Poll, "Thirty-nine percent of Americans admit to holding prejudice against Muslims," and "the same percentage of respondents think Muslims — US citizens included — should carry special IDs" (Bayoumi par. 19). Ironically, but tellingly at the same time, "almost 60 percent of all Americans have never met a Muslim. One in ten thinks Muslims believe in a moon god" (Bayoumi par. 20). To be sure, it is easier to demonize and be fearful of a group with which one is not familiar.

30. After the September 11 attacks, "across the country, there were well over 1,000 reported hate incidents and hate crimes, including murders, arson, vandalism, physical and verbal assaults, and telephoned threats" (Abdelkarim, "American Muslims and 9/11" 83). Abdelkarim also argues that after September 11, Muslims like himself "have had our loyalty to our country challenged, our patriotism questioned, our institutions raided, and our civil liberties stomped upon" ("Arab and Muslim Americans" 55). Specifically, he identifies the "mass interrogations of Arab Americans and American Muslims," as well as how "several thousand people were rounded up in mass detentions, without charge and without having access even to an attorney" (55).

31. Similarly, Abdelkarim argues that the events of September 11 "resulted in a more rapid maturation of the American Muslim community" and that "Sept. 11 forced American Muslims to emerge from their cocoons of isolation" ("American Muslims and 9/11" 84). Specifically, he suggests that "Muslims began to reach out to their neighbors and to other faith and ethnic groups. Mosques and Islamic centers around the country began to hold open houses for their non–Muslim neighbors. Muslims have participated in earnest in interfaith gatherings and in town hall meetings with local, state and federal government officials" (84). Also, Anny Bakalian and Mehdi Bozorg-mehr argue, "Perhaps the most unexpected consequence of the 9/11 backlash against Muslims was their mobilization. Instead of capitulating to hate crimes and bias incidents, as well as a series of government executive orders, initiatives, and legislation that targeted Muslim immigrants, this group moved to claim its rightful place in American society" (9).

32. Indeed, immediately after September 11, Lala stops her socializing and she continues to avoid socializing with others for the duration of the novel.

33. Another significant post–September 11 event is that, at this time, Lala also hears from her long-lost brother, Bob, who, Lala discovers, is somewhere in New York City. As Khakpour explains, "Bob's letter ushered in the first season of happiness that they could remember since Tehran" (248). Lala's happiness even infects Darius, who now sees "the potential for being *saved*" (250). Lala ends up trying to find Bob in New York City, later in the novel, and while she doesn't find him then, Khakpour implies that she does eventually find Bob later.

34. To some extent, this may be seen in how Darius romanticizes Iran. As Khakpour explains, "He [Darius] fantasized about arriving in the streets of Tehran on the big day itself too ... amid streams and firecrackers" (303)

## Chapter 4

1. The memoir form could also be seen as running parallel to the re-emergence of the diary form (another form that seems to capitalize on the reading public's desire for something that appears real), which was made popular once again largely by Helen Fielding's *Bridget Jones's Diary* (1996).

2. Sarah Palin's autobiography, *Going Rogue* (2009), reportedly sold 700,000 copies in its first week, whereas Bill Clinton's *My Life* (2004) sold 900,000 in its first week (Italie, par. 2 and 4).

3. Along similar lines, Darznik writes, "To an increasing number of critics, meanwhile, the popularity of books by Iranian women in America, particularly memoirs, constitutes a pernicious outcome of contemporary military campaigns in the Middle East: a restaging of Orientalist and imperialist ideologies by a cadre of 'native informers'" (55).

4. This portrayal of a veiled Iranian woman or women is particularly evident in the cover of Azadeh Moaveni's *Lipstick Jihad* (2005), to be explored in a subsequent chapter, and in *RLT*'s cover as well.

5. Perhaps the most effusive praise of *RLT* comes from National Book Award winner Gloria Emerson, who not only described *RLT* as a "brilliant book," but said that "you have to spend a lifetime reading to write as well as Nafisi does. She is incapable of writing a trite or bad sentence" (12).

6. Part of this might have been prompted by former secretary of the treasury Paul O'Neill and counter-terrorism czar Richard Clarke's tell-all memoirs, *The Price of Loyalty* (2004) and *Against All Enemies* (2004), both of which were highly critical of the Bush administration, as well as the release of the *9/11 Commission Report* (2004) which was also critical (although not quite as much as O'Neill or Clarke's books) of the Bush administration.

7. Even though Nima's essays are unfinished, the fact that Nafisi calls them "brilliant" is important as it demonstrates that Nafisi does not completely generalize about or debase Iranian men.

8. For instance, Anne Donadey and Huma Ahmed-Ghosh suggest that "the memoir comes dangerously close to confirming a set of stereotypes about Islam for readers who are already saturated with them: that it is a theocratic, evil religion that should be allowed no place in the public sphere; that it oppresses women; and, finally, that it stands in stark contrast to the American way of life, thus justifying further foreign military intervention and U.S. political dominion over the world" (643–4).

9. To support her argument for the division of church and state, Nafisi describes her grandmother "who was the most devout Muslim I had ever known ... and still she shunned politics" (103). She says that her grandmother, a pious Muslim, resented "the fact that her veil, which to her was a symbol of her sacred relationship to God, had now become an instrument of power, turning the women who wore them into political signs and symbols" (103). Along these lines, Nafisi suggests that she doesn't object to the veil but to the requirement to wear one. She argues, "We had to have more respect for that 'piece of cloth' than to force it on reluctant people" (165).

10. Specifically, Bahramitash argues, "Western political domination over the Muslim world and military action against it throughout the colonial period was legitimized on the assumption that Muslim societies were inferior to those in the West. Civilizing the Orient through whatever means was deemed appropriate and was the pretext under which colonization of the Middle East and North Africa took place. Historically, the status of women was invoked as an indication of the Muslim world's backwardness, even though in the late nineteenth and early twentieth centuries women in Western countries had few legal rights and were not allowed to vote" (223–4).

11. For instance, see Hamid Dabashi's article, "Native Informers and the Making of the American Empire."

12. Bahramitash also implicates *RLT* for contributing to the Orientalist notion "that all societies in the Orient are the same and all Muslim women there live under the same conditions" (222)

13. Probably the clearest expression of this came during a McCain rally in which a woman expressed her fear and disdain of Obama because she believed him to be a Muslim. Also, polls from 2008 suggested that, on average, about 10–12 percent of Americans believed that Obama was Muslim (Burke, par. 1; Dimock, par. 1).

14. For instance, Donadey and Ahmed-Ghosh argue, "Unwittingly or not, Nafisi's book provides an ideological rationale to help Americans of various political persuasions stand behind a conservative political agenda" (643). Similarly, Bahramitash argues that *RLT* "reinforces what many North Americans want to believe about the 'oppression' of Iranian women while the United States is at the height of its war on terror and Iran has been signaled out by the US president as a member of an 'axis of evil' and an 'outpost of tyranny'" (230).

15. Dabashi implicates *RLT* for being at least "partially responsible for cultivating the US (and by extension the global) public opinion against Iran" (par. 9).

16. Further, Dabashi never specifies what he considers to be these "U.S. imperial moves for global domination." They could, for instance, be his interpretation of the primary motivation behind the first Gulf War, for the U.S.–backed Shah's regime, or the subsequently U.S.–backed Iraq during the Iraq-Iran war. However, would these really be "moves for global domination," or attempts to balance power in the Middle East (albeit towards U.S. interests), or something entirely different? Dabashi also argues that *RLT* demonstrates a "conspicuous absence of the historical and a blatant whitewashing of the literary" ("Native Informers," par. 13). Nafisi does gloss over the Iran-Iraq war to some degree, suggesting at first that "for me, as for millions of ordinary Iranians, the war came out of nowhere one mild fall morning: unexpected, unwelcome, and utterly senseless" (157). She then acknowledges that part of the rationale was that "the enemy had attacked our homeland" (158). However, she suggests that "many were not allowed to participate fully" because "from the regime's point of view, the enemy had attacked not just Iran; it had attacked the Islamic Republic, and it had attacked Islam" (158). While it is true that certain groups (e.g., Jews) may not have felt as much invested in the war because of its religious overtones, it is also true to some extent that Iraq held some animosity towards Iran since the former is predominantly Sunni while the latter is predominantly Sh'ia.

17. As Dabashi explains, "From Edward Said to Amy Kaplan and Gauri Viswanathan, we now have a sustained body of scholarship, extended from the US, through Europe, to India and by theoretical implication all around the colonized world, a persuasive argument as to how the teaching of English literature has historically been definitive to the British, and now by extension American, imperial proclivities" ("Native Informers," par. 19).

18. Dabashi believes that Nafisi "sought to save the soul of a nation by teaching a privileged few among them 'Western Classics'" ("Native Informers," par. 23). Dabashi also criticizes Nafisi's choices to use these classics as running contrary

to the struggles of ethnic and racial scholars. He writes, "After decades of consistent struggles, Native-Americans, African-Americans, Latin-Americans, Asian-Americans, feminists, and scores of other denigrated and disenfranchised communities, have successfully engaged the white male supremacist canon of the US higher education, against all odds and against powerful opposition from Christian fundamentalism and other conservative bastions upholding this empire. With utter disregard for this struggle across the nation, across the globe in fact, Azar Nafisi squarely places yet another non–European culture outside the fold of the literary — of the sublime and the beautiful" ("Native Informers," par. 24).

19. Keshavarz includes Nafisi's book in this as well as Asne Seierstad's *The Bookseller of Kabul* and Khaled Hosseini's *The Kite Runner* (3).

20. For a book that presents itself as *Reading More Than Lolita in Tehran, Jasmine and Stars* actually is more of a personal narrative than a literary study. Keshavarz does explore Shahrnush Parsipur's novel *Women without Men*. She also considers the female Iranian poet Forough Farrokhzad in a chapter she calls "The Eternal Forough: The Voice of our Earthly Rebellion." Interestingly, Nafisi also mentions the influence and importance of Farrokhzad in her follow-up to *RLT*, *Things I've Been Silent About* (2008), although she does not focus on Farrokhzad or any other Iranian writer in *RLT*. It is possible that she aimed to directly address critics like Keshavarz who accused Nafisi of debasing and ignoring Persian and Iranian literature and culture. Here Keshavarz's point is more convincing in that one can see how *RLT* and books like it overlook "these women's contributions" (36). In addition, the fact that Nafisi calls Farrokhzad a large influence but doesn't seem to teach her (at least not as detailed in *RLT*) helps support Keshavarz's point.

21. In fact, Kesharvarz functions as her own salesperson, commodifying her book as a product, promising that the reader will "laugh and cry with me" (6) while meeting "ordinary Iranians" (6). However, the people that Kesharvarz tends to focus upon are members of her extended Iranian family. Are they really any more "ordinary" than the Iranians on whom Nafisi focuses?

22. Ironically, this is exactly what Keshavarz suggests that Nafisi's book did: "The teaching of Western literary works to Iranian students was presented as a groundbreaking act or as something on the order of taming the savages" (19).

23. Indeed, one of Nafisi's students, Mr. Nyazi, represents the administration in his claim that *The Great Gatsby* is "immoral. It taught the youth the wrong stuff; it poisoned their minds" (120).

24. Nafisi also claims the Regime "banned ballet and dancing and told ballerinas they had a choice between acting or singing. Later women were banned from singing, because a woman's voice, like her hair, was sexually provocative and should be kept hidden" (108).

25. Keshavarz also states that "human sexuality is complicated and detecting its abuse is a challenge, particularly during times that bring shifts in cultural values. Iranians are not an exception when it comes to abusive human behavior" (50). While this may be true, she does not establish that sexual abuse occurs at the same or lower rate (or of the same magnitude) as in other countries

26. She also explains, "Living in the West, faced with demeaning stereotypical representatives of myself as an Iranian Muslim woman, I needed women who stood out in my memory, who made me feel empowered" (Keshavarz 154). Keshavarz believes that *RLT* paints a simplistic picture of Iran that caricatures Iranians as ugly (religious fundamentalists), faceless (oppressive men) and victims (women). She also argues against *RLT*'s "oversimplified world that posits good on the side of the West and evil squarely in the Muslim Camp. The book's villains are often reduced to their faith, hatred of progress (exemplified by the West), and the oppression of women" (Keshavarz 112). In general, this is a sentiment echoed by Reza Aslan, who suggests that the war on terrorism has been "described on both sides of the Atlantic in stark Christian terminology of good versus evil" (*No God but God* xv).

27. Donadey and Ahmed-Ghosh also suggest that "it is not possible for her to be unaware of the emergence of the various women's journals and movements, given the elite, educated background Nafisi shares with their most active participants, such as Shirin Ebadi, Mehrangiz Kar, and Shahla Lahiji" (628–9). They further suggest that "a lack of acknowledgment of such efforts feeds into western stereotypes of Iranian women as passive and helpless. It further reinforces the west's rhetoric that such oppression of women and backwardness are rooted in Islam" (629).

28. When Keshavarz mentions Ebadi, she also glosses over the death threats Ebadi has received and the many difficulties she faced and continues to face, stating that she took on "considerable risk," without any elaboration of the kinds of risks she took (125). In fact, Ebadi begins her own book with an account of how she saw herself in a report as a target for an assassin because she is not religious (*Iran Awakening* xv).

29. It is not clear if Nafisi encourages their tastes or if they come to their preferences on their own. While it has been established that American popular culture has been embraced by Middle Eastern youth, Nafisi seems to do little to counteract the predilections of her children for Western/American culture over Iranian/Persian culture. Rather, Nafisi states more matter of factly that not only did her children have "little

affection for Persian music" but they identify Persian music "with political songs and military marches — for pleasure they turned somewhere else" (60–1).

## Chapter 5

1. In addition to *Lipstick Jihad,* Moaveni has contributed to Shirin Ebadi's *Iran Awakening* (2006).

2. According to Moaveni, "Demand is highest for Persian translations of Danielle Steel (with intimate scenes either blotted out or obliterated by euphemism) and her Iranian equivalents, Fahimeh Rahimi and M. Moaddabpour, neither of whom has ever been seen on television (used in Iran mainly to promote state ideology, soap and rice). The most popular novel of the last two decades, Fattaneh Haj Seyyed Javadi's *Listless Morning,* about an idle aristocratic family under the 19th-century Qajar monarchy, has sold an unheard-of 185,000 copies since 1998 and spawned dozens of imitations" (*Honeymoon in Tehran* 27).

3. Moaveni sees the youth of Iran associating American items with "the freedoms they were denied," such as "Coke and Barbie" (209). She also relates how "American fast food was taking over Tehran. That fake Hardees, KFCs, and McDonaldses were swarming with teenagers thrilled to be tasting and participating in a ritual they associated with openness — eating a burger and fries" (210). In fact, she concludes, "All over the capital, it seemed Iranians were craving consumer symbols of American culture. The scarcity of supply only drove more demand, even for faux versions of everything you could imagine" (210).

4. To some extent, Moaveni sees some hope in this younger generation. As she explains in an interview: "Tehran now belongs to this new generation that was very young during the revolution, and happily missed out on all that trauma. They came of age in the period when the revolution had become ridiculous, all the clerical kitsch had zero legitimacy among the majority of society. The key point is that no one is scared anymore, and everyone is just mocking the elephant in the living room. People say whatever they want, bribe to get their way, and live whatever sort of life they want, juggling when required, coasting when not" ("A Q&A," par. 3).

However, Moaveni feels that the George W. Bush administration has made things more difficult for young people in Iran who seek reform. As she explains: "The Axis of Evil speech ruined any medium-term change for liberal politics in Tehran. Newspapers mute their criticism; intellectuals have quieted down; there's a real sense that the regime is in survival mode, and will no longer tolerate any dissent. So intellectual

life, city politics, which was so vibrant before, is now shaded by cautious self-censorship" ("A Q&A," par. 4).

5. Dunk also suggests that Moaveni "is willing to celebrate both Iran's cultural heritage and its modern political and social dynamics rather than offering a blanket ode to the past or diatribe aimed at the Islamic Republic," and she also praises *Lipstick Jihad* for "reaching past stereotypes and ex-pat nostalgia into the guts of modern Iran" (252).

6. Along similar lines, *Kirkus Reviews* suggests that *Lipstick Jihad* "is beautifully nuanced, complex, and illuminating," and that "Moaveni makes Iran a distinct entity" ("*Lipstick Jihad*" 106).

7. Toumani also suggests that *Lipstick Jihad* may not have been received very well by both Iranian and non–Iranian readers due to its humor and satire, or "irreverence and introspection," which, according to Toumani, "makes her sound uniquely American" (30). Specifically, Toumani describes how Moaveni read a selection from *Lipstick Jihad* to an audience, and how the audience did not respond well to Moaveni's humor (30).

8. As Alexandra Starr writes, "Moaveni writes unusually well and perceptively. She was obviously miserable in Iran, and with reason. It is humiliating to live in a repressive culture. It is disjunctive to feel alienated from a society you have a blood stake in. But she might have fared better beating back the black dogs — and written a better book — had she stopped ruminating on her predicament and more closely observed the plight of people around her" (29).

9. Similarly, Karim and Khorrami argue, "Many Iranian-Americans have often felt concerned, ambivalent, and at times even ashamed about revealing their heritage in an atmosphere steeped with media images portraying Iranians as hostile, as fanatical, and above all as terrorists during the period of the revolution, the Iran-Iraq War, and as recently as the 1991 conflict known as the Persian Gulf War" (21–22).

10. As Moaveni explains: "We weren't reflected anywhere — not on television, not on radio; we didn't have our own ethnic slur (the ones for Arabs didn't count), let alone a spoof on *The Simpsons*" (Moaveni 26).

11. For example, Moaveni describes how a non–Muslim American tries to call the police after seeing a Muslim reading the Koran in public (235).

12. In a subsequent chapter, we will see how even these "small magazines" which had "circulations of 2,000 to 5,000" have generally been replaced by blogs written by Iranians.

13. An Iranian friend suggests that what marks Moaveni as a foreigner and an American is that she laughs "whenever you want," that she smiles

"too much," and that she doesn't "alter" herself "in public" (69).

14. Moaveni also sees a lack of sympathy on the part of some Iranians who view the United States "as a greedy, heartless uber-power in pursuit of domination of the Middle East, indifferent to its civilians," and who feel that the U.S. may have just gotten a taste of its own medicine (223–4).

15. According to Moaveni, other changes can be seen in a kind of "grassroots women's movement of considerable vigor," which fights "for equitable legal rights in parliament" and against "issues from polygamy to domestic abuse" (17).

16. As Moaveni explains, "A modest flat was now beyond the budget of the average middle-class couple; only Iranians supported by their parents, or those few who belonged to the upper middle class, could afford to own their own place before their forties" (18–9).

17. Moaveni concludes that "the real story of modern Iran, what would drive the country's politics and future, was its failing economy and how it was sinking the prospects of millions of young people, who cared far more about finding jobs and raising their living standards than about whether Islam would become compatible with western-style democracy during their lifetime" (110).

18. Moaveni herself seems to agree that theirs was flawed logic or a rationalization. She writes, "We had all been wrong. Desperately, fatally, irretrievably wrong. The election had mattered after all, and so had voting" (57).

19. At a time (2005) in which "Iranians had grown increasingly skeptical of U.S. power in the Middle East," Ahmadinejad becomes more appealing through his supposed strength in dealing with other countries (most notably the United States), and his willingness to confront other political leaders and countries, but even to stay on equal ground with Iran's Arabic neighbors (105). Moaveni doesn't even exclude herself and her peers from Ahmadinejad's initial charm as she writes, "We were all taken in" (108).

20. At the same time, Moaveni suggests that Ahmadinejad would not have been elected were it not for his eventual backing by religious authorities. Indeed, once they turn their support to Ahmadinejad, he goes from winning "just 12 percent of the electorate" in the first round of voting to winning the election (193).

21. According to The Washington Post, the program was aimed at "expanding broadcasting, funding nongovernmental organizations and promoting cultural exchanges." The program also ended up being funded by $19 million dollars less than the originally proposed $75 million (Baker and Kessler).

22. As a journalist, Moaveni gets caught in the crossfire as her contacts become less willing to speak and her stories are severely scrutinized and even condemned by Moaveni's main contact, Mr. X, a government official who tells her that legal proceedings have started against Moaveni for her supposedly blasphemous news stories. Another government official tells Moaveni that she needs to "avoid subjects the government deemed provocative and instead focus on more neutral subjects, such as film and women's high rates of university attendance" (297).

23. Rather, according to Moaveni, the "Iranian government had grown pragmatic. It also distributed clean syringes to heroin addicts, and condoms to prostitutes and prison inmates. This was rather astonishing, given that it also punished drug use and homosexuality with anything from flogging to death" (126).

24. As Moaveni explains, "As odd as this might sound, most women in Iran consider marriage greatly liberating. The adjectives they use to describe their married lives — 'independent,' 'unbound,' 'carefree' — are similar to those western women would apply to being single" (204). They tend to connect marriage with freedom (205).

25. Unlike Nafisi, who invokes Western literature and Gatsby as she leaves Iran at the end of RLT, Moaveni ends Honeymoon in Tehran by seeking solace in traditional Persian literature and poetry, "grateful for the heritage in books that offers Iranians a place to retreat from the uncertainty of the present. They are a reminder that though today Iranians are diminished by the cruel laws of unjust tyrants, it has not always been so, and thus will not always be" (334). In many ways, this foreshadows the 2009 demonstrations in Iran.

26. In 2008 Iran, she notices an even greater discrepancy between the rich and poor. As she explains, "In all my years I had never seen Tehran like this before. So urbane and openly hospitable to people with money to spend, yet so hard-edged and ungenerous to those who were struggling" (329).

27. Dumas's website explains that "Funny in Farsi was on the SF Chronicle and LA Times bestseller lists" ("About Firoozeh Dumas," par. 2).

28. Instead, in an interview, Dumas explains her motivation for writing: "When I was about 36 years old, and I had two children by then, I wanted my children to know my stories just like I knew my father's stories" (Simon).

29. In a way, this is what may have led reviewers like Debra Moore to praise Funny in Farsi. Moore writes, "Today, as Middle Easterners in the United States are subject to racial profiling, stereotyping, and sometimes violence, this book provides a valuable glimpse into the immigrant experiences of one very entertaining family" (128).

30. As Dumas's website relates, "Orange County Reads One Book (California) selected Funny in Farsi for Community Reads 2004, the

City of Whittier (California) in 2005, Cape Ann (Massachusetts) in 2006, Palo Alto and Berkeley (California) in 2006, and Dayton (Ohio), Lamorinda (California), Wood Dale, Itasca and Bensenville (Illinois) in 2008, Brentwood (California) in 2009 and in 2010, Concord (New Hampshire) selected both *Funny in Farsi* and *Laughing Without an Accent. Funny in Farsi* is now on the California Recommended Reading List and is used in many junior high, high schools and universities across the country" ("About Firoozeh Dumas," par. 4).

31. While it may be hard to believe, her website suggests that "everywhere she has gone, audiences have embraced her message of shared humanity and invited her back for more" ("About Firoozeh Dumas," par. 5).

32. Specifically, Dumas states that Iranian-Americans "love" *Funny in Farsi* and that they "keep thanking me for showing another side of the Iranian people to the world. Most Westerners think Middle Easterners just discuss politics and religion all day. We're actually quite fun" ("*Funny in Farsi*— Author Interview," par. 11).

33. As Dumas further explains, "In Iran, if a book sells two thousand copies, it has done well. In the first year of publication, thirty thousand copies [of *Funny in Farsi*] were sold" (9) and it "won the Readers' Choice Award from a magazine for twentysomethings" (*Laughing Without an Accent* 10).

34. In all fairness, Dumas does describe her father as growing up rather impoverished, and this may have something to do with his desire for wealth.

35. At Disneyland, even Dumas's father's overwhelming fear of "child kidnappings" in the United States dissipates when Dumas gets lost at Disneyland but is easily rescued and reunited with her family.

36. Further, even after this incident, Dumas is quick to point out to the reader that this treatment is more the exception rather than the rule. She explains, "But almost every person who asked us a question asked with kindness. Questions were often followed by suggestions of places to visit in California" (34).

37. In her own words, "When my parents and I get together today, we often talk about our first year in America. Even though thirty years have passed, our memories have not faded. We remember the kindness more than ever, knowing that our relatives who immigrated to this country after the Iranian Revolution did not encounter the same America" (36).

## Chapter 6

1. Miller further explains, "At least five anthologies of contemporary prison literature (edited by Bell Gave Chevigny, H. Bruce Franklin, Wally Lamb, Janine Pommy Vega, and Judith Scheffler) have been published in the past decade; the PEN prison writing program is flourishing, and two stories that arose from the PEN program are represented in the first collection (2000) of *The Best American Voices*, edited by Tobias Wolff. Popular films of the past decade such as *The Shawshank Redemption, American History X, Dead Man Walking, The Green Mile,* and *Hurricane,* and the acclaimed HBO television series *Oz* attest to the fact that the American public is increasingly interested in stories of imprisonment" (1).

2. This especially comes through after the guards shave Ghahramani's head as punishment for her outburst against them. As she explains, "Nothing that has happened to me in prison has distressed me like the shearing of my head. And I know it is shallow. I know it is all to do with vanity. But I was the pretty one. I liked being pretty. So what is this? A character-building opportunity? A chance to accept how superficial being pretty is? I don't want the opportunity! I want to be a pretty Persian girl dutifully attending to her studies and having nothing to do with politics. Nothing" (73).

3. Clawson's support for this is that "Ghahramani shows how the regime is determined to control even the smallest aspects of each person's life. She is shown pictures of her entering and leaving a male student's apartment—a grave offense against the state even though they were simply friends studying together" (88).

4. Along similar lines, Carolyn Leavitt describes the Islamic Republic as a "fundamentalist regime" (58).

5. In an interview with *Mother Jones* magazine, Ghahramani explains her own fears while living in Iran, after her arrest: "There was always an unspoken fear between us that they would take me again. Sometimes I would come back a little bit late, and I would find my mom shivering and screaming, 'Where have you been? Why didn't you call me or pick up your phone?' She would basically freak out. So it was really hard to go back to a normal life. There was always that paranoia for them and for me, and it stopped us from living life like we used to" (Butler, par. 11). Ghahramani also explains, "I wasn't giving any speeches or writing anything, but I would see my other friends arrested again and again, and I thought eventually that would happen to me, too. Even if you've just contacted an old friend, that could be a reason to get arrested if you have a previous record" (Butler, par. 13).

6. For instance, Ghahramani retaliates against her especially vicious and demeaning interrogator by screaming, not putting her blindfold on, and ultimately saying he has "a disgusting face" (70). His response is to completely shave her head, and Ghahramani's continued defiance

helps lead to a particularly vicious beating that results in broken ribs, bruises, and presumably, internal bleeding.

7. Along these lines, reviewer Patrick Clawson also suggests in a non-critical way that Ghahramani's general apolitical views seem "very much like an average American student" (88).

8. In truth, despite Ghahramani's profession of being mostly apolitical, she does have some strong beliefs and critiques of the Islamic Republic. Beyond using Islam to help prop up their largely totalitarian regime, Ghahramani suggests that the Islamic Republic has turned a blind eye to poverty, even to "war widows" during the Iran-Iraq war (30).

9. As James Buchan explains, "for the purposes of the Islamic Republic, she [Ghahramani] already has three strikes against her. Her doting father was a military officer under the Shah and a Kurd, while her mother was a Zoroastrian and brought Zarah up in that ancient faith" (par. 4).

10. In all fairness, there is no reason to consider that Ghahramani would be writing for an Iranian audience as Iranian prison narratives like hers are among the least likely works to be published in Iran.

11. This is, of course, subjective. Esfandiari herself argues that "solitary confinement is a kind of torture" (qtd. in Havemann 47). However, during this time she does have some interactions with her guards every day, so she is not completely isolated from other people.

12. In another article, Rubin describes Esfandiari as "a petite, soft-spoken grandmother" ("Is Iran Jailing"). While Estafandiari was 67 years old at the time of her incarceration, this article was published two years afterwards, when she was 69.

13. For instance, Sorcha Hamilton writes: "She [Esfandiari] weaves her personal experience with the political and historical background of Iran, which makes the book a little dense and uneven. Best are the more personal descriptions: the white rose from a guard, as a gesture of hope; the strength of her mother, tirelessly waiting at the prison gates with food and clothes; how Esfandiari got down on her knees and cleaned the foul, nauseating toilet herself in an attempt to maintain some sense of dignity."

14. Esfandiari also argues that "under President Ahmadinejad, who had been elected a little over a year before, the security services had cracked down on writers and academics. We all knew of newspaper closures and arrests. The well-known intellectual and political philosopher Ramin Jahanbegloo had been arrested at the airport on his way to Europe, and spent four months in Evin Prison" (3).

15. When listening to Ja'fari on the phone, Esfandiari concludes that "he was some kind of teacher, maybe, I thought, in night school" (77).

Later, she explains that he claims to be "a university professor" (77). Given Esfandiari's own academic background (she possesses a Ph.D.), the Islamic Regime may have chosen a different kind of interrogator for her — one that they felt could match her intellectually, or at least, one that possessed the credentials to potentially do so.

16. Along similar lines, Laura Secor, writing for the *New York Times*, argues, "At a time when the Bush administration had made no secret of its desire to forge ties with the Iranian opposition, it was hardly irrational for the unpopular regime to fear that it would come to a similar end" (8).

17. However, she also has an unpleasant guard whom she calls Sour Face, who seems angry and resentful, and also seems to believe all the inmates are guilty (161).

18. Esfandiari might be receiving better treatment if we believe one of the guards who claims that in Esfandiari's section, the inmates "were served the same food as the Intelligence Ministry's staff" (166).

19. Part of the way Esfandiari keeps her strength up is through a continual process of denial and self-control. In a way, the paucity of comforts she has strengthens her resolve to fight against her interrogators. For this reason, when guards come to install a television in Esfandiari's cell, instead of being overjoyed, she describes herself as being "furious," because "this was my prison, a hellhole," and she "didn't want my interrogators to boast to my mother and the world that I was comfortable and had what I needed" (180).

20. A good, recent example would be the much publicized case of three young American who were imprisoned after straying into Iran. While the hikers claimed that they did so accidentally, while hiking, the Islamic Regime imprisoned them on the accusation of espionage.

21. Specifically, the program is entitled, "In the Name of Democracy," and, according to Esfandiari, it sought to implicate the U.S. for "orchestrating the revolutions," primarily in countries in the former Soviet Union as well as in Iran (178). According to James Bone, writing for *The Times*, Esfandiari directly "claimed that she was involved in the Velvet Revolution" in this program.

22. As Sorcha Hamilton explains, "Ten thousand signatures were collected during Esfandiari's imprisonment calling for her release, while her family, colleagues and supporters waged a tireless campaign with the backing of the UN, Human Rights Watch and others. Then senators Barack Obama and Hillary Clinton called for her release, and her situation was widely reported in the US and European media." Specifically, according to Robin Wright of the *Washington Post*, "The turn-

ing point in Esfandiari's eight-month ordeal appears to have been a letter from Lee H. Hamilton, Wilson Center president and former congressman, to Iranian supreme leader Ayatollah Ali Khamenei."

23. Indeed, according to the *Washington Post*, "Diplomats from more than 20 governments in Europe, Asia and the Middle East delivered strong messages to Iran's foreign ministry. More than 100 former officials from several countries used personal connections to Iranian officials, Hamilton said" (Wright).

24. As Esfandiari explains, "Through the Internet, an international civil society had come into being, ready to be mobilized in cases like mine" (205).

25. One reason Esfandiari refuses to come back to Iran is that, according to her, "True to form, the Islamic Republic has not brought closure to my case" (221).

26. Specifically, Esfandiari claims that "Iran's leaders are heedless of the damage they do to their own citizens and the havoc they inflict on the lives of the individuals and families. They assume everyone else is as indifferent to basic human decency as they. They pretend to forget what they did to me—and the worse torment they inflicted on countless others. But I cannot forget" (219).

27. According to Bahari, he is not the only one to be arrested: "The other Iranians interviewed in Jason's report—a former vice president and a former foreign minister—had been arrested a week before me as part of the IRGC's sweeping crackdown" (par. 52).

28. In his own words, Bahari explains, "I was born in Tehran and lived there the first 19 years of my life, before going to Canada and Britain for my studies and to begin my career as a journalist and documentary filmmaker. I returned in 1998, making movies and reporting for *Newsweek*" (par. 40).

29. One reason Bahari capitulates is that he is told and believes that his "investigation" would otherwise take "between four and six years," and he "could be sentenced to death" (par. 60).

30. According to Bahari, "Mr. Rosewater didn't beat me while asking me questions. He beat me before or after, simply to show he was in control. He pretended not to enjoy it. At one point he told me he beat me mainly because he was angry. "What you have done, Mazi, makes my blood boil. I don't want to raise my hand against you, but what do you suggest I do with someone who has insulted the Leader?" (par. 69).

31. As Bahari explains, "Once or twice a year I am felled by devastating migraines. Mr. Rosewater knew that, from the medication I'd brought with me to Evin, and he took particular pleasure in pounding the back of my head." (par. 70).

32. For instance, as Bahari explains, Mr. Rosewater tells him that his "days are numbered," and that "the next time I saw him, he promised, I'd be standing on a chair with a noose around my neck. He would personally kick the chair out from under me. I would not know the date of my execution in advance. But, he assured me, it would take place after morning prayers, around 4 A.M." (par. 71).

33. Bahari explains this with the following: "The Guards see real enemies all around them — reformists within the country, hundreds of thousands of U.S. troops outside. Even worse are the shadows — supposed agents of Britain, the United States, and Israel — upon whom they impose their own fearful logic and their reinvented history. Only Muslims, only they, are victims" (par. 40).

34. They also try to intimidate Bahari into naming conspirators in this supposed planning of a Velvet Revolution by telling him, "No names means the noose" (par. 86).

35. For her part, Esfandiari is very aware of the damage that these prisons have done to the image of the United States in the Muslim world. In an interview, she explains, "I was always very cautious not to complain to my interrogators because if I said something they would immediately come back and say, 'What about Guantánamo? What about Abu Ghraib?' There are hundreds, maybe thousands, of people who went through Evin Prison and were beaten up or tortured or harassed" (qtd. in Havemann 48).

36. Another reason Mr. Rosewater may focus on New Jersey is that the show that Bahari appeared on, *The Daily Show*, which initially got him into trouble, has a New Jersey connection in the sense that the host, Jon Stewart, is from New Jersey, and frequently makes light of that fact (and of the state itself) on the show.

37. Mr. Rosewater also claims that Bahari has "a secret American network. A New Jersey network" (Bahari, par. 39).

38. According to Bahari, "the multilayered pressure campaign that *Newsweek* and others had put together on my behalf— the editorials and petitions, the diplomatic démarches, the quiet personal efforts of world leaders," helped him get released (par. 102).

39. One way they attempt to do this is by forcing Bahari to "sign documents saying I would 'cooperate with the brothers in the Revolutionary Guards' once outside the country. He'd given me a list of names to report on, including most of my Iranian friends in London and other Western cities. He'd given me the e-mail address to use" (par. 105).

40. For a specific list of the charges brought against Bahari as well as his responses to these charges, see Maziar Bahari, "Justice Iranian Style," *Newsweek*, 10 May 2010, 27 May 2010, http://www.newsweek.com/2010/05/10/justice-iranian-style.html.

41. Batebi was also arrested three times for participating in student-led demonstrations (Shane and Gordon, par. 19).

42. Specifically, in this demonstration, "hundreds of students demonstrated against the closing of a newspaper, *Salam*" (Shane and Gordon, par. 20).

43. According to the *60 Minutes* interview, "Trying to help, Batebi took his friend's shirt off. 'To put pressure on the wound. It was bleeding. And so I tried to use his shirt to keep the blood in. Then we took him to the medical facility,' he recalled.... After helping his friend, Batebi returned to the protest, and waved the bloody shirt to show what police had done. That's when a photographer took a picture of Batebi that would appear on the cover of *The Economist* and was seen around the world. Just days after the picture appeared, the government arrested him" ("How Ahmad Batebi," par. 8–9).

44. During the time he spent in solitary confinement, Batebi was reportedly "trapped in a tiny cell not much bigger than a bathtub" ("How Ahmad Batebi," par. 15). As he further explains, "They kept the light on 24 hours a day. You have no information about the outside. You have no contact with the outside, and after a while you become mentally disoriented. This kind of torture doesn't affect you physically, but it does affect you mentally and emotionally" (qtd. in "How Ahmad Batebi," par. 15).

45. While the sources do not directly state this, given Batebi's age and his treatment in prison, it would not be at all surprising if his incarceration was mainly or at least partially responsible for his strokes.

46. Through his work with Voice of America, Batebi describes himself as committed to help "people imprisoned in Iran whose human rights are being violated" ("How Ahmad Batebi," par. 57–58).

## Chapter 7

1. Indeed. as Trevor Mostyn argues, "Some modern Muslim writers blame Salman Rushdie for sparking off the witch-hunt by so-called Islamists against writers" (28).

2. Iran is not the only predominantly Muslim Middle Eastern country that employs censorship. As Mostyn argues, "In most of the Islamic world press freedom remains a dream. In Libya, Iraq, and Saudi Arabia almost complete control by the government ensures a compliant press.... In Algeria, Egypt, Sudan and the Israeli-Occupied Palestinian Territories emergency legislation gives the authorities draconian powers of censorship. The head of state, the ruling party and, of course, the Islamic environment itself are usually forbidden targets for the writer" (159).

3. Specifically, Mostyn points to how in late 1999, "some of pop art's greatest treasures, including Andy Warhol's 1973 silkscreen print of Mick Jagger and James Rosenquist's portrait of Marilyn Monroe, were being shown at the Museum of Contemporary Art in Tehran" (25).

4. Also according to Mostyn, "By 1994 forty-eight writers and journalists had been executed by revolutionary courts, including the 28-year-old Said Soltanpour, who was abducted in front of his bride at his wedding and later shot, and the novelist Rahman Hatefi, who was left to bleed to death in prison after interrogators opened his veins. There were then a thousand Iranian intellectuals in prison and twice that many in exile" (25).

5. As Mostyn argues, there are additional cultural reasons for censorship in Islamic countries that go beyond the mere political structure of the country. One such reason is the perceived importance in Islamic countries of the community as opposed to the more Western (especially American) championing of the individual. As he details, "In the West freedom of expression exists, goes the argument, to liberate the creative self from the constraints and limits imposed by the community, yet it is this community — this Arabic *umma*— which is so crucial to traditional Islamic society" (20).

6. Historically speaking, there is some truth to this claim. As Gail Riley explains, in the United States "the government is allowed wide latitude with respect to freedom of press during times of war" (26). Not only has this restriction of the press and speech gone into effect with the earlier Espionage and Sedition Acts, more recently, as Riley explains, "during the Persian Gulf War, limitations were again placed on reporters. Censors read stories before they could be submitted for print, and the censor's word, with rare exception, was the law" (26).

7. Some of the last well-known American censorship trials revolved around works published by members of the Beat Generation in the 1950s and early 1960s, such as Ginsberg's *Howl* and Burroughs's *Naked Lunch*.

8. Another way censorship can actually benefit the writer is by increasing a writer's notoriety. Indeed, as Mostyn explains, "In Egypt writers have even been reporting advertising *fatwas* against their books in newspapers in order to publicize them" (13).

9. Specifically, it has been suggested that Mandanipour served in the Iran-Iraq war in part "because of a belief that the experience would make him a better writer" (Baghramian, par. 1).

10. This was "the 1998 Golden Tablet Award for best fiction in Iran during the previous two decades" ("Shariar Mandanipour," par 2). Mandanipour has also won "the Mehregan Award for the best Iranian children's novel of 2004 ... and Best Film Critique at the 1994 Press Festival in Tehran" ("Shariar Mandanipour," par. 2).

11. Specifically he has published "nine volumes of fiction, one nonfiction book, and more than 100 essays in genres such as literary theory, literature and art criticism, creative writing, censorship, and social commentary" ("Shariar Mandanipour," par. 3)

12. Baghramian also suggests, "The recent events in Iran make his immediate return unlikely but he continues writing perceptive commentaries on the unfolding political turmoil" (par. 3).

13. For example, Wood suggests, "One of the great successes of this book is how thoroughly it persuades the reader that a novel about censorship could not help also being a novel about fiction-making; and it thus brings a political gravity to a fictive self-consciousness sometimes abused by the more weightless postmodernism" (74). Along similar lines, another reviewer describes *CILS* as "magisterial metafiction that makes an ordinary love affair astonishing and provides a rich understanding of life under repressive Islamic rule" (Hoffert 85).

14. It is also quite possible that Mandanipour's use of comedy and satire helped to defuse his bleak portrayal of life in contemporary Iran, whereas Nafisi rarely ever employed comedy or satire in *Reading Lolita in Tehran*.

15. Kakutani, for instance, describes Iran as "a totalitarian state" ("Where Romance," par. 3).

16. Wood critiques *CILS* for its awkward introduction of oddly placed allusions like a seemingly random appearance of "Gogol's Akaky Akakievich, the clerk from the story 'The Overcoat,' who asks the narrator, 'Have you seen the thief who stole my cloak?'" (74). Along similar lines, Kakutani critiques *CILS* for "the intermittent appearances of a hunchbacked midget," which she finds "annoyingly gratuitous and contrived" (par. 10).

17. This claim is supported by Marjane Satrapi's *Persepolis* and *Persepolis 2*, as well as by Azadeh Moaveni's *Lipstick Jihad* and *Honeymoon in Tehran*, which depict how Iranian women generally do not wear the hijab in private.

18. For Mandanipour, the use of figurative language (especially metaphors and similes) not only is a hallmark of Iranian literature, but also makes the process of reading and interpreting it especially challenging.

19. At greater length and as evidence of the extent of his paranoia, the instructor also tells his class: "The people you students know as today's writers and poets fall into three groups. They are either spies for the West, drug addicts, or homosexuals. It is every Muslim's duty to spill the blood of such people" (217).

20. Along similar lines, according to the narrator, a censor can likewise deem the mere mention of the word 'breast' in an asexual context problematic. For example, while driving through Tehran, the narrator writes that he sees a banner that reads: "MEDICAL SEMINAR ON THE CAUSES SND PREVENTIONS OF BREAST CANCER" (41), as if to dare Mr. Petrovich to censor something that clearly has no sexual implications (which he presumably would censor).

21. However, when the narrator tells his publisher, "Mr. Petrovich forgave us three breasts and two thighs" (40), it indicates the further objectification of women, in this case as analogous to cut-up chicken.

22. Specifically, Coetzee writes, "Writing under censorship is like being intimate with someone who does not love you, with whom you want no intimacy, but who presses himself in upon you. The censor is an intrusive reader, a reader who forces his way into the intimacy of the writing transaction, forces out the figure of the loved or courted reader, reads your words in a disapproving and *censorious* fashion" (38).

23. Mandanipour also suggests that when it comes to writing about women, it is even more difficult for an aspiring writer. In a scene in which the narrator debates which character (Sara or Dara) should call the other first, he imagines an Iranian pseudo-feminist criticizing him if he has Sara call Dara first as it would make her look weak in comparison, but if he has Dara call first "hard-line political activists" would suggest that this is not realistic and that he has "been paid off by the government to write that political activists are weak" (169).

24. As other contributing factors, Mandanipour suggests a decreasing number of brothels in contemporary Iran and increasing rates for prostitutes (58).

25. It is possible that Mandanipour named this character Mr. Atta as an allusion to one of the primary September 11 hijackers, Mohammad Atta, as Mandanipour's Mr. Atta seems to be a rather vicious villain. However, there is no direct evidence that this was his intention.

26. In fact, the narrator clearly portrays Mr. Petrovich's disdain for Dara in how Mr. Petrovich tells the narrator that Dara, being a worthless character, should just commit suicide (263). What Mandanipour suggests here is that through his position as a censor and years of indoctrination by the Islamic Regime, Mr. Petrovich has lost his ability to genuinely love another, or even appreciate love.

## Chapter 8

1. Sufism is particularly well suited to poetry because basic Sufi tenets, which suggest a primary difference between a visible and invisible world, mirror the difference between literal and figurative language. William Chittick explains that in Sufi poetry and Sufisim in general, "the universe can be pictured as kernel and husk. The

kernel represents the invisible realm, which is the domain of souls, spirits and angels; the husk represents the visible realm, which is the domain of sense perception and bodily things. The kernel is essentially light, life, knowledge and awareness; the husk is essentially darkness, death, ignorance and unconsciousness" (424).

2. The importance of poetry in Iran may also be due to how "of all the countries overrun by the Arabs in their seventh-century expansion, only Persia retained its own language; in all other countries defeated by the Arabs at that time the dominant (and in many cases only) language is now Arabic. In Persia it is still Persian, a language which has wholly different roots from Arabic (Persian is an Indo-European language, Arabic a Semitic one)" (Davis 147).

3. Khatreh Sheibani argues that "the idea of changing Persian poetry to accommodate new social and political poetry" began in the "late nineteenth century," with the poem standing "against traditionalist conceptions, which aimed at preserving the old Persian prosody along with relatively traditional concepts and beliefs" (509–10). Sheibani also claims that Persian poetry was largely "dormant" from "the fifteenth to the nineteenth century," and these newer twentieth century poets helped make poetry popular again (510). Some of the better known of these less formulaic, modern poets include ma Yushij (1897–1960) and his immediate followers, Ahmad Shamlu (1925–2000), Mehdi Akhavan-Saless (1928–1990), and Forugh Farrokhzad (1935–1967) (Karimi-Hakkak 212).

4. As Karimi-Hakkak argues, "In order to propagate unorthodox notions of civilization, progress, and the rule of law, Persian poets had to scrap the elitist conventions that had brought nothing but harm to the people, and to inculcate the desire for liberty and equality in their fellow countrymen. The search for modernity in Persian poetry was aligned with Iran's efforts to forge a modern state, a forward-looking culture, and a society modeled along European lines. Iran was thought to have stagnated in part because previous generations of poets had not guided the people to modernity" (212).

5. However, this can be seen as, by and large, a more recent literary development as argued by Persis Karim, who suggests that "long before the prominence of Iranian American memoirs, poetry was the first genre of writing that registered the tenor of Iranian immigrant sensibility, and was infused with experiences of alienation, exile, loss, and a sense of reckoning with new locale(s) in North America" (111).

6. As Mozaffari and Karimi-Hakkak suggest, "In spite of the censorship imposed by the strict religious ideologues and by various organs of state, writers and poets have multiplied and literary magazines have flourished." The kind of literature published in Iran tends to be apolitical or clouded in metaphor (xx).

7. Mozaffari and Karimi-Hakkak echo Karim by suggesting that "no twenty-first-century account of Persian poetry will be complete without taking note of the poetry produced by Iranian expatriates in the last two decades" (369).

8. In the forward, Desi Di Nardo suggests that the collection "does not distinguish among class, race, gender, or age, but appeals to audiences on a mass scale" (v). Indeed, the collection does represent women of different ages and includes work by both Iranian and expatriate Iranian women. While it may be true that the collection contains a diversity of topics from the more universal discussions of love, to "innocence of childhood," to "resistance to an interminable war and a defective regime" (v), it does seem that most of the poetry from Iran in the collection is more domestic and less political in nature whereas the poetry from Western countries is often more politically charged. As mentioned previously, this could be attributed to Iranian censorship and the West's predilection for poetry that displays Iranian oppression if not backwardness. To some extent Di Nardo contributes to this supposition by suggesting that poetry is especially important "to those who suffer through alienation, suppression, and discrimination and apply poetry as a medium to be heard, as a vehicle of escape, or purely as a wing of support" (vi). The implication, then, is that these poets included in this collection are largely the Iranian women who suffer through the kinds of oppression she mentions. In fact, Di Nardo writes, "In a region plagued by war and uproar, and in a country where women continue to be suppressed and at times persecuted, it is no marvel so many Iranian women resort to poetry to communicate feelings, experiences, and messages of love and hope" (vii–viii).

9. Indeed, as Erika Friedel argues, "Men were/are privileged over women in law, in economics, in everyday practices, in the division of labor" (30).

10. Reportedly, stonings were rare in Iran before 1997 and there were no stonings in Iran from 1997 to 2001. Since then there have only been a few cases of stonings. In 2001, Maryam Ayoubi was stoned to death for adultery and murder of her husband (Theodoulou 6). Also, in 2007, Zohreh and Azar Kabiri-niat (who are sisters) were "sentenced to execution by stoning in Iran for being accused of infidelity by Zohreh's abusive husband," despite the fact that both women professed their innocence ("Iran: Abusive Husband's" 6). According to Amnesty International, their sentence was commuted in late 2008 ("Good News," par. 1). In summer 2010, an Iranian woman, Sakineh Mohamamadi e Ashtian, "a 43-year-old mother of two in the northwestern Iranian city of Tabriz, was accused of having ex-

tramarital relations with two men who ended up killing her husband" and consequently sentenced to be stoned to death ("Iranian Woman Faces Death," par. 1).

11. For a more detailed description of a stoning in Somalia, see the article "Somali Woman Executed by Stoning," BBC News, 27 Oct 2008, 1 Sept 2010, http://news.bbc.co.uk/2/hi/Africa/7694397.stm.

12. Along these lines, other poems tend to be more domestic accounts of love and relationships such as Arezou Mokhtarian's "Tonight," in which she writes, "Tonight / you do not love me / you are tired and bored / to play with these cords" (lines 1–4). Another example would be Mehri Rahmani's poem "With You" in which she writes, "I am thirsty / Place the skies in your eyes / Blaze out the star / So I can see you" (lines 9–12).

13. There is definitely an historical basis for how Iran has backed and supported Hezbollah (Samuels 49; Dilanian A08; Wall and Fulghum 31).

14. While it is difficult to find support for how the Hezbollah played a role in the discrimination against those of the Baha'i faith, Iran's exclusion of the Baha'i has been documented. For instance, Firuz Kazemzadeh argues that primarily because Iran tends to exclude religious groups originating after Islam, Baha'is literally have "no civil rights" and "cannot hold government jobs, enforce legal contracts, practice law, collect pensions, attend institutions of higher learning, and openly practice their faith" (537).

15. While they may not have experienced as much discrimination as the Baha'i, Kurds have also not been fully integrated or accepted by Iranian society. This is perhaps best exemplified in how "five Iranian Kurds, one of them a woman, were hanged for alleged terrorism by the Iranian authorities in Tehran's Evin prison, probably to warn dissenters of the punishment they may expect" ("Politics" 8).

16. The first part of *Dear Regime* is entitled "Part A(s If Change Were Possible)" and it immediately suggests not only that Sedarat might want change for Iran (presumably cultural, if not governmental change), but that he believes such change may not be possible.

17. At the same time, Sedarat's use of the ghazal may be in line with that of Hafiz, whose ghazals reportedly worked "toward a moralizing conclusion," but would also "simultaneously, subvert it" (Davis 171).

18. Freud's best-known case of sexual repression would be that of Dora.

## Chapter 9

1. For an in-depth exploration of Iranian blogs, an excellent resource is Nasrin Alavi's *We Are Iran* (2005), which details the widespread popularity and importance of blogs in Iran. *We Are Iran* was the first full-length book that investigated this subject matter, and for the most part, it was met by praise from reviewers. However, one reviewer did critique Alavi for not explaining how she chose the blogs she included in her study (Javanshir 213). This critic felt that Alavi may have chosen blogs most aligned with her own political perspectives (Alavi appears to be a liberal reformer) as opposed to a purely random selection of blogs (Javanshir 213). The point may be valid; however, at the same time, it would be simply impossible for any writer to cover anything approaching a majority of the thousands upon thousands of Iranian blogs.

2. According to Dayem, "Between 20 and 25 million Iranians have regular digital access, giving the country the highest Internet penetration rate in the region" (42).

3. China appears to have the highest numbers of bloggers with a 2008 governmental estimate of 107 million and another non–Chinese government late 2007 estimate of approximately 47 million (Lewitt 29; Zha and Perlmutter 279; "CNNIC Releases").

4. Dayem further explains, "Iran's filtering and blocking regime has been described by various experts as second only to China's. In late 2008, the government boasted that this committee had filtered upward of five million sites, though most independent observers believe that this number is inflated. A cybercrimes law introduced by the government in 2006 effectively put all forms of expression on the Internet on the same footing as other forms of journalism, which are governed by Iran's restrictive and highly punitive press law of 2000" (43).

5. In detail, the Berkman study revealed "four major networks (what they call 'poles'), with subclusters of bloggers within each one. The poles they identify are: 1. Secular/Reformist: Contains expatriates and Iranians involved in a dialogue about Iranian politics and other issues. 2. Conservative/Religious: Two subclusters are focused primarily on religious issues; the other sub-cluster is on politics and current affairs. 3. Persian Poetry and Literature. 4. Mixed Networks" (Ludtke 45).

6. Other critics suggest that "Religious blogs of various kinds are expanding too. There are more than 3,000 blogs registered on persianblog as religious. The second biggest weblog provider in Iran also lists over 3,000 blogs as dealing with ideas and religion. Mihanblog, another weblog service provider, even offers the domain name of muslimblog.ir. Parsiblog was launched in 2005 with the aim of promoting and encouraging religious blogs and currently hosts around 4000 blogs" (Sreberny and Khiabany 282).

7. As Jared Cohen explains, "The Internet is

growing in Iran, and while owning a computer remains the luxury of the upper classes, the growing number of Internet cafes has made the Internet widely accessible to a broad swath of Iranians. The Internet is a place where Iranian youth can operate freely, express themselves, and obtain information of their own terms" (56). Alavi also argues that blogging "provides a safe space in which people may write freely on a wide variety of topics, from the most serious and urgent to the most frivolous. Some prominent writers use their blogs to bypass strict state censorship and to publish their work on-line; established journalists can post uncensored reports on their blogs; expatriate Iranians worldwide use their blogs to communicate with those back home; ordinary citizens record their thoughts and deeds in daily journals; and student groups and NGOs utilize their blogs as a means of coordinating their activities" (1).

8. Dayem further explains, "Since the turn of the century, when blogging started taking a foothold in Iranian society, Tehran has detained dozens — and possibly hundreds — of bloggers. Some were held for months before being acquitted, but others have had to serve lengthy prison terms. What is most peculiar is that those who feel the wrath of the state often don't fit the mold of the pro–Western, anticlerical youth. For instance, theology student and blogger Mojtaba Lotfi was sentenced to a multiyear prison term after he posted a sermon by renowned theologian Hossein Ali Montazeri in 2004" (43). Multiple reports suggest that an Iranian blogger, Omidreza Mirsayafi, died "under mysterious circumstances in Tehran's notorious Evin prison" ("Death to Bloggers" 16; Dayem 43). Mirsayafi was sentenced to two years in prison "for 'insulting' the Islamic Republic's leaders," and he was also sentenced to an additional six months in prison for "publicity against the government" ("Death to Bloggers" 16). While prison officials claim that Mirsayafi committed suicide, many Iranians think that he was put to death. Along similar lines is the case of Hossein Derakhshan, generally thought to be the Iranian "blogfather" due to his "development of a guide and a piece of software that enabled Farsi speakers to blog in their native tongue without having to resort to transliteration in the Roman alphabet." Presumably due to his critical views about the Islamic Regime, Derakhshan's blog was banned by the Islamic Regime, but "his articles have been published by many international publications, including *The Guardian* and *The New York Times*" (Dayem 43). He was arrested in late 2008 purportedly for comments made on his blog "about a key Shi'a cleric and the third infallible Imam of Shi'ism" (Dayem 43). He has been imprisoned since then ("Iranian Political Detainee").

9. Alavi also suggests that "At the time of registering, private information such as name, family name, and identity card and telephone numbers would be recorded. This ruling indicates, among other things, the state's perception and recognition of the significance of blogging. It has, of course, produced a big response from bloggers" (276).

10. The extent to which blogging has become important to Iranians can perhaps be best illustrated through the following comment by an Iranian blogger: "I blog ... therefore I ... exist" (Alavi 5).

11. Similarly, Morozov argues, "In the first days after the protests, it was hard to find a television network or a newspaper (never mind the blogs) that didn't run a feature or an editorial extolling the role of Twitter in fomenting and publicizing the Iranian protests" (10).

12. Realizing the importance of Twitter as a communication tool, in June 2009 during the Iranian demonstrations, the Obama administration "asked Twitter to delay routine system maintenance that would have temporarily cut off service. Twitter complied, the demonstrations continued" ("Cyber Technologies").

13. However, as Baumann argues, "in truth, the Iranian security forces probably could have shut down Facebook and Twitter within Iran's borders, if they had chosen to do so. Instead, it is likely that they deliberately allowed the tweets and Facebook messages to get through as a means of identifying malcontents" (53). Similarly, Dayem suggests the Islamic Regime has recently introduced "new laws and technologies to regulate it [blogging]" (43). Still, he also argues that "most observers of Iran concur that the government is not trying to end or disrupt blogging per se; rather it is involved in a constantly evolving engagement with bloggers to define the boundaries of what can be said in Iran. Weblogistan remains a place where a vigorous exchange of ideas does occur — yet it is the place where the limits of free expression in Iran are being tested" (43).

14. Janet Alexanian explains, "Iranians in the United States, like many immigrant groups, have been active in using media to create a sense of community, share information, react to events in Iran, and articulate their identities and particular experiences in a new country" (134).

15. As Alexanian describes, "Iranian websites such as Iranian.com and Persianmirror.com attract almost half a million unique viewers monthly and post new submissions every day" (135). In addition, Alexanian suggests that "websites such as Iranian.com have functioned as a kind of virtual community, one that has served the needs of Iranian Immigrants dealing within feelings of displacement and longing and, at the same time, allowed for the public expression of feelings that have generally been seen as belonging to the private realm" (130).

16. Dayem suggests that there are two main reasons why there has been a significant increase in the number of Iranian blogs. First, "the ability of women, ethnic minorities, and other otherwise marginalized groups — not to mention print journalists who have lost their jobs due to newspaper closures — to express themselves with relative freedom cannot be overstated." The second reason is the "high rates of Internet penetration coupled with a highly literate and very young population (70 percent of Iran's population is under 30 years of age)" (42).

17. While www.iraniansblogs.com may contain the largest number of Iranian blogs written in English, one of the most popular websites for Iranian bloggers and independent journalists is the U.S.–based site Balatarin or http://balatarin.com/en. According to the site, "Many Iranian bloggers rely on Balatarin for publicizing their articles. Balatarin's 35 million page views is an indicator of its success in bringing a lot of audience for what bloggers produce. There have been more than half a million story submissions to Balatarin. Users have left more than 8 million comments so far" ("About Balatarin," par. 8). They also suggest, "Balatarin also is a place where a number of Iranian-born journalists and bloggers are present and directly talk to their audience" (par. 9). While Balatarin suggests that they are "testing a new service to translate its stories to English," very few of the links are in English, making it virtually impossible for a reader to utilize Balatarin unless she or he has at least a rudimentary knowledge of Farsi (par. 6).

18. A good example of this kind of blog is "I Am an Iranian Daughter" (http://iraniandoughter.blogspot.com/), written by Eftekhar (presumably her user name). "I Am an Iranian Daughter" details Eftekhar's life as a graduate student, and she also provides the reader with a general introduction to her family as well as to Iran and Iranian customs. Her innocuous entries do not indicate that she is anything other than a well-adjusted, although generally apolitical, young adult.

19. A good example of this kind of blog is "Faith Today" (http://cyberfaith.blogspot.com/), with its impressively precocious entries by a young Iranian (born in 1991) named Kourosh Ziabari (if the blog is accurate). Ziabari's blog contains a number of entries about subjects such as sanctions against Iran, interviews with academics, and accounts of lesser known areas of Iran such as Giulan, as well as pro–Palestinian blogs. It is hard to know, as is the case with most blogs, the extent to which Ziabari's descriptions (the more objective ones) are generally reliable or accurate, and he does not typically use multimedia forms (e.g., streaming video and pictures) to back up his claims and information.

20. Another similar blog is "Brooding Persian" (http://broodingpersian.blogspot.com/), which was active from 2003 to 2009, with a peak in entries during 2005. This blog was also highly critical of the Islamic Regime, perhaps best evident in the final entry from August 2009, which begins with: "The Reigning Imbecility in Iran has been up to its old despicable tricks again, and is conducting show trails [*sic*] and broadcasting taped forced confessions on TV" (par. 1).

21. This account is corroborated by a story in ADN Kronos International (AKI); however, in this story, one is identified as a "convicted robber" and the other as an "accomplice" ("Iran: Four Hanged"). While this doesn't make the punishment any better, it is evidence that the author of the blog, at least in this case, wanted to either hold the Islamic Republic culpable or demonize it.

22. Kamangar was executed in May 2010 (Valadbaygi).

23. According to an article in France 24 International, also arrested at this time were four other accused members of "the Kurdish rebel group, PJAK (The Party of Free Life of Kurdistan)." The Islamic Regime convicted the five "of being 'moharebs' or 'enemies of God' — a crime punishable by death under Iran's sharia-based Islamic law," and "of carrying out terrorist acts, including bombings of government centres and public properties in several Iranian cities" (France 24).

24. See "Iran Hangs a Little Fish," *The Washington Times*, 11 May 2010, 3 Nov 2010, http://www.washingtontimes.com/news/2010/may/11/iran-hangs-a-little-fish/. In this article, the *Washington Times* suggests that Kamangar was "wrongly accused of being a terrorist by the Islamic regime in Tehran," that he "spent almost four years of physical and mental torture in Iran's prison system," and that his ultimate "crime was being a Kurd" (par. 1).

25. For instance, an entry for May 2, 2010, notes that "women cracked his nerves so bad that he hung his (c)ondoms for good" (par.1), while an entry for April 25, 2010, comments, "Wasn't even scared of God! The only thing he feared in life was her missed periods" (par. 1).

26. "Tehran Post" may be referring to the claims made by the Bush administration around August 2007 that the Iranians had been supplying Iraqi insurgents with weapons (Jackson A10).

27. There is also some support for this claim as well (at least from the time of the entry in August 2007 when "some legislators," accusing "Saudi Arabia, in particular, of 'tacit approval' for Islamist terrorism." These legislators included "Zalmay Khalilzad, America's representative to the United Nations," who "recently hinted that Saudi support for some Sunni political parties in Iraq has weakened the Shia-dominated, American-backed government" ("Arming Its Friends" 40).

28. In more detail, "Tehran Post" writes, "yes. once again the same old story. Israel does whatever it wants, the world turns blind, and just another nightmare for Palestinians. 300 people killed. But who cares? they were a bunch of radical muslim terrorists, better to be wiped off the earth. bad bad palestinians. they are an existential threat to us, we democrat, refined, prosperous, lived-in-this-land-since-Adam Israelis" (par. 2).

29. Specifically, "Tehran Post" writes that, "even reading a short piece news from Ahmadinejadist websites and newspapers is a real torture for me. standing all their audacity and hypocrisy truly needs nerves of steel, and i can't understand how brazenly they can deny realities and run all this smear campaign against people who have a (sometimes even the slightest) different point of view? Pooh!" (par. 2).

30. A day of mourning for Shi'a Muslims, commemorating the death of one of Mohammad's grandchildren.

31. Specifically, "Tehran Post" describes how on the "27th of December 2009, in the day of Ashoura, people gather in Enghelab (Revolution) Street in Tehran to continue the series of protests starting since the day after the election. Clash between people and police, anti-riot forces and plain cloth agents rapidly turns into violence. In one scene, a police patrol car breaks into a crowd, killing at least two citizens. According to official reports, at least 8 people are killed, one of them Mir Hossein Musavi's nephew" (par. 2).

32. Specifically, "Under Underground" writes, "They are insisting in the news that how Bush administration couldn't help people who suffer from this disaster. I know that rescue mission was not good in Katrina hurricane. But what they try to say is that if we (as Iran government) face with this kind of disaster we were better" (par. 3).

33. Specifically, Shamshiri suggests, "I used to get loads of death threats. I should confess that I never got used to them probably because I am all for life and of course I am not religious. They were agitating, pushed me back every time and stopped me for awhile to think again and reassess my position and standing but at the end, none of them could hold me back until this time. For obvious reasons I should not go into details" (par. 5).

34. Shamshiri also claims that Ayatollah Khamenei has directly targeted the Internet and that "American authorities say they have approved a 45 million dollar budget to defeat the Islamic Republic through the Internet." He also claims that the "Iranian government agencies took it seriously and they are working measures to fight on Internet environment" (par. 2).

35. A good example of this kind of blog is "For a Democratic Secular Iran," written by Azarmehr, an Iranian living in England (http://azarmehr.blogspot.com/).

# Works Cited

Abdelkarim, Riad Z. "American Muslims and 9/11: A Community Looks Back ... and to the Future." *Washington Report on Middle East Affairs* 21.7 (2002): 82–84.

_____. "Arab and Muslim Americans: Collateral Damage in the Wars on Terrorism, Iraq." *Report on Middle East Affairs* 22.4 (2003): 55–57.

"About Azadeh." *Azadeh Moaveni*. 12 Oct 2010. http://www.azadeh.info/?page_id=2.

"About Balatarin." *Balatarin*. n.d. 17 Oct 2010. http://balatarin.com/about.

"About Firoozeh Dumas." *Firoozeh Dumas-Bio* 2007. 15 Aug 2010. http://firoozehdumas.com/about-firoozeh-dumas/.

"About the Sami Rohn Prize." *Jewish Book Council*. 13 Aug 2010. http://www.jewishbookcouncil.org/page.php?22.

"The Adventures of Mr. Behi." 21 July 2010. 2 Oct 2010. http://mrbehi.blogs.com.

_____. 16 Feb 2010. 2 Oct 2010. http://mrbehi.blogs.com.

_____. 29 June 2009. 2 Oct 2010. http://mrbehi.blogs.com.

_____. 14 June 2009. 2 Oct 2010. http://mrbehi.blogs.com.

_____. 8 June 2009. 2 Oct 2010. http://mrbehi.blogs.com.

_____. 6 Feb 2009. 2 Oct 2010. http://mrbehi.blogs.com.

Afshar, Koorosh. "The Burnt Generation." *National Review Online*, 12 June 2003. 30 June 2009. www.nationalreview.com/comments/comment-afshar061203.asp 10 June 2009.

Afshin-Jam, Nazanin. "Someday." *The Poetry of Iranian Women*. Ed. Sheema Kalbasi. Reel Content Publishing (www.reelcontent.org), 2009. 21–22.

Ahmadinejad, Mahmoud. "President Ahmadinejad Delivers Remarks at Columbia University." *The Washington Post Online*, 24 Sept 2007. 11 May 2009. http://www.washingtonpost.com/wpdyn/content/article/2007/09/24/AR2007092401042.html.

Alavi, Nasrin. *We are Iran: The Persian Blogs*. Brooklyn: Soft Skull Press, 2005.

Alexanian, Janet A. "Publicly Intimate Online: Iranian Web Logs in Southern California." *Comparative Studies of South Asia, Africa and the Middle East* 26.1 (2006): 134–145.

Alfoneh, Ali. "Mixed Response in Iran." *Middle East Quarterly* 18.3 (2011): 35–39.

Amini, Asieh. "Battle of the Blogs." *New Statesman* 137.4913 (2008): 34–35.

Armengol-Carrera, Josep M. "Where Are Fathers in American Literature? Re-visiting Fatherhood in U.S. Literary History." *Journal of Men's Studies* 16.2 (2008): 211–226.

"Arming Its Friends and Talking Peace." *Economist* 384.8540 (2007): 39–40.

Asayesh, Gelareh. "I Grew Up Thinking I Was White." *My Sister, Guard Your Veil; My Brother, Guard Your Eyes*. Ed. Lila Azam Zanganeh. Boston: Beacon Press, 2006. 12–19.

Associated Press. "US Will One Day 'Beg' Iran for Ties: Ahmadinejad." *Hindustan Times*, 18 Oct 2010. 28 Oct 2010. http://www.hindustantimes.com/US-will-one-day-beg-Iran-for-ties-Ahmadinejad/Article1-614565.aspx.

Azarmina, Pejman. "In Iran, Gender Segregation Becoming a Fact of Medical Life." *CMAJ: Canadian Medical Association Journal* 166.5 (2002): 645–647.

Azlan, Reza. "From Here to Mullahcracy." *My Sister, Guard Your Veil; My Brother, Guard Your Eyes*. Ed. Lila Azam Zanganeh. Boston: Beacon Press, 2006. 24–29.

_____. *No God But God*. New York: Random House, 2005.

Baer, Robert. *The Devil We Know*. New York: Crown Publishers, 2008.

Baghramian, Maria. "Censorship and Sensibility." *Irish Times*, 8 Aug 2009. 15 Apr 2010. http://www.irishtimes.com/newspaper/weekend/2009/0808/1224252206052.html.

Bahari, Maziar. "118 Days, 12 Hours, 54 Minutes." *Newsweek*, 21 Nov 2009. 23 Feb 2010. http://www.newsweek.com/id/223862.

Bahramitash, Roksana. "The War on Terror, Feminist Orientalism and Orientalist Feminism." *Critique: Critical Middle Eastern Studies* 14.2 (2005): 221–235.

Bakalian, Anny, and Bozorgmehr, Mehdi. "Muslim American Mobilization." *Diaspora: A Journal of Transnational Studies* 14.1 (2005): 7–43.

Baker, Peter, and Kesler, Glenn. "U.S. Campaign Is Aimed at Iran's Leaders." *The Washington Post,* 13 Mar 2006. A01.

Baumann, Michael. "A Political Revolution Goes Viral ... Not So Fast." *Information Today* 26.9 (2009): 51–54.

Bayoumi, Moustafa. "Arab America's September 11." 8 Sept 2006. 12 Feb 2011. http://www.thenation.com/article/arab-americas-september-11.

Bearman, Joshua. "Interview with Marjane Satrapi." *The Believer.* Aug 2006. 9 June 2009 http://www.believermag.com/issues/200608/?read=interview_satrapi.

Benson, Heidi. "An Irreverent Memoir Gains Toehold in Iran, Despite Censors." *San Francisco Chronicle,* 3 Feb 2007. Daily Datebook, E1.

Bigonah, Roshanak. "If the Earth Was a Farm." *The Poetry of Iranian Women.* Ed. Sheema Kalbasi. Reel Content Publishing (www.reelcontent.org), 2009. 42.

"Bingala." n.d. 28 Sept 2010. http://bingala.blogspot.com/.

_____. 28 June 2010. 28 Sept 2010. http://bingala.blogspot.com/search?updated-max=2010-0710T14%3A38%3A00%2B04%3A30&max-results=30.

_____. 20 June 2010. 28 Sept 2010. http://bingala.blogspot.com/search?updated-max=201007-10T14%3A38%3A00%2B04%3A30&max-results=30.

_____. 2 May 2010. 1 Oct 2010. http://bingala.blogspot.com/search?updated-max=2010-0710T14%3A38%3A00%2B04%3A30&max-results=30.

_____. 25 Apr 2010. 1 Oct 2010. http://bingala.blogspot.com/search?updated-max=2010-0710T14%3A38%3A00%2B04%3A30&max-results=30.

_____. 23 Feb 2010. 29 Sept 2010. http://bingala.blogspot.com/search?updated-max=201003-28T09%3A02%3A00%2B04%3A30&max-results=30.

_____. 11 Feb 2010. 29 Sept 2010. http://bingala.blogspot.com/search?updated-max=201003-28T09%3A02%3A00%2B04%3A30&max-results=30.

_____. 20 Jan 2010. 30 Sept 2010. http://bingala.blogspot.com/search?updated-max=2010-0328T09%3A02%3A00%2B04%3A30&max-results=30.

_____. 3 Jan 2010. 1 Oct 2010. http://bingala.blogspot.com/search?updated-max=2010-0105T15%3A32%3A00%2B03%3A30&max-results=30.

_____. 5 Dec 2009. 1 Oct 2010. http://bingala.blogspot.com/search?updated-max=2010-0105T15%3A32%3A00%2B03%3A30&max-results=30.

_____. 10 Nov 2009. 1 Oct 2010. http://bingala.

blogspot.com/search?updated-max=2010-0105T15%3A32%3A00%2B03%3A30&max-results=30.

_____. 13 May 2009. 1 Oct 2010. http://bingala.blogspot.com/search?updated-max=2009-0620T14%3A30%3A00%2B04%3A30&max-results=30.

Block, Allison. "My Life as a Traitor." *Booklist* 104.19/20 (2008): 118.

Bone, James. "Documentary Exposes 'Plot' by Academics." *The Times* (United Kingdom), 17 July 2009.

Bordewich, Fergus. "Veiled Threat." Smithsonian 34.8 (2003): 118–119.

Brison, Susan. "Trauma Narratives and the Remaking of the Self." *Acts of Memory.* Ed. Mieke Bal, Jonathan Crewe, and Leo Spitzer. Hanover, NH: University Press of New England, 1999.

Brooding Persian. 8 Aug 2009. 27 Oct 2010. http://broodingpersian.blogspot.com/search?updated-min=2009-01-01T00%3A00%3A00-08%3A00&updated-max=2010-01-01T00%3A00%3A00-08%3A00&max-results=4.

Brown, L. Carl. "My Prison, My Home: One Woman's Story of Captivity in Iran." *Foreign Affairs* 89.2 (2010): 169.

Buchan, James. "Veiled Threats." *The Guardian,* 1 Mar 2008. 22 Feb 2010. http://www.guardian.co.uk/books/2008/mar/01/featuresreviews.guardianreview26

Burke, Daniel. "Poll: 1 in 10 Think Obama Is Muslim." *USA Today,* 1 Apr 2008. 15 Oct 2010. http://www.usatoday.com/news/religion/2008-04-01-obama-muslim_N.htm.

Burns, John F., and Somaiya, Ravi. "WikiLeaks Founder on the Run, Trailed by Notoriety." New York Times, 23 Oct 2010. 27 Oct 2010. http://www.nytimes.com/2010/10/24/world/24assange.html.

Bush, George W. "State of the Union Address." CNN.com, 29 Jan 2002. 10 May 2009. http://archives.cnn.com/2002/ALLPOLITICS/01/29/bush.speech.txt/.

Butler, Kiera. "Thirty Days in Iran's Worst Prison." *Mother Jones,* 4 Jan 2008. 27 Apr 2010. http://motherjones.com/politics/2008/01/thirty-days-irans-worst-prison.

Byrd, Christopher. "Reading Lolita in Tehran." *Wilson Quarterly* 27.3 (2003): 126–127.

Campbell, Eddie. "What Is a Graphic Novel?" *World Literature Today* 81.2 (2007): 13.

Chin, Frank, and Chan, Jeffrey Paul. "Racist Love." View Larger Image *Seeing Through Shuck.* Ed. Richard Kostelanetz. New York: Ballantine Books, 1972. 65–79.

Chittick, William. "The Pluralistic Vision of Persian Sufi Poetry." *Islam and Christian Muslim Relations* 14.4 (2003): 423–429.

Clawson, Patrick. "My Life as a Traitor." *Middle East Quarterly* 15.3 (2008): 88–89.

"CNNIC Releases 2007 Survey Report on China

Weblog Market Number of Blog Writers Reaches 47 million Equaling One Fourth of Total Netizens." China Internet Network Information Center. 27 Dec 2007. 12 Sept 2010. http://www.cnnic.cn/html/Dir/2007/12/27/4954.htm.

Coetzee, J.M. *Giving Offence: Essays on Censorship.* Chicago: The University of Chicago Press, 1996.

Cohen, Jared. *Children of Jihad.* New York: Gotham Press, 2007.

Cooper, Julie. "Funny in Farsi." Random House Inc. Academic Resources. 15 Aug 2010. http://www.randomhouse.com/acmart/catalog/display.pperl?isbn=9780812968378&view=tg.

Costantino, Manuela. "Marji: Popular Commix Heroine Breathing Life into the Writing of History." *Canadian Review of American Studies* 38.3 (2008): 429–447.

"Counterterrorism in the Obama Administration: Tactics and Strategy." Woodrow Wilson International Center for Scholars. 2 Apr 2010. 27 May 2010. http://www.wilsoncenter.org/ondemand/index.cfm?fuseaction=media.play&mediaid=1782996E-F794-8311-AFD1DC4E64A713AC.

"Cyber Technologies Encourage Long-Wanted Change to Iran." *Newsday* (Melville, NY), 19 Jun 2009.

Dabashi, Hamid. *Iran: A People Interrupted.* New York: The New Press, 2007.

_____. "Native Informers and the Making of the American Empire." Al-Ahram. 1–7 June 2006. 8 Mar 2011. http://afpakwar.com/blog/archives/2611.

Darznik, Jasmin. "The Perils and Seductions of Home: Return Narratives of the Iranian Diaspora." *MELUS* 33.2 (2008): 55–71.

Davaran, Ardavan. "Iranian Diaspora Literature Since 1980: Contexts and Currents." *The Literary Review* 40.1 (1996): 5–13.

Davis, Dick. "Spells to Fascinate the Angel Gabriel: On Classic Persian Poetry." Parnassus: Poetry in Review 25.1/2 (2001): 146–175.

Dayem, Mohamed Abdel. "Attempting to Silence Iran's 'Weblogistan.'" *Nieman Reports* 63.2 (2009): 42–44.

"Death to Bloggers." *The Washington Times,* 23 Mar 2009: 16.

DePaul, Amy. "Re-Reading Reading Lolita in Tehran." MELUS 33.2 (2008): 73–92.

"Development: Global Sponsors." Woodrow Wilson International Center for Scholars. 11 Aug 2010. http://www.wilsoncenter.org/index.cfm?fuseaction=awards.sponsors.

Dilanian, Ken. "Iran: 2-State Solution Possible." *USA Today,* 27 Apr 2009. A08.

Dimock, Michael. "Belief That Obama Is Muslim Is Durable, Bipartisan — but Most Likely to Sway Democratic Votes." Pew Research Center Publications. 15 July 2008. 17 Nov 2010, http://pewresearch.org/pubs/898/belief-that-obama-is-muslim-is-bipartisan-but-most-likely-to-sway-democrats.

Donadey, Anne, and Ahmed-Ghosh, Huma. "Why Americans Love Azar Nafisi's Reading Lolita in Tehran." Signs: Journal of Women in Culture & Society 33.3 (2008): 623–646.

Dumas, Firoozeh. "A Spoonful of Humor Gets the Pages Turning." *Firoozeh Dumas — For Educators.* 12 June 2010. http://firoozehdumas.com/educator-guide/.

_____. *Funny in Farsi: A Memoir of Growing Up Iranian in America.* New York: Villard, 2003.

_____. *Laughing Without an Accent.* New York: Villard, 2008.

Dunk, Malina. "Lipstick Jihad." *Iranian Studies* 41.2 (2008): 251–253.

Ebadi, Shirin. *Iran Awakening.* New York: Random House, 2006.

_____. "Shirin Ebadi's Nobel Prize Speech." Muslim Women's League. 10 Dec 2003. 23 Feb 2009. http://www.mwlusa.org/news/shirin_ebadi_acceptance_speech.htm.

Edwards, David, and Brynaert, Ron. "Unplugged McCain Sings 'Bomb Bomb Bomb, Bomb Bomb Iran.'" *The Raw Story,* 19 April 2007. 6 Jan 2010. http://www.rawstory.com/news/2007/McCain_unplugged_Bomb_bomb_bomb_bomb_0419.html.

Eisenmenger, L.E. "Boston College's Iranian Writer in Residence Mandanipour Speaks on FIFA's Ban on Headscarves." *Boston Examiner,* 9 Apr 2010. 22 May 2010. http://www.examiner.com/x-4128-Boston-Pro-Soccer-Examiner~y2010m4d9-Harvards-Iranian-writer-in-residence-Mandanipour-speaks-on-FIFAs-ban-on-headscarves.

Elliott, Andrea. "Muslims in America: Creating a New Beat." *Nieman Reports* 61.2 (2007): 55–56.

Emerson, Gloria. "The Other Iran." *Nation* 276.23 (2003): 11–12.

Esfandiari, Haleh. *My Prison, My Home: One Woman's Story of Captivity in Iran.* New York: Ecco Press, 2009.

Fang, Bay, and Whitelaw, Kevin. "Talking the Talk to Tehran." *U.S. News & World Report* 135.1 (2003): 20–22.

Farjami, Leila. "The Balloons in Declaration of War." *The Poetry of Iranian Women.* Ed. Sheema Kalbasi. Reel Content Publishing (www.reelcontent.org), 2009. 12–13.

Filkins, Dexter. "Iran Is Said to Give Top Karzai Aide Cash by the Bagful." *New York Times,* 23 Oct 2010. 12 Dec 2010. http://www.nytimes.com/2010/10/24/world/asia/24afghan.html?_r=1&hp.

Flanigen, Bill. "Iranian Rebellion Grows on the Web." *Reason* 41.6 (2009): 14.

Forbes, Clark. "Girls Score Over Sexism." Sunday Herald Sun (Melbourne), 8 Oct 2006. E08.

Foucault, Michel. *Discipline and Punish: The Birth of the Modern Prison.* New York: Vintage, 1977.

Friedl, Erika. "New Friends: Gender Relations within the Family." *Iranian Studies* 42.1 (2009): 27–43.

"Funny in Farsi." *Kirkus Reviews* 71.9 (2003): 654–655.

"*Funny in Farsi*—Author Interview." Random House, Inc. 15 Aug 2010. http://www.random house.com/catalog/display.pperl?isbn=978030 7430991&view=auqa.

Gannon, Martin. *Paradoxes of Culture and Globalization.* Los Angeles: Sage Publications, 2008.

Ghahramani, Zarah. *My Life as a Traitor.* New York: Farrar, Straus, and Giroux, 2008.

Gilderhorn, Joseph B., and Hamilton, Lee H. "The Ordeal of Haleh Esfandiari." *Wilson Quarterly* 31.3 (2007): 6.

Gonyea, Don. "Jesting, McCain Sings: 'Bomb, Bomb, Bomb' Iran." National Public Radio. 20 April 2007. 7 Jan 2011. http://www.npr.org/templates/story/story.php?storyId=9688222.

Gonzalez, Rigoberto. "Small Press Spotlight: Roger Sedarat." *Small Press,* 16 Mar 2008. 6 July 2009. http://bookcriticscircle.blogspot.com/2008/03/small-press-spotlight-roger-sedarat.html.

"Good News: Iranian Sisters Have Their Sentence of Death by Stoning Overturned." *Amnesty International* 29 Oct 2008. 1 Sept 2010. http://www.amnesty.org.au/adp/com ments/18635/.

Gordon, Michael R., and Lehren, Andrew W. "Leaked Reports Detail Iran's Aid for Iraqi Militias." *New York Times,* 23 Oct 2010. 27 Oct 2010. http://www.nytimes.com/2010/10/23/world/middleeast/23iran.html?scp=2&sq=%22iran%22&st=nyt.

"Graphic Novel by the Numbers." *Publishers Weekly* 254.10 (2007): 9.

Grossman, Lev. "The Moment." *Time* 173.25 (2009): 9.

Hakakian, Roya. *Journey from the Land of No.* New York: Crown Publishers, 2004.

Hamilton, Sorcha. "Eight Months in Iran's Notorious Evin Jail." *Irish Times,* 28 Jan 2010.

Harrison, Frances. "Women Graduates Challenge Iran." *BBC News, Tehran,* 19 Sept 2006. 12 Aug 2010. http://news.bbc.co.uk/2/hi/mid dle_east/5359672.stm.

Hassanzadeh, Farideh. "Matrimony." *The Poetry of Iranian Women.* Ed. Sheema Kalbasi. Reel Content Publishing (www.reelcontent.org), 2009, 90.

Hattenstone, Simon. "Confessions of Miss Mischief." *Guardian UK,* 29 March 2008. 9 June 2009. http://www.guardian.co.uk/film/2009/mar/29/biography.

Havemann, Judith. "Ordeal in Iran." *Wilson Quarterly* 32.1 (2008): 45–49.

Hewett, Heather. "Reading Lolita in Tehran." *Christian Science Monitor* 95.99 (2003): 21.

Hickey, Dave. "Pagans." *Art in America* 96.9 (2008): 37–38.

Hillman, Robert. "Beyond Pity." *Griffith Review* 15 (2007): 1–9.

Hoffert, Barbara. "Censoring an Iranian Love Story." *Library Journal* 134.7 (2009): 85.

Hosenball, Mark. "Wired for a Revolution." *Newsweek* 153.26 (2009): 14.

Houshmand, Zara. "Invitation to the Hungry Ghosts." *The Poetry of Iranian Women.* Ed. Sheema Kalbasi. Reel Content Publishing (www.reelcontent.org), 2009. 5.

Hout, Syrine C. "Memory, Home, and Exile in Contemporary Anglophone Lebanese Fiction." *Critique* 46.3 (2005): 219–233.

"How Ahmad Batebi Survived Torture in Iran." *60 Minutes,* 5 Apr 2009. 12 June 2010. http://www.cbsnews.com/stories/2009/04/03/60mi nutes/main4917310.shtml.

Huntley, Kristine. "*Funny in Farsi: A Memoir of Growing Up Iranian in America.*" *Booklist* 99.19/20 (2003): 1731–1732.

"Iran: Abusive Husband's Testimony Leads to Stoning Sentence for Sisters." *Off Our Backs* 37.4 (2007): 6.

"Iran: Four Hanged, Thief's Hand and Leg Amputated." ADN Kronos International. 14 Apr 2009. 30 Oct 2010. http://www.adnkronos.com/AKI/English/Security/?id=3.1.250839768.

"Iran Hangs a Little Fish." *The Washington Times,* 11 May 2010. 3 Nov 2010. http://www.washingtontimes.com/news/2010/may/11/iran-hangs-a-little-fish/.

"Iran Hangs Woman, Four Other 'Enemies of God.'" *France 24: International News 24/7.* 9 May 2010. 1 Nov 2010. http://www.france24.com/en/20100509-iran-hangs-woman-four-other-enemies-god.

"Iran Has No Capacity for Reforms; Gozaar Interviews Ahmad Batebi." Gozaar: A Forum on Human Rights and Democracy in Iran. 29 Oct 2008. 12 Apr 2010. http://www.gozaar.org/english/interview-en/Iran-Has-No-Capacity-for-Reforms.html.

"Iran: Over 400 Women Protest Constitutional Sexism." *Off Our Backs* 35.5/6: 7.

"Iranian Political Detainee Gets His First Trial." Radio Zamaneh in English. 23 Jun 2010. 17 Dec 2010. http://www.zamaaneh.com/enzam/2010/06/iranian-political-detaine-1.html.

"Iranian Woman Faces Death by Stoning." *The Jerusalem Post,* 30 June 2010. 1 Sept 2010. http://www.jpost.com/MiddleEast/Article.aspx?id=180005.

Italie, Hillel. "Palin Book Sales: She's No Bill Clinton." *Huffington Post,* 23 Nov 2009. 23 Sept 2010. http://www.huffingtonpost.com/2009/11/23/palin-book-sales-shes-no_n_368 549.html.

Izadi, Dina; Araste, Afshin Moseni; and Fadaei, Azita Seied. "Activities to Attract Girls to Physics in Iran." *AIP Conference Proceedings* 1119.1 (2009): 122–123.

Jackson, David. "Bush Aims to Halt Iranians from Arming Iraqis." *USA Today*, 29 Aug 2007: A10.

Javanshir, Maryam. "Who's the 'We' in We Are Iran?" *Journal of International Affairs* 60.2 (2007): 213–218.

Kakutani, Michiko. "*Reading Lolita in Tehran*." *New York Times*, 15 Apr 2003. 12 Jan 2010. http://query.nytimes.com/gst/fullpage.html?res=9C04E7DC103BF936A25757C0A9659C8B63&scp=1&sq=reading%20lolita%20in%20tehran&st=cse.

_____. "Where Romance Requires Courage." *New York Times*, 29 June 2009. 22 June 2010. http://www.nytimes.com/2009/06/30/books/30kaku.html.

Kalbasi, Sheema. *Echoes in Exile*. Martinez, GA: PRA Publishing, 2006.

_____. "Kaddish." *The Poetry of Iranian Women*. Ed. Sheema Kalbasi. Reel Content Publishing (www.reelcontent.org), 2009. 9.

_____, ed. *The Poetry of Iranian Women*. Reel Content Publishing (www.reelcontent.org), 2009.

Kaminer, Debra. "Healing Processes in Trauma Narratives: A Review." *South African Journal of Psychology* 36.3 (2006): 481–499.

Kaplan, Hasan. "Muslims in America and the Question of Identity: Between Ethnic Heritage, Islamic Values, and the American Way." *Ekev Academic Review* 11.32 (2007): 1–10.

Karim, Persis, ed. *Let Me Tell You Where I've Been*. Fayetteville: The University of Arkansas Press, 2006.

Karim, Persis, and Khorrami, Mohammad, eds. *A World Between*. New York: George Braziller, 1999.

Karim, Persis, and Rahimieh, Nasrin. "Introduction: Writing Iranian Americans into the American Literature Canon." *MELUS* 33.2 (2008): 7–16.

Karimi-Hakkak, Ahmed. "Speaking to the Jasmine, a Scythe in Hand: A Selection of Modern Persian Poetry." *Parnassus: Poetry in Review* 25.1/2 (2001): 211–229.

Kaya, Ilhan. "Identity Across Generations: A Turkish American Case Study." *Middle East Journal* 63.4 (2009): 617–632.

Kaye, Dalia Dassa, and Wehrey, Frederic. "Arab Spring, Persian Winter." *Foreign Affairs* 90.4 (2011): 183–186.

Kazemzadeh, Firuz. "The Baha'is in Iran: Twenty Years of Repression." *Social Research* 67.2 (2000): 537–538.

Keshavarz, Fatemeh. *Jasmine and Stars: Reading More than Lolita in Tehran*. Chapel Hill: University of North Carolina Press, 2007.

Khakpour, Porochista. *Sons and Other Flammable Objects*. New York: Grove Press, 2007.

_____. "What I Saw at the Revolution." *The Daily Beast*, 11 Feb 2009. 14 Oct 2010. http://www.thedailybeast.com/blogs-and-stories/2009-02-11/what-i-saw-at-the-revolution/.

Kutschera, Chris. "Every Picture Tells a Story." *Middle East* 322.49 (2002): 49–50.

Lamb, Christina. "I Would Not Let Them Break Me." *The Sunday Times*, 3 Jan 2010. 6.

Lagerfeld, Steven. "A Prisoner in Iran." *Wilson Quarterly* 31.3 (2007): 2.

"*Laughing Without an Accent*." *Kirkus Reviews* 76.5 (2008): 228.

Leavitt, Caroline. "My Life Is a Traitor" *People* 69.3 (2008): 58.

Levine, Michael. *Writing Through Repression*. Baltimore: The Johns Hopkins Press, 1994.

Lewitt, Adam. "A Hundred Million Blogs." *New Statesman* 137.4908 (2008): 29.

"Lipstick Jihad." Kirkus Reviews 73.2 (2005): 106.

Lopez, Tiffany Ana. "Critical Witnessing in Latina/o and African American Prison Narratives." *Prose and Cons: Essays on Prison Literature in the United States*. Ed. D. Quentin Miller. Jefferson, NC: McFarland, 2005.

Ludtke, Melissa. "Publishing and Mapping Iran's Weblogistan." *Nieman Reports* 63.2 (2009): 45.

Lumsden, Michael. "*Lipstick Jihad*: An Interview with Azadeh Moaveni." *Mother Jones*, 9 Mar 2005. 12 May 2009. http://motherjones.com/politics/2005/03/lipstick-jihad-interview-azadeh-moaveni.

Lydon, Christopher. "Shariar Mandanipour: The 'Love Cure' for Iran." Radio Open Source. 24 July 2009. 11 Apr 2010. http://www.radioopensource.org/shahriar-mandanipour-the-love-cure-for-iran/.

Lyons, Stephen. "Lolita in Tehran Lifts a Veil on Oppression." *USA Today*, 23 May 2003. D05.

Malek, Amy. "Memoir as Iranian Exile Cultural Production: A Case Study of Marjane Satrapi's *Persepolis* Series. *Iranian Studies* 39.3 (2006): 353–80.

Mandanipour, Shariar. *Censoring an Iranian Love Story*. New York: Knopf, 2009.

Masliyah, Sadok. "Persian Jewry — Prelude to a Catastrophe." *Judaism* 29.4 (1980): 390–403.

"Middle East Center." Woodrow Wilson International Center for Scholars. 22 Aug 2010. http://www.wilsoncenter.org/index.cfm?topic_id=1426&fuseaction=topics.intro.

Miller, D. Quentin, ed. *Prose and Cons: Essays on Prison Literature in the United States*. Jefferson, NC: McFarland, 2005.

Moaveni, Azadeh. *Honeymoon in Tehran*. New York: Random House, 2009.

_____. "Letter from Tehran: Seeking Signs of Literary Life." *New York Times*, 27 May 2007. 14 Aug 2010. http://query.nytimes.com/gst/

fullpage.html?res=9F05E4DA1031F934A1575 6C0A9619C8B63&sec=&spon=&pagewant ed=all.

_____. *Lipstick Jihad*. New York: Public Affairs, 2005.

Mobasherat, Mitra. "Iranian Reporter, Sentenced in Absentia, Lashes Out Against Regime." CNN World. 21 May 2010. 27 Aug 2010. http://www.cnn.com/2010/WORLD/meast/05/20/iran.journalist.sentence/.

Mokhtarian, Arezou. "Tonight." *The Poetry of Iranian Women*. Ed. Sheema Kalbasi. Reel Content Publishing (www.reelcontent.org), 2009. 46.

Momeny, Leyla. "Persian Princess Insania." *Let Me Tell You Where I've Been*. Ed. Persis Karim. Fayetteville: The University of Arkansas Press, 2006. 442–443.

Moore, Debra. "*Funny in Farsi*." *Library Journal* 128.6 (2003): 108–109.

Morozov, Evgeny. "Iran: Downside to the 'Twitter Revolution.'" *Dissent* 56.4 (2009): 10–14.

Mostyn, Trevor. *Censorship in Islamic Societies*. London: Saqi Books, 2002.

Motlagh, Amy. "Towards a Theory of Iranian American Life Writing." *MELUS* 33.2 (2008): 17–36.

Mozaffari, Nahid, and Karimi-Hakkak, Ahmad, eds. *Strange Times in Persia*. London: I.B. Tauris, 2009.

Muedini, Fait. "Muslim American College Youth: Attitudes and Responses Five Years After 9/11." *Muslim World* 99.1 (2009): 39–59.

Munson, Sam. "The Book Club." *Commentary* 116.2 (2003): 72–74.

"*My Life as a Traitor*." *Kirkus Reviews* 75.21 (2007): 1140.

Nafisi, Azar. Reading Lolita in Tehran. New York: Random House, 2003.

_____. "The Stuff That Dreams Are Made of." *My Sister, Guard Your Veil; My Brother, Guard Your Eyes*. Ed. Lila Azam Zanganeh. Boston: Beacon Press, 2006. 1–11.

Naghibi, Nima, and O'Malley, Andrew. "Estranging the Familiar: 'East' and 'West' in Satrapi's *Persepolis*." *ESC: English Studies in Canada* 31.2–3 (2005): 223–247.

"New Faculty in English." Bucknell University. 14 Aug 2010. http://www.bucknell.edu/x37399.xml.

Notkin, Debbie. "Growing up Graphic." *Women's Review of Books* 20.9 (2003): 8–16.

Parsons, Claudia. "Accused of Anti-Semitism, Ahmadinejad Meets Jews." Reuters. 24 Sept 2008. 13 Aug 2010. http://www.reuters.com/article/2008/09/25/us-un-assembly-iran-jews int-idUSTRE48O00E20080925.

Pena, Aisha. "American Muslims' Civil Liberties and the Challenge to Effectively Avert Xenophobia." *Muslim World* 99.1 (2009): 202–220.

Peterson, Scott. "In Ahmadinejad's Iran, Jews Still Find a Space." *Christian Science Monitor* 99.106 (2007): 1–4.

Pevere, Geoff. "Stark Study of Oppression Banned in Iran." *Toronto Star*, 9 Mar 2001.

"Politics." *Economist* 395.8682 (2010): 8.

Pomeroy, Robin. "Chavez and Ahmadinejad Say United to Change World Order." Reuters Africa. 21 Oct 2010. 28 Oct 2010. http://af.reuters.com/article/worldNews/idAFTRE69K137 20101021.

Pusateri, Chris. "Sons and Other Flammable Objects." *Library Journal* 132.13 (2007): 70.

"A Q & A with Azadeh Moaveni, the Author of Lipstick Jihad." *Public Affairs*, 1 Mar 2005. 12 Apr 2010. http://www.parstimes.com/books/moaveni_qa.pdf.

Rahmani, Mehri. "With You." *The Poetry of Iranian Women*. Ed. Sheema Kalbasi. Reel Content Publishing (www.reelcontent.org), 2009. 53.

Ratliff, Ron. "Reading Lolita in Tehran." *Library Journal* 128.6 (2003): 98.

Rassapour, Mehrangiz. "Stoning." *The Poetry of Iranian Women*. Ed. Sheema Kalbasi. Reel Content Publishing (www.reelcontent.org), 2009. 32–33.

Razavain, Shirin. "Dying Young." *The Poetry of Iranian Women*. Ed. Sheema Kalbasi. Reel Content Publishing (www.reelcontent.org), 2009. 6.

"Reading Lolita in Tehran." *Kirkus Reviews* 71.4 (2003): 289–91.

Riley, Gail Blasser. *Censorship*. New York: Facts on File, 1998.

"Roger Sedarat." 6 July 2009. http://sedarat.com/home.html.

Roncevic, Mirela. "Daring to Imagine." *Library Journal* 128.6 (2003): 100–101.

Rosenberg, Scott. *Say Anything*. New York: Crown Publishers, 2009.

Rubin, Trudy. "Iran Cannot Silence Its Opposition." *The Philadelphia Inquirer*, 17 Sept 2009.

_____. "Is Iran Jailing a Ploy to Retain Power?" *The Philadelphia Inquirer*, 23 May 2007.

Ruether, Rosemary. "The Lie that Barack Obama Is a Muslim Won't Go Away." *National Catholic Reporter* 44.30 (2008): 12–16.

Samuels, David. "The Spy Who Loved Hamas and Hezbollah. And Iran." *Mother Jones* 34.5 (2009): 48–51.

Satrapi, Marjane. "How Can One Be Persian." *My Sister, Guard Your Veil; My Brother, Guard Your Eyes*. Ed. Lila Azam Zanganeh. Boston: Beacon Press, 2006. 20–23.

_____. *Persepolis*. New York: Pantheon, 2004.

_____. *Persepolis 2*. New York: Pantheon, 2005.

_____. "Why I Wrote *Persepolis*." *Writing* 26.3 (2003): 9–12.

Schjeldahl, Peter. "Words and Pictures: Graphic Novels Come of Age." *The New Yorker* 81.32 (2005): 162–68.

Secor, Laura. "Prisoner of Tehran." *New York Times Book Review,* 22 Nov 2009. 8.

Sedarat, Roger. *Dear Regime: Letters to the Islamic Republic.* Athens: Ohio University Press, 2007.

Seifoddini, Farnoosh. "Dokhtar-e Amrika-I." *The Iranian,* 17 Dec 2002. 25 Oct 2011. http://www.iranian.com/Arts/2002/December/Dokhtar/index.html

Shamshiri, Fariborz. Rotten Gods. 29 Jun 2010. 16 Oct 2010. http://www.rottengods.com/2010_06_01_archive.html.

_____. Rotten Gods. 23 Jun 2010. 16 Oct 2010. http://www.rottengods.com/2010_06_01_archive.html.

_____. Rotten Gods. 6 Jun 2010. 16 Oct 2010. http://www.rottengods.com/2010_06_01_archive.html.

_____. Rotten Gods. 3 Jun 2010. 16 Oct 2010. http://www.rottengods.com/2010_06_01_archive.html.

_____. Rotten Gods. 7 May 2010. 17 Oct 2010. http://www.rottengods.com/2010_05_01_archive.html.

_____. Rotten Gods. 20 Apr 2010. 17 Oct 2010. http://www.rottengods.com/2010_04_01_archive.html

_____. Rotten Gods. 13 Apr 2010. 17 Oct 2010 http://www.rottengods.com/2010_04_01_archive.html

_____. Rotten Gods. 10 Mar 2010. 16 Oct 2010. http://www.rottengods.com/2010_03_01_archive.html.

Shane, Scott and Gordon, Michael R. "Dissident's Tale of Epic Escape from Iran's Vise." *The New York Times,* 13 July 2008. 2 July 2010. http://www.nytimes.com/2008/07/13/world/middleeast/13dissident.html?_r=2&fta=y.

"Shariar Mandanipour." *PEN World Voices.* 12 May 2010. http://www.pen.org/author.php/prmAID/155.

Sheibani, Khatereh. "Kiarostami and the Aesthetics of Modern Persian Poetry." Iranian Studies 39.4 (2006): 509–537.

"Shorn of Dignity and Equality." *Economist* 346 (2003): 23–25.

Simon, Scott. "Firoozeh Dumas: '*Laughing Without an Accent.*'" *Weekend Edition Saturday,* 21 June 2008.

Solomon, Deborah. "The Way We Live Now: Questions for Dalia Sofer; Tales From Tehran." *The New York Times Online,* 26 Aug 2007. 23 June 2009. http://query.nytimes.com/gst/fullpage.html?res=9D00E1DE103FF935A1575BC0A9619C8B63

"Sons and Other Flammable Objects." *Publishers Weekly* 254.25 (2007): 33.

Sreberny, Annabelle, and Khiabany, Gholam. "Becoming Intellectual: The Blogestan and Public Political Space in the Islamic Republic." *British Journal of Middle Eastern Studies* 34.3 (2007): 287–286.

Starr, Alexandra. "The Mullahs and Me." *The New York Times Book Review,* 13 Mar 2005. 29.

Stewart, Rory, and Allardice, Lisa. "Secret Texts." *New Statement* 132.4645: 53–56.

"Stop Torturing Us." n.d. 24 Sept 2010. http://stop.torturing.us/.

_____. 23 June 2010. 24 Sept 2010. http://stop.torturing.us/.

_____. 8 May 2009. 24 Sept 2010. http://stop.torturing.us/search?updated-max=2010-0620T04%3A58%3A00-04%3A00&max-results=6.

_____. 26 Apr 2010. 24 Sept 2010. http://stop.torturing.us/search?updated-max=2010-0620T04%3A58%3A00-04%3A00&max-results=6.

Talattof, Kamran. "Breaking Taboos in Iranian Women's Literature." *World Literature Today* 78.3/4 (2004): 43–46.

"Tehran Post." User Profile. n.d. 5 Oct 2010. http://www.blogger.com/profile/14347271388052099044.

_____. 29 Dec 2009. 8 Oct 2010. http://ord-per.blogspot.com/search?updated-max=2010-09-12T03%3A13%3A00-07%3A00&max-results=20&reverse-paginate=true.

_____. 19 Dec 2009. 8 Oct 2010. http://ord-per.blogspot.com/search?updated-max=2010-09-12T03%3A13%3A00-07%3A00&max-results=20&reverse-paginate=true.

_____. 11 July 2009. 8 Oct 2010. http://ord-per.blogspot.com/search?updated-max=2010-09-12T03%3A13%3A00-07%3A00&max-results=20&reverse-paginate=true.

_____. 20 June 2009. 8 Oct 2010. http://ord-per.blogspot.com/search?updated-max=2010-09-12T03%3A13%3A00-07%3A00&max-results=20&reverse-paginate=true.

_____. 4 June 2009. 8 Oct 2010. http://ord-per.blogspot.com/search?updated-max=2010-09-12T03%3A13%3A00-07%3A00&max-results=20&reverse-paginate=true.

_____. 29 Dec 2008. 7 Oct 2010. http://ord-per.blogspot.com/search?updated-max=2009-05-30T12%3A23%3A00-07%3A00&max-results=20&reverse-paginate=true.

_____. 1 June 2008. 7 Oct 2010. http://ord-per.blogspot.com/search?updated-max=2008-07-20T04%3A07%3A00-07%3A00&max-results=20&reverse-paginate=true.

_____. 1 Apr 2008. 6 Oct 2010. http://ord-per.blogspot.com/search?updated-max=2008-07-20T04%3A07%3A00-07%3A00&max-results=20.

_____. 9 Oct 2007. 7 Oct 2010. http://ord-per.blogspot.com/search?updated-max=2008-01-21T12%3A15%3A00-08%3A00&max-results=20.

_____. 28 Aug 2007. 5 Oct 2010. http://ord-per.blogspot.com/search?updated-max=2007-10-

09T08%3A38%3A00-07%3A00&max-re
sults=20.

Theodoulou, Michael. "Uneasy Times for Iran's
Jews." *Christian Science Monitor* 91.231 (1999):
6.

Toosi, Nahal. *"Funny in Farsi: A Memoir of Growing up Iranian in America."* *The Milwaukee
Journal Sentinel* 2 Jul 2003.

Toumani, Meline. "Another Country." *Nation*
280.17 (2005): 25–30.

Tully, Annie. "An Interview with Marjane Satrapi."
*Bookslut*, October 2005. 9 June 2009. http://
www.bookslut.com/features/2004_10_003261.
php.

"Under Underground." User Profile. n.d. 12 Oct
2010. http://www.blogger.com/profile/06715
267717783097327.

Under Underground. 10 Sept 2009. 15 Oct 2010.
http://yaserb.blogspot.com/search?updated-
min=2009-01-01T00%3A00%3A00%2B03
%3A30&updated-max=2010-01-01T00%3
A00%3A00%2B03%3A30&max-results=5.

Under Underground. 24 June 2009. 15 Oct 2010.
http://yaserb.blogspot.com/search?updated-
min=2009-01-01T00%3A00%3A00%2B0
3%3A30&updated-max=2010-01-01T00%3
A00%3A00%2B03%3A30&max-results=5.

Under Underground. 9 Apr 2010. 12 Oct 2010.
http://www.blogger.com/profile/06715267717
783097327.

Under Underground. 5 Feb 2007. 14 Oct 2010.
http://yaserb.blogspot.com/search?updated-
min=2007-01-01T00%3A00%3A00%2B03
%3A30&updated-max=2008-01-01T00%3
A00%3A00%2B03%3A30&max-results=11.

Under Underground. 4 Jan 2006. 13 Oct 2010.
http://yaserb.blogspot.com/search?updated-
min=2006-01-01T00%3A00%3A00%2B0
3%3A30&updated-max=2007-01-01T00%3
A00%3A00%2B03%3A30&max-results=40.

Under Underground. 9 Sept 2005. 13 Oct 2010.
http://yaserb.blogspot.com/search?updated-
min=2005-01-01T00%3A00%3A00%2B
03%3A30&updated-max=2006-01-01T00%3
A00%3A00%2B03%3A30&max-results=50.

Under Underground. 18 June 2005. 13 Oct 2010.
http://yaserb.blogspot.com/search?updated-
min=2005-01-01T00%3A00%3A00%2B03%
3A30&updated-max=2006-01-01T00%3A00
%3A00%2B03%3A30&max-results=50.

"US Behind Terror Acts in Iran." Press TV, 17
Oct 2010. 27 Oct 2010. http://www.presstv.ir/
detail/147094.html.

"US: Iran Took Hikers on Iraq Side of Border."
*New York Times*, 22 Oct 2010. 28 Oct 2010.
http://www.nytimes.com/aponline/2010/10/2
2/us/politics/AP-US-Iran-Hikers.html?sc
p=3&sq=%22iran%22&st=nyt.

Vala, Lobat. "The Epic of Stoning." *The Poetry
of Iranian Women*. Ed. Sheema Kalbasi. Reel
Content Publishing (www.reelcontent.org),
2009. 34–35.

Valadbaygi, Saeed. "Farzad Kamangar and 4
Other Political Prisoners Executed!" *Street
Journalist*, 9 May 2010. 5 Nov 2010. http://
www.astreetjournalist.com/2010/05/09/farzad-
kamangar-and-4-other-political-prisoners-
executed/.

Wall, Robert, and Fulghum, David A. "Fighting
Under Fire." *Aviation Week & Space Technology* 170.13 (2009): 31–32.

Wallace, David Foster. "E Unibus Pluram: Tel-
evision and U.S. Fiction." *A Supposedly Fun
Thing I've Never Do Again*. 21–82. Boston:
Back Bay Books, 1997.

Weich, Dave. "Marjane Satrapi Returns." Pow-
ells.com Interviews. 17 Sept 2004. 9 June
2009. http://www.powells.com/authors/satrapi.
html.

Weissman, Benjamin. "A Sleek and Brilliant
Monster." *L.A. Weekly*, 6 May 1999. 12 March
2010. http://www.laweekly.com/content/print
Version/30794.

Williams, Armstrong. "A War on Terror, Not a
War on Muslims" *KRLA 870*, 27 Feb 2006. 11
Jan 2011. http://www.krla870.com/column.
aspx?id=1c3187d0-316f-4b6a-a293-f09ef6
30f2d3.

Wolpe, Sholeh. "It's a Man's World to the End
of the End." *The Poetry of Iranian Women*, Ed.
Sheema Kalbasi. Reel Content Publishing
(www.reelcontent.org), 2009. 1.

Wood, James. "Love, Iranian Style." *New Yorker*
85.19 (2009): 72–75.

Woodcock, Susan H., and Gropman, Jackie.
*"Funny in Farsi: A Memoir of Growing up Iran-
ian in America."* *School Library Journal* 49.11
(2003): 172–173.

Wright, Robin. "Iran Frees U.S. Scholar from
Prison." *The Washington Post*, 22 Aug 2007.

Yong, William. "In Iran, Future of University Is
in Flux." *New York Times*, 16 Oct 2010. 27
Oct 2010. http://www.nytimes.com/2010/10/
16/world/middleeast/16iran.html?scp=17&sq=
%22iran%22&st=nyt.

Zandian, Mandana. "The State of Red." *The Poetry of Iranian Women*. Ed. Sheema Kalbasi.
Reel Content Publishing (www.reelcontent.
org), 2009. 15.

Zanganeh, Lila Azam. *My Sister, Guard Your Veil;
My Brother, Guard Your Eyes*. Boston: Beacon
Press, 2006.

Zha, Wei, and Perlmutter, David. "Blogs as
Stealth Dissent?" *International Media Communication in a Global Age*. Ed. Thomas J. John-
son. New York: Routledge, 2010.

# Index